New York's Family Grocer

NEW YORK'S FAMILY GROCER

The Story of D'Agostino Supermarkets

Paul Schmitz

EMPIRE STATE EDITIONS

AN IMPRINT OF FORDHAM UNIVERSITY PRESS

NEW YORK   2026

Copyright © 2026 Fordham University Press

All rights reserved. No part of this publication may be reproduced, stored in a retrieval system, or transmitted in any form or by any means—electronic, mechanical, photocopy, recording, or any other—except for brief quotations in printed reviews, without the prior permission of the publisher.

Fordham University Press has no responsibility for the persistence or accuracy of URLs for external or third-party Internet websites referred to in this publication and does not guarantee that any content on such websites is, or will remain, accurate or appropriate.

Fordham University Press also publishes its books in a variety of electronic formats. Some content that appears in print may not be available in electronic books.

Visit us online at www.fordhampress.com/empire-state-editions.

For EU safety / GPSR concerns: Mare Nostrum Group B.V., Mauritskade 21D, 1091 GC Amsterdam, The Netherlands, gpsr@mare-nostrum.co.uk

Library of Congress Cataloging-in-Publication Data available online at https://catalog.loc.gov.

Printed in the United States of America

28 27 26   5 4 3 2 1

First edition

This book is dedicated to the memory of my beloved parents, Dennis and Loretta Schmitz, and to all those who made this story possible but never got to see it in print.

CONTENTS

1. Italian Immigration and the Currency of the Ethnic Merchant   1
2. Immigrant Grocers and American Dreams (1880–1946)   30
3. The Grocer in the Gray Flannel Suit (1946–60)   74
4. One of the Nice Things About New York (1960–82)   129
5. New York's Family Grocer (1982–2025)   177

   Acknowledgments   245

   Notes   247

   Bibliography   301

   Index   321

New York's Family Grocer

Figure 1. "Only in New York" (1995). Courtesy of D'Agostino Supermarkets.

CHAPTER 1

Italian Immigration and the Currency of the Ethnic Merchant

"Only in New York," proclaims a 1995 advertisement for D'Agostino Supermarkets (fig. 1). Set against an eight-by-eleven-inch, black-and-white portrait of the business's founder, the text of the ad continues: "New York is the world's dream factory. Like everything else dreams are bigger here and some of them do come true. Ours began in 1932 when 21-year-old Nick D'Agostino, Sr. sold his pushcart and, with his brother, opened the small grocery store that grew into today's unique chain of D'Agostino Supermarkets." The ad then announces that the company is celebrating its sixty-third year in business "in the shadow of imposing neighbors who this year are observing milestone anniversaries"—including the New York Public Library, the Metropolitan Museum of Art, the American Museum of Natural History, and the United Nations.

In establishing D'Agostino's* landmark status, the text seeks to communicate a sense of eminence and stability, especially to those consumers who may be less aware of the company's history—a necessity in a city whose public life is simultaneously dynamic, transient, and anonymous. D'Agostino's is the only merchant in this pantheon of cultural institutions, however. The firm declares its pride "to stand in this august company." Who besides the company itself would set D'Agostino Supermarkets alongside the UN

---

* While the organization and its stores are officially branded as "D'Agostino Supermarkets" or "D'Agostino" in signage, advertising, and media, I also refer to them as "D'Agostino's" throughout the book—which reflects popular usage among New Yorkers.

or the Met as a New York institution? And yet, what are dreams but the most hopeful of self-projections?

The top of the circular bears the caption "D'Agostino Supermarkets, family owned and family operated since 1932." The label of "family business" signals to customers that merchants are neither faceless nor heartless but will act in the customers' best interests—what management would term as being the "consumer's agent"—because they share their domestic values and traditions. The advertisement's notion of family also acknowledges Americans' fascination with their own heritage. While New York is the celebrated home of Broadway and Wall Street, the city's identity is rooted in its immigrant character. A family that has ascended from humble beginnings is a ready symbol for the mythology of American striving. The ad imagines the immigrant family as an institution and a product, as well as a source of ancestry. Here, this family name, embodied in a patriarchal visage, serves as a mark of identity that doubles as an article of commerce.

New York's Family Grocer: The Story of D'Agostino Supermarkets centers on founding figures Nicola ("Nicholas") and Pasquale ("Patsy") D'Agostino, who were part of the legion of foreign-born fruit and vegetable merchants who tried to parlay their knowledge of produce into a living. The society of urban merchants followed a hierarchy, from grocery store owners to clerks to produce vendors and pushcart peddlers. Butchers, bakers, and fish men usually had their own shops, forming close-knit societies that guarded the secrets of their respective trades. Nicholas and Patsy negotiated an economic landscape crowded with independent, ethnic grocers who scraped out small profits while staving off a return to the pushcart. Italian peddlers, delivery boys, clerks, and grocers formed a network that helped their countrymen obtain work and pool capital to start new businesses. Recently arrived relatives and "paesani" from Italy continually strengthened this collective.

How did Nicholas and Patsy D'Agostino establish a business in 1932—during the depths of the Great Depression—that not only survived, but also flourished? In seeking to answer this question, I will consider the history of Italian Americans in New York City and the evolution of the grocery business more generally. "Frank Tucciarone and Company"—the predecessor to the first D'Agostino's market—had enjoyed the advantage of a prime Manhattan location (83rd Street and Lexington Avenue) with a well-heeled clientele labeled the "silk-stocking trade." The D'Agostino brothers also benefited from a revolutionary approach to the grocery business: the now-common notion of offering produce, meats, and dry goods under one roof. Nicholas and Patsy thus became pioneers of the supermarket model.

By 1939, the brothers had two relatively successful stores on Manhattan's Upper East Side and one in suburban Mount Vernon (which would close within a decade). Their success, and perhaps the wealth and status of their customers, made them well-known public figures, especially among reporters looking for a quote about the latest developments in food retailing.

Throughout the Second World War, the D'Agostino brothers presented themselves as standard-bearers for small businesses struggling to escape the tentacles of larger competitors and the federal government's Office of Price Administration (OPA). Patsy D'Agostino became a leading voice in various local and national grocery associations, including the New York State Food Merchants Association and the National Association of Retail Grocers. In 1943—the same year Congress called Patsy to Washington to testify on the OPA's effect on small business—he was the subject of an article in *The New Yorker*. The profile highlighted his ethnicity, his love for vegetables, and his disdain for chain stores and government bureaucrats. Then in the 1950s, as the postwar boom launched D'Agostino's to the top of New York's retail hierarchy, Patsy was hailed as an emblem of free enterprise by *American Magazine* and *Business Week* and as a model of religious devotion by *Catholic Digest*. The ethnic publication *Italamerican* called the brothers symbols of the "inborn nobility" of Italians, yet also celebrated their success as proof of Italians' ability to attain a fully assimilated American dream.

The press often portrayed the D'Agostinos' story as a confirmation of the virtues of American society, making the brothers increasingly aware of the cultural and economic value of their history. Patsy D'Agostino was the focus of early articles on the company. In addition to heading the produce department, Patsy had the title of president and therefore oversaw management and press relations—a role that apparently suited him. As vice president, Nicholas supervised meat and fish and spent much of his time in his white butcher's coat, behind the counter, or in the stockroom. Nicholas seemed to begrudge the attention given to his older brother, as it overshadowed his own role in building the business, and he was wary of Patsy's ability to charm customers and members of the press. The brothers had an intimate but complicated relationship. Their success strained their fraternal ties, especially when Patsy contracted cancer and the brothers had to decide the future of their enterprise. After Patsy's death in 1960, Nicholas assumed the presidency and pushed the business's growth to new levels, while claiming its rags-to-riches tale as his own.

When Nicholas's son Stephen succeeded his father in the 1970s, he modernized the operation, expanded to seventeen stores, and initiated advertising campaigns to enhance the company's status. *New Yorker*–style cartoons paired D'Agostino stores with landmarks such as the Central Park Zoo and the Brooklyn Bridge, while other ads associated D'Agostino groceries with the lifestyle of young sophisticates. Company advertising thus showed the store to be integral to the cultural life of the city. When Stephen's younger brother, Nick D'Agostino Jr., became the CEO in 1982, he continued to grow the business's reach and reputation, especially with yuppies, foodies, and upper-income consumers. But Nick also embraced the concept of family as a managerial principle and a source of the company's identity. Throughout the 1990s, new advertising campaigns would celebrate the family's origins as New York grocers, using historic photographs to promote the D'Agostinos as an immigrant family that had made good in a city that relished its heritage. In the new millennium, however, D'Agostino Supermarkets would struggle to maintain its place in New York's ultracompetitive marketplace—as the grocery business was transformed by the rise of big-box stores, online retailing, and the Whole Foods revolution. While the city itself was remade by gentrification and generational change, the company and its narrative would begin to fade from public consciousness. This book seeks to chronicle this storied business and the circumstances that enabled it, for a time, to prosper.

"The Forty D'Agostinos": On the Writing of Family History

> "I was recently pleased to get into a cab which was driven by an opera lover," writes Don Wigal. "On his radio, he was sharing with me music from the opera *La Forza del Destino*. I told the driver that I appreciated the music. He replied, 'Yeah. It's my favorite opera: *The Forty D'Agostinos*.'" It could only happen in New York.—*D'AGs Consumer Newsletter*, September/October 1982[1]

The process of writing this story began in 1996, during my first semester of graduate school at Boston University. Earlier that year, my grandfather, Nicholas D'Agostino Sr., had died after a long, slow decline. My grandfather was a person of great strength and intensity, who despite a childhood of dire poverty in the mountains of Italy, had the audacity and the ego to dream of wealth and status in the United States. He possessed unshakable faith, a relentless work ethic, and the ability to devote himself completely to a task. Like many immigrant-entrepreneurs of his generation, his life was shaped by hunger—for food, for success, and, ultimately, for social legitimacy (evidenced by the extended monologues on proper table manners he directed at his grandchildren). With only a fourth-grade education, he had carved a fortune out of the New York streets through blood, sweat, and the grace of God (a simple equation to his mind). And yet, Nicholas D'Agostino wanted nothing more than to provide for future generations of his family. Despite his peasant beginnings, Nicholas's American Dream was not only to pull his family out of poverty but also to give his children and grandchildren the chance to become businessmen, lawyers, and college professors and to have their surname rank with the finest names in New York.

A few months after his funeral, as my grandmother, Josephine D'Agostino, was in the process of moving to a new residence, I visited their home on Long Island one last time. I took the train down from Boston to see my mother—who was visiting from California to help close the house and catalog its contents—and to interview my grandmother's caregivers for a project on recent immigration to the US. While my aunt and my mother deliberated over which furnishings and heirlooms to pass along, sell, or donate, I sat interviewing my grandmother's Salvadoran nurse at the kitchen table. She quietly testified to her struggles and hopes in this strange new country as my aunt and my mother sorted through artifacts from my grandparents' life—objects that signified the aspirations and achievements of a passing generation of American immigrants.

The original source materials for this book came from a cardboard box that had been stuffed with a vast and unruly collection of artifacts—yellowed newspaper clippings and grocery-industry magazines, advertisements, and pamphlets; worn invitations and programs from banquets and conventions; personal letters and journals; dozens of black-and-white family photographs—that my grandmother had compiled over the course of five decades. For years, she served an uncredited role as archivist for her husband and sons, their business, and their families. As my relatives prepared the house for sale in the wake of my grandfather's death, this neglected trove was passed first to my mother and then to me. Here was a complete merging of "the personal" and "the professional"; or rather, in this box, the multigenerational stories of the family and the family business became one intermingled narrative of identity. I was sentimental about the provenance of these materials; my grandmother was necessarily moved into an assisted living facility after the loss of her husband, as age and dementia slowly eroded her faculties. My mother was anxious to share these dusty treasures with her own children and have them put into some kind of coherent order—perhaps to draw a larger moral or message from their contents.

Having grown up in northern California, the son of an English professor at the local state college, I had sometimes struggled to connect with the figures and family melodrama of the D'Agostino story. Scholarship is often an act of autobiography, and by undertaking this project, perhaps I was seeking to understand my own relationship to my extended family and its patriarch, as well as my sublimated Italian American heritage. After Nicholas D'Agostino's passing, I found it curious how my grandfather's public identity subsumed his personal life, with his obituary reading like a kind of advertisement for the business that he and his brother, Patsy, had founded, his face plastered across the shop windows of the small chain of grocery stores in Manhattan he had helped to build. I wondered at his inability to have a life apart from the company he created, which eventuated in a family whose relationships were shaped by the legacy of his business.

It is now over two decades since I began my expedition and again, a cloud of mortality has cast a shadow over the writing of this book. My uncles, who helped expand D'Agostino Supermarkets across New York City, have entered their sunset years while my mother, who was the book's inspiration and chief promoter, has since died. She contributed hundreds of pages of notes and journal reflections on the history of the D'Agostino family and its business in the hopes that their narrative (and the perspective of the women who had been left out of the public record) would finally be heard, perhaps healing the divisions in her family in the process.

Here I must recognize the many challenges of composing a family history, given the fluidity of memory and the personal stakes involved. I care deeply for the principal figures in this narrative, both past and present, and am aware of the bias endemic to these projects. One must be vigilant in maintaining objectivity and a sense of perspective, even as one is managing the sentiments and agendas of the subjects. I admit that in researching, writing, and revising this book, I felt the weight and anguish of my own family's history, which were matched by a sense of responsibility to the living and the dead. Yet my connection to D'Agostino Supermarkets has not only supplied me with a rich collection of texts and materials, but has also reinforced my commitment to a full and faithful telling of its story. Additionally, my "insider status" has furnished me with a rare perspective, as the internal dynamics of a family business—particularly one born from immigrant struggle—is one of the central themes of this work.

This book also contemplates the premise that businesses, like the individuals that birth and nurture them, follow a cycle of life and death. Business models and innovations spring from cultural and historical moments, serving the needs of the buying public while playing to their dreams, anxieties, aspirations, and sense of identity. In this regard, the retail giants of an era can seem immortal, their potential demise difficult to contemplate. Who could have foreseen the decline of Woolworth's, A&P, Detroit's "Big Three" automakers, or even McDonald's? And yet, over time, most businesses begin to suffer from stale ideas, declining resources, and the inability to evolve and innovate when facing a new generation of competitors. They begin to fall out of step with the times, to lose their connection to the larger culture. Like the people who construct them, they age and, eventually, expire.

This, too, is the story of D'Agostino Supermarkets, which, for decades, successfully reinvented itself to maintain a prime position in one of the nation's toughest markets, enabling it to become a touchstone in the cultural life of the city. Over the years, its stores had appeared in numerous films and television programs, with the company advertising itself as "the place where Will met Grace." Since the 2010s, D'Agostino's has faded as a business of note in New York, however. In a city that has continued to grow younger, hipper, and more moneyed, consumers have turned away from traditional supermarkets, instead favoring gourmet grocers, Whole Foods and Trader Joe's, online retailers, and even Manhattan's ubiquitous network of drugstores. Meanwhile, D'Agostino's urban footprint has continued to shrink even as the family has migrated to the suburbs of Connecticut and Westchester or relocated to Florida—a great literal and metaphoric distance from its immigrant origins as pushcart peddlers, greengrocers, and butchers. The organization has grappled with the same challenges (both operational and domestic) that have brought down thousands of family firms before them—issues that I will contemplate in the chapters that follow. In order to stave off its financial woes and bolster its prospects, D'Agostino's joined with former rival Gristedes under the mantle of the New York Food Group (which is part of the Red Apple Group conglomerate) in 2016. In 2021, the head of Red Apple, John Catsimatidis, replaced Nicholas D'Agostino III as the company's president and COO. For the first time in its ninety-year history, "New York's Family Grocer"[*] would not have one of its descendants at the helm.

My engagement with the family archive that provided much of the primary-source material for this project has involved taking its many individual pieces—including newspaper clippings, articles from industry newsletters and popular magazines, personal journals, photographs, and

---

[*] This appellation combines D'Agostino's slogan "New York's Grocer" and the tagline "Family Owned and Family Operated Since 1932"—embodying the company's history, its bond with New York, and its identity as a family business.

company advertising—and putting them into dialogue with the larger world of scholarship. In doing so, I hope to elucidate the import of D'Agostino's as it relates to the story of Italian Americans, ethnic entrepreneurship, the grocery business, and New York City itself. This book thus engages several areas of scholarly discourse through the narrative of the D'Agostino company. As an account of an Italian family's struggles with marginalization and assimilation, *New York's Family Grocer* serves as a microhistory of ethnicity in twentieth-century America. Italian immigration to New York is one of its necessary topics, so I begin by analyzing the conditions of the Italians' collective passage and settlement. Many of the Italians who came to the US initially had no desire to stay on—they hoped to earn enough in America to buy land or houses in their native Italy, a country that was struggling with a host of environmental, social, and economic issues. In the early twentieth century, Italian immigrants often lived on the periphery of American society. Over the next four decades, however, Italians slowly integrated themselves into America's larger population of white ethnics. With marriage and settlement in the US, they became more engaged in the public life of their adopted homeland, while their diligence as laborers earned them stable blue-collar positions.

Some of the more ambitious members of the community bettered their prospects by joining New York's network of ethnic merchants. But involvement in the food trade allowed Italians to transform their identities as well. Before Nicholas and Patsy D'Agostino settled in New York, their father, uncles, and cousins had already suffered the prejudice of an American society that questioned their ability to assimilate. Italian immigrants' worst critics viewed them as gangsters, subversives, and primitives, while a host of sympathetic social workers and journalists wondered if their Mediterranean character was out of step with the demands of a modern capitalist society. Yet over time, the figure of the Ellis Island immigrant would replace the iconic Yankee farmer as the incarnation of prototypically American values like independence, self-reliance, and determination. This process would be aided by Italians' continued movement into the postwar middle class, and by the politics of the ethnic revival that began in the late 1960s. But I argue that ethnic entrepreneurship played a fundamental role in the immigrants' transformation from an alien underclass to symbols of American enterprise.

Success in the marketplace not only converted immigrants into proto-Americans, but also allowed them to fuse culture with commerce. In the case of Italian merchants, this exchange sometimes involved the marketing of their traditional image. In the popular imagination, the immigrant-peddler embodied an elemental set of values—a sense of craft, authenticity, and a dedication to family—that belied the crass materialism of modern America. The myth of the pastoral Italian had remarkable endurance, following ethnic merchants across the twentieth century as they moved from the pushcarts to ownership of grocery stores and import shops. This characterization tended to sentimentalize Italian identity, but it also became a way for retailers to differentiate themselves from their more anonymous competitors. As pushcart peddlers and small-time grocers, the D'Agostino brothers had carried the ethnic mantle, though they would embrace the latest innovations within their industry. When Patsy and Nicholas made their fortunes during the postwar boom, their humble origins, as well as their story of immigrant striving, had great appeal for journalists who regarded the brothers as cultural emblems. While its operation took a decidedly modern turn in the 1960s and '70s, the company would later return to the narrative of the "Old World" family, with historic ties to the city of New York.

Because their fortunes were closely aligned with those of New York, the stories of the family and the company also provide a chronicle of the city's evolution. I recount New York's primacy as a center for Italian immigration amid its own modernization, then discuss Manhattan's post–World War II prosperity as well as its transition to a postindustrial economy. Ensuing chapters illustrate the ascendance of New York's white-collar sectors in the 1960s and '70s even as the city suffered the onset of urban decay. Finally, I examine the city's revival since the 1980s in the context of new immigration, Wall Street, and gentrification. The D'Agostinos took great pride in their civic identity and understood that their profitability was contingent on New York's continued vitality. I will explain how the city became a necessary partner in the company's success while feeding its image.

Business history provides an additional subject of this narrative, as I analyze the evolution of the retail food trade and the development of the modern supermarket. I begin by surveying the crowded landscape of pushcart markets and ethnic grocery stores in early twentieth-century New York that provided Italian immigrants with a ladder of upward mobility, while also serving as an emblem of identity. I then delineate how the supermarket signified the glories of postwar America—described by its boosters as accessible, based in the "something for everyone" notion of consensus, offering seemingly unlimited choice, and enabled by the nation's industrial might and technological innovations. As part of this discussion, I will consider how independent and ethnic grocers opposed or assimilated themselves into this commercial paradigm.

In the second half of the book, I recount America's growing discontent with the supermarket, beginning in the 1960s. The decade's politics influenced consumer activists and helped create the green-minded "whole foods" movement that migrated from funky co-ops and health food stores to high-end malls and Main Street. I also contemplate how the burgeoning gourmet food trend began to alter the tastes and buying habits of middle- and upper-income shoppers. My final two chapters examine the demise of the neighborhood grocery during the urban crisis of the late 1960s and '70s, and its subsequent resurrection with new immigration. I will also detail how consumers now turn to small ethnic markets, "gourmet" groceries, Walmart, Costco, and online shopping rather than the traditional supermarket, as the assumptions of mass marketing, and the notion of a "typical" American family, have begun to founder.

This book also provides a careful investigation of the fraught culture of family-owned companies. Family firms must overcome steep challenges to maintain their viability—including external threats from well-funded corporate competition and internal tensions between relatives seeking ultimate control over the operation. If these businesses can maintain their talent pool and the integrity of their mission through succeeding generations of management, their heirs may then carry the burden of the family name. Yet, the case of D'Agostino Supermarkets also illustrates how a family-owned company can capitalize on the name recognition and sense of heritage conferred by its identity—wielding a valuable form of currency. Since the 1990s, D'Agostino's has sought to differentiate itself from a host of competitors and promote its historic status with the new urban gentry by identifying as New York's family grocer, even as the D'Agostino family sometimes struggled to preserve domestic peace and civility. Indeed, many of the company's issues illustrate the difficult realities that family businesses must confront in sustaining themselves.

My treatment of D'Agostino's corporate identity and its relationship with New York consumers necessitates an analysis of its advertising. Patsy and Nicholas D'Agostino had seen marketing as an extravagance, like many retailers of their generation. Before the mid-1960s, magazine and newspaper articles and ribbon-cutting ceremonies served, for all intents and purposes, as the business's most common forms of promotion. But despite the modest size of its operation, D'Agostino's sought recognition as the city's grocer of choice. As part of this strategy, new president Stephen D'Agostino, and his brother Nick, enlisted a talented advertising agent to create one of the first image-based branding campaigns ever undertaken by a supermarket company.

In the late 1960s, D'Agostino's began an innovative campaign of *New Yorker*–style cartoons that celebrated its association with the sophisticated life of Manhattan. Throughout the 1970s and '80s, clever newspaper ads and radio slogans made D'Agostino Supermarkets the most renowned food retailer in the nation's most populated market—even though it had fewer than twenty locations, each operating in less than nine thousand square feet of commercial space. In the 1990s, however, the company's advertising assumed a more historical character. These ads featured black-and-white images of Nicholas D'Agostino and his wife, romanticizing their roots as part of an immigrant New York that had made good. One could read this campaign as a response to the ethnic renaissance that had come into vogue with middle- and upper-class consumers. Yet as New York's own identity was destabilized by economic and demographic change, D'Agostino's tried to represent itself as an immutable part of the life of the city. These ads not only were visually attractive, but also personalized D'Agostino's story for two generations of shoppers—older residents who wondered at the city's transformation and new urbanites who had little sense of the stores' reputation. As marketing assumed the role of personal narrative, it blurred the lines between the private and the public, between family and commerce.

Finally, throughout this text, I will explore the value of narrative as a means of establishing identity for individuals as well as business entities. The careers of Patsy and Nicholas D'Agostino illustrate the ways in which personal history can become a form of public representation, especially for those ethnic figures who have overcome humble beginnings to win wealth and distinction. "Rags-to-riches" tales have an established place in the lore of American democracy, even if contemporary audiences view texts such as Horatio Alger's *Ragged Dick* as sentimental and outdated. American culture continues to venerate those citizens who triumph over poverty, a lack of education, or the supposed impediment of foreign birth to affirm the national parable of opportunity. My narrative analysis thus examines how Ellis Island immigrants and their descendants have sought to inherit America's "rags-to-riches" legend.

As the D'Agostino brothers achieved success as entrepreneurs, magazine and newspaper writers used their struggles with poverty and marginalization to identify them to a larger audience. Of course, interpretations of their life stories shifted according to the era and the orientation of the publications that featured them. In a 1943 article in *The New Yorker*, for example, Patsy D'Agostino emerged as a struggling, sincere Italian immigrant; in the 1950s, publications like *American Magazine* used his story to emphasize the openness and optimism of a probusiness America. But as Patsy became a public figure, he came to understand that just as his life story had appeal for journalists, it could also promote his company. Although Nicholas D'Agostino was initially skeptical of his older brother's profiling, he too began to assume the mantle of the archetypal self-made man after Patsy's death in 1960. The transformation of individuals into icons can exact a cost, however. As the arc of one's public life is told and retold, the reality of one's interior life may be upstaged by the legend. The brothers eventually "became" their stories, and the barriers between their private and public selves became harder to distinguish. And just as Patsy and Nicholas adapted their personal history to create an identity, their company and its inheritors would eventually use their narrative as part of their brand. The case of D'Agostino Supermarkets illustrates the power of these "rags-to-riches" tales in American culture, as well as the burden of maintaining such iconic legacies.

To synchronize these many themes, I have structured *New York's Family Grocer* chronologically. Following a summary of the chapter contents, the remainder of chapter 1 provides an overview of Italian immigration and settlement in the US in the late nineteenth and early twentieth centuries, and then examines the evolution of Italians' cultural identity. This first chapter also details the development of New York's pushcart and retail food trades, which fed the ambitions of ethnic entrepreneurs while playing an essential role in the history of D'Agostino's. Chapter 2, which covers the period from approximately 1880 to 1946, begins the narrative of Patsy and Nicholas D'Agostino—recounting their troubled family lineage, their childhood in rural Italy, their migration to the US, and their early tribulations before they acquired their first store. Much of chapter 2 focuses on D'Agostino's existence as a small business negotiating economic depression and wartime bureaucracy, as well as larger competitors. These struggles influenced the company's image, as the brothers were viewed as both proto-American strivers and ethnic curiosities by such authorities as *The New Yorker* magazine and the United States Congress.

The third chapter documents the business's rise from independent grocery to supermarket in the post–World War II era (1946 to 1960), as the D'Agostino brothers became icons for the era's veneration of free enterprise and citizenship, and its supposed assimilation of working-class ethnics into prosperous, suburban lifestyles. In this period, differing versions of the company's history were circulated and manipulated by the print media. Patsy D'Agostino was initially circumspect about the firm's changing identity, having once professed his disdain for the impersonality and motives of larger competitors. Yet he also became increasingly aware of the "currency" of the company narrative and began to capitalize on its public image. The growing influence of successful immigrants in philanthropy and religion will also be a supporting theme in this chapter. By the mid-1950s, the brothers had become leaders in Italian American and Catholic benevolent societies, activities that connoted assimilation *and* heightened ethnic consciousness as well as charity. Along with the shifting fortunes of immigrants in the postwar years, this section will also examine the development of American food culture, especially as it relates to the supermarket.

In the fourth chapter, covering 1960 to 1982, I document the transition in company leadership first from Patsy to Nicholas D'Agostino, and then to Nicholas's son Stephen. In the 1960s and 1970s, D'Agostino's continued to expand and prosper, as Stephen D'Agostino adopted a number of innovative strategies to modernize its business model and grow its brand. To that end, management initiated large-scale advertising campaigns to distinguish D'Agostino Supermarkets from its competitors. These campaigns identified D'Agostino's as one of the principal pleasures of life in Manhattan, appealing to the city's young, literate, and fashionable residents. Much of this chapter will consider how company advertising allied D'Agostino's with the cosmopolitan spirit of New York, even as the city struggled with the growing decay of its core.

In my concluding chapter, which extends from 1982 to the present, I will examine D'Agostino's efforts to maintain its profitability and relevance in an evolving city. Under the leadership of Nick D'Agostino Jr., the firm reasserted its historic identity as a family grocery through advertising campaigns, civic-minded philanthropy, and a revitalized corporate culture. This strategy was designed to address changes in the lifestyle and economics of the city caused by gentrification and new immigration. Here, I also consider how economic and demographic shifts revolutionized food marketing in New York, as a host of new rivals—from Korean greengroceries to gourmet retailers like Whole Foods and Fairway Market—threatened D'Agostino's status with consumers. As the food business grew more unforgiving, D'Agostino Supermarkets struggled to uphold its "family owned and family operated" motto and its legacy as a company.

"Jerusalem the Golden":
Italian Immigration and the Birth of Modern New York

A presentation of the startling facts of Italian immigration and its role in the development of modern New York. As the capital of the Italian diaspora, the city becomes a symbol of immigrant dreams and self-making, even as the newcomers contend with their marginal status in American society. Later, a meditation on identity and agency within the Italian community.

The narrative of D'Agostino's originates in the migration of millions of immigrants to New York during America's industrial age, as the family, like so many other newcomers, allied their own ascent with the city's mythology. There were only about 12,000 Italians living in New York City in 1880, but over the next four decades, Italian immigrants made it their primary destination and their mythical homeland.[2] The census of 1910 found that the city now hosted over 340,000 foreign-born Italians—one-fourth of the national total. By 1920, this figure had risen to 400,000, though one could number the city's Italian population at 800,000 if the children of immigrants were added to the count.[3] In his highly regarded 1947 memoir of life in the villages of southern Italy, Carlo Levi wrote, "New York, rather than Rome or Naples, would be the real capital of the peasants of Lucania." He explained that while New York was "indifferent" to Italian peasants, treating them like beasts of burden, they viewed the city as "Jerusalem the golden."[4] According to one observer, New York had thus become the "world's greatest Italian city," with a population that exceeded even Naples if this second generation was included.[5] The vast majority of these new Italian immigrants were poor peasants and rural laborers from the southern regions known as the "Mezzogiorno."[6] Collectively, they were virtually illiterate, possessing few professional skills besides their capacity for toil.[7] By one estimate, Italians had the highest proportion of manual workers of any population that arrived in the US between 1880 and 1924, with laborers composing up to two-thirds of the annual count of Italian immigrants—a statistic that gives some indication of their humble status, as well as their dramatic rise later in the twentieth century.[8]

At the height of Italian immigration, from 1880 to 1910, almost 80 percent of the migrants were men, most of whom were hoping to maximize their earnings in America to aid their families and purchase land and houses back in Italy.[9] By the mid-twentieth century, successful Italian immigrants like Nicholas and Patsy D'Agostino would present themselves as symbols of assimilation and the possibilities of the American Dream. But the generations that preceded them staked their futures in Italy, not

America, and their lifestyles reflected their modest aspirations. As part of this approach, the migrants often lived in crowded, substandard housing, ate humbly, and abstained from any extravagances. It was an effective strategy, as in 1907—the peak year of their immigration to America—the Italian Immigration Commission estimated that its exiled population remitted $85 million to Italian citizens.[10] Often these immigrants worked seasonally in the United States, shuttling so frequently between Italy and America that they acquired the moniker "birds of passage." Nearly half of the Italians who came to the US between 1880 and the First World War returned to Italy at some point—though many of these "ritornati" eventually settled in America.[11] The immigrants' transnational existence complicated their notion of identity.[12] As a result of their frequent movement, Italian immigrants had little motivation to affiliate with labor unions, political clubs, or religious institutions in the US. As peasants, they had a historic antipathy toward the State, and tended to identify with their families and local villages since the national unification of Italy had only begun in 1861. The sojourners' permanent settlement—and their subsequent investment in the American community—often corresponded with their decision to bring wives to the United States.[13] Of course, it was only after they had spent considerable time in the US that the immigrants began to even consider themselves Italian (rather than identifying by region or village), as their categorization by the majority population and their need to form social alliances and new families flattened provincial boundaries.[14]

Where did many of the new immigrants find employment? In the early twentieth century, New York City was experiencing a construction boom to meet its needs for modern infrastructure and housing. The explosion of the city's population and its economy necessitated the completion of hundreds of miles of new tunnels, sewers, streets, and streetcar tracks, as well as scores of new office buildings and apartments for the thousands of white-collar employees who were joining the expanding middle class. These projects required a massive labor force to perform "pick and shovel" work, and because Italian immigrants had few professional skills suited for the urban-industrial economy, they often found themselves performing the basic, brutal tasks of construction—such as digging ditches and hauling bricks and cement—that were nonetheless crucial for the building of modern New York.[15] In 1890, one city official testified to Congress that Italians formed 90 percent of the labor for New York's public works.[16] Thousands of Italians dug the New Croton Aqueduct (completed in 1890) and the Lexington Avenue subway (which opened between 1904 and 1918), while helping to build the Williamsburg Bridge (1903), the Manhattan Bridge

(1909), and Grand Central Terminal (1913). By 1910, over 20 percent of the Italian men in New York worked in the construction industry.[17] In succeeding decades, Italians would also find work as dockworkers and longshoremen, and would form the backbone of New York's municipal labor force, often serving in the sanitation department.[18]

New York City had also become the center of the nation's clothing industry, and it offered immigrants ready employment in dozens of factories and sweatshops. Unmarried women were particularly active in the garment industry, with 85 percent of young, single Italian women working in clothing factories and assembly shops by 1905.[19] Once Italian women married, cultural taboos usually forced them to stop working outside the home. But married women often "finished" the sewing of pants, shirts, coats, and dresses in their tenement apartments, or stitched artificial flowers and feathers for hats and garments. Between unmarried and married groups, Italian women composed over one-third of the laborers in the city's women's wear industry by 1905.[20]

Once they arrived in New York, Italians usually followed the immigrant masses into the cramped neighborhoods below 14th Street—some of which housed as many as a thousand people per acre. Because they lacked money and mobility, immigrants had to live near shops, factories, and warehouses to have ready access to employment opportunities.[21] New York's main Italian districts thus coincided with the city's industrial nexus. Immigrants also gravitated toward established ethnic neighborhoods to be in the company of their familiars. Between 1880 and the 1920s, Italians steadily populated the tenements of Lower Manhattan as well as East Harlem, where Nicholas D'Agostino would first learn the pushcart trade.[22]

Despite their numbers, Italians lived on the margins of American society even through the first two or three decades of the twentieth century—which made the D'Agostino brothers' eventual ascendance even more remarkable. Immigrants' intense loyalty to their families and home communities made them wary of those they perceived as outsiders. Even within Italian neighborhoods, their sense of parochialism prevented the formation of unitary ethnic and social organizations, as they preferred the company of fellow Abruzzesi, Calabrians, Sicilians, and Neapolitans instead.[23] And here, their story mirrors the plight of more recent migrants to the US, most notably those from Mexico and Central America. Because so many Italian laborers were essentially sojourners in America, they were far less likely than their immigrant counterparts to learn English or become citizens or join civic or religious institutions.[24] Most Italian immigrants would only fully participate in political organizations or the Catholic Church with upward mobility and generational change.²⁵ Italian immigrants' reluctance to engage civil society extended to New York's public and parochial schools. In another sign of their alienation and indigence, according to a 1908 government commission, Italians had the largest number of children who had left school for work of any of New York's ethnic groups.²⁶

In recent years, scholars such as Donna Gabaccia, James Barrett, David Roediger, and Matthew Jacobson have puzzled over the liminal status of Italians as "racially ambiguous 'in-between people.'"²⁷ According to the convoluted logic of the nineteenth and early twentieth centuries, Italians, along with other Mediterranean peoples, were racially distinct and inferior to those from northern and western Europe. Writers frequently described the immigrants as "swarthy," while one of the most common epithets for Italians—"guinea"—was a derivative of a nickname for West African slaves.²⁸ As such, critics also charged that Italians were prone to criminality and vengeance while associating them with the specter of the Mafia (a stereotype that would later be cemented in the public mind with Prohibition and the infamy of Al Capone).²⁹ These characterizations were given academic credence by the new pseudoscience that corresponded with modern immigration. Italians' position on the racial hierarchy corresponded with their status as migrant workers—granted the right to exchange their labor for wages and given free rein in their own ethnic ghettoes, but not fully recognized by America's civic community. This was evidenced by the Immigration Act of 1924 in which the federal government capped the annual immigration at 165,000 a year while establishing a quota that discriminated against southern and eastern Europeans.³⁰

Yet Italians were officially designated as "white" and thus able to enjoy the benefits of naturalization and citizenship (as determined by the Naturalization Law of 1790). Thus, as Matthew Jacobson asserts, for much of the nineteenth and early twentieth centuries, Italians were part of "a system of 'difference' by which one might be both white and racially distinct from other whites."³¹ Here, one must acknowledge that despite prevailing social prejudices, Italians did ultimately benefit from their legal status as whites. Thomas Guglielmo contends that despite their "racial undesirability," Italian émigrés were essentially "white on arrival," as they experienced no restrictions to citizenship, employment, education, or marriage, nor did they experience segregation in their access to housing, accommodations, or transportation.³² In the coming decades, as Guglielmo and Stefano Luconi have demonstrated, Italian Americans pursued the privileges afforded to the nation's white population, particularly in accessing housing, education, and industrial employment.³³

While the gangster image would continue to plague Italian Americans, the perception of Italian delinquency was moderated by the figure of the steadfast ethnic laborer, which one progressive journalist declared "represents the Italian in America."[34] Yet even as Italians' ability to use a shovel or a hammer earned them a place in industrial society, their very status as the anonymous construction workers, ditchdiggers, and street cleaners of the urban economy placed them on the margins of the American consciousness—a condition that was accentuated by their constant relocation. At the turn of the century, one sociologist mused "the Italian immigrant as a laborer, alternating only between stone-breaking and ditching, remains an alien to the country," adding "he remains a machine, pure and simple, furnishing only brute force, and no special interest can be felt in the work he accomplishes."[35] And with the absence of an educated middle class, it seemed as if Italian immigrants lacked the literati to author their story. Robert Foerster, the period's foremost scholar of Italian Americans, mused:

> Of the externals of the emigrant's life much has been written. How he thinks and feels, however, what kindles and chills him, what his deeper moods are and the springs of his action are matters mainly hidden, guarded, and unconfessed. A Cellini, a Rousseau, a Goethe bares the record of his life's course; but the emigrant, besides lacking the faculty of literary expression, accepts the fact that for the world he is a supremely unimportant person. What is more, he is less to be thought of, after all, as an individual than as a composite. Hence he cannot speak. And we can only guess.[36]

Without the cultural agency to author their story, Italian immigrants would continue to have their identity determined by xenophobes, labor contractors, social workers, academics, and government officials. Not only did Italians appear primarily as figures of labor, or social problems, or ethnic curiosities to members of the establishment, but they also lacked any individuality. How would Italian immigrants gain authority over their own narrative? Patsy and Nicholas D'Agostino's own father, who began his life in America as a migrant laborer, complained of the anonymity that accompanied the oppression he experienced in the US. Crucially, as Patsy and Nicholas's story would later suggest, success in the marketplace and fluency in the lexicon of entrepreneurship could lead to rule over the public self.

"Another Bit of Old New York":
The Pushcart as Enterprise and Identity

Those Italian immigrants who hope to elevate themselves above the category of laborer see their best opportunity in the pushcart trade. As the pushcart trains generations of future grocers in the basic lessons of the marketplace, it signifies ambition, the democracy of the streets, and enterprise in its purest form. Yet even as the pushcart becomes a symbol of immigrant New York, its demise prefaces the rise of the supermarket, urban renewal, and post–World War II assimilation.

After the First World War, Italians began a slow climb up the socioeconomic ladder. While the community would continue to be predominantly working class for the next several decades, its members moved into more secure positions throughout the 1920s. A Works Progress Administration (WPA) survey of birth and marriage records, conducted between 1916 and 1931, found that "laborer" continued to be the leading occupation for New York's Italians, followed by tailor, barber, shoemaker, driver, and carpenter. But the proportion of Italians who designated themselves simply as laborers changed significantly over the life of the survey. In 1916, 50 percent of the Italian fathers of children born in New York had claimed that occupation; by 1931, only about 30 percent did, as Italians moved into skilled blue-collar professions as bakers, mechanics, carpenters, and clerks. The survey also indicated some upward mobility between generations—while over 30 percent of the loosely defined "younger generation" of Italians claimed to be laborers in 1916, only about 10 percent were part of this demographic in 1931.[37] By the end of World War I, a solid middle class of white-collar workers, shopkeepers, bankers, musicians, lawyers, physicians, and newspaper publishers had also established itself in the city's Italian quarters.[38]

This social mobility was also evident in the cohort's geography. A previous generation of Italian workers had begun to migrate up from Lower Manhattan along the new subway corridors in Brooklyn, the Bronx, Queens, and East Harlem to be closer to jobs building transit lines or residential buildings in these same communities.[39] Now, successful members of the Italian community continued this slow exodus, with their search for more desirable housing leading them to middle-class neighborhoods in Upper Manhattan and the Bronx. By 1913, the city's five boroughs hosted more than twenty-five individual Italian districts, with populations ranging from 2,000 to 100,000 people. By 1930, East Harlem became the most populous "Little Italy" in the city—home to around 80,000 Italian immigrants and their children—while Brooklyn housed the greatest number of New York's Italians.[40]

Yet in the early twentieth century, the ethnic merchant would emerge as the most visible symbol of the community's ascendancy. Social critics had once typified Italian immigrants as lacking the competitiveness to achieve success in America, as evidenced by an 1881 article in *Harper's Magazine*: "The idyllic life of an Italian hill-side or of a dreaming medieval town is but poor preparation for the hand-to-hand struggle for bread of an overcrowded city."[41] Other observers had wondered if the Italians' "emotional nature" would impede their ability to prosper in an American culture that valued "a practical and opportunist spirit, a nature that is sharp in business but in other things narrow and matter-of-fact."[42] But Italian peddlers and shopkeepers served to dispel myths about the culture's lack of compatibility with America's capitalist ethos, becoming models of the power of free enterprise. Within the community, owning a small grocery became an accessible means of achieving prosperity and respectability, and a welcome escape from shoveling dirt or swinging a pickaxe in a subway tunnel. With a few words of English and the aid of a family member or two, an Italian laborer might begin on a pushcart, then work up to owning a fruit or vegetable stand, and even open his own shop. The mercantile impulse was tremendously important for Italian immigrants because it was a ready avenue for improving their fortunes. But the pushcart and the fruit stand had special significance in the American context, as they enabled Italians to transform themselves from alien drones to artisans and, later, protocapitalists in line with the entrepreneurial spirit of their adopted country.

Peddlers and pitchmen had been consistently represented in the many waves of Italian immigration, and their ubiquitous presence established the notion that Italians possessed a "natural affinity" for fruits and vegetables. As early as 1870, as many as one in nine Italians were active dealers in wines, groceries, and produce, and by 1890 it was estimated that there were over 10,000 Italian merchants and peddlers in the city of New York. The Italian consul general reported in 1892 that Italians "owned most of the produce stands in New York and ran them profitably."[43] As this commercial class emerged, it refashioned Italian identity in America by selling an aesthetic as well as a product, thus merging sentiment with enterprise. One can find several depictions of pastoral Italian figures—marked by their dusky features and flamboyant costumes—in urban newspapers and magazines of the late nineteenth and early twentieth centuries.[44] According to these accounts, immigrants would bring the conviviality and artistry of the Old World to the barren environs of the industrial city through food and music. And as much as Anglo-American critics and consumers enjoyed the fruits of the peddler's craft, they also seemed drawn to the spectacle of the marketplace. One writer mused:

> The fruit trade is in the hands of Italians in all its branches, from the Broadway shop with its inclined plane of glowing color, to the stand at a street corner. Among the last the well-to-do fruit-merchant has a substantial wooden booth . . . and in summer dispenses slices of water-melon and *aqua cedrata* to the *gamins* of the New York thoroughfares, just as he once did to the small lazzorini of Naples or the fisherboys of Venice. . . . At night the flaring lamps make the dusky faces and the masses of fruit glow in a way that adds much to the picturesqueness.[45]

Another remarked that the Italian peddler "exhibits his wares dressed in such neatness of design that the customer almost hesitates to disturb the picture."[46] In the journal *Charities*, author and social reformer Lilian Brandt concluded that the "attractive arrangement of fruit stands, the picturesque gayety of the Italian quarters in our cities . . . these are familiar evidences of a racial characteristic which should be recognized as a distinct contribution to American life."[47] The food trade thus became a means for the immigrants to project—perhaps unwittingly—a cultured sensibility that Americans had long associated with Italy, but not with the humble ditchdiggers of the Lower East Side.[48] Future generations of ethnic food merchants—including Patsy D'Agostino—would play on these sentimental associations to win favor with magazine writers and customers.

The growth of Italian retailing also stemmed from a generational divide within the immigrant community, however. Commentators noted that one of the qualities that separated second-generation Italian Americans from their immigrant parents was their nascent entrepreneurial spirit. The first generation of immigrants had directed their wages and their concerns toward their families and their home villages in Italy and hesitated to invest in the promises of America. Their conservative economic strategies often merged with a pessimism based in their lack of occupational security and the centuries of hardship that the peasantry had endured. But young Italian Americans seemed particularly attuned to the possibilities of the marketplace. Brandt argued that in the Italian community, the "most striking manifestation of the American spirit" could be found "in the economic aspirations of the children." She explained, "The ambition which in Italy would have been kept dormant by social traditions, is roused in America by the all-pervasive and generally effective idea of 'getting ahead.'"[49]

Robert Foerster concluded that pushcarts and corner stores embodied this notion of striving—"a special incarnation of the individualist impulse for self-redemption."[50]

When reflecting on his career as a grocer, Patsy D'Agostino would argue that his experiences on a pushcart were foundational to his understanding of the free market and his success as an entrepreneur. Perhaps no other economic body, public institution, or organization was as vital to the development of ethnic business in New York City as the pushcart. For those immigrants determined to escape more brutal vocations, it represented opportunity—as they could go into business with a minimum of capital and, with a steady run of profits, work toward ownership of their own shops. Generations of future grocers and shopkeepers would thus learn the fundamental laws of the marketplace selling their wares to the city's masses. Yet the history of the pushcart also offers a vivid biography of New York and its immigrants. In the late nineteenth century, the pushcart trade became an emblem of ethnic culture and the gritty, egalitarian ethos of the city itself. By the advent of the New Deal, however, public officials would wrangle the pushcart trade into enclosed markets as part of a larger strategy of urban planning, just as tenement districts were merging into broader blue-collar communities. The narrative of the pushcart thus encompasses the immigrants' passage from ghettoization to assimilation, and "Old" New York's evolution into a modern metropolis—a journey that would be lived out by Patsy and Nicholas D'Agostino and their descendants.

The first pushcart peddlers served the peculiar needs of the city's ethnic and laboring classes, while supplying them with fresh produce and perishables at affordable prices.[51] Over time, the pushcarts began to satisfy the appetites of the city's more adventurous residents, a place where "the American of longer standing could experiment to his heart's—or stomach's—content."[52] Yet the pushcart also represented opportunity for thousands of ambitious immigrants; according to an estimate made in 1925, more than 90 percent of the city's 7,800 peddlers were foreign-born.[53] By the mid-1920s, New York had fifty-three pushcart markets, with "enough carts to line one side of Broadway for the whole length of the island." In terms of numbers, the city's pushcart vendors did an annual business of $35 million, selling about two hundred different commodities, "from apples to umbrellas."[54] The food trade, however, was the foundation of the pushcart business, as approximately 1.5 million New Yorkers bought some portion of their fruit, vegetables, dried fruits, nuts, and cheese from a peddler.[55]

Despite the pushcarts' established role in the life of the city, there was vigorous debate among administrators, store owners, and consumer groups about the regulation, and possible elimination, of the pushcart trade by the first decade of the twentieth century. Pushcarts were criticized for the discarded produce they left rotting in the streets—which in the summer months attracted hordes of flies and gave off a thick odor—and the "rabble" they attracted. Shopkeepers also complained that peddlers blocked their stores and drove away customers.[56] The city's failure to effectively register and regulate peddlers added to their reputation for lawlessness.[57] As a result of public pressure, officials began to discuss the possibility of herding the pushcarts into enclosures or vacant lots or under bridges and viaducts.[58] Finally, in 1918, the New York Municipal Assembly used a series of ordinances to establish the majority of the city's public markets.[59] Aided by this new legislation, the pushcart trade seemed to enter a proverbial "golden age" in the 1920s, when Patsy and Nicholas began their own careers. Greater regulation and the establishment of permanent market spaces removed the more unsavory aspects of the trade, while licensing provided hundreds of thousands of dollars of revenue for the city. New York's Department of Markets issued over 10,000 permits a year for its permanent markets in the mid-1920s.[60]

Yet the economy of the "Roaring Twenties" also changed the character of New York, as it expanded its middle and professional classes and brought new wealth to thousands. Against this backdrop, store owners, urban planners, politicians, and power brokers squared off against peddlers, social workers, and urban romantics in the kind of battle that would define New York's cultural politics for years to come. By the end of the twenties—the same decade that saw rates of immigration plummet with the passage of the Immigration Act of 1924—the political tide would turn against the pushcart. In 1929, all peddlers were banned from doing business in Midtown Manhattan.[61] In 1930, a citizens committee established by the mayor found that the sanitary conditions at open-air markets were "deplorable and a potential menace to the city."[62] By the early 1930s, there were reports in the local press that administrators had targeted the pushcarts as an impediment to civic progress.

Public officials, as well as the peddlers' adversaries, proposed a variety of strategies for controlling New York's organic marketplace.[63] Throughout the next decade, the city campaigned to further condense the approximately fifty street markets that were spread throughout the five boroughs into a handful of enclosed, government-owned terminal markets.[64] With his commitment to public works and modernizing infrastructure, Mayor Fiorello La Guardia made the construction of these markets—and the eradication of the pushcart—a priority.[65] In 1934, La Guardia ordered that no licenses be issued to pushcarts except for the sale of "staple food products" to eliminate the pushcarts' competition with taxpaying stores.[66] Three years later, the mayor, with the assistance of the commissioner of markets and the Merchants Association, redoubled his efforts to incorporate the pushcart trade into new terminal markets in East Harlem and the Bronx. He explained that this "reform" would eliminate unnecessary middlemen, make commerce more efficient, and bring the consumer and the farmer closer together.[67] Despite these efforts, 6,000 to 7,000 pushcart peddlers continued to ply their trade in the city of New York in the mid-1930s.[68] But the Department of Markets' requirement that all licensed merchants rent permanent stalls in the terminals dealt a heavy blow to the notion of the itinerant peddler.

In 1937, *The New York Times* eulogized the pushcart's passing, even if a lonely few remained on the streets to sell hot dogs or trinkets. *The Times* mused that in the future, the city might "have a pushcart wing in the Metropolitan Museum, with samples of carts, awnings, simulated fruits, vegetables, shoes, aprons, dishes, hot dogs, and even pants, and perhaps a few lifelike effigies similar to those of the slaves who long ago rowed the Egyptian lords and ladies up and down the Nile."[69] The paper concluded that "one pauses to drop a reminiscent tear—farewell to a busy, animated incident of the street scene; farewell to the cries of the hawkers; farewell to the bright colors of fruits and flowers; farewell to the smell of decaying fish; farewell to lovely lack of sanitation and glowing inefficiency; farewell to another bit of old New York."[70]

Even as city officials and the peddlers sparred over the future of the pushcart, a revolution in food merchandising was occurring on Long Island. In 1930, Michael Cullen opened his massive King Kullen Market—often credited as the world's first supermarket. Cullen believed that with the onset of the Great Depression, consumers would flock to stores that sold a high volume of goods at low prices. His massive operation offered several innovations—including a plentiful stock of inexpensive dry goods, available in neat piles and open bins throughout his store. Cullen encouraged patrons to examine and choose their own groceries (a concept first introduced by Piggly Wiggly of Memphis in 1916), and then to proceed to crude counters at the front where they would be "checked out" with the aid of an adding machine. By 1936, King Kullen had seventeen stores doing $6 million worth of business.[71]

Other major retailers followed Cullen's example and began to convert their conventional groceries to "supermarkets." In the 1930s, Safeway shuttered thousands of its locations and reopened them according to a modified version of Cullen's plan, while the Great Atlantic & Pacific Tea Company closed three traditional stores for every new supermarket it opened. While innovations in the production of tin cans and cardboard boxes in the late nineteenth century were fundamental to A&P's early success, the company also benefited from a vast network of warehouses and unparalleled purchasing power to save on distribution costs and keep prices low. By 1930, A&P's "profit through volume" strategy would allow it to become the first company to sell $1 billion in merchandise in a year.[72] In the crowded, high-rent environment of New York City, independent grocers would come to view the local A&P as the figurative bully on their block.

As noted by scholars such as Marc Levinson and Richard Tedlow, the rise of the modern supermarket was prefaced by a handful of innovations that stimulated revolutionary changes in consumer behavior. For grocers, the development of commercial-sized electric refrigerators enabled the sale of meat and dairy, while advances in the use of cellophane allowed longer shelf life for candy and baked goods (including the new-fangled sliced bread), and the attractive display of precut meat.[73] The soaring popularity of the automobile and access to refrigerators in the home also allowed shoppers to venture outside their immediate neighborhoods to find the best prices and selection of products and "stock up." All these developments hastened a dramatic expansion in the size of stores. Relatedly, in the 1930s, Kroger opened the first grocery that was surrounded on all four sides by a parking lot, while Sylvan Goodman of Standard Foods introduced the first shopping cart.[74] The supermarket concept would not make its full impact on the retail landscape until after World War II. But stores like King Kullen and Safeway would inspire the next generation of entrepreneurs, and Michael Cullen's presumptions about consumer behavior would shape retail strategies for the next fifty years.[75] Historian Tracey Deutsch has thus argued, "Supermarkets became a model for how all retailers, not just grocers, might sell larger amounts of goods at lower prices than they had thought possible."[76]

The pushcarts had bestowed a sense of earthy charm and "Old World" vibrancy on New York. For the next couple of decades, terminal markets would continue their legacy in a more contained, regulated fashion. One could argue that places like the Bronx Terminal Market served as extensions of the pushcart, in function if not impulse. But the enclosure of the pushcart trade signaled the supremacy of the supermarket paradigm. The Bronx Terminal Market functioned mainly as a supplier to grocers and restaurants, whereas the pushcarts had once provided shoppers with a wide variety of inexpensive food items and domestic goods. Within these spaces, individual traders tended to specialize in particular fruits or vegetables, complementing the compartmentalization of the supermarkets. In his remarks to commemorate the opening of the new markets, Mayor La Guardia even advised vendors to remember "you are now longer peddlers. You are now merchants."[77]

The pushcart's eventual decline would also close an avenue of social mobility for thousands of immigrants looking to escape the tyranny of manual labor. Many successful peddlers had moved from the pushcart to jobs as grocery clerks, produce buyers, and store managers. The trade had a particular significance for New York's Italian population. According to the city's commissioner of markets, 90 percent of its 1,300 licensed peddlers were Italian-born even in the mid-1930s.[78] But the pushcart's value as a training ground for entrepreneurs is borne out by the remarkable number of Italian-owned groceries in New York City—ten thousand by the late 1930s—many of which were owned by former peddlers.[79]

For thousands of immigrants, the pushcarts provided an apprenticeship in the rudiments of the food trade while holding the promise of independence and advancement. The skills that aspiring retailers like Patsy and Nicholas D'Agostino developed on the pushcart—how to find the best locations, assess the quality of produce, haggle with suppliers and soothe customers, calculate the amount of merchandise to stock, and run a dynamic operation in a limited space—became their best assets as entrepreneurs. In a sense, Patsy and Nicholas would always be pushcart men, as they continued to apply its lessons even after they became executives. Years later, Patsy D'Agostino would claim that as a peddler, he became an independent businessman in the purest sense—thus achieving a quintessentially American identity—even while mired in the ethnic ghetto. In the coming decades, the D'Agostino family would emerge from its own humble beginnings to join a larger narrative of enterprise, assimilation, and generational mobility out of New York's immigrant neighborhoods—which is the subject of this book.

Figure 2a. Nicola "Nicholas" (*left*) and Pasquale "Patsy" D'Agostino (*right*) as children in Italy (ca. 1914). Personal collection of the author.

Figure 2b. Nicholas (*left*) and Patsy (*right*) with their mother, Loreta (D'Espinosa) D'Agostino (ca. 1916). Personal collection of the author.

Figure 3. Nicholas D'Agostino as a teenager in New York at the beginning of his career in the food business (ca. mid-1920s). Personal collection of the author.

Figure 4a. Frank (*left*) and Adolph Tucciarone (*right*), in front of their grocery at 83rd Street and Lexington Avenue in Manhattan. Young Josephine Tucciarone is visible behind the glass, to the right of her uncle (ca. 1920s). Personal collection of the author.

Figure 4b. Adolph (*left*) and Frank Tucciarone (*right*) inside their store. The placement of their wares behind the counter was standard practice for grocers before the advent of self-service (ca. 1920s). Personal collection of the author.

Figure 5. Tommy Mazzucco and Gerard Carcone's Butterfield Market. Nicholas D'Agostino stands second from the left. Note the new meat counter at the back of the store—a revolutionary concept for the grocery business (ca. 1930). Personal collection of the author.

Figure 6. Patsy and Nicholas D'Agostino, and their families, at the opening of their new store on 85th Street in Manhattan (1945). Personal collection of the author.

CHAPTER 2

Immigrant Grocers and American Dreams (1880–1946)

In May 1943, *The New Yorker* profiled Pasquale "Patsy" D'Agostino in a ten-page article oddly titled "If Trouble Can Be Avoid," introducing the grocer's story to a national audience while establishing the company's mythology. The feature's title came from an incident in which Patsy—already harried by wartime deprivation and regulation—chastised one of his employees for failing to order white eggs, with the warning "If trouble can be avoid, let us avoid it."[1] On its surface, the article was a human-interest story, detailing one person's struggles with the chaos of the home front. Author Mark Murphy solicited his readers' sympathy for the familiar figure of the neighborhood grocer, commending his modest triumph over adversity and celebrating his relentless work ethic. Yet in his portrayal of Patsy D'Agostino's habits, speech, and aspirations, Murphy also reflected the public's assumptions about Italian identity. The story's title advertised the immigrant's broken grammar, while Murphy described Patsy as loud and colorful, but earthy:

> Patsy is a vigorous fellow of thirty-eight, with big shoulders, crisp black hair, glittering black eyes, and an energetic and confident manner. He has a smile which more than one of his customers has described as charming. Recently he has been feeling rather tired, but he doesn't blame the war; he thinks that possibly he needs more sleep than the five or six hours he is in the habit of getting. He is

disturbed about not being able to jump out of bed as quickly as he used to. Nowadays he wakes up around five, lights a cigarette, and lies in bed smoking and anticipating the day ahead with foreboding. At about five-twenty, he gets up, puts a pot of coffee on the stove, shaves, dresses painstakingly, drinks a cup of black coffee laced with a jigger of whiskey. He then sets out for the market in a maroon Pontiac sedan; being a food distributor, he has a B card. He arrives at the market in full voice.[2]

Throughout the article, Murphy showed Patsy blustering at his store clerks' "maltreatment of vegetables" and having profane outbursts about the quality of produce:

Patsy returned to the vegetables and asked Tony if he had any peas. Tony showed him an open bushel, and Patsy took a pod, broke it, and flipped a piece of it into his mouth. He spat, and several peas rolled across the floor. "My God, Tony," he said, "is them things bullets? They should use them in North Africa, boom, boom, in the foxholes. To hell with your goddam peas. You could kill a man throwing those peas at him. My customers come in and I sell them those peas, Tony, what would they think? Such merchandise!"[3]

Historian Mary Corey has argued that in the 1940s and '50s, *The New Yorker* carried dozens of feature articles, short stories, and cartoons in which ethnic figures were valorized as more authentic, noble, and soulful than America's white middle class.[4] To the readers of *The New Yorker*, the ethnic grocer served as a type of pastoral "other"—part sage and part buffoon. Here, the magazine's sentimental gaze recalls an earlier generation of Italian immigrant subjects in popular journalism. Much of Murphy's article is set at the Bronx Terminal Market, a major supplier of fruits and vegetables for New York City grocers. As a type of capitalist frontier, the market was not without menace—it was populated by several unsavory characters, including a "tall, gloomy-looking man," who claimed to "know the right fellows downtown" who could get Patsy turkeys illegally and punctuated his offer by continually poking his finger into Patsy's chest. But Murphy ultimately characterized the Bronx Terminal Market as a haven of rustic immigrants, plying their trade—an idyllic alternative to Manhattan's stifling realm of financiers, stockbrokers, and white-collar functionaries. The market thus served as a window into the "Old World," where the clerks and wholesalers called Patsy "Boss"—an honorable title in the grocery-and-meat business. Murphy wrote:

> The market is a pleasant place. On cool mornings, the store clerks build fires in large cans on the platform and toss spoiled apples into the flames. They give off a sweet, woodsy smell.... In the stores there are great piles of fruit in a variety of colors and vegetables in many shades of green and yellow. The intimacy the men have with vegetables and fruit gives them a profound respect for things that grow in the earth.[5]

The writer seemed captivated by Patsy D'Agostino's identity as an artistic type, privy to a deeper knowledge because of his bond with the soil's harvest. He noted that Patsy was "much more finicky and querulous when he is buying vegetables than the average housewife is," as the grocer scrutinized boxes of broccoli and teased his supplier that, as with children, no two boxes of broccoli were exactly alike. Murphy also spent one-third of a page cataloguing Patsy's shopping list of seventy varieties of fruits and vegetables, which ranged from the ordinary ("two bags white onions," "five pounds garlic," "one crate California carrots") to the exotic and obscure ("half bushel Jerusalem artichokes," "six bunches oyster plants," "a basket escarole," "five pounds root horseradish"). Murphy then observed that while Patsy bought most of the produce quickly, his sentimentality emerged when "over several things obviously close to his heart he lingered and haggled about price and quality."[6]

Throughout the article, Patsy recalled his difficult passage from teen-aged immigrant to failed tradesman to prosperous merchant—an account that became foundational for the future telling and retelling of the brothers' ascent from rags to riches. In the postwar era, after their operation had become a million-dollar business, the early struggles of Patsy and his brother Nicholas were usually described as a prelude to their ultimate triumph as entrepreneurs. In Murphy's feature, Patsy survived his many tribulations to attain a modest version of the American dream. Yet *The New Yorker* profile also makes him into a symbol for the virtues of the city's immigrant class—who quietly endured through a mix of hard work and perseverance. And although Patsy had survived a lifetime of challenges, the article noted that his native grit would continue to be tested by the instability of wartime America.

In this story, Patsy recounted that when he first arrived from Italy in

1921, his father, Ignazio ("Ignatius") Stephen D'Agostino,* brought him to Norwood, Massachusetts. Unfortunately, the nation's industrial economy was suffering through a recession that began soon after Warren G. Harding was elected president. With few prospects, Patsy and his father went to Ambridge, Pennsylvania, and then to New York, where they manned a pushcart at 141st Street and Eighth Avenue in Harlem.[7] For two years, he and his father averaged $30 in weekly profits (their receipts ranged from $125 to nothing) and slept in the unheated back room of a friend's store. Still, Patsy tried to save his wages, and by the time he turned eighteen, he had collected $900. He then bought two pushcarts at 106th Street and Broadway but lost his money through a combination of inexperience and misfortune.

Despondent at his inability to succeed on his own, Patsy quit the pushcart business altogether and began to work as a pipe fitter in the Bronx maintenance shop of the New York, New Haven, and Hartford Railroad. Murphy presented this period as Patsy's exile from the rudiments of his ethnic identity—his family, his freedom, and the fruits of the soil. Murphy explained that Patsy "didn't want to face his father, who was disappointed at his son's giving up the independent existence of pushcart peddling," so Patsy gained a transfer to a railroad shop back in Norwood, where his mother's family lived. But when he arrived, Patsy discovered that he could not work in the shop because of a strike—"One cousin was among the strikers, and his relatives pointed out to Patsy that it would not look well for him to take a job under these circumstances." Patsy subsequently took a job painting shingles in a shop in Norwood. Murphy interpreted this episode through the prism of ethnic sentimentality, writing, "In the months away from green vegetables and fresh fruit, Patsy was miserable." Patsy himself remembered his anguish stemming from the separation from his family. He said, "I was lonely. I was away from my father. My mother and brother were in Italy. And it was cold in Massachusetts."[8] His relatives convinced him to return to his lonely father and to life on the pushcarts.

Patsy then shared one of his favorite anecdotes with Murphy—a story that was featured in several articles on his life—which he used to explain his ultimate exile from the pushcart. He and his father bought twenty-five bushels of string beans at sixty-five cents a bushel and started to sell

---

*To associates and his family, Ignatius Stephen D'Agostino was known by his middle name, Stephen, but for the sake of narrative clarity (as two of his grandchildren bore his first and middle names) I will refer to him as Ignatius.

them at three pounds for a quarter. "Then it starts to rain, thunder and lightning like cats and dogs," Patsy recalled, "and by dark we are selling the beans two pounds for a nickel. I quit the pushcart business right then."[9] By this time, Patsy had decided that his ultimate ambition was to become a clerk in a grocery store because they worked inside and were treated with respect. While contemporary readers might regard this as a modest objective, it seemed an act of great hubris to Patsy's "Old World" father, who argued that his son lacked the English and the polished manners to get hired. Patsy worked as a plasterer for half a year before he could get a job as a delivery boy in the grocery store of Mr. Gennaro Gentile (the only man Patsy ever called "Boss," he asserted). In Gentile's store, Patsy did achieve his goal of becoming a clerk, but in 1926 he quit once again, this time so that he could marry Irene Salemme in Dedham, Massachusetts. He went to work for the chain store First National in Boston but walked out, Murphy recalled, after being "unjustly reprimanded." Patsy moved back to New York, where he dug ditches for a year, before going back to work for Mr. Gentile.[10]

Then, in 1930, after nine exhausting years of switching jobs and localities, Patsy became a partner in Frank Tucciarone's grocery at 83rd Street and Lexington Avenue. Two years later, Patsy's brother, Nicholas D'Agostino, bought out Tucciarone, and the two partners reopened the store as a new type of operation. Yet, despite his status as a founder and partner in the company, Nicholas was nearly absent from Murphy's feature. Nicholas was mentioned only as "Patsy's brother, Nick, a bouncing, friendly fellow" who "had come to this country in 1924, and Patsy had advised him to become a butcher."[11] The article's lack of regard for Nicholas's role in the business, and its misrepresentation of Patsy's role in directing his career, would be a source of tension between the brothers for years to come.

Murphy ended his piece by returning to the subject of vegetables. He described Patsy D'Agostino carefully monitoring his store's operation, even chastising his employees for such offenses as mistreating the cauliflower. On his drive home, Patsy reflected on his wishes for his children. He did not express the grandiose visions of a would-be mogul or empire builder, but of a simple man who wanted to pass his beloved trade to another generation:

> My children, they can do what they want to do, because this is a free country, and I want them to do what they want to do, but I would like one of them to take up the grocery business. Meats and groceries is good, and there is fresh vegetables. Fresh vegetables are green and

beautiful. You have to know them. You have to know how to treat them, so they will stay fresh, and people will buy them, and the fruit and the vegetables will look beautiful on the table, and the people will be healthy because fruit and vegetables are good for them. Fruit and vegetables are from nature. They are beautiful, like nature.[12]

The "Other" Italians: Lost Ancestors and Historical Contingencies

The personal narratives of Nicholas and Patsy D'Agostino begin with a remembrance of lowly origins before celebrating the brothers' climb from proverbial rags to riches. But their immigrant forebears, whose efforts are lost to the public record, set the stage for their triumph. What are the historical factors that limited this generation's ambitions? Must the narratives of our modern-day Horatio Algers consider, "What if?"

In the annals of American business, biographies that celebrate the glories of individual enterprise tend to suggest that their protagonists had a sure path to success—that victory was destined by superior skill, will, or vision. These narratives often suffer amnesia about history's many contingencies and counterfactuals while obscuring the contributions of minor characters who once seemed bound for starring roles, particularly if they are women. At the time of the profile in *The New Yorker*, Patsy D'Agostino and his brother, Nicholas, had already overcome poverty, their lack of education, an unstable family life, cultural marginalization, and an uncertain command of English to become respected merchants. In the ensuing decades, they would continue to distinguish themselves from their peers through a combination of talent and industry. Yet a recounting of the brothers' family history shows that their parents, uncles, and in-laws also seemed poised to capture their own versions of the American dream. Why did the aspirations of this earlier generation founder? In the larger chronicle of ethnic entrepreneurship, is it possible for one to view their earlier ventures as prototypes that failed? How did their experiences prepare the way for Nicholas and Patsy's own ascendance? And what do their fates reveal about the limited horizons of the city's Italian population at this point in history?

Most versions of Patsy and Nicholas D'Agostino's rise from pushcart peddlers to supermarket magnates begin in the remote mountain town of Bugnara, in the province of L'Aquila and the region of Abruzzi (now known as Abruzzo).[13] With the Apennine Mountains serving as an effective barrier, the region had little contact with the outside world—leading one commentator to muse that Abruzzi had experienced less modernization than any region in Italy, with its residents "remaining the same as they were centuries ago."[14] Throughout Abruzzi, the landscape was bounded by "tratturi"—sheep trails that led in and out of the mountains—that dated from Roman times. To outsiders, Abruzzi's harsh terrain and isolation seemed to endow its natives with a rugged, resilient character. After centuries of privation, they had earned the label "forte e gentile," which roughly translates as "strong and kind."[15]

In Bugnara, the symbols and customs of the premodern world held sway. The system of primogeniture continued to determine authority and property ownership for the town's families, while the local economy was based on small-scale agriculture, including the cultivation of corn, olives, and hay and the raising of goats and sheep. Every day, the women of the town—some dressed in starched headdresses and black dresses with petticoats and aprons—would gather at the well to gossip and draw water. Later, they would hike to rivers and streams in the mountains to do their laundry, beating the clothes on rocks to wash away the grime. The town's population was ostensibly Catholic, but its religious practices incorporated the superstitions, folk rituals, and anticlericalism known to the Italian peasantry. While the Apennines offered stunning vistas and a certain rough grandeur, Bugnara itself suffered from dismaying poverty. Throughout the town, chickens, dogs, and goats wandered among the human residents, even sharing their lodging on occasion.[16] Before World War II, most houses in Bugnara lacked electricity, and so a family's meals were usually cooked over an open fireplace.[17] Thus, the interiors of the stone and stucco houses tended to be dim and blackened with smoke. Homes in Bugnara also did not have running water or indoor plumbing, and Nicholas D'Agostino joked that the town water supply offered a choice in drinking water: "One to make you 'go' [to the bathroom] and another to stop you from 'going.'"[18]

In *The Italian Emigration of Our Times*, Robert F. Foerster observed, "Emigration has wrought in Italy what once the Black Death wrought in England."[19] Foerster noted that even with Italians' tendency to shuttle between America and Italy, in the fifty years from 1870 to 1920, "four million persons have been permanently lost to Italy and twice as many temporarily."[20] As with scores of other Italian villages, between 1880 and 1930 Bugnara sent most of its adult males to America to work in construction, manual labor, or the lower levels of the food trade. The "push" factors for emigration from towns like Bugnara were clear: gnawing hunger, desperate living conditions, and limited social advancement. The late nineteenth century was a particularly difficult period for the villages of southern Italy. The region struggled to maintain its agrarian economy on a cruel landscape, with a climate that featured blazing summers and infrequent rainfall. The modernization of the system of feudal agriculture earlier in the century eliminated common lands and privatized large agricultural estates while causing widespread deforestation. The clearing of wooded areas eliminated key methods of survival for the peasantry, contributed to soil erosion, and made malaria a widespread threat. Moreover, the unification of Italy in 1861 had fostered the growth of the country's industrialized northern regions at the expense of the agrarian south. The establishment of a national state meant heavier taxes for the creation of an army and navy and the building of infrastructure and modern public works, as well as a proliferation of local bureaucrats looking for bribes. Meanwhile, the peasantry saw their fates determined by powerful absentee landlords and local gentry. Finally, Italy struggled with overpopulation, as even into the 1930s, Italy's population density was greater than that of China, India, and all but three European countries. This confluence of factors, as well as the uncertainties of farming itself, meant that Italians suffered widespread malnourishment.[21] Conversely, the emigration of adult males could bring long-term economic benefits to a community if the émigrés sent their wages back home.

Who remained to continue the work of farm, family, and community? As in most agrarian societies, work in rural Italy had always been a family enterprise. In regions such as Abruzzi, where men typically traveled miles from the home to tend fields or flocks of livestock, and could be absent for days or even weeks, women already had some authority over the management of the household. The women in these communities cultivated corn, wheat, olives, flax, and vegetables and hauled them to market; raised chickens and pigs; and usually made their families' clothing—a responsibility that included spinning and weaving, as well as sewing.[22] And in the homes of peasants and artisans, children were expected to work by age eight, leading one historian to comment that in Italy "work was children's primary education."[23] But the massive emigration of Italian men in the late nineteenth and early twentieth centuries cemented the crucial role of women and children in keeping their communities alive—as well as the sense of abandonment felt by those who had been left behind—as seen in the narrative of the D'Agostino family.

Since so many of the husbands and young men in the village had gone to America and returned only seasonally, if at all, Bugnara often functioned as a matriarchal society. This system of migrant labor and settlement put tremendous strain on marriage and family life, however. In the case of Nicholas D'Agostino, his father's emigration meant that he was essentially denied the pleasures of childhood because he began working at such a young age. Until he was fourteen, Nicholas's mother and aunts served as his main parental figures, and he remained devoted to them for the rest of his life. At the same time, Nick's separation from Ignatius seemed to instill in him a longing to prove himself worthy of the world's respect. One might argue that his grand ambitions began with a desire for recognition from his absent father.

In the early 1980s, Nicholas D'Agostino began to compose an autobiography, which he never completed.[24] Nicholas foregrounded his narrative in the hardships that shaped his family's history and left him with deep psychic wounds. He wrote that when his mother, Loreta D'Espinosa, was ten years old, her mother died. Soon thereafter, Loreta had to get her first job, hauling bricks for the building of a railroad bridge.[25] Though their father was the town blacksmith, the family's financial circumstances forced him to hire out Loreta's younger brothers and sisters to various gentry just so they could get enough to eat. Nicholas remembered his mother "telling me how cruel some of the masters and mistresses were. Sometimes they would send a child of four or five up into the mountains with snow on the ground to tend the sheep with only cloth shoes to wear."[26]

Loreta remained unmarried until she was in her thirties—which might indicate a dedication to her siblings, her distaste for the demands of marriage, or even a certain rebellious spirit. Her own family remembered her as quite a prickly character. Yet according to her son, when Ignatius D'Agostino heard about Loreta's "beauty, strength and good character" from his compatriots (including Loreta's brother, Tony D'Espinosa) on a railroad gang in Youngstown, Ohio, he was immediately intrigued. Ignatius then sent Loreta a parcel containing his picture, a small monetary gift, and a proposal of marriage. Loreta, in turn, invited the stranger to visit her in her hometown. Nicholas wrote that the courtship created a small scandal in Bugnara: "Our town of 1500 souls was shocked. One of the leading citizens of the town, a doctor, said to her, 'Aren't you making a mistake, promising to marry a man from America without knowing his habits? My girl, you are buying a cat in a bag!'" Apparently, the doctor's violated sense of propriety only encouraged Loreta's curiosity, as she "replied without hesitation, 'When the cat in the bag arrives, I will examine the merchandise, and if I don't like what I see, I will let the cat go!'"[27]

Perhaps Loreta D'Espinosa was genuinely drawn to Ignatius, or maybe she saw marriage as a means of escape from small-town poverty, because soon after meeting him, she accepted his proposal. But the transient condition of immigrant laborers diminished the couple's relationship. After winning Loreta's hand, Ignatius went back to America to work for a short interval and returned to Bugnara in 1904 to marry Loreta in the village church. Then, after a brief period of cohabitation that resulted in the birth of his first son, Ignatius returned to the US. Loreta and four-year-old Patsy followed him to America in 1909.

All immigrants face daunting challenges—from finding work and lodging, to learning a new language and customs—when trying to adapt to the demands of living in the US. Still, even if Italian immigrant men were marginalized within the social hierarchy, their work gave them access to the world beyond the ethnic ghetto. Since most unmarried immigrant women worked for wages, often in the city's booming textile industry, they also had opportunities for socializing with their peers and having some exposure to the larger culture. But the peasant wives who were brought to New York by their itinerant husbands faced unique difficulties in acclimating to America. In Italian culture, social taboos discouraged married women from working outside the home, even if the demands of raising children and keeping house would allow it. With few opportunities to participate in the public life of the city, married Italian women had little exposure to American culture or language. Moreover, the nature of women's domestic duties in the US, even in the immigrant districts of Lower Manhattan, contributed to their isolation.[28] Many of the daily tasks in their home villages, such as washing clothes and baking bread, had a communal aspect that was lacking in America. Though immigrant women would visit in the halls and stairwells of their buildings, they performed many of their chores (cooking, laundry, and sewing work to supplement the family income) within the confines of their private apartments.[29]

Loreta must have found the adjustment to life in New York City extremely difficult. She went from living with her family in a tranquil mountain town of fewer than two thousand residents, to a cramped city apartment, amid millions of strangers whose language she could neither write nor speak. Moreover, her own husband was a stranger to her and her son, as he had lived thousands of miles away for most of their marriage. How could she not have felt isolated or even depressed by her new situation? Is it surprising that she contemplated an immediate return to Bugnara, especially when one considers her reputation for defiance? She is likely not the first immigrant bride to reconsider her decision to leave the shelter of her village for the uncertain hazards of marriage and migration. While the immigrant's encounter with the American dream is often cast as a tale of masculine triumph, Loreta D'Agostino's disappointments may have been more typical, especially for women.

Still, in the few months she was living in New York, Loreta became pregnant with Nicholas. Soon afterward, with one son in tow and another still in the womb, she took the boat back home. Years later, her children would address their mother's decision with brevity and tact. Patsy D'Agostino would say of his mother's return, "From the very beginning America did not agree with Mom, or vice versa. She always said it had something to do with the water."[30] Nicholas wrote in his autobiography that in New York, "I became a gleam in my father's eye. While she was carrying me, my mother became lonely for home, so she took Patsy back to Italy, and I was born in Bugnara."[31]

Loreta's decision had serious consequences for herself and her children. Her "loneliness" for home meant a return to the dire poverty of Bugnara with the additional challenge of raising two sons without much support from her angry husband. The family was sustained through financial and physical hardship—including a catastrophic earthquake in 1915—by the efforts of Loreta and her sisters, and by contributions sent by her brothers working in America. Her children also had to grapple with divided loyalties; as Nicholas later admitted, "I had a foot in both worlds."[32] At the conclusion of the Great War, Ignatius returned to Bugnara, and Nicholas, already nine years old, met his father for the first time. The story of Ignatius's arrival would become a seminal memory for his two sons. Years later, Patsy would recall that he had joined a pack of boys who were tormenting a grubby stranger who had stumbled into their village, drunk. Later that day, Patsy discovered that the stranger was, in fact, his own father. These anguished memories of childhood and their parents' rocky marriage likely fueled the two brothers' feverish desire for success and social recognition.

Ignatius stayed in Bugnara for nearly a year before returning to New York. In 1921, he returned to Italy to retrieve fifteen-year-old Patsy and bring him back to the US. Up until this time, Patsy and Nicholas had been attending their local school. But after Ignatius and Patsy left, Nicholas observed, his mother "realized that she could no longer afford to send me to school, so at the age of ten, my formal education ended." Nicholas got a position as an apprentice to a cabinetmaker, doing his master's bidding by performing tasks as varied as carrying bricks and shining shoes.[33] As part of his duties, Nicholas was sometimes required to make a fifteen-kilometer round trip into neighboring Sulmona for supplies; he would pocket his train fare and walk in order to contribute to the family's coffers.

In his writings, Nicholas D'Agostino remembers his childhood in Italy mainly with fondness and nostalgia. But considering the size of his dreams and his ego, he must have struggled against the limitations of life in Bugnara. Young Nicholas was aware of the stifling class distinctions that characterized Italian life, even in a town as small as Bugnara. He told the story of a baron, also with the surname D'Agostino but unrelated to his father, who asked his mother to change their last name because, as a noble, he did not want to share a name with a "poor D'Agostino." The baron even offered to buy sole ownership of the D'Agostino name. Nicholas remembered:

> One day, my mother received a box of fruit from her mother-in-law in Tufo di Minturno, which was delivered by mistake to the baron. The baron was so upset that he sent for my mother; and told her to write to her husband in America, and ask how much money he would take to change his name, because he did not wish to have a poor D'Agostino in the same town with a baron D'Agostino, it would be too much of a conflict! My mother quickly said "I am now a D'Agostino, and I shall stay one—you stay in your own house and I will stay in mine."[34]

When he reached adolescence, Nicholas was deemed ready for the adult demands of an immigrant's life in America. In his autobiography, he explained his migration to the United States as an effort to heal a growing rift between his older brother and his father. Nicholas recalled that in 1924, his brother Patsy wrote to their mother complaining that "it was almost impossible for him to get along with my father; and that the only salvation would be for me to come to America to repair the situation. When I think now what was expected of me, that at 14, I was expected to reconcile these two grown men, it is almost unbelievable." For the voyage to America, Nicholas's mother bought him fresh cheese and mortadella and a new suit, his first. Loreta even paid to upgrade his passage to second class and, through her tears, explained to Nicholas that while his brother had been allowed to go to school into his teens, Nicholas "never demanded or asked for anything; and I have given you so little that I am ashamed and mortified."[35]

Nicholas's account of his departure indicated his own ingenuousness. He recalled that in his last week in Bugnara, his mother "counseled me as tenderly as if I had been a bride preparing for her marriage. She told me never to force a girl to do anything against her will, for it would come back upon me, and since I did not have a sister, my own children or grandchildren would pay for it." Of course, the self-made millionaire concluded his recollection of this episode with a declaration of his masculinity: "I reminded her that when I first started carrying bricks on [a] hod on my shoulder, she would look at my bleeding shoulder and say, 'What is that man doing to you?' And I would answer her, 'This is what makes me tough. This is what makes me a man! The reason I can now travel alone is that I am not afraid.'"[36] Within a couple of years of her younger son's departure, Loreta took to bed with a mysterious "illness." Over the last three decades of her life, she rarely left the confines of her upstairs room, even to relieve herself. And when her husband returned to Bugnara, the couple essentially lived apart.

D'Agostino Supermarkets dates its origins to 1932, the year Nicholas "co-founded" the business with his brother Patsy and, not coincidentally, married Josephine Tucciarone. Yet the story of D'Agostino's reveals a continuous process of mythmaking that has buried the influence of several figures who helped shape the company's identity. Reviewing the narrative of the business and the family, it is notable how Patsy and Nicholas's father, uncles, and in-laws laid the groundwork for the brothers' success. In published accounts of the company's history, however, these relatives often symbolized the "Old World" types who were unable to adapt to their new country—a first generation of ragged immigrants who never attained riches. While these forebears built a foundation that enabled the advancement of their children, their very failures indicate how fragile the American dream was for the first generation of Italian immigrants.

In 1888, the brothers' father, Ignatius D'Agostino, left his home in Tufo di Minturno, a town in southern Lazio not far from the Tyrrhenian Sea. He had already had a painful childhood, as his impoverished parents had hired him out to a wealthy family so that he could get enough to eat. In his early years in the US, he lived out the prototypical existence of the Italian immigrant of the late nineteenth century—following friends and relatives to whatever industrial employment was available in hopes of earning enough money to build a more prosperous life in Italy. In Wheeling, West Virginia, he worked on the railroad and slept in boxcars with his fellow "braccianti," sometimes rising in the middle of the night to kill the lice that swarmed over him. His work on the railroad eventually took him to Youngstown, Ohio, where he labored alongside the brothers of his future wife. Later, Ignatius worked briefly in Ambridge, Pennsylvania, at a factory that manufactured parts for bridges. He eventually settled among his relatives in New York City and began a career as an itinerant fruit peddler.

Ignatius was part of a generation of migrants who suffered the brunt of anti-Italian prejudice. He tired of being labeled as a "dago" by the "Americans," but Ignatius became particularly bitter about the dehumanizing treatment suffered by Italian laborers.[37] For years, he would grouse to his sons about the discrimination he endured in his early years in the US. His son Patsy once quoted Ignatius as remarking that in America, "you could earn a dollar but were treated like a pig doing it."[38] Although he eventually became a citizen, Ignatius would never consider the United States his home.

The insecure condition of the Italian worker also affected Ignatius's opportunities for economic and domestic stability. As previously noted, Loreta D'Espinosa bore the couple's first child in Italy while Ignatius was back in America. His wife and child stayed in Italy for about five years while Ignatius continued to work in various capacities. And when Ignatius finally brought Loreta and little Patsy to the US, they stayed for only a few months. After this difficult split from his wife and children, Ignatius's fortunes continued their rise and fall, as he moved from peddler to grocer and back to peddler, his struggles exacerbated by his taste for alcohol and gambling. When he returned to Bugnara after the Great War, he thought he was staying "for good," having earned a fair sum in America. But in the inflationary climate of post–World War I Italy, his savings evaporated, prompting another return to America.

Ignatius introduced Patsy to the world of pushcart peddling and gave him a piece of the partnership he had formed with another acquaintance. Patsy would later recall that as a businessman, his father seemed to lack vision, focusing on the day's receipts without a thought for long-term strategy or investment. Ignatius carried the psychic traits of first-generation immigrants—including a hardened "peasant mentality." His sons noted that in his "Old World" business strategies, Ignatius tended to be conservative and pessimistic about the future. When Patsy and Nicholas began to develop their own aspirations, their father was critical to the point of being derisive. Yet Ignatius had some success as a merchant and a grocer throughout the 1920s and early 1930s. When he finally returned to Italy in 1939, he had nearly five thousand dollars in his possession, making him a modest success for an immigrant of his generation.

In their accomplishments, Nicholas and Patsy D'Agostino would also be indebted to Ignatius's contemporary—and Nick's future father-in-law—Francesco ("Frank") Tucciarone and to his brother, Adolpho ("Adolph"). The Tucciarone brothers established the store that later became the first D'Agostino's, and thus could make some claim to the title of founders of the supermarket chain. In the late 1920s, it seemed that the Tucciarones' climb from obscurity to prosperity would be worthy of its own legend. But like Ignatius D'Agostino, Frank and Adolph exemplified the limits, rather than the fulfillment, of America's promise to ethnic entrepreneurs.

Like Ignatius, Frank Tucciarone came to the US from Tufo di Minturno. Although the Tucciarone family had once been members of the gentry, they suffered financial difficulties that limited the brothers' prospects. Frank first tried to join the Franciscans, following in the footsteps of two of his brothers, but was asked to leave after one of them died of typhoid. (The friars suspected he might be a carrier of the disease.) He was so desperate to secure a position with the order that he lingered about the seminary for three days, filling his empty stomach with snow, even offering to clean the friary's toilets if he was allowed to stay. Eventually, the Franciscans put him on a train and sent him back home. Frank then decided to go to America, where he slept in a stable and supported himself by selling apples on the street. Through the sweat of his brow and the aid of his "paesani," Frank Tucciarone steadily advanced in the food business, working on pushcarts and small groceries throughout Manhattan. For a brief time, Frank actually went into business with his friend and fellow townsman, Ignatius D'Agostino. On more than one occasion, Frank (who had some education because of his family background) would read aloud from Alessandro Manzoni's novel *The Betrothed* while Ignatius would prepare vegetables for sale, tears streaming down his face.[39]

Once he had achieved some financial stability, Frank sought a bride. He "crossed the ocean three times" to win the hand of Celeste Mazzucco, a girl from back in Tufo. After her family moved to New York, Frank romanced seventeen-year-old Celeste by taking her to hear Enrico Caruso sing at the Metropolitan Opera House. The couple married in 1908 and had two daughters and two sons over the next eight years. Soon after he was wed, Frank and his brother, Adolph, founded a grocery store at 83rd Street and Lexington Avenue, where they enjoyed modest profits serving the posh neighborhood. But Frank's success was tempered by an unfortunate turn of events. In 1918, Celeste died during childbirth, throwing his family life into chaos. Single parenthood proved overwhelming for him, and he sent his children to live with various relatives. His children struggled with this arrangement, and after his eldest daughter, nine-year-old Josephine, was found sleepwalking down the block from a relative's Staten Island home, Frank began to seek a new bride.[40] Less than a year after his first wife's death, Frank Tucciarone remarried.

By the mid-1920s, the lives of Frank Tucciarone and his children seemed to have steadied. With the continued success of the Tucciarone Brothers store, Frank moved his family to a house in a stable middle-class neighborhood in the Bronx. By all accounts, he was a gentle soul with few vices, but he did enjoy playing poker and "the numbers"—the underground lottery that was part of the fabric of most working-class neighborhoods. Perhaps it was this love of gambling or, more likely, Frank's middle-class aspirations that then drew him to the booming stock market, where he began to invest a significant share of the profits from the grocery business. He also bought a Packard sedan that was nicknamed "six rooms and a bath," which he had to push out of parking spaces because he did not know how to drive in reverse.[41] As the nation's fortunes climbed to exhilarating heights, this immigrant must have believed that he had attained his American dream, unaware that the looming depression would erase his accomplishments from the historical record.

Despite their prosperity, the Tucciarone brothers struggled to maintain family harmony—foreshadowing the D'Agostinos' own acrimony and in-fighting when future generations sought to claim credit for the business's success. Following a particularly nasty dispute, Adolph Tucciarone decided to split with his brother after nearly two decades of working together, and Frank was forced to look outside the family for a partner. Ignatius D'Agostino then helped broker a deal to bring in his son Patsy as Frank's partner. It seemed as if the family grocery, now called "Frank Tucciarone and Company," had been saved. Unfortunately, Frank had invested heavily in stocks, perhaps even buying "on the margins," and the market crash of 1929 eventually wiped out his savings and his capital.[42] By 1931, he was looking for someone to buy *his* share of the business to save the operation. After finally selling to young Nicholas D'Agostino, Frank and his family moved out to the Jersey Shore to foil his creditors; he lived out his days there working as a clerk in a food store.

Frank Tucciarone's sagging fortunes also affected his children's prospects in the food business (another unfortunate trend in this family saga). His sons would work in the middling levels of the grocery industry, serving in various capacities as fruit buyers, dairy supervisors, and store managers for D'Agostino's. But the decline of the Tucciarone grocery also changed the course of another promising career, that of Frank's eldest daughter, Josephine. While it is unlikely, in that era, that Josephine Tucciarone would have risen to a position in management or ownership, or that the social norms of motherhood would have allowed her to focus on a profession, as a teenager, she was already her father's principal lieutenant. Josephine's life as a woman toiling in a business dominated by men serves as another example of an American dream deferred and a reminder of the limitations young women of her generation faced.

In many ways, Josephine had a prototypical Italian-immigrant childhood. Her family moved so frequently that she attended more than a half dozen grammar schools, and after graduating from the eighth grade she was forced to drop out. The family eventually resettled near her father's store in Yorkville, a move that reflected her father's own ascendance from pushcart peddler to shopkeeper. Then, as Frank Tucciarone's store continued to prosper, he took the family to a middle-class residential neighborhood in the Bronx. But wherever the Tucciarones lived, a network of relatives and ethnic cohorts played a major role in the girl's development. After her mother's death, neighbors and relatives took responsibility for her upbringing until her father remarried. In her teenage years, the family regularly attended events sponsored by the Minturno Aid Society, the mutual aid organization associated with the Tucciarones' hometown.[43]

Yet Josephine's aspirations made her more representative of the "new woman" of the 1920s than of the matrons of the immigrant community. For the previous three decades, it had been common for single Italian women to be employed in the garment industry, as well as in candy, tobacco, and paper-box factories.[44] Josephine had the good fortune to work in her father's store, and she was part of a generation of young Italian American women who were beginning to access low-level, white-collar jobs in groceries and department stores. After Josephine left school to work in Adolph and Frank Tucciarone's store in 1923, she was allowed to attend a neighborhood "continuation" school to learn bookkeeping. This coursework enabled her to sharpen her business acumen to the point that she played a major part in the Tucciarone brothers' operation. Because of her skill balancing the store's finances, Josephine knew it was a sound business with great potential. She saw a fancy fruit and vegetable operation with a wealthy, loyal clientele, but with relatively low overhead despite its favorable location.

Josephine Tucciarone complemented her business savvy with social charms that drew customers, who would ask to be waited on by the "Little Boss." She even began to imitate the styles of the ladies of Park Avenue after hours of observing them parade through the neighborhood. Customers also appreciated her speed at adding figures and her graceful handling of the merchandise, while her employers valued her artful produce displays—a vital skill in the trade. Josephine was not above employing a few tricks not uncommon among ethnic grocers; with her wealthier customers, she might keep her finger on the scale when weighing produce or add the numbered address or date to the tally on receipts to pad the bill. While Josephine maintained close ties to her relatives and Italian neighbors, she also seemed to embody a generational shift in her social habits. She enjoyed the pleasures of the new mass culture, regularly using a portion of her wages to go to movie houses, shop for a new hat or dress, or have an evening out with her friends.[45] Like many Italian American girls, Josephine enjoyed a freedom to date and interact in public with young men that was unknown to her female predecessors. Once it came time for Josephine to consider a husband, she was no longer constrained by the "Old World" rule of arranged marriages. This sense of liberation would lead to Josephine's courtship with Nicholas D'Agostino and to her pivotal role in the founding of his company, as she brokered the sale that saved the grocery from ruin. Yet even as she embodied modern ambitions and tastes, Josephine's career also represented the professional ceiling for women of her ilk—especially in the male-dominated provinces of ethnic commerce. Her father's new partner, her future brother-in-law Patsy, limited her role in the grocery's day-to-day operations, often treating her like a subordinate. When her husband later joined the business, Josephine grew exasperated with the contentious relationship between the two brothers; she may have felt some relief when motherhood ended her duties in the store.[46]

"And the Rest Is History":
The Difficult Birth of the D'Agostino Brothers' Grocery

When young Nicholas D'Agostino arrives in the US, he joins the mass of Italian merchants struggling to emerge from the ethnic ghetto. Nicholas remembers the achievements and failures of this older generation, including his own frustrations with their lack of vision. He then reveals the slights that motivated his dreams of success. Finally, he recounts his apprenticeship in the food business, as well as the family drama that led to the founding of the first D'Agostino's market.

Throughout the 1940s and 1950s, Patsy D'Agostino became the face of the brothers' venture, as his charm and charisma attracted customers, salesmen, and reporters. Patsy began to develop an identity through their discourse, bartering pieces of his life story in the service of building the business. His persona eventually defined the company's image, as he used interviews and magazine stories to author its history—as in the 1943 profile in *The New Yorker*. Meanwhile, Nicholas D'Agostino saw work as foundational to his identity. He loved his older brother, but he sometimes viewed Patsy's role in the business as more style than substance.

In the early 1980s, on the heels of being honored by the Horatio Alger Foundation, Nicholas began to dictate a memoir that would include his own version of D'Agostino's history. Like many autobiographies, Nicholas's effort began as an act of retrospective self-creation—an attempt to literally represent himself as a "self-made man." As the surviving member of the original partnership, Nicholas seized the opportunity to validate his own contributions (though his interest and energy in composing the memoir soon faded, and his account was left incomplete). While the resulting text consists mainly of Nicholas's fond recollections of his home village and the kin who raised him, it provides a critical perspective on the early struggles of this immigrant business as well as on the competing narratives of family-owned firms.

Nicholas D'Agostino would remember his arrival in the US in 1924 as one of the most disappointing moments of his life. If one were to draw comparisons with Orson Welles's *Citizen Kane*, this episode might serve as the "Rosebud" that continued to drive Nicholas's ambitions and haunt his successes. Ignatius D'Agostino had become an American citizen in 1901, so fourteen-year-old Nicholas traveled to the US on an American passport, with his money sewn into his underwear and shirt. Before Nicholas left Italy, his mother recalled how on her voyage to America, Ignatius had rowed out into New York Harbor to meet her ship, sending flowers and fruit aboard to welcome her. While her tale may have been apocryphal, she encouraged her son to expect a similar reception. When Nicholas's boat arrived in New York Harbor, he looked for his father, "but as much as I strained my eyes, I could not see him, and this was my first disappointment in the New World." When Nicholas spotted two of his uncles waiting for him, he took some consolation that his older brother was probably there, too. But when he asked for Patsy, his uncles told him that his brother had gone up to Boston to be with his girlfriend. Nicholas called his brother's failure to greet him after nearly four years apart his "second disappointment in the new land."[47]

Where was the young immigrant's father? Apparently, Ignatius's thirst for liquor had begun to affect his health, and he was back at a relative's apartment, bedridden and delirious. Nicholas remembered that his father "was so ill, he did not even know me; and the next day he was taken to Bellevue Hospital." Young Nicholas's sense of rejection, and his humiliation at seeing his father so addled by drink that he had to be hospitalized, stayed with him the rest of his life. Patsy's decision to visit his girlfriend, Irene (who would later become his wife), rather than welcome his sibling, would also fuel Nicholas's resentment of his older brother. Though

Nicholas and Patsy developed a close bond, an underlying sense of competition always shaped their relationship. In his autobiography, Nicholas recalled the confrontation that followed his arrival:

> The next day, Tuesday, my brother came back from Boston. . . . He came running into my room to kiss me and embrace me, and I said to him, "You wanted me to come to America so bad, and you knew that I would arrive on the first of September; and instead of meeting me, you went to Boston to see your girlfriend! Things can't be that serious because you are only 19." The next thing I asked him was, "You wrote us all the news of the faults of our father, that he was drinking and gambling—tell me, how much money have you saved in five years?" He answered simply, "I have no money. But I would like to see how much you will have saved in five years." Without hesitation, I answered, "It will have to be more than you have saved, since you have nothing!"[48]

Simone Cinotto has written about the necessity for recent arrivals from Italy to form "flexible and contingent households with extended family members" while depending on family networks as sources for jobs, places to stay, or credit.[49] Nicholas's domestic situation in his first years in America illustrated the communality and chaos that shaped the lives of Italian immigrants in New York City. Immediately after his arrival, Nicholas moved into the apartment of his Uncle Philip Mazzucco. It was already crowded because Philip lived there with his wife and three sons, two of his brothers, and his nephew. The confines of the apartment grew even tighter when Nicholas's portly uncle, Tony D'Espinosa, moved in after a few months. The boarders paid "Zio Pipo" a weekly fee for food, lodging, and laundry while trying to combine their meager resources in pursuit of business opportunities. Soon after Tony D'Espinosa's arrival, he, Ignatius D'Agostino, and another partner bought a pushcart and produce stand at 141st Street and Eighth Avenue in Harlem. It was on this pushcart that Nicholas got his first experience in the food business. Within the year, Uncle Philip and one of his sons had also pooled enough money to buy a fruit store on 180th Street, near Jerome Avenue in the Bronx. While Nicholas, his father, and his Uncle Tony continued to labor at their pushcart, they followed Philip and his family into a large private house half a block away from their store. Six months after this move, Ignatius D'Agostino again returned to Italy, so in 1926 Nicholas and his Uncle Tony moved to 141st Street in Harlem to be closer to their stand.[50] Later that year, Ignatius returned to New York and moved back in with Nicholas and Tony up in Harlem.

Nicholas's recollections of his early days in the food business also demonstrate the opportunities and hazards facing ethnic merchants in an era of unchecked, bare-knuckled capitalism. Italian immigrants who worked in the produce trade had to cope with an unstable business climate in which individual fortunes suffered the uncertainty of constant peaks and valleys. If immigrants could earn enough money toiling on the pushcarts and fruit stands of their relatives or countrymen, they might be able to purchase their own stands. If they prospered as peddlers, they might be able to then combine resources with their associates and buy a small grocery. But most groceries made only slim profits, and many aspiring shopkeepers facing a lack of capital found themselves returning to work as clerks and peddlers if their ventures failed. The immigrants' system of financing their operations added to this climate of instability, as business arrangements in which relatives and "paesani" pooled their dollars often bred discord between the principals. Several members of the Mazzucco and Tucciarone families had small groceries on the Upper East Side—a situation that might stimulate conflict, as well as employment and investment. The agreements that bound potential partners were often provisional at best and could collapse if one party became disgruntled or received a better offer. Once a venture was launched, partners often tried to claim authority over one another, even as the roles and responsibilities within the organization remained murky.

For a young employee like Nicholas, the disorganization and despotism of the older generation of ethnic merchants was maddening. Working at the stand and pushcart on 141st Street, he remembered that he had "four bosses on top of me and they would all want me to bring them water, bags, bananas, etc.; until the only way I could do for all of them was to work one at a time." Nicholas's frustrations came to a head one day, when "my Uncle Tony called to me to bring him some water. I called back that I would as soon as I finished bringing bags to my Uncle Alex. He was furious, since he wanted the water immediately, and he called me a s.o.b. I said to him 'I am not a s.o.b., and that is not a nice name to use about your sister!'"[51]

Tired of this abuse and infighting, Nicholas took a job working for his Uncle Philip Mazzucco in the Bronx. Nicholas received an astounding $25 a week—a $10 raise from the salary his father paid him. Then, about a year later, Nicholas's cousin, Tommy Mazzucco, and Mazzucco's brother-in-law, Gerard Carcone, opened the Butterfield Market at 90th Street and Lexington Avenue. The two young entrepreneurs offered neighborhood shoppers a novel concept—meat, groceries, and produce sold under the same roof, anticipating the industry's dramatic evolution over the coming decades. Mazzucco and Carcone offered Nicholas a small raise to come work for them.[52] He accepted and set about learning the basics of store operations—including packing and delivering groceries, cleaning and stocking, organizing merchandise, and working in the produce department. Nicholas then asked Carcone for the opportunity to also train as a butcher in exchange for a $10 reduction in his weekly wages (and the pledge that he would continue to perform the rest of his menial duties).

The butchers' trade was a closely guarded, if prosperous, fraternity. In his autobiography, Nicholas explained: "In those days, no butcher would let you cut so much as a pork chop or a leg of lamb because to some extent, they were jealously guarding their self-preservation." Carcone agreed to his proposal, and Nicholas began an apprenticeship that would be crucial to his future. Then, when the Butterfield Market moved down to larger quarters on 89th Street, Nicholas also got the chance to learn the fish business. Nicholas attributed this opportunity to a mix of diligence and serendipity, explaining, "A large percentage of fish men did not show up for work on Mondays and even Tuesdays, because they were traditionally heavy drinkers, so they would exploit my willingness to learn by letting me cover for them on those days."[53]

Nicholas's array of skills and his sense of opportunity allowed him to continue to improve his prospects. During the summers, most Manhattan groceries drastically reduced their hours of operation because so many New Yorkers went to the shore or the lakes to escape the heat. Most grocery employees were forced to take their vacations or find other work during this fallow period. In the summer of 1930, Nicholas was short on cash after he had lost $100 betting on a prizefight, so he used his August vacation to find a position at a grocery in North Asbury, New Jersey. Nicholas was able to work as a butcher, fish man, and grocer in his new place, and thus was well compensated for his efforts. At the end of his first week, when he opened his pay envelope, he was "delighted to find the sum of $45! Remember that I was 20 years of age, and in 1930, men with families were working for $8 a week. A lawyer fresh out of law school would be happy to earn $15 a week." As the nation suffered through the onset of the Great Depression, the cocky young grocer felt "great satisfaction to do as well as I did. As the man said, 'All you need is a strong back and a weak mind!'"[54]

In Nicholas's absence, Tommy Mazzucco and Gerard Carcone's enterprise began to founder. They contacted Nicholas and offered to bring him back with a significant raise in pay. He accepted their offer, but back at the Butterfield Market, he found himself in the middle of another personality conflict, as "soon friction began again between the owners." First, Tommy sold his shares to his partner's brother, Charlie Carcone. After six months, Charlie then sold his shares to Gerard Carcone's brother-in-law, John Tucciarone. This partnership also failed.[55] As the owners faced financial ruin, Nicholas, then only twenty-one years of age, brokered a deal to have another acquaintance, a salesman named Gus Tamm, buy Tucciarone's stake and save the grocery.[56]

Initially, the new partnership was a great success for all concerned. Yet Nicholas soon found himself seeking new employment after a dispute with his superiors. In 1932, Nicholas was engaged to Josephine Tucciarone, and he had received permission from one of his bosses (Mr. Carcone) to take time off in August to get married. One afternoon in May, Gus Tamm told Nick that June would be his month off. When Nicholas protested that he had already set his wedding date, Gus told him that the business was having some problems, and that he would have to take two months off. Nicholas remembered that in a fit of temper and defiance, he told Tamm to "take his job and shove it." Nicholas also recalled that he felt disrespected by Gerard Carcone, who was out at lunch and had left Tamm to deliver the bad news. Declaring that Carcone did not "have the guts" to face him, Nicholas "went on to say that if I had to take this sort of abuse now, what would it be like when I got married? I would be nothing but a slave and this is not what I was born for."[57]

How should one interpret the story of Nicholas D'Agostino's departure from the Butterfield Market? From one perspective, it seems as if his youthful temper and fragile ego were clouding his judgment. After all, Nicholas was abandoning a steady paycheck during the depths of the Great Depression, even as he was planning to marry. Perhaps he sensed that Tamm and Carcone's venture was doomed. Yet, one might wonder if his temperament was actually setting Nicholas apart from his peers. In Nicholas's recollection of the episode, his defiant sense of independence, as well as his resentment at perceived slights, spurred his ambitions and his willingness to take risks. Similarly, in recalling his own origins as an entrepreneur, Patsy D'Agostino—rejecting ethnic stereotypes and the "Old World" mindset of his father—would credit his departure from a dead-end job at a grocery chain in Boston to his determination to be more than "a number."[58] In both episodes, the generational divide between the uncompromising young strivers and their more conservative, long-suffering elders is clear. The brothers had volatile tempers and tended to be contrarians, but in these qualities, one could already detect the sense of ego, drive, and destiny that defined their careers as entrepreneurs.

The story of Nicholas D'Agostino's engagement and marriage to Josephine Tucciarone provides further insight into the generational issues that catalyzed the brothers' emergence from the larger immigrant community. In 1926, Patsy D'Agostino had married Irene Salemme and moved to Boston to be near his bride's family. After four years of struggling on the margins of the food business, Patsy then returned to New York to try his luck among his friends and relatives. Soon after his return, he was able to purchase Adolph Tucciarone's share of Tucciarone Brothers market, which almost immediately improved his prospects. Patsy also invited his younger brother to board in his new apartment. Nicholas accepted his brother's offer, but after a few months, he became discontented with his sister-in-law's "sharp tongue" and her refusal to "do [his] laundry." He began to seek the counsel of his brother's coworker, and his old friend, Josephine.[59]

By 1931, Nicholas was making a healthy wage as a butcher and enjoying the benefits that came with his newfound prosperity in America. As a young man who loved a good time and had few responsibilities, he dedicated a large portion of his salary to his social life and his wardrobe. In his autobiography, Nicholas explained:

> In those days, I had started to play cards a couple of nights a week. I was also going out with girls two or three times a week; and many Saturday nights, after I took the girl home at one or two in the morning, I would go and find my cronies and play poker until seven or eight Sunday morning, and we would play pretty heavily. To lose or win two or three hundred dollars was very easy, and the few thousand dollars I had accumulated began to dwindle. I was burning the candle at both ends and in the middle, too!

During an argument over Nicholas's social habits, his concerned older brother asked him why he couldn't "settle down and get a nice girl 'like Josephine?'" With a swagger, Nicholas replied, "What are you talking about? There isn't a girl in the world that I couldn't have!"[60]

Whether he read Patsy's question as a warning or a challenge, Nicholas soon began taking Josephine out. The couple spent their courtship enjoying all the social activities that were luring the children of immigrants in cities like New York, including trips to the movies and the beach, and picnics and boat rides held by the Tammany-sponsored Democratic Club. In February 1932, Nicholas proposed to Josephine at a dinner at Frank Tucciarone's home. He had been sampling some of Mr. Tucciarone's fine homemade wine that evening, so he finished his proposal with the assurance: "To prove I mean it—[that it was] not just your father's muscatel—I will come back in the morning."[61] The following Sunday, in a display of Old World hospitality, Josephine's stepmother cooked an engagement supper for the couple and about eighty friends and family members.

At the party, Nicholas discovered that his own father, Ignatius D'Agostino, had been the best man at the wedding of his prospective father-in-law, Frank Tucciarone, and was the godfather of his fiancée. This odd revelation angered Nicholas, as he connected it with past efforts by his parents to control his destiny. Though he was born into a European culture in which parents wielded great power in arranging their children's marriages, Nicholas saw himself as independent and capable of earning his own way in the world—a young American in the making. Nicholas recalled that after he first witnessed his father call his wife-to-be "godchild" and Josephine call his father "compare," he made sure to express his displeasure at this discovery:

> "What is this joyful talk, godchild and compare?" And in front of Josephine I said to him, "How is [it] you never told me? In fact, you wanted me to get married in Italy because this one had so much land, or this girl had so many meringues [gold pieces]!" My mother also wished me to marry in Italy to some girl whose family we knew. My answer to her was that she had not told me who she was going to marry, and I did not think she had the right to tell me who to marry. I told her I had made my choice, and that I had made the bed and would have to lie in it. At least the responsibility would be all mine.[62]

This incident, along with Josephine's desire for an engagement ring, strained Nicholas's relationship with his family and propelled him to make his own way. Nicholas wrote that the diamond ring his bride-to-be picked out was $500 and "although I made a good salary of $48 a week, what with sending a little to my mother, and always loving good clothes, I only had about $400. I asked my dad to lend me $100. . . . He refused me." Nicholas then went to his maternal uncle, Tony D'Espinosa, who had lent Patsy a sizable sum so that his favorite nephew might buy into Tucciarone Brothers grocery. Nicholas remembered that his Uncle Tony gave him a terse response: "You mean to tell me you are making $48 a week, and haven't saved $500? It isn't what a man makes, but what he saves that make him worth his salt." Nicholas saw his uncle's condescending response as another example of his family's accommodation of his older brother, and its lack of respect for his own worth. He fired back, "You loaned my brother seven or eight thousand dollars without all this talk, and you refuse me $100?" Nicholas then borrowed from a $50,000 life insurance policy to get the money for the ring, but he did not forget the slights by his father and his uncle. Defying the code of the Old World family, he concluded, "What I learned from these experiences was very valuable—that you do not depend on anybody."[63]

In the months leading up to his wedding, Nicholas D'Agostino began working at the Grand Royal market at 86th Street and Lexington Avenue. Then one afternoon, Josephine Tucciarone presented him with a business opportunity that would change his life. Patsy had purchased her Uncle Adolph's share of the family grocery and kept it solvent, but Frank Tucciarone had continued to take heavy losses in the stock market. Nicholas recalled that Frank was "mortgaged to the hilt" and had also received a letter from one of his "cronies" about an outstanding debt. The situation down at the Tucciarone market had grown so dire that Patsy and Frank could only afford to draw salaries of $35 a week in the winter and $25 in the summer, while Nicholas was making $50 a week at Grand Royal.[64] Frank was even forced to take a summer position at a grocery in Long Branch, New Jersey, to supplement his income.

Out of desperation, Frank asked Josephine to convince her fiancé to buy her father's shares of the grocery for two or three thousand dollars. Nicholas was reluctant to give up his $50-a-week salary and invest in a struggling business, especially as he was preparing to wed. But his brother begged him to accept Frank's offer, as Patsy still owed his Uncle Tony several thousand dollars and could not afford to see the store fold. Josephine Tucciarone also advocated for the sale, not only to save her father but, as her bookkeeping experience had shown her, because the grocery had great potential owing to its location and its well-to-do customer base. But Josephine insisted that Nicholas pay her father $5,000—the full value for his share—causing a dispute that nearly ended the couple's engagement.

Before making his final decision, Nicholas had one last meeting with Patsy. The brothers dissected "all the mistakes our former bosses had made" and tried to chart a new path for their venture. Nicholas recalled that unlike their predecessors, he and Patsy "agreed that we would charge our own food bills . . . and neither would touch so much as a dollar without the knowledge and consent of the other." Nicholas offered to work without a salary for a couple of months, and the brothers then promised each other that once they had paid their debts and replenished their inventory, they would put in a meat and fish department. The strategy of the "all-in-one" store would differentiate their operation from the scores of traditional groceries in Manhattan. But Nicholas also believed that his training would give the D'Agostino brothers an advantage regarding quality and operating costs, explaining that "in other stores the owner would [only] know produce or groceries or whatever, and the head of the other departments would take advantage of the owner's ignorance, and abuse their power." Years later, Nicholas recalled that even with their healthy ambition, he and Patsy could not know the ultimate destiny of their project: "The cellar was bare, the store was smaller than small, 25 feet by 50 feet at most. . . . We named the market the Yorkville Food Shoppe, and although we had high hopes for it, we little realized that it was the beginning of an era."[65]

In August 1932, Nicholas and Josephine did marry at St. Raymond's Church in the Bronx. Satisfying Nick's sense of style and splendor, the couple rejected the immigrants' typical "hall" wedding for a catered affair with no children allowed. The couple then honeymooned in Lake George. But all the profligate spending caught up with the couple, and they had to wire home for more money. At the end of their trip, they had to take a humble horse and buggy to the local train station, holding only their return tickets and a precious nickel for the subway.[66]

The D'Agostino brothers' market would not even carry their names until the late 1930s, as Nicholas and Patsy first called their grocery the Yorkville Food Shoppe. The brothers' decision to keep their names off the marquee was not unusual: Their relatives had given their own markets titles like the Florence, the Butterfield, and the Grand Royal (which often corresponded with their designated phone exchanges). As these groceries served a wealthy Anglo-American clientele, the issue of store identification showed that Italians were still guarded about their identity in WASP America, even if they were no longer the itinerant peddlers of the immigrant ghetto.

Yet Nicholas and Patsy's enterprise also marked a new era for the ethnic merchant and the city's Italian community. While Ignatius D'Agostino and Frank Tucciarone had prospered in the food business, their generation's modest vision of success ranged from mere survival to control over a particular city block. Even when they owned their own stores, they saw themselves as independent operators serving a limited niche. Their business model and their inventory were derived from the daily buying habits of their regular customers and the advice of salesmen; they had no sense of long-term growth or the economic trends outside their own neighborhoods. The older generation's limited English and lack of social polish prevented them from serving a larger clientele, at a time when Italians were still viewed as a marginal population. One can argue that both Ignatius and Frank reached the ceiling for immigrants of their era: Ignatius returned to Italy in 1939 with a few thousand dollars in his pocket and Frank owned a home and a luxury auto before the stock market crashed.

Nicholas and Patsy, however, had mastered all the elements for leading a new era of marketing. Because Nicholas and Patsy apprenticed on pushcarts and in small groceries, they had an expert understanding of the produce business as well as the laws of supply and demand. Nicholas's training as a butcher and fish man allowed the brothers to offer quality in these now-necessary categories of food retailing. Nicholas also possessed a vision of his future as a new kind of entrepreneur, fed by his union with Josephine; he had an unwavering sense of independence and the need to distinguish himself from the immigrant masses. And their store would benefit from a hidden intangible—Patsy's genius for cultivating friendships and alliances with customers, salesmen, fellow grocers, and the press corps of New York City.

The D'Agostino brothers' market would also distinguish itself from other groceries because their ideas and identity corresponded with a crucial moment in food history—a synergy of vision and circumstance. Nicholas and Patsy had an innovative concept—meat and groceries sold under one roof—which the city and the nation were ready to embrace. They had a favorable location and a partnership that would allow them to survive the privations of the Great Depression and the Second World War. They had the means to free themselves from the problematic alliances that chained an earlier generation of Italian entrepreneurs. Finally, Nicholas and Patsy were ready to move up from the pushcart just as the larger Italian community was poised to raise itself out of America's literal and figurative ghetto. The arc of their story suggested that, ultimately, a type of selective evolution guided the marketplace and allowed certain generations of immigrants to climb into the American mainstream.

At the time of the 1943 *New Yorker* article, the D'Agostino brothers were harboring ambitions for expanding their operation, which had enjoyed steady growth since the inception of their partnership. The brothers' first store at 83rd Street and Lexington Avenue was only eighteen and a half by thirty feet, but it had several wealthy patrons—including the Gimbel family, who supposedly spent upwards of $2,000 a week on food.[67] Patsy and Nicholas had spent $8,000 to enlarge their store in 1935 to allow for the installation of a meat counter. After a second expansion, the brothers moved their operation to 77th Street and Third Avenue in 1939, when their landlords threatened to hike their rent. Although the family celebrated this move as a milestone, the store was overshadowed by the tracks of the Third Avenue Elevated (which would be torn down in the 1950s). In 1940, they opened a second store on Lexington Avenue (near their original location) and a third, in Mount Vernon, in 1941.[68] Despite its characterization of Patsy D'Agostino as an independent underdog, *The New Yorker* related that the brothers "would still be expanding but for the war."[69] In fact, in 1945, Patsy and Nicholas opened their fourth store at 85th Street, between Lexington and Park Avenues.

"Italy Will Always Be 'Sunny Italy' and England Will Always Be 'Foggy England'": D'Agostino's in the Second World War

While Italian immigrants grapple with the meaning of World War II, the D'Agostino brothers face down scarcity, OPA bureaucrats, chain stores, and a skeptical American public. Patsy emerges as a spokesperson for independent grocers and the rights of the "little guy," while Nicholas labors in the back. But when he is profiled in the esteemed *New Yorker* magazine, Patsy becomes both a public character and an ethnic caricature.

World War II was a period of struggle for the D'Agostino brothers, despite their ownership of a stable, prosperous business. Like many independent retailers, Nicholas and Patsy had difficulty retaining an able workforce, as the draft and war industries drained the labor pool. By 1942, they had already lost sixteen of their employees to the armed forces.[70] Also, the primacy of the war effort meant that grocers had to scramble to stock their inventories. Within months of the attack on Pearl Harbor, the government announced that product deliveries would be cut by 25 percent to save gasoline and rubber for the war effort.[71] During this period, Nicholas and Patsy often left for the marketplace at 5 a.m. to have a chance at obtaining quality meat, fish, or produce. Because of gas rationing, Nicholas had to use his Dodge sedan to pick up and deliver meat and fish, which left the family car with an indelible smell.[72]

But the nation's wartime economy also meant that retailers had to maneuver a web of regulations and bureaucracy just to keep their doors open. Food rationing required customers to have the proper paperwork to acquire limited amounts of staples like coffee and sugar, which, in turn, made them a prickly lot. The system of rationing was a particular challenge for D'Agostino's since the butcher's art was central to its business model and meat was now a rare commodity. Nicholas later claimed that the company's ability to "take care" of customers during this time of scarcity engendered tremendous loyalty and set the stage for the company's meteoric rise after the war was over. Every Christmas during the war, Nicholas and Patsy received from grateful patrons dozens of pricey gifts, from wool scarves, to leather gloves and wallets, to bottles of scotch.[73]

In addition to the constraints of wartime bureaucracy, the D'Agostino brothers also faced cultural impediments, as their native country waged war against their adopted homeland. Like thousands of other immigrants, Nicholas and Patsy had balanced their Italian and American identities in a sort of transnational equilibrium. They maintained deep affection for both countries, while placing their loyalty to family above all other considerations. Still, a host of factors pressured Italian Americans to clarify their allegiances. Before 1914, a constant stream of new arrivals had allowed Italian communities in the US to maintain their ethnic character as well as ties to their native villages. However, as the establishment of legal quotas, World War I, and the interwar depression limited passage to and from Europe, Italians became more rooted in America.[74] Then, with the onset of World War II, the governments of Italy and the US each made formal claims on the loyalties of Italian immigrants and their progeny. The Italian government had once encouraged the migration of its peasantry while allowing them to retain their citizenship, a strategy meant to relieve overpopulation and bring capital into Italy (as laborers sent money back to their families overseas). In the 1930s, however, Benito Mussolini campaigned against emigration and called for those living abroad to declare their fealty to Italy and to return home with the skills and resources they had acquired while in exile. Meanwhile, with its entry into the war, the United States promoted the need for patriotism and loyalty among its ethnic citizens.[75]

Initially, several prominent Italian Americans—including the leaders of national organizations like the Sons of Italy, the editors of *Il Progresso Italo-Americano* (the top Italian newspaper in the US), and the entrepreneur Generoso Pope—praised Mussolini as a symbol of national pride and progress. By 1941, however, the Italian community (including the aforementioned figures) had disavowed the dictator and thrown themselves firmly behind the American war effort.[76] In 1943, the Italian American

Grocers Association even raised $451,000 to buy a B-29 bomber, which was named "The Spirit of the IAGA."[77] Moreover, Italian Americans did not face the same legal discrimination suffered by their Japanese compatriots once hostilities began. While Italian nationals living in the US were required to register with the government as "enemy aliens," citizens of Italian descent were not.[78] Some Italians on the West Coast—the region where anxieties were highest—suffered the indignities of curfews and relocation, and had their fishing boats and radios confiscated, but they were not subject to mass imprisonment on the basis of their ethnic identity.[79]

Of course, Italians sometimes endured milder forms of suspicion. Even the D'Agostino brothers, after years of serving the Yorkville community, had to suffer questions about their loyalties. The brothers had little use for the political regimes of Italy, but they never wavered in their love for their native country, which transcended governments and nation-states. Nicholas recalled one instance in which an angry customer called the store to tell him that she could no longer be a customer, since America was at war with Italy. Nicholas calmly and cryptically replied, "Italy will always be 'sunny Italy,' and England will always be 'foggy England,'" before hanging up the phone.[80]

By the onset of World War II, Patsy D'Agostino had become a public figure, as witnessed by the 1943 feature in *The New Yorker*. Author Mark Murphy characterized Patsy as "a figure in the trade" whose "pronouncements carry weight" with fellow grocers, "many of whom go to him for advice or encouragement."[81] Patsy was named president of the New York State Food Merchants Association in 1941 and director of the National Association of Retail Grocers in 1942. His position of leadership in the industry was quite an accomplishment, considering that two decades earlier, he was working on a pushcart and could barely speak English. He had also become a favorite of local reporters; a review of *The New York Times* articles dedicated to food rationing shows that Patsy D'Agostino was quoted in eighteen separate stories.[82]

The war effort caused scarcity and spurred inflation, with the soaring cost of consumer goods becoming a chief concern for the Roosevelt administration. In response to public sentiment, the president established the Office of Price Administration to stifle profiteering and stabilize prices, enlisting a paid and volunteer staff of over 250,000 while creating a host of arcane regulations to govern the behavior of merchants and farmers.[83] In his *New Yorker* piece, Murphy dedicated several paragraphs to Patsy's battles with the Office of Price Administration and his profane denouncements against its system of price controls and point rationing. He related that Patsy spent many nights discussing the OPA with his fellow grocers "at clamorous meetings" in which he spoke "not only loudly but well."[84] Throughout the article, Murphy described Patsy giving advice to grocers confused by regulations, supporting those who doubted their ability to stay in business, warning off the black marketeers who seem to be lurking behind every market stall with an offer of cheap turkeys, and cursing at employees who sold cocoa to A&P customers, all the while expounding on a range of subjects, from coffee rationing to the idiocy of caviar being branded an "essential food."[85]

Patsy believed that the OPA favored larger merchants over independent operations like his, especially with its method of publicizing the prices and offerings of competing retailers.[86] He explained how, initially, he "ran all over the state making speeches at meetings all about how the government was going to protect the little man in the grocery business." Both Murphy and D'Agostino seemed acutely aware that the label of "small businessman" carried heavy political symbolism, as Patsy reflected on his own struggles:

> Patsy talks about "little business" with emotion. He considers himself a little business man, and he thinks that he and men like him are pillars of American civilization, which they probably are. He sometimes feels that he is being conspired against, a matter naturally open to question. The confusion that has come into his life because of the war affects him deeply, and once, when he was exceptionally depressed at finding that the wholesale price of chickens was seventeen cents above his own retail ceiling price, he said, "Put me to jail. Take away my business. This is the end of free enterprise. Make the end of free enterprise and you got the end of democracy. I like it here in America. I've done better here than a man could anywhere else in the world. I know what it is to slave for a dollar. I own my own home. I have my business, and I got a wife and three children. Now what the hell kind of a future are they going to have?"[87]

Then, on June 7, 1943, Patsy was called as an expert witness before a House of Representatives select committee investigating the plight of small businesses in the United States under the National Defense Program. Serving on the committee were such notable political figures as representatives Wright Patman, Estes Kefauver, and Adlai Stevenson, while senators such as Robert La Follette Jr. and James Michael Curley observed the proceedings.[88] Congress had called Patsy to comment on the Office of Price Administration, the Emergency Price Control Act (which was designed to stabilize prices and protect against inflation), labor unrest, and the growth of the black market during the war.[89]

Patsy D'Agostino's appearance before Congress was a landmark event in the formation of his public identity for several reasons. Testifying before the nation's greatest legislative body certainly highlighted Patsy's incredible rise from obscure poverty in rural Italy and his undistinguished beginnings as a tradesman and a peddler. And becoming the voice of the grocery industry proved Patsy's charisma, political savvy, and business instincts, especially when one considers his lack of education and late acquisition of English. But Patsy's congressional appearance also signified the maturation of his public self. In his testimony, Patsy spoke confidently about the issues affecting his industry and refused to back down under the aggressive questioning of his political inquisitors. Moreover, he seemed fully aware of the value of his own identity as an immigrant and an entrepreneur, as he claimed the language of public image.

Throughout his testimony, Patsy criticized the government's program of price controls, its system for classifying food retailers, and its unwitting promotion of the black market.[90] Patsy was also critical of organized labor's effect on wartime food policy. He spoke frankly about the Office of Price Administration's flaws and provided evidence to support his analysis. But, more significantly, he tried to win the committee's sympathy—and make himself a more credible witness—by employing the legend of American freedom and opportunity. In his remarks, Patsy revised the figure of the immigrant, whose patriotism was proven not through the absolution of his ethnic roots, but by his love for, and flight from, a homeland that had fallen under an oppressive totalitarian regime. He presented the Italian merchant, selling fruits and vegetables from a cart or storefront, as being as fiercely independent as the Yankee farmer, and therefore as thoroughly American. In his opening statement, he described his own passage from lowly migrant to pushcart peddler to shopkeeper, concluding:

> I always had one purpose in mind—that some day I would become my own boss and be in business for myself.... The reasons for these few words regarding my past is another way of saying that I appreciate the fact that, as an immigrant, this country has offered me the opportunity to take my place amongst many other respectable American businessmen and become a self-supporting citizen, and enjoy as many others do the freedom of private enterprise.[91]

During the session, Patsy used his identity strategically, playing the role of humble ethnic to prove his authority as an American. He portrayed the mass of grocers as simple and industrious, and when asked to confirm a garbled portion of his testimony, he apologized: "I am only an immigrant and I cannot pronounce all of my words the way I should probably." Patsy recalled a meeting with government officials in which they conceded that the established maximum price regulations (particularly the system for marking up prices) had become too complex for grocers. His remarks contrasted his own authenticity with the pretensions of bureaucrats, lawyers, and economic theorists:

> In other words, they realized the mistake that they made in printing 40 or 50 pages of regulation . . . that the average retail grocer, not being a college professor . . . could never understand—and I want to say to you now that more grocers have to pay lawyers and accountants on their pay roll in the last year or so than ever in history because of trying to comply and trying to be a good American, not because he does not want to respect the law.[92]

Later, Patsy tried to validate his critique of government policy by manipulating the rhetoric of the war effort. These allusions were often heavy-handed, but the efficacy of Patsy's remarks is less significant than their recognition of the nation's symbolic vernacular. When testifying about the OPA's system of categorization, for example, he stated, "I do not think it is the American way of doing things. . . . Those boys are fighting to preserve the American way of life, and why should we want to destroy the small businessman?" He also loaded his criticisms of the OPA with references to Nazis and fascists, remarking that its legislation "seemed bent on creating a regimented food industry at the cost of destroying thousands upon thousands of independent retailers in a blitzkrieglike manner."[93]

Patsy was especially critical of the OPA's decision to publish its classifications of merchants, and the differences in their prices, services, and product lines, in the local newspapers—with his anger often leading to moments of hyperbole.[94] Although the OPA intended to keep the public informed about its policies and their own shopping options, Patsy and his peers viewed their announcements as free advertising for their larger rivals. Patsy called the announcements the "latest stab in the back received by small merchants" since they informed potential customers about the lower prices and wider inventory of stores like A&P. He derided these policies as "un-American" and "undemocratic," and in an unfortunate attempt at political theater, presented as evidence a March 1943 report from the Office of War Information that described how German businesses had gradually fallen under the control of government-sanctioned monopolies.

Regrettably, Patsy went so far as to ask the committee why he needed a classification system that would "brand me the same as Hitler branded people in Germany 'Jew' or 'Jewish.' I do not think that is necessary."[95]

Over the course of his testimony, Patsy and the congressmen each tried to manipulate the symbolic associations of the immigrant and the American merchant to bolster their political positions. Moreover, for the congressmen, Patsy's hyphenated identity cut both ways. For Patsy's supporters, his ethnicity presumed an understanding of the true workings of fascism while his American citizenship confirmed his ambition and his integrity. For his critics, Patsy's Italian birth meant an ignorance of American principles and his naturalization proved his disconnection from European affairs.

Patsy seemed to comprehend these biases—and the contingency of his own identity—and turned them to his advantage. A sympathetic Adlai Stevenson implied that because Patsy was an Italian immigrant, he might be an authority on the conditions that existed when Hitler and Mussolini came to power and know "whether the small businessman was in the same condition and same class as is now going on in this country." Patsy gave his definite assent, arguing that the "pattern was practically the same" when Hitler and Mussolini came to power as when the US government established its wartime food policy. Although Patsy made sure to voice his support for the existence of the OPA, and for limited regulation, he declared, "We are in war and I would not want to brand any agency of our Government as being anything like the Fascists or nazi-ism [sic], but, by God, we are on the way."[96]

Estes Kefauver, however, attempted to nullify Stevenson's line of inquiry by questioning Patsy's credibility, as well as his motives. After one difficult exchange, Patsy declared, "All of us have somebody fighting and giving their blood to our country just as much as the lawmakers" and then described soldiers, presumably of an ethnic background, receiving "letters after letters that their fathers' businesses have been washed away" and how these troops would have to "start thinking now where they are going to work when they come back."[97] Kefauver then suggested that D'Agostino's American residency and the fact that he had not returned to Italy since 1921 proved his ignorance of the fascist regime, as if citizenship had dissolved all his native ties. After Kefauver had the temerity to make this assertion, Patsy fired back, "I beg your pardon. I have a brother who came here in 1924; my father has been back three times; I get letters from boys I went to school with.... My father went back before the war because of sickness, and I do hope some day that I will be able to see them when they are free again. So I do know something about it."[98]

Patsy D'Agostino's visit to Capitol Hill provided a watershed moment for him and for the company the brothers were building. Patsy's appearance before Congress showed that although his identity—"Italian immigrant," "small businessman," "grocer"—had specific connotations, it was also the product of dialogue and context. Here, the contingencies of business and cultural politics helped shape his public image. Through his testimony, Patsy showed that he understood the lexicon of political and social metaphor and the figurative meaning of his identity. One must recall Robert Foerster's statement that the Italian immigrant, "lacking the faculty of literary expression, accepts the fact that for the world he is a supremely unimportant person. What is more, he is less to be thought of, after all, as an individual than as a composite. Hence he cannot speak."[99] While Patsy never composed a formal autobiography, through the *New Yorker* article, his work as an industry spokesman, and his appearance before Congress, he had begun to find his own voice and craft a public persona.

Seen in the context of a broader paradigm, the D'Agostino brothers' progression from pushcart peddlers to entrepreneurs can be framed as a prototypical story of Americanization. While Patsy and Nicholas were trained by an older generation of ethnic merchants on pushcarts and in corner groceries, their ambitions lead them to reject the conventional wisdom of their elders—as well as their sense of limits—to establish a new type of operation. Theirs was a classic immigrant's tale of children rejecting their fathers and resolute individuals separating themselves from their communities of origin to achieve self-actualization and professional success. Patsy and Nicholas, in pursuing their dreams, had become disciples of the American principle of self-determination.

Robert Foerster's observation about the immigrant's lack of individualism and agency also provides insight into Patsy D'Agostino's emergence as a successful entrepreneur and emissary. Ignatius D'Agostino and Frank Tucciarone were part of a generation of ethnic merchants that dominated food retailing in terms of sheer numbers but could not advance beyond their neighborhood fiefdoms because of limitations of culture as well as capital. In one of the many circulated versions of his early career in the food business, Patsy D'Agostino recalled his frustration with his life as a pushcart peddler and how he told his father that he aimed to get a respectable job as a grocery clerk. Ignatius D'Agostino scoffed and told his son that he lacked the manners, the grooming, or the verbal skills to land a coveted "inside" job—a reaction that mirrored his own perceptions of Italian identity rather than the capabilities of his son.[100]

As historian Simone Cinotto has documented, by the late 1920s, the Italian business community witnessed a "new generation of American-born entrepreneurs educated . . . fluent in English and equipped with professional skills [that] was able to overcome the barriers that had often kept the previous generation within the relatively safe boundaries of the ethnic marketplace."[101] To some degree, Patsy and Nicholas would always be pushcart folk like their elders, as the pushcart gave them the basic skills that enabled their future success. But Patsy and Nicholas were able to "cross over" and build a small chain of markets that served the city at-large because they understood the modern idiom of business. Patsy and Nicholas had begun to differentiate themselves from their ethnic predecessors because they had mastered a business model that now required proficiency in the produce trade, merchandising, and the butcher's art—under the rubric of the "all-in-one" market. Furthermore, Patsy D'Agostino recognized that relationships, promotion, and image would be crucial for the next generation of entrepreneurs.

Despite his father's skepticism, Patsy D'Agostino was well suited for the "inside" life of a merchant. He had a basic understanding of etiquette and manners, he knew how to dress, and, most importantly, he could communicate effectively despite his uneven English. Patsy's gift for charming customers, salesmen, reporters, politicians, and his peers in the industry allowed him to continually grow the company, especially in terms of its reputation. He seemed to intuit that in this new culture of business, language itself had a commercial value—serving as a form of exchange between retailer and customer.

On a literal level, language acquisition—whether in terms of learning English, earning a formal education, or mastering the symbols that define a society—is a fundamental component of assimilation. If one were to extend this analogy, the early chapters of Patsy and Nicholas D'Agostino's "rags-to-riches" tale recall another trope of ethnic narratives—the quest for literacy. Many of these autobiographies describe the narrator's escape from the limitations of their given racial, ethnic, or socioeconomic status through the mastery of language or the experience of education. In forms like the slave narrative, literacy frees protagonists and brings them distinction, but, paradoxically, often makes them a representative voice for an entire cultural group. In the case of Patsy D'Agostino, literacy was not about schooling, or reading and writing with great skill; rather, Patsy came to master the vernacular of the marketplace.

In 1943, *The New Yorker* had represented Patsy D'Agostino as a folk hero and an ethnic token. But Patsy had shone in the spotlight, defying the magazine's condescension. It is apparent from the article that he had the "gift of gab"—as he offered several lengthy dissertations on war and the food business that the author found amusing and insightful. His comprehension of the issues that were facing his industry, and his ability to command respect, had made him a leader among his peers. Patsy embodied the trajectory of the immigrant experience. Before he had truly established himself in the food business, he had sampled the life of the industrial laborer when he worked in the shop of the New York, New Haven, and Hartford Railroad. Later, he had trained as a plasterer in an attempt to learn a trade. He had worked as a humble pushcart peddler and a grocery clerk. Now, with an array of talents and experiences, and a new vision for the industry, Patsy and his brother, Nicholas, were poised to make another evolutionary leap—from immigrant strivers to ethnic icons.

Figure 7. The grocers as executives: Nicholas (*left*) and Patsy (*right*) in the late 1940s. Personal collection of the author.

Figure 8. From pushcart to supermarket: Nicholas and Patsy pose in front of the 20th Street store at Stuyvesant Town (ca. 1950s). Personal collection of the author.

Figure 9. The opening night crush in front of the new D'Agostino Brothers' store on 20th Street, February 1950. Personal collection of the author.

Figure 10a. One of the D'Agostino clerks shows off the supermarket's deluxe dairy counter as the store entered a new era of food retailing. Note the formality of his appearance (ca. 1950s). Personal collection of the author.

Figure 10b. Grocery clerks inventory the wide selection of canned goods sold at the D'Agostino Brothers' stores in the 1950s. Personal collection of the author.

Figure 11. Patsy D'Agostino, grocer about town (ca. 1950s). Personal collection of the author.

Figure 12a. The immigrants "get religion": Nicholas and Patsy, with an unnamed priest, at one of their store openings (ca. 1950s). Personal collection of the author.

Figure 12b. Nicholas and Patsy D'Agostino with Monsignor John Carroll-Abbing. The brothers are holding a rendering of one of the buildings for Boys' Town of Italy (ca. 1950s). Personal collection of the author.

Figure 13a. Nicholas D'Agostino and his family before their trip back to the "Old Country" in 1951. Personal collection of the author.

Figure 13b. The D'Agostino brothers and their spouses at one of the many banquets they attended in the 1950s and '60s as members of various ethnic, charitable, and retail organizations. Participation in philanthropic and ethnic societies allowed successful Italians to "give back" while asserting their social ascendance (ca. mid-1950s). Personal collection of the author.

Figure 14a. Nicholas D'Agostino (*right*) poses with New York's Terence Cardinal Cooke in the late 1960s. Personal collection of the author.

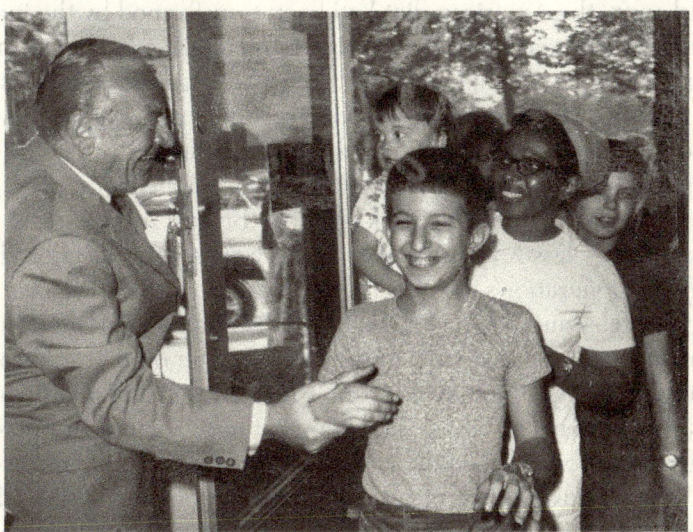

Figure 14b. Company president Nicholas D'Agostino greets customers at yet another store opening (ca. late 1960s). Personal collection of the author.

CHAPTER 3

The Grocer in the Gray Flannel Suit (1946–60)

In 1955, *Life* magazine documented American postwar abundance with an issue devoted to food. With a cover headline that declared that food was now a "mass luxury," *Life* chronicled the advances in agriculture, shipping, and storage that allowed Americans to process and consume an astounding $73 billion worth of food annually.[1] According to the magazine, between 1935 and 1955, the American diet had been transformed by the introduction of frozen foods, a dramatic increase in the intake of red meat, and the growing dominance of supermarkets. In 1954, supermarkets constituted only 5 percent of the country's 360,000 grocery stores, but accounted for 50 percent of the business, grossing about $17 billion.[2]

A page-length photo of a D'Agostino's market appears on page 30 in a feature article on food in New York entitled "Biggest Appetite."[3] A photograph in middle-class America's favorite magazine—a publication that had provided the generation's most iconic images—marked a new level of recognition for Patsy and Nicholas D'Agostino's operation. Yet, the company's inclusion in an edition that used food as a barometer of national prosperity was fitting, as D'Agostino's own fortunes rose on this tide of affluence. As the 1950s commenced, the D'Agostino brothers began a run of success that must have shocked even them. Years later, Nicholas D'Agostino would credit the company's fair treatment of its customers during the "difficult war years" as the primary reason for its new status. The introduction to his unpublished autobiography makes the ingenuous claim that as other merchants exploited consumers, D'Agostino's, "knowing the war would someday be over, decided to buy at only the right price and sell at a fair price. As a result, their reputation as a friend of the consumer grew and, after the war, their sales soared. The rest of the story . . . is history."[4]

Despite Nicholas's recollection, the company's claim on the "mass luxury" celebrated by *Life* rested largely on Patsy D'Agostino's 1950 procurement of a store on 20th Street, between Peter Cooper Village and Stuyvesant Town. Built by the Metropolitan Life Insurance Company, these housing developments were supposed to herald a new age in the city's storied history—as New York sought to counter the looming decay of its tenement neighborhoods and give itself a more modern visage. Like the city itself, D'Agostino's used the Met Life projects as a source of prosperity and a means of remaking its image.

The company's postwar evolution is a story of difficult and often masterful negotiation. As the war ended, independent grocers were besieged by chain supermarkets, while the "mom and pop" grocery seemed poised for extinction. One might think that a family-owned retailer could be doomed by this hostile climate. But Patsy and Nicholas D'Agostino were able to use the inventiveness and flexibility of their modest operation to maximize their advantage over would-be Goliaths. Through the formation of wholesale cooperatives and their adoption of the industry's latest innovations, for example, the brothers were able to counter the heft of their corporate competitors. They also used their familiarity with their customers' buying habits and their expertise with meat and produce to win the loyalty of shoppers. As Patsy and Nicholas's fortunes continued to ascend, several magazines used the brothers' life stories to affirm the merits of postwar society. Initially, the D'Agostinos were the subjects of stories by *Business Week*, *American Magazine*, *Italamerican*, and *Catholic Digest*, with each publication adapting the brothers' tale of immigrant striving to confirm its own agenda. Over time, the brothers became cognizant of the value of their stories as a source of identity and a commercial advantage.

Like thousands of other working-class and ethnic Americans who saw their fortunes lifted by the economy of the 1950s, Patsy and Nicholas D'Agostino grappled with the price of affluence and assimilation as they enjoyed the rewards of their postwar success. When Patsy and Nicholas moved their families to Queens and, eventually, the suburbs of Long Island and Westchester, they struggled to maintain their connection to old ethnic cohorts. Membership in a network of ethnic and charitable organizations superseded traditional ties to extended family and local provincial societies, even as these affiliations signaled growing financial and social agency within the American establishment. Similarly, the brothers' return to Abruzzi after the war renewed their bond with the land of their birth even as it showed their distance from their humble origins. Finally, Patsy D'Agostino's death in 1960 at the age of fifty-five led to a protracted legal fight within the family over the true ownership of the company and its legacy. In the courts, the natural tension between family and business came to an ugly conclusion, while Nicholas defended his ownership of the company's holdings and his own role in its celebrated rags-to-riches story.

If You Can't Beat 'Em, Be Them: Independent Grocers and the Struggle for Postwar Survival

At the end of World War II, merchants confront food shortages, recession, labor issues, and the growing reach of the supermarket. Patsy D'Agostino counsels his peers on how to incorporate the latest marketing strategies in order to stave off the "big boys." As thousands of "mom and pop" stores become obsolete, retailers who successfully adapt the supermarket paradigm survive and prosper. By the beginning of the 1950s, the brothers appear ready for another evolutionary leap.

Once the Second World War came to an end, the grocery industry did not immediately begin to rake in easy profits, nor were its members poised for some imagined suburban gold rush. In the late 1940s, most American retailers were concerned about a possible recession, their lack of available inventory amid continued food shortages, and the transition from stringent government regulation to an uncertain market economy.[5] In succeeding years, grocers coped with escalating prices, labor unrest, and the nation's migration to the suburbs. But the food industry's most volatile issue concerned the growing dominance of the supermarket model.[6] World War II had been a trying time for independent merchants, as they dealt with a maze of Office of Price Administration (OPA) restrictions; the shortage of butter, sugar, and meat; and the loss of their workforce to the armed forces. Many commentators have maintained that conditions on the home front actually protected the independent grocers from larger predators, however. Federally mandated restrictions on construction and materials impeded the building of new stores, while gas rationing discouraged patrons from shopping outside their neighborhoods. Independent grocers also benefited from consumers' expanded incomes and limited choices during wartime.[7]

After the war, as shoppers increasingly used automobiles to shop for the lowest prices, independent and urban retailers became anxious about their long-term prospects. Smaller competitors complained that chain stores often enjoyed hidden volume discounts and advertising allowances from grocery suppliers based on the grand scale of their purchases.[8] The major chains had also started to acquire prime locations in the new suburbs, while initiating a series of mergers that abolished many of their smaller competitors. In cities like New York, larger, "all-in-one" ventures also eliminated hundreds of independent butcher shops and bakeries. According to one survey, between 1948 and 1951, the number of supermarkets in the New York area increased by a whopping 60 percent, while their volume of business grew to five times the 1948 level.[9] A&P reported annual sales of almost $3 billion in 1950—second only to General Motors—while receiving ten cents of every food dollar spent in the US.[10] By the early 1950s, the industry had divided into three rival categories—the "Big Three" national food chains, which included A&P, Safeway, and Kroger; regional chains and local supermarkets such as Grand Union; and, at the very bottom, the smaller independents.[11]

The tenuous position of independent merchants in this era revived a contentious public debate about the symbolic place of small business in American society. Throughout the 1940s, Patsy D'Agostino made several impassioned speeches on behalf of his fellow independents. In his 1948 address to the National Association of Retail Grocers convention, he declared that the independents "must be permitted to compete on an equal basis with everyone in the business, or else the real backbone of America—the free enterprise system—will no longer exist."[12] These concerns extended to another venerated commercial institution—the family-owned grocery. In a 1951 letter to *The New York Times*, one of Patsy's allies, Marcel Martino, the founder and former president of the Bronx Terminal Market Merchants Association, warned shoppers that this local merchant "who stood steadfastly by your side throughout years of adversity, the man who took care of your needs while he patiently waited for your husband's pay check to come in, is doomed to disappear from the American scene." Martino then concluded, "Unless some corrective measures are taken he will soon become a relic of the past—like the wooden Indians in front of the cigar shops."[13]

Over the next decade, smaller retailers either adopted the practices of the supermarket or perished, while medium-sized merchants solidified their positions in cities like New York. Meanwhile, Patsy D'Agostino led the call for his fellow independents to evolve. During the war, the New York State Food Merchants Association—an organization of five thousand independent grocers that had Patsy as its president—had issued a three-point plan for meeting chain store competition. This strategy called for the expansion of smaller stores to handle a much larger volume of sales, the extension of food lines to include "all edibles, including meat" (a service that many grocers still considered prohibitively expensive), and, most significantly, the conversion of all stores to self-service retailing.[14] After the war, Patsy again recommended that his fellow association members incorporate the self-service model.[15] Then, in a 1949 lecture at City College of New York, he warned that the future belonged to medium-sized markets, rather than the traditional "papa-mama" store or the giant retailer. He explained that the "papa-mama" had been lost to many communities because they could not offer the price or variety that modern consumers had come to expect, while larger chains were hamstrung by high fixed costs.[16]

In 1952, the National Association of Retail Grocers announced that independent stores still operated almost two-thirds of the nation's groceries.[17] Yet merchants struggled to upgrade and expand their operations, as the cost of doing business continued to escalate throughout the decade. One grocer complained to a *New York Times* reporter that to survive under prevailing conditions, "you have to have a supermarket." This particular grocer was presiding over "the chromium and glass glories" of nearly $8,000 in renovations, like thousands of other independent merchants who were adding new refrigeration systems, freezers, shelving, and checkout equipment in order to be competitive.[18] Because of these alterations, the American grocery store of the early 1950s occupied three times the area of the 1940 model while costing twelve times as much to operate.[19]

It seemed as if the forces of competition and demand were driving grocers into some type of retailing arms race, as they desperately sought to evolve. In 1951, supermarkets throughout the country spent $375 million for new and remodeled spaces.[20] By the middle of the decade, one industry source reported that smaller chains and independent operators were building over 50 percent of new "supers" on a national level.[21] In cities such as New York, resourceful merchants were forced to modify the supermarket ideal to fit the urban landscape. Retailers like D'Agostino's began to adopt the "superette"—a "streamlined" version of the supermarket that offered modern amenities within the confines of neighborhood geography.[22] Advocates of the superette praised its ability to adjust to the fluctuations of the market more effectively than the chain stores.

Paradoxically, smaller retailers also survived the rigors of the marketplace by imitating the corporate mindset of their feared rivals. In his impassioned defense of the family grocery, Marcel Martino had argued that family firms should form "buying groups" to gain access to the same volume discounts and publicity enjoyed by larger adversaries. The D'Agostino brothers led other independent retailers in forming voluntary associations and wholesale cooperatives to combat chain store competition. Grocers would purchase stock in these warehouses and use their collective buying power to obtain mass quantities of name-brand dry goods. The warehouses would then supply the retailers several times a year, providing them with the same savings that large chains enjoyed with their volume purchasing.[23] By 1947, Patsy and the members of the New York State Food Merchants Association had founded over twenty wholesale warehouses.[24] The brothers then organized the Buy-Low Grocery Company and the Joint Merchants Produce Co-Op (which in 1951 sold $1.5 million worth of dry goods and $1.6 million worth of fruit and vegetables to their respective members).[25]

At the end of the 1940s, it appeared as if the "Big Three" supermarket chains (A&P, Safeway, and Kroger) were poised for national dominance. But modest, regional firms continually surprised analysts by maintaining their market shares.[26] In urban areas, local supermarkets actually expanded their sales faster than the national chains—signaling the endurance of a particular model of neighborhood merchant.[27] In New York, local operators like D'Agostino's held a secure portion of the city's food dollar, even as larger predators eliminated many of the city's smallest groceries.[28] Patsy D'Agostino even maintained that the supermarket had proved to be a great leveler for independent grocers, giving them "buying equity" with chain stores. He claimed that the chains no longer had an apparent buying advantage, musing, "In carload lots it's the same for me as for anyone else. In some ways we independents are even better off than the big fellows, because we have less handling of goods and a lot less red tape. So by the time we get the stuff into the store it costs the same as it costs the chains."[29] At this stage of their development, the magnitude of chain supermarkets also stifled innovation, invited the oversight of the federal government, and attracted union organizers.

In 1950, Patsy D'Agostino was one of twenty-two merchants featured in *Food Marketing*, a book whose ostensible purpose was to explain the inner workings of the nation's largest industry through the eyes of the entrepreneurs who represented its various branches. *Food Marketing* portrayed the modern supermarket as a model of American democracy because shoppers now consumed more than 1,600 pounds of food a year and could choose from between 2,000 and 4,000 items at their supermarkets. The text also celebrated advancements in transportation and technology (including the nation's 50,000 food processing plants, and its production of canned and frozen goods) that had made the food business the incarnation of America's industrial superiority. Its editor, Paul Sayres, went so far as to claim that the history of the supermarket, "born in crisis, tested through war, and maturing in prosperity," was "the story of America." Sayres explained that the supermarket was the truest embodiment of the "American way of life" not merely because of its material power, but because it represented an authentic spirit of community and cooperation (versus the false merits of communism):

> We call it the world's biggest business, and surely annual retail sales in the neighborhood of 31 billion dollars give it the right to that title. Yet this vast industry is not great because of any unified power or monopolistic control. It is not great because a government has legislated it into greatness. It is great because millions of Americans are working together to unify hundreds of diverse strands into a strong chain from farm to table.[30]

Patsy D'Agostino's chapter can be found in a section labeled "40 Million Housewives Can't Be Wrong." Its title, "Independents on the Band Wagon," implied that merchants such as the D'Agostino brothers had been incorporated into the grand system espoused by Sayres. In this piece, Patsy muted his criticism of chain store competition, although he began by describing the satisfactions of the independent merchant. For Patsy, the success of the independent stemmed from "his love of people" and his ability to practice his trade as a kind of creative art. With all the poetry of an expert copywriter, he mused: "There is glamour in food, there is drama in people, and there is romance in merchandising. It is in merchandising that the independent operator, who is not restricted by instructions coming from remote headquarters, can use all of his individual and original ideas."[31]

Patsy proceeded to give the hard facts behind the evolution of the modern grocery. He noted that while independent merchants had continued to own a 60 percent share of retail food distribution in the previous two decades, they would need to evolve to maintain their place in the economy.[32] He then explained how in the 1940s, the substantive differences between independent operators and chain stores had steadily diminished. Patsy observed that both independents and chains now offered meat and fish, produce, dairy products, bakery items, candy, and ice cream—items that were all handled by specialty stores twenty years before. More important, both independents and chains had implemented self-service retailing; only 13 percent of independents had adopted this system in 1939, but over 64 percent had made the shift by 1949.[33] The adoption of the self-service model (where customers selected their own items from open shelves, rather than relying on clerks to retrieve them from behind the counter) had sped the expansion of individual outlets. D'Agostino cited a *Progressive Grocer* survey that showed that in 1939, fewer than 5,000 independent stores earned sales volumes above $100,000; by 1949, that number had increased to 36,000. Over the same period, the number of small stores decreased, with both chain stores and independents having both fewer and larger outlets.[34]

Despite his humble beginnings as an immigrant grocer, Patsy D'Agostino spoke as one converted to the methods of the supermarket, warning his more conservative colleagues: "There are, of course, those who are satisfied to remain small. There is a risk in that, because the food business today calls for men who try to grow and go forward with the times. Those who grew have fared well in the vast majority of cases." In his analysis for *Food Marketing*, Patsy went so far as to attribute much of D'Agostino's postwar success to its adoption of a modern business model, casting his achievements as "an illustration" of three major trends: the growth of "one-stop" shopping centers, self-service retailing, and the movement toward larger stores.[35] These comments seemed to represent a paradigm shift both in Patsy's thinking about the grocery business and in his own operation.

In 1945, the D'Agostino brothers opened their fourth store at 85th Street, between Lexington and Park. According to Patsy, the 85th Street store represented a revolutionary step for the company, as they attempted to merge their traditional "silk-stocking" customer base—a demographic that usually commanded a retailer's full attention—with the philosophies of self-service. As one of the few self-service markets on the Upper East Side, the brothers were able to offer better prices and, despite the skepticism of their peers, their traditional customers seemed to enjoy this novel form of shopping. The new store enjoyed a sales volume of more than $750,000 in 1946. Patsy mused that the gamble "taught us that it pays to change as time and habits change." He then advised his independent brethren, "In the grocery business, as in other fields, one cannot start anything without taking chances, but this is one field where taking chances may pay off. No one who operates his own store can rest today on what he was able to do 15 years or even 10 years ago."[36]

Throughout his essay, Patsy sounded as if he were shilling for the modern supermarket. At other moments in the text, however, his voice became more personal and authentic—as when he seemed to consider his eventual succession by his own son and nephews. At the conclusion of the 1943 article in *The New Yorker*, Patsy had spoken wistfully about his dream of having at least one of his children follow him into the grocery business, since fruits and vegetables "are beautiful, like nature."[37] His description of the next generation in *Food Marketing* is not some imagined descendant of the ethnic peddler, but an entrepreneur weaned on college business courses and trained for life in the boardroom rather than behind the butcher counter. Patsy appeared to be reminding himself and his brother, Nicholas, to show regard for the next generation's ideas when he admonished his peers to accept the new breed of merchant:

> Today, we find many younger men coming into retail food stores. . . . Their fresh viewpoint may not always be readily accepted by older retailers, but in more intimate acquaintance they will find it welcome. Twenty years ago few sons of retailers seemed to be attracted to their father's business. Today we find them returning to it, even after long years of study, often with college degrees. They sense that backbreaking routines have been replaced with brainwork and with more promising and profitable tasks. They come in with new courage. The admonition to the seasoned merchant is not to close his mind to the contribution that may come from young men and young thinking.[38]

"From Pushcart to Super-Market": D'Agostino's and the Postwar Boom

In the 1950s, New York aspires to become a "world city" through an ambitious program of construction and investments in the institutions of culture and finance. In remaking the city's identity, public officials stake their fortunes on the new middle class. The D'Agostino brothers also hitch their star to New York's celebrated act of urban renewal, opening a new chapter in the company's history.

In the decade following World War II, as millions of Americans left cramped neighborhoods for the promise of greener pastures at the end of suburban cul-de-sacs, the grocery industry sought a business model that could exploit this shift. While suburban shopping malls became the new centers of civic life in the 1950s, D'Agostino's stayed true to the city—maintaining a profitable niche with New Yorkers. Because its customers were typically prosperous residents of Manhattan, the company had little incentive to change its geographic orientation. Despite a brief foray into suburban Westchester County in the 1940s, the brothers were reluctant to continue to expand into that territory. Patsy D'Agostino explained to one reporter, "Westchester is overexpanded. Out there they expect service at self-service prices."[39] Moreover, because the brothers had learned their trade on the city streets, they were much more comfortable with urban commerce.

The city that had drawn Patsy and Nicholas and thousands of other immigrants was changing, however, even as it entered a decade of celebrated cultural and civic achievement. Since the 1940s, New York had witnessed an incredible blossoming of literature, music, theater, painting, and architecture. As new institutions of culture, like the Museum of Modern Art, were transforming the city's image, traditional venues, such as the theaters of Broadway, experienced a glorious period of creative production. Meanwhile, by the beginning of the 1950s, New York would host the most visible symbol of cosmopolitanism, the United Nations building. In this period, a host of commentators labeled New York the "world city" and a "global cultural capital."[40]

And yet, at the conclusion of World War II, members of the political and commercial establishment were anxious about New York's long-term future. Their discussions focused on the decay of the city's infrastructure and housing stock—compounded by the return of 750,000 veterans to aging tenement neighborhoods—and the impending flight of the middle class.[41] Residents and merchants complained about New York's prohibitive real estate taxes and its traffic issues. At the same time, new communities in New Jersey, Long Island, and Westchester became more alluring, as improvements in the commuter rail system and the proliferation of automobiles allowed thousands of New Yorkers to decamp to the suburbs while continuing to work in the city. Civic leaders understood that the flight of residents to new subdivisions and townships would result in the out-migration of business, threatening the coffers of a city desperate for revenue. To secure its middle class and to protect itself from a mass exodus, the city began to invest in the philosophies of urban renewal—including a corporate partnership to provide housing—which would have a dramatic impact on D'Agostino's fortunes.

City officials feared that they lacked the resources to build enough new units or attract a private investor who could complete a major housing development. But Robert Moses, New York's all-powerful parks commissioner and a member of the exclusive City Planning Commission, and the Metropolitan Life Insurance Company came forward with a unique solution—offering a public-private partnership with the city.[42] In the late 1940s, Metropolitan Life was the world's largest insurance firm and, with assets of $7.5 billion, one of its largest private companies. Moses believed it had the resources to build apartments in the middle of Manhattan, where land acquisition costs were prohibitive, but where the stratagems of urban renewal—including the clearance of dilapidated neighborhoods—would have maximum effect. Moreover, Metropolitan Life already had experience with large-scale housing projects, having built the massive

Parkchester complex in the Bronx in 1938.[43] Stuyvesant Town, along with a subsequent venture called Peter Cooper Village, became a national model for public-private collaborations, while marking a new era in American urban governance. Acting on the Met Life and Moses proposal, state and city authorities took unprecedented steps to subsidize the land acquisition and tax payments for the company. New York thus became the first municipality in America to use public funds to aid private entities in performing duties that were once the sole province of government.[44] With the building of Stuyvesant Town, Met Life would become the world's largest nongovernmental investor in real estate development.

Robert Moses and Metropolitan Life decided to build just above 14th Street by the East River. While the population of this district had shrunk by more than half over the previous two decades, 11,000 people still lived in the area slated for redevelopment.[45] Of course, the neighborhood was associated with the city's immigrant past, and at the time of Stuyvesant Town's conception, nearly 60 percent of its residents were still "foreign born."[46] When it learned that the city was pursuing a massive redevelopment scheme, *The Saturday Evening Post* declared:

> The life and fate of Americans are entangled with the destiny of New York. So . . . there is a gleam of light for all cities, because New York is working now to develop a slum-clearance project which is likewise a housing project for middle-income self-supporting people; and, moreover, it is a project of free enterprise.

Placing a middle-class housing development in one of Manhattan's former immigrant hubs signaled the city's transition from a community defined by gritty tenements and close-knit ethnic neighborhoods to one that was ruled by urban planning and white-collar aspirations. *The Saturday Evening Post* even wondered if "New York could be reconstructed steadily so as to become eventually an assemblage of neighborhoods similar in conception to Stuyvesant Town."[47]

To stem the prevailing tide of outward migration, Metropolitan Life sought to mimic the characteristics of suburban design by providing potential tenants with units that offered all modern conveniences, ample living space, lawns, and respite from the grime and noise of the city. When plans for the Stuyvesant Town development were announced, *The New York Times* labeled the $50 million project an East Side "suburb in the city."[48] Frederick Ecker, the president of Metropolitan Life, termed the Stuyvesant Town undertaking "a plan to make it possible for persons, at medium rentals, to live in a park—to live in the country in the heart of New York."[49]

The project's uniform apartment buildings covered only about 30 percent of the development's total area, with the rest of the grounds devoted to private parks, gardens, and roadways.[50]

Stuyvesant Town and Peter Cooper Village were also designed to be self-contained and exclusive, with their buildings and walls serving as ramparts that effectively blocked passersby from even viewing their interiors. In a 1943 public hearing at City Hall, opponents of the project termed it a "medieval walled city, privately owned, in the heart of New York." These opponents, who included civil rights and education advocates, were especially critical of Met Life's failure to provide any public schools, day nurseries, libraries, or public playgrounds within Stuyvesant Town, and its explicit exclusion of African Americans from residency.[51] Designers had also eliminated the grid of streets around the development and widened the bordering thoroughfares in order to aid automobile travel and parking.[52] These design details distanced Stuyvesant Town from its neighbors while creating an effective social barrier against the poorer communities below 14th Street.[53] Even the project's thirteen-story buildings offered residents a far greater degree of anonymity than did the city's other neighborhoods.[54]

The construction of Stuyvesant Town and Peter Cooper Village created an immediate sensation among New Yorkers. The company received 200,000 applications for Stuyvesant Town's 24,000 spots. Peter Cooper Village, which targeted a higher class of tenant, received 20,000 applications for its 3,000 apartments when it opened its application process in 1947.[55] *The New York Times* declared that these new projects, along with the proposed United Nations site, were part of a "renaissance" and an "architectural revolution" along Manhattan's East River.[56] The *Times* later reported that that the two developments had upgraded the state of commerce in the neighborhood, as half of the 151 stores along the projects' boundaries were renovated.[57] Meanwhile, the value of buildings along First Avenue, between 14th and 23rd Streets, had nearly doubled by 1950.

The D'Agostino brothers' own postwar boom began when they won a contract from Metropolitan Life to open a store on 20th Street between Stuyvesant Town and Peter Cooper Village—a tremendous coup for the company. Metropolitan Life had considered putting chain stores in the new developments, as they had in their Parkchester project in the Bronx. However, Patsy convinced Met Life that D'Agostino's was a better choice because of its experience working with a more prosperous customer base, and he agreed to pay a steep rent to assuage any lingering concerns. He later explained that he "sold them on letting me in there on the grounds that Peter Cooper had a higher income group than Parkchester. I guess they're not sorry. My rent is two percent of gross sales, so last month I paid them $3,000."[58]

If the fanfare that Nicholas and Patsy D'Agostino brought to the opening of their new store is any indication, the brothers must have sensed that their fortunes were about to be made. Nicholas and Patsy had previously celebrated store openings with a simple ribbon cutting and family photographs. For the 20th Street location, the brothers organized a cocktail party and invited several food executives, local politicians, and radio and television stars, after which the guests were driven to the store in limousines. One of D'Agostino's corporate clients, Arnold Bakers, reported in its trade journal, "The opening of D'Agostino Bros. beautiful market on February 14th in Stuyvesant Town certainly will go down in history as one of the most spectacular openings of modern times." The baking company's representative then gave a blow-by-blow description of the festivities:

> To begin with, Patsy and Nick (two grand guys), operators of this rapidly rising chain, sponsored a cocktail party at the Sert Room of the Waldorf-Astoria Hotel where we rubbed elbows with Tex McCrary and Jinx Falkenberg, Arlene Francis, Jack Sterling, John Reed King, and Robert Smallwood, President of Lipton Tea, as well as other celebrities of food and radio fame. At 4 p.m. with police escort, we were whisked to the market in ten English Minx cars where an elaborate ribbon cutting ceremony, headed by N.Y.C. Commissioner of Markets, Mascheralli [sic], was held.

The writer concluded that despite the fanfare, "the most outstanding tribute to the occasion was the more than one thousand tenants of both Peter Cooper Village and Stuyvesant Town who waited in driving sleet and cold to seek admission."[59]

The spectacle surrounding the 20th Street store opening reflected the brothers' new aspirations and emboldened sense of identity. Nicholas and Patsy had called their first store the "Yorkville Food Shoppe" because they were reluctant to advertise their ethnicity to their affluent customers. In 1950, however, Nicholas and Patsy changed the names of all their stores to "D'Agostino Brothers."[60] A week after the gala opening, the company also took out a full-page announcement in *Town & Village*, the development's newspaper, which used the brothers' own history to introduce them to potential customers—wedding the brothers' personal narrative to their public identity. "From Pushcart to Super-Market" read the headline, followed by three awkward paragraphs that began: "Your store in the heart of Town & Village has a history . . . a history that dates back to a windy day in 1921 when two boys named Nick and Patsie [sic] D'Agostino set foot in this country from Italy. That was a big day—it was the beginning of your store in Town & Village."[61]

When Patsy noted the sizable rental fee the brothers paid to Met Life, he also mentioned that the new store did $2 million dollars' worth of business that first year—which meant a healthy profit, even by today's standards.[62] The store's receipts became the engine of the company's growth, causing Patsy and Nicholas to adopt a more ambitious strategy. As the brothers contemplated further expansion throughout Manhattan, they decided to compete for top recognition among the city's shoppers, even if the company maintained its independent, regional orientation.

In the coming decades, D'Agostino's would remain rooted in the city, operating out of its modest commercial spaces while targeting a discerning consumer. Yet, just as Stuyvesant Town and Peter Cooper Village marked a shift in New York's cultural identity, Patsy and Nicholas's new venture took them another step from their origins as ethnic grocers. In its earliest incarnation, D'Agostino's was essentially a neighborhood operation, even if it had targeted a wealthier segment of the population. Because their livelihood was dependent on the residents of the Upper East Side, the brothers had tailored their retailing strategies to upper-income patrons, offering them charge accounts, telephone ordering, and delivery service. In the 1950s, Patsy and Nicholas had brought their business downtown and widened its appeal—a move that corresponded with the modernization of the food industry. Like the city itself, the D'Agostinos now staked their company's future on New York's expanded white-collar middle class.

The new location offered shoppers the most current amenities and services in a relatively small space (well under 10,000 square feet). But serving a broader clientele forced the brothers to reexamine their assumptions about merchandising a grocery store. The continued evolution of middle-class life, especially for young professionals, required a new calculus. Years later, Nicholas's son Nick D'Agostino Jr. explained:

> In the past, it was more the maid would come in and do the shopping. Now the customer was doing the shopping and even the husband was doing the shopping and a lot of single people were living in the city and they were working people—even in the '50s and '60s—who were pressed for time.[63]

The D'Agostinos had already enjoyed their first successful experiment with self-service a few years earlier at their 85th Street store. Now, postwar prosperity, new packaging technologies, and consumer demand led the company to apply this model on a grander scale, beginning with the installation of new self-service meat counters, deep freezers, and refrigerated produce sections.[64] Customers appreciated the convenience and speed this mode of shopping provided. But the D'Agostinos and their fellow grocers found that consumers also preferred self-service shopping because they were free to touch and examine the merchandise and make their choices without the influence of a store employee—all of which resulted in a higher volume of purchases per customer.[65] Moreover, retailers like Nicholas and Patsy discovered that the mass and variety of supermarket offerings created a fortuitous paradox in consumer behavior—by having a wider exposure to different brands and types of food, shoppers often "traded up" for higher-priced staples rather than searching for the best bargain.[66]

At the end of the 1950s, one *New York Times* reporter would say of the new food industry, "The revolution in merchandising, of which the supermarket is the glittering symbol, is inseparable from the revolution in the merchandise itself."[67] Because so many of their customers at 20th Street were working professionals with new families, the former pushcart peddlers had to first change their approach to the sale of produce. D'Agostino Brothers offered a wide selection of prewrapped fruits and vegetables to shoppers who now preferred to "take a package with four oranges in it rather than . . . go to somebody to have them select them, put them in a bag, and weigh them."[68] In addition, D'Agostino Brothers carried an expansive selection of canned goods, as customers began to buy everything from baked beans to fancy mushrooms in tins.[69] Yet one of the clearest signs that the company was targeting a new demographic was in the broad array of frozen foods now available in its stores.

Frozen foods, which were developed in the 1920s but perfected during World War II, transformed the American diet in the 1950s. Advances in refrigeration and packaging had their perfect marriage in the millions of units of frozen orange juice, creamed spinach, peas, and corn, and recently invented "TV dinners" that were sold in the postwar era. By 1952, Americans were annually consuming eighteen pounds of quick-frozen products per capita.[70] Although the D'Agostinos had received their initiation into the food business through the produce trade, they had carried a limited supply of frozen foods even at their Yorkville shop.[71] With the soaring popularity of frozen foods in the 1950s, however, Patsy made this market segment a retailing priority. Toward the end of the decade, he even penned an article in which he asserted that, although analysts viewed "frozens" as the province of the suburban supermarket, they were a crucial part of his own inventory because of the "large percentage of working husbands and wives" in the city's "higher-than-average income areas."[72] Here, D'Agostino's again acknowledged the changing dynamic of the middle-class family (as a growing number of married women were joining the labor force) and the ascendancy of the city's white-collar class in the postwar era.[73]

As much as this new retail paradigm was forcing merchants to reconsider their methods of merchandising, it was also transforming their notion of store design. While the prohibitive cost of urban real estate, high overhead, and lack of parking prevented suburban superstores from conquering New York, the supermarket concept altered the physical scheme of the city's major groceries.[74] The early supermarket had been considered the "poor man's store," as retailers like Long Island's King Kullen operated out of former warehouses and displayed their wares "factory-style" in industrial stacks and crude bins.[75] Even a high-end grocery like the Yorkville Food Shoppe had been narrow, cramped, and dark. As the supermarket became an institution of middle-class life, however, retailers added sleek décors, air-conditioning, indirect lighting, mood music, and bathrooms to their stores. Increasingly, they came to resemble department stores in terms of design and inventory while aiming to define the retail life of the city in the same way that department stores had for a previous generation.[76]

In the 1950s, D'Agostino's began to promote its stores' "spotless cleanliness" and paid new attention to presentation and displays.[77] In 1943, *The New Yorker* had used the rustic setting of the Bronx Terminal Market to idealize Patsy D'Agostino as an ethnic grocer with an organic sensibility. A decade later, one writer could have been invoking poet Allen Ginsberg's iconic supermarket in California when he described the interior of a D'Agostino Brothers' store:

> We looked down through dazzling fluorescence at mountains of food between spacious aisles, at gleaming counters, some refrigerated the length of the store. Pleasant mood music flowed from the amplifiers; conveyor belts sped the work at the checkout counters. Today, all the meat is prepackaged and many vegetables and fruits are pre-wrapped. But Patsy still pinches the produce regularly, and Nick, who began as a butcher, keeps a close check on all the meat.[78]

The concept of the supermarket as department store also altered shoppers' expectations of what a grocer should sell. In the 1950s, Patsy and Nicholas would begin to offer their customers a limited supply of the personal items typically found at the corner drugstore, including bath and beauty products, soap and toothpaste, and domestic cleaning supplies.[79] Supermarket merchandisers found that they could charge much higher markups on popular items such as cigarettes, paper towels, floor wax, and candy than they could on food. Facing down larger competitors, grocers around the country felt pressured to stock an array of nonfood items, with one survey finding that at the dawn of the 1950s, from 40 to 60 percent of all markets now carried drugstore items.[80]

The notion that the modern supermarket was the descendant of the department store also carried implications of class. By offering to fulfill whatever conceivable need a consumer could have, in a forum that was made accessible by self-service shopping and modest prices, the supermarket became an institutional representation of the 1950s ideal of consensus.[81] Proponents of the supermarket promoted it as a common meeting place for different classes of Americans. One writer remarked, "Supermarket shopping has been a democratizing influence. The wife of the workingman and the wife of the man in gray flannel both shop in the same supermarket and buy the same frozen canapés."[82] Yet even as the supermarket allegedly broke down class distinctions, its conception of a democratic marketplace carried notions of status. The image of housewives buying frozen canapés communicated the idea that at the supermarket, Americans of different means could get a taste of luxury. This was particularly potent for the thousands of Americans who now had expanded buying power because of postwar prosperity, as over one-third of American families were categorized as "middle-income" by 1957.[83] And with its experience serving a wealthy clientele on the Upper East Side now joined to the popular retail strategies of the supermarket, D'Agostino Brothers was poised to be the merchant of choice for New York's new middle class.

In her study of the newly affluent readership of *The New Yorker*, Mary Corey observed that although the postwar economy brought this group unprecedented financial clout, it was unsure of how to spend its money. This cohort's desire for social status was balanced by its significant intellect, its interest in culture, and its nascent sense of taste—in short, the ideal audience for the magazine's sensibility. Corey adds that these would-be cosmopolitans sought "the earmarks of aristocratic taste" through consumer goods, as well as through their selection of reading matter. She argues that their "discriminating consumption" became "a means of displaying personal identity and social authority," against the "tasteless homogeneity" of the mass market (which, of course, had aided their own prosperity).[84] The urban sophisticates described by Corey bear a striking resemblance to the demographic that Patsy and Nicholas targeted at their 20th Street store. Stephen D'Agostino, Nicholas's son and the future president of the company, explained that in the 1940s, the typical D'Agostino customer was "'old money,' educated, probably more WASP than anything else." But with the greater social mobility of the 1950s, people "getting $100 a week jobs . . . the 'upscalers'—now that becomes the demographic we're looking for. And we stayed with that group of people, and they stayed with us. And if *they* went upscale, *we* went upscale and we all traveled together."[85] Indeed, as these (implicitly white and middle-class) strivers continued to prosper, moving from Stuyvesant Town and Peter Cooper Village to the Upper East Side, there were already D'Agostino stores in their new neighborhoods to serve them.

D'Agostino Brothers' high-end reputation enhanced its charm for shoppers who were somewhat ingenuous about matters of taste and status, but ready to enjoy their own good fortune. In the 1950s, Nicholas and Patsy even began to advertise their stores as "markets of distinction."[86] Of course, the great success of the brothers' new ventures was not simply the result of location or image. Even though D'Agostino's continued to incorporate the methods of the self-service supermarket, it could provide its customers with a superior product because its principal managers had extensive training in the meat, fish, and produce trades. As a smaller operation, the company had better quality control than its larger competitors.[87] More important, through their inventory and expertise, Nicholas and Patsy were uniquely positioned to exploit their customers' desire for a taste of the "good life."

As noted earlier, after the scarcity and rationing of the Depression and World War II, American consumers made red meat a staple of their diet and a mark of their own prosperity. The nation's annual per capita consumption of red meat reached a forty-six-year peak in 1954, at a stunning 156 pounds.[88] Throughout the decade, D'Agostino Brothers used this hunger for beef to maximize its profits and build its reputation.[89] Because of Nicholas's mastery of the butcher's trade, the company offered the best selections of steaks, chops, and prime-cut meats of any major retailer in the city. In addition, the 20th Street store offered customers a broad selection of fine imported and domestic cheeses, as well as a host of other products in its deluxe new dairy case. It should be noted that before World War II, grocers offered a limited dairy selection since shoppers purchased their milk directly from a dairy retailer, bought their ice cream at the local soda fountain, and had little knowledge of cheese beyond the most basic, durable types. By providing a figurative beachhead for middle-class strivers, Stuyvesant Town and Peter Cooper Village had already transformed the retail culture of the community by the time D'Agostino's arrived. *The New York Times* observed that the area's new residents had "introduced a different scale of living" to the area. The newspaper noted that the neighborhood's old groceries now carried pâté de foie gras, canned lobster, and crabmeat, while liquor stores that had once sold "gallon jugs of wine to local Italian families" carried more than a hundred wines as well as scotches and cordials, to keep pace "with the discriminating taste of the projects."[90]

By the end of the decade, D'Agostino Brothers also began to embrace the "gourmet" culture that was emerging among the budding sophisticates of Manhattan. Like other savvy supermarket retailers, the company noticed that a segment of their customers had developed an interest in such epicurean delights as European sausages, artichokes, imported olive oil, capers, and crepes, and were looking for them in their local supermarket rather than in the traditional import shops.[91] According to *Fortune* magazine, urban supermarkets were even beginning to stock "fancy staples" like shrimp, crab, lobster tail, endives, artichokes, and cans of lobster bisque for those customers who viewed them as standard offerings.[92]

Who were these aspiring epicures? According to *Fortune*, they tended to be young couples with "more money than they used to have" and a full calendar of cocktail and dinner parties. They were often looking to impress their friends with fancy hors d'oeuvres, but tended to purchase gourmet items in attractively packaged cans and jars—which suggested that they were not yet connoisseurs. The young social climbers' appetite for exotic dishes suggested an ironic turnabout from the early twentieth century, when artichokes and capers were the province of ethnics. One merchant explained, "The immigrants used to support the import business. . . . Now it's the younger generation. . . . They are the reason for fancy foods in small packages in supermarkets and chain stores."[93]

One might dismiss their new appetites as a fad, especially since these consumers were buying gourmet items in prepared, packaged forms. Yet, this dalliance with cocktail party exotica suggested the beginnings of a culinary revolution. *Fortune* predicted that "the man who tries French sardines in olive oil is apt to develop a taste for them, if only as an occasional treat. However shallow the original impulse to buy, the lasting result may be a greater sophistication of American taste."[94] Over the next the decade, this generation would become devotees of Julia Child and *Gourmet* magazine and transform the nation's food culture. Moreover, these would-be connoisseurs would continue to change the complexion of the supermarket and become a precious resource for those retailers—such as D'Agostino's—who could win their loyalty.

Despite its apparent success, the supermarket revolution was not without cost. Like many other independent retailers, Nicholas and Patsy spent thousands of dollars installing refrigeration systems and lighting, widening aisles for shopping carts, and installing larger, more "shopper-friendly" shelving. The new system of retailing also significantly altered Americans' connection to their food sources, as the very packaging and processing of meat, produce, and dry goods transformed them into commodities. This meant that consumers had a less intimate connection to their food on both a global and a tangible level.

Of course, both the consumer and the producer were responsible for this development. Self-service meat departments had been made feasible by the development of cellophane and Styrofoam and the refinement of factory-cut meat. Once self-service meat departments became the rule, however, many shoppers overlooked the inherent quality of certain cuts of meat in the name of expediency and price. In the produce department, retailers sold lettuce, tomatoes, and apples wrapped in cardboard and plastic, rather than in the rustic pyramids of the old grocery. Customers not only seemed to appreciate this convenience, but also began to expect produce that was durable and not subject to the whim of the seasons. As a result, dozens of varieties of fruits and vegetables that had been sold by pushcart peddlers like Patsy and Nicholas began to disappear from grocery stores. In other cases, shoppers began to reject fresh produce altogether for the ease of frozen fruits and vegetables.

This growing disconnect was also manifest in the social habits of American consumers. The new store at the site of New York's grand experiment in urban renewal anticipated a shift to more modern, anonymous methods of retailing which, in turn, reflected the city's changing identity. Previously, when most grocers ran neighborhood operations, personal relationships and trust were essential aspects of maintaining a customer base. Before the 1950s, most shoppers went to the counter of their corner store and asked the grocer and his clerks to retrieve the items on their shopping lists. The clerks not only fetched the shoppers' dry goods, but also chose and weighed their produce. For customers purchasing meat, the butcher hacked sections from enormous sides of beef or pork, and then sliced those cuts according to the customer's specifications. Because of their intimacy with customers, grocers of this generation had to be experts in their trade and salesmen of both the merchandise and themselves. In their first stores on the Upper East Side, Nicholas and Patsy knew most of their regular customers by name, as well as their addresses and buying habits, especially since their clients demanded a higher grade of service. In this context, Patsy's ability to charm their patrons was vital to D'Agostino's success, as was the customers' belief that the brothers offered a higher grade of produce, meats, and fish than the competition.

In the anonymous environment of the supermarket, shoppers were often reluctant to ask clerks for their advice on the freshness of products, or to learn how to prepare unfamiliar cuts of meat or exotic vegetables. Instead, consumers tended to opt for familiar, standardized, prepackaged items. This inclination not only affected America's eating habits but also changed the role of the grocer. Retailers began to view experienced clerks as an expensive luxury rather than an extension of their own expertise. They also came to realize that the modern supermarket functioned more efficiently with a strict division of labor. Over time, the responsibilities of clerks thus became uniform and limited, while the grocers' pool of employees grew younger and more replaceable. The nominal transition from "grocery clerk" to "employee" signaled the position's declining prestige. And as supermarkets began to adopt the hierarchies of corporations, grocers began to acquire the management philosophies of executives. To stave off the dominance of larger competitors, they had to ultimately learn the principles of the boardroom.[95] In fact, this development would be seen in the next generation of D'Agostino company leadership when Patsy's and Nicholas's sons assumed management positions in the 1960s.

By offering a vast line of nonfood items on their shelves, supermarkets imperiled such retail institutions as newsstands, tobacconists, floral shops, stationery stores, neighborhood drugstores, and soda fountains.[96] Yet, for grocers, the move to incorporate the drugstore trade into their operations was a burden as well as a benefit. By 1953, food stores often carried 3,500 to 4,000 items, nearly tripling the offerings of the typical store twenty-five years earlier. While supermarkets gained a lucrative source of revenue, expanding their inventories meant needing to continually shift their focus away from food. Moreover, those merchants unable to expand and adapt were often forced into obsolescence—as over this same twenty-five-year period, the number of American grocery stores shrank by 17 percent.[97]

Finally, the transformation of the grocery industry in the 1950s meant the decline of some of the most romantic aspects of New York's food culture. The family grocery on the corner was increasingly forced to modernize and expand or go out of business. In 1957, a congressional subcommittee investigating the price of food distribution paid a visit to New York's Washington Street fruit and vegetable market. Rep. Harold Cooley (D-NC) called the wholesale food markets of New York—once mythicized as havens of rustic authenticity by *The New Yorker* and *The New York Times*—"obsolete, antiquated ratholes" that were "a disgrace to the city and the nation." Attributing rising food prices to "the inefficient and excessive handling at wholesale," *Business Week* noted that retailers had begun to bypass these markets to deal directly with growers.[98] In 1958, the city's Markets Commissioner Anthony Masciarelli recommended to Mayor Robert F. Wagner Jr. that the city close its eight remaining open-air pushcart markets. Masciarelli asserted that the markets had outlived their usefulness as an outlet for housewives in low-income areas with the emergence of supermarkets, and now were simply an economic drain on the city's budget.[99]

New York was spared some of the consequences of the supermarket revolution. At the end of the decade, the state government outlawed the sale of drugs at its groceries. Meanwhile, the cost of real estate, rent, overhead, and construction, as well as traffic issues and the lack of ample retail space continued to prevent chain retailers from taking over the city. In Manhattan, most shoppers could not drive to 20,000-square-foot superstores and load up on two weeks of groceries because they lacked automobiles, accessible parking, or large apartments. Still, the future of the "little guy" in the retail food business seemed in peril, especially from a national perspective. At the end of the 1950s, approximately 200,000 "mom and pop" stores still existed in the US, but they managed to retain only 6 percent of the grocery business and were closing at the rate of 6,000 a year. One *New York Times* writer mused, "Thus is the last stronghold of traditional American 'rugged individualism' being breached. Time was when an ambitious young man could start a career in retailing with a small store, or even a pushcart. Now he is more likely to become a corporation employee, an organization man in what has become one of the biggest of big businesses."[100]

At the same time, the proliferation of the supermarket model provided the D'Agostino brothers with the opportunity to build their reputation with those shoppers who felt alienated from the latest developments in the food industry. Over the next few decades, the company would pitch itself as the store that cared about its customers while offering the finest meats and produce in New York. As part of an older generation of grocers, Nicholas and Patsy did have genuine affection for their trade. As the business continued its steady growth across the city, its "reputation as a friend of the consumer" (as the company literature later termed it) was a key part of maintaining a relationship with its customer base. The notion that D'Agostino's had a deeper, time-honored commitment to food—reflected in the brothers' own narrative of their origins as pushcart peddlers—would be an asset in the grocery's negotiation of the cold, hard world of modern retailing. And yet, the transformation of the industry seemed to parallel the D'Agostino brothers' own evolution. Like many of their socially mobile clientele, Patsy and Nicholas had gone into the Second World War with fixed identities based in their ethnicity and their trades. Now, the brothers were being swept up in the tide of postwar prosperity and the ancillary social benefits that it carried. Over the next decade, like their customers, these former immigrants would have access to new luxuries, new neighborhoods, and new connections to the mainstream of American culture.

"To See America with His Own Eyes": The Many Narratives of Patsy D'Agostino

As his fortunes rise, Patsy D'Agostino becomes a favorite subject for members of the press. His life story becomes a commodity—signifying America's many virtues—though the tale shifts according to the orientation of its teller. As the D'Agostino brothers' "rags-to-riches" story continues to build the company's reputation, it also heralds their new social status.

During the 1950s, Patsy D'Agostino remained a favorite source of quotes for local journalists seeking to understand the latest developments in food retailing. And he continued to emerge as a leading voice in the industry through his work with national and regional grocers' associations. Throughout the decade, Patsy's profile would also be elevated by a series of magazine features that chronicled his rise from pushcart peddler to prominent entrepreneur. While Patsy's growing celebrity reflected and fed the expansion of the D'Agostino brothers' business, his status as a darling of the press revealed a growing fascination with his "rags to riches" success. A comparative reading of these articles—each highlighting or omitting key narrative details, in keeping with the thematic agenda of the respective publication—reveals how Patsy D'Agostino's life story was being adapted as a morality play about the virtues of postwar America. For some of these publications, Patsy's narrative reflected the opportunity for all Americans to prosper under the free-market system; for others, his achievements signified the ability of immigrants and Catholics to fully assimilate and gain civic respectability. At the same time, through these various accounts, one can see the brothers' personal history evolving into a form of public identity.

Despite the fanfare for the opening of the 20th Street store, the brothers were still considered "small" businessmen in the period immediately following the war. In a 1951 *Business Week* feature, "A Gospel for Independent Grocers," Patsy D'Agostino outlined his philosophy for independent merchants.[101] In the opening paragraph, Mr. D'Agostino warned, "For those big overgrown supers . . . is coming a day of reckoning." *Business Week* observed that D'Agostino "has none of the average independent's gnawing fear of the big chains. What he lacks in size and stockholders' money, he makes up for in ingenuity and speed." Under the heading "All Classes," *Business Week* defended the democratic character of D'Agostino's clientele with the observation: "In any of his stores you will find women in worn coats rubbing elbows with women in mink."[102]

In the piece, Patsy emphasized the independent grocer's need for flexible, innovative strategies to compete with the industry's Goliaths. He advised his peers to offer a varied product line to bring in "a range of customers" and to meet the chain store prices on staples, but he encouraged them to "clean up" on a limited stock of items that chains refused to carry, such as caviar and pickled mushrooms. Patsy also counseled his fellow independents to be cautious in their marketing strategies, arguing that they should not offer shoppers private label merchandise (except coffee), credit, delivery service, or expensive packaging (policies that would all necessarily change as management grew more ambitious). One of Patsy's "commandments" was particularly ironic considering the subsequent direction of the operation. He was forthright about his reluctance to advertise, a venture that would become essential to the company's iconography throughout the 1970s and '80s. *Business Week* noted that D'Agostino "has never spent a cent for such matters himself. Yet the New York press displays an enviable interest in all his enterprises." Patsy argued, "Why do you spend all your money on men to tell everybody your company is something it isn't? Pay your employees well instead, and they will tell the world how wonderful you are."[103] Of course, Patsy's outgoing personality and his ability to cultivate relationships were effective means of drawing customers and winning the loyalty of employees. He embodied the hands-on character of an older generation of entrepreneur, suggesting that would-be merchants know "everything possible about your business," concluding, "God forbid somebody is working for me and I don't know what they're doing."[104]

True to D'Agostino's reputation, meat and fish (which accounted for 27 percent of its sales) and produce (which made up another 12 percent) were the focus of its business.[105] At the time of the article, the three D'Agostino markets continued to prosper—each generating between $800,000 and

$2 million worth of business. The company maintained a steady rate of 3 percent profit (about 1 percent higher than that of A&P).[106] Even if the brothers were harboring plans for conquering the New York market, Patsy worried about expanding too quickly, telling *Business Week*, "We like to chew our meat as we go along. We have no stockholders."[107]

As the D'Agostino brothers' fortunes rose, however, their image as humble greengrocers began to shift as well, beginning with a 1952 feature in *American Magazine*: "I Found $5,000,000 in a Pushcart." In polished English, the article communicated both the promise of American society and Patsy's distance from the Old Country.[108] But with a title that implied that riches were just waiting to be bagged by those willing to take initiative, this version of Patsy's story—conveyed with the likely aid of a ghostwriter, in a middlebrow publication whose motto was "Successful Living for the Family"—affirmed postwar America as a country of enterprise and prosperity.

In the piece's opening, Patsy claimed that unlike most Italian immigrants, he did not want to come to the United States. He admitted that his perceptions had been shaped by the prejudices of his elders. His father convinced him that in America, he could make enough ($1,000) to return to Italy, finish high school, and have a secure career as a government bureaucrat.[109] Patsy remembered, "I didn't want to come to America, because I was afraid you would put a label on me," after hearing Ignatius D'Agostino describe the prejudice typical of American society. He explained that while his father "pined for the Old Country," he ultimately "blamed his failures on the fact that native Americans kept putting a label on him. They called him a Dago. I didn't want to be called a Dago." Patsy then recalled a teacher who described the US as "a cold world of skyscrapers, giant factories, and department stores" where the "individual was lost":

> It was my grade-school teacher back in the Abruzzi district of Italy who made me afraid Americans would put a number on me. He was a solemn man who seemed to know all about the world. America, he warned, was a land where, if you were lucky enough to rise above ditch-digging, shining shoes, or tending a pushcart, you worked for a giant corporation and became a number.[110]

To contemporary readers, these warnings might appear to be thoughtful advice. Ignatius D'Agostino did belong to a generation of Italian immigrants who lived on the periphery of American society, while Patsy's teacher clearly understood the exploitation Italian laborers suffered in the industrial age. Beyond this historical reality, however, the introductory tale used these two figures as a symbolic warning to the readers of *American Magazine*. In Patsy's story, Ignatius committed the sin of blaming society's supposed prejudices for his own lack of success. Patsy's other "father"—a learned man from stuffy Old Europe—was damned for his cynicism, when he claimed that individual ambition might be stymied by the harsh realities of modern existence.

Patsy's anecdote seemed to be directed at a readership struggling to defy the limitations and anomie of middle-class life in the 1950s. Patsy then hinted that those citizens lacking in profit motive, satisfied with their fate, or dependent on state-instituted security were even vulnerable to the overtures of a totalitarian state:

> My ambition in those days was very modest. In fact, I was, by my present standards, dismally lacking in enterprise. Ambition was discouraged by Italy's rigid class lines. . . . In Italy during those days everyone harped on security, much as they harp on it in America today. We were ripe for the dictatorship of Benito Mussolini when he appeared a year or so after I left.[111]

Unlike the 1943 profile in *The New Yorker*, the narrative in *American* paid scant attention to Patsy's early failures. It mentioned that he was supposed to go to Pittsburgh to work in the steel mills but ended up in Harlem when a job failed to materialize. However, *American* attributed Patsy's difficulties to the "Old World" mentality of his father, Ignatius, who grumbled that in America "you could earn a dollar but were treated like a pig doing it." Patsy explained that this mindset limited his father's enterprise:

> Every time some acquaintance from the Old Country wandered by, Father would embrace him, and soon we had a new partner for our pushcart or sidewalk fruit stand. . . . Father would expansively split any profits with his "partner" and give me, "the boy," a few dollars, depending on how good business had been. Several Monday mornings I would find we didn't even have a pushcart. Father had lost it the night before in friendly gambling.

Frustrated, Patsy "bought" himself in as a partner and pestered his father to run four pushcarts at once. The result was a quick profit of several hundred dollars, but father and son clashed. At the age of eighteen, he convinced one of his associates, Domenick Clemente, to join him in opening a fruit and vegetable store. Their friends advised the boys that they would stand a better chance of succeeding if they anglicized their names. Patsy thus took the name "Pat Austin," and his partner became

"Dick Clements." The two Italians called their store "Austin & Clements." Patsy recalled that the new mantle seemed "Very English. Within three months we had failed disastrously."[112]

It is likely that Austin & Clements went under because Patsy and his partner lacked experience. They may have suffered from a poor location, a lack of capital, or pure bad luck. The episode certainly indicated the ambiguity of Italian identity in America, as the young merchants were afraid to use their own names on the store's marquee.[113] Yet in this instance, Patsy D'Agostino used this recollection to validate the notion that America is an open society for those with ambition, no matter their ethnic background. As the article noted, Patsy was too proud to return to his father and too afraid to return to Italy empty-handed, so he went to Norwood, Massachusetts, where his cousins, the D'Espinosa family, promised to find him a job. Patsy D'Agostino recalled that in Norwood, his cousin Bill D'Espinosa made the "deepest impression" on him. D'Espinosa was one of ten children whose father was a blacksmith's helper. Mornings he attended Northeastern University in Boston, afternoons he worked in a tannery, and between 11 p.m. and 2 a.m. he studied. D'Espinosa eventually gained admittance to West Point, where he finished in the top fourth of his class. "Bill D'Espinosa convinced me that in America there is a chance for the humblest immigrant," proclaimed Patsy. He then told how Bill gave him "the soundest advice I ever received":

> He was going through the mail and came across a letter addressed to "Pat Austin." It was from my old partner, "Dick Clements." I hadn't told Bill about my alias. "Who on earth is Pat Austin?" he yelled. Sheepishly I reached for the letter. I explained that "Pat Austin" was the name I had concocted to make myself sound like a 100-per cent American. Bill snorted his disgust. "Did the name D'Espinosa keep me out of West Point?" he asked. I had to admit it had not. He added, "Patsy, you don't have to have an English-sounding name to be a good American. Don't be something phony. Just be yourself—for all you are worth."[114]

In this version of his story, Patsy returned to New York—"so anxious to make good in the American way that I began relishing the wildly insecure life of the pushcarts." Here, the pushcart was symbolically reimagined, as it no longer represented a doomed existence but was instead emblematic of a frontier mentality—equated with free enterprise and judged as "typically" American. Patsy shared that he and his brother Nick, largely absent from the piece, "owe nobody money. We are in complete control of our stores, as I was when I had my own pushcart." Patsy also noted that he now lectured on economics once a week at the City College of New York (CCNY)—quite a distance from his origins as an immigrant peddler—and that from his perspective the "best laboratory in the world for learning the basic economic laws of food merchandising is on a fruit-and-vegetable cart" because it was a pure reflection of the laws of supply and demand.[115]

The account also merged American opportunity and the mass prosperity of the 1950s. Patsy's father eventually went back to Italy, where he died, "still disgruntled with America." His son, however, grew to love his new homeland, explaining that their two perspectives were the product of generational difference and the possibilities of assimilation:

> I believe the opportunities of America in recent decades have been broadening rather than shrinking. The nasty labels, I'm sure, were flung more loosely in his day. They embittered him so much that he was blind to the opportunities America offers to even the humblest immigrant. As for me, I have been blessed with more good things than I ever dreamed of.

Among the blessings that Patsy counted in the *American* article are the friends he had in "every state of the Union" and his "typically American 8-room stucco home on a winding, tree-lined street in New Rochelle, N.Y." He toasted his "four closest neighbors" who represented a cross-section of American society: Charlie Clausen, an industrial sales manager; George Anderson, an engineer; Jimmy Tyson, a manager for Tommy Dorsey's band; and Harry Caldwell, who sold real estate. Patsy concluded:

> All four are helping make America the wonderful place to live in that it is. And all four know that their neighbor Patsy D'Agostino is an immigrant with no schooling to speak of who began as a pushcart peddler in Harlem. But they have put no label on me. We're all fine back-and-forth friends.

Consistent with the tenor of the postwar period, this tolerant, authentic spirit of community was linked to individualism—a nation in which everyone was free to pursue their dreams—while the populism at the heart of American culture was tied to entrepreneurship. Patsy concluded that America had given him the chance to "express myself successfully in a very individual, D'Agostino way. The fact that there is still plenty of room in this huge country for you and me to express ourselves as individuals through independent enterprise, is what I cherish most about my homeland."[116]

Here, one can detect a shift in the meaning of "independent." In

The New Yorker piece and in Patsy's 1943 congressional testimony, "independent" had connotations of defiance. It was used in opposition to corporations—the "small" businessman defending himself against the vultures of big business. The "independent" of the *American* feature—rooted firmly in the mindset of the 1950s—enjoyed secure ties to the establishment. Patsy called the small merchant "the backbone of American society," adding that the independent grocer sold two-thirds of all food sold in America. Yet Patsy still advocated a modest prosperity, maintaining:

> Our own D'Agostino enterprise may grow a bit more, but not too much, I hope. Right now we have about 100 employees. Our New York stores sell $5,000,000 worth of groceries every year. Ever since we started being successful I have had a dread of becoming too big. Once I begin to forget the names of any of my employees, I no longer want to grow. I might get careless and start putting numbers on them.[117]

Patsy recalled how at twenty-two he moved to Massachusetts, married Irene Salemme, and went to work for First National as a clerk. *American* chose Patsy's disenchantment with his situation as a climactic moment in its story. Patsy made thirty dollars a week at First National (ten dollars less than he earned as a clerk in Gennaro Gentile's New York store) and noticed that they made "the same mistakes some other great corporations were making in their passion for 'efficiency.'" He noted that on his check was printed "#7,543."

Even several months after Patsy was named the manager of one of First National's neighborhood locations, the name of the previous store manager remained posted. He grew tired of being called "Mr. Cash." After he was reprimanded for arriving late one snowy morning, Patsy quit: "My wife was about to have a baby. But I could not take being 'Mister Cash,' Number 7,543 any longer. I shouted to the supervisor that I would rather dig ditches."[118] Patsy's tale reflected postwar anxieties about a loss of individuality, with the decade's promotion of the "organization man" as a model for the white-collar workforce.[119] And yet, was the store's reluctance to replace the nameplate of "Mr. Cash" also an act of veiled anti-Italian discrimination? In a 1950 interview with a columnist from the *New York Daily Mirror*, Patsy had explained that he "didn't stay in Boston long. There was a lot of prejudice then against Italians."[120]

In fact, Patsy would be forced to dig ditches before returning to work for his mentor, Gennaro Gentile in New York. For three years, Patsy studied under Mr. Gentile while saving enough to buy his own store. Frank Tucciarone, described as an "acquaintance," sold him a partnership in his store at 83rd and Lexington for $4,000, which Patsy had saved and borrowed from his uncle. Patsy characterized Mr. Tucciarone (his brother's future father-in-law) as suffering from the same cultural issues as his father—his allegiance to the "old ways" impeding his optimism and his ability to see opportunities. Patsy claimed that as the depression "deepened" Mr. Tucciarone became gloomy and declared, "Patsy, there is no more hope for the independent. He is finished." Patsy explained that *he* knew the store could compete if they "offered highly personalized service and kept prices down." However, "Mr. Tucciarone couldn't see it. His thoughts were tied to the old-fashioned specialty approach. He was delighted when I offered to buy him out, and my brother Nick became my partner July 1, 1932."[121]

American Magazine had a stake in characterizing Patsy's success as the product of design and ambition rather than luck or providence because it proved the magazine's very premise. Patsy described himself as a man of vision, perhaps revising the two brothers' personal history:

> For years I had been planning in my own mind the kind of store I wanted. One important new trend, as I saw it, was toward bringing all home foods under one roof to simplify the housewife's shopping, instead of having separate butcher shops, fruit markets, and dry groceries. In the late twenties, with a view towards this kind of setup, I encouraged Nick to become a butcher and learn the meat business. I studied the fruit-and-vegetable merchandising problem by spending a great deal of time at the Bronx wholesale market in the early morning.[122]

This rendering of the Patsy D'Agostino story would form the basis for a chapter in *How I Made a Million*, a collection of twenty-two biographical sketches of self-made millionaires telling the "True, inside stories of how 22 fabulous fortunes were built from pennies." *How I Made a Million* clearly sold itself as a guide to easy wealth for a determined, but dim, audience.[123] In the body of his chapter, Patsy detailed his rise from humble beginnings. He did not offer much in the way of practical advice for millionaires-in-training, and the business philosophies expressed in the chapter are conservative and lacking in originality. He recalled that when he and Nick began their grocery, they were without the capital to expand or add a meat department, so "both our families combined forces and living quarters, so we could save and save and save. . . . We took only enough money out of the business to eat and support ourselves simply." Even though the company opened its first meat department in 1935 and grossed $100,000 in its first year, Patsy claimed that the operating philosophy was "To expand only as much as we could keep our hands on the reins of the business, never to depend on strangers making our decisions for us."[124]

In a testament to the value of self-education, Patsy shared that as a young immigrant, he had refined his English by reading comic strips and the dialogue screens at silent movies.[125] He also remembered his apprenticeship at one New York market in which his boss left several unread grocery trade bulletins out on the counters. The episode recalled Ben Franklin's autobiography, as Patsy asked for the circulars and that very night "with the help of my dictionary I tried to learn what the periodicals had to say. And from that day to this I have read every issue cover to cover." He then linked this practical knowledge to upward mobility: "They [the periodicals] told me how to do my job, and I might add that in later years I received much of the additional 'education' I got by attending meetings of my local, state and national trade associations, which ultimately honored me with their presidencies." Later, Patsy, who had left school in his midteens, proudly discussed his appointment to give a series of lectures on the food business at CCNY as proof of the unlimited possibilities of American society. He mused that when students called him "Professor" D'Agostino, "I couldn't help but know that nowhere else can someone without a diploma be a 'professor' of his own kind of economics."[126]

Like the *American Magazine* feature, the article for the October 1954 issue of *Italamerican*—"The D'Agostino Brothers" by Vittorio de Fiori and Enrica Laglia—preached the trinity of business, national pride, and family in keeping with the tenor of the times.[127] De Fiori and Laglia were, however, partial to the Italian in *Italamerican*. They were quick to celebrate their countrymen (and the Abruzzesi in particular) as being blessed with deep reserves of spirituality and character. The article opened by naming the inherent nobility of the D'Agostino brothers as a source of their success:

> Of all the attributes that mark the distinguishing traits of the people of the various regions of Italy, there are none finer than those traditionally used to describe the people of Abruzzi: "forte e gentile"—strong and courteous . . . for this people has a moral fortitude and strength of character as well, which, enhanced by an instinctive kindness and courteusness [sic], mark it with an inborn nobility that needs no crest or coat of arms to prove itself. This is the hereditary spiritual wealth that the D'Agostinos brought with them to America.[128]

Italamerican briefly summarized Patsy's period of migration and struggle. The magazine was brazen about claiming the D'Agostino story as its own, however. For example, it chose to cast Patsy's frustrations with his father as a cautionary tale for young Italians not only to cherish their original homeland, but also to invest themselves in the possibilities of America. When Patsy began the story of quitting his father's pushcart to start his own enterprise, the magazine reinterpreted his motives. It explained to an audience that had a foot in two worlds that while Patsy may have had some frustration with his old-fashioned father and still longed to return to Italy:

> By this time, Patsy was almost 18 years old and it is here that we like to differ slightly from his own recounting of the story, especially as regards to the driving force that led to his resolve to strike out on his own. It must have been about this time that Pasquale D'Agostino reached the decisive moment that was to drastically change the already made plans for his future. . . . Patsy was beginning to see America with his own eyes and while his conscious mind remained faithful to the modest ambition he had cherished on his arrival, while he continued to believe that his only goal was to accumulate faster the money needed to go back to Italy, we suspect that he was, in reality, awakening to the possibilities of free enterprise. He was beginning to derive pleasure from his work and, unlike his father, he was on the way to finding the true heart of America.[129]

Thus, by implication, the magazine located the moral of Patsy's tale and the "heart of America" in the possibility of wealth, which it also equated with assimilation. The article did quote the stories of Austin and Clements, and Patsy's cousin, Bill D'Espinosa, to emphasize America's openness to Italians. Like the feature in *American Magazine*, *Italamerican* had no interest in dramatizing Patsy's fortitude or his misfortunes as an immigrant. Rather, *Italamerican* made a concerted effort to suppress any evidence of the immigrant's dissatisfaction:

> Having supplied this much background on Patsy's peregrination from the time of his arrival in America to the time when he finally recognized his desire to become an American citizen, we can afford to skip over the subsequent years of hardship he experienced after he left Norwood to return to New York. It is enough to know that in his desire to make good he began to relish even the insecurity that preceded his ultimate success.[130]

In making Patsy and Nicholas D'Agostino the public face of ethnic pride, de Fiori and Laglia also provided a glowing portrait of their relationship. *Italamerican* was the first magazine that gave extensive coverage to Nicholas, describing him as "a stocky, friendly man whose eyes often twinkle with a mischivious [sic] smile," while allowing him to comment on the secret of the company's success. *Italamerican* even called the brothers an "ideal partnership," seemingly unaware of any underlying rivalry between them:

> Whatever one may decide to be the secret of the extraordinary success of the D'Agostino Brothers, one thing was so obvious during our interview that we must refer to it especially. It is, simply, the strong bond of affection and complete understanding between two brothers, deepened by a common background of experience. Both have a most profound respect for each other's ability and for the duties they have assigned to themselves. . . . They take equal shares of the responsibilities and never fail to consult one another on any problem arising. As a result they have established an ideal partnership—one that is rare even between brothers.

The magazine certainly had a stake in the notion that the traditional Italian family was the culture's endowment to America. In accordance with this theme, in a section entitled "Proud Husbands and Fathers," Patsy and Nicholas both articulated their wishes that their sons would eventually become their successors in the business.[131]

The article also did not discuss patriarch Ignatius D'Agostino's troubled existence in America, ignoring his gambling, drinking, depression, and financial struggles. Instead, de Fiori and Laglia concluded that he later returned to Italy out of undying affection for his country of birth: "Father D'Agostino finally went back to Italy. He had never been able to forget the lofty mountains of the Gran Sasso and La Maiella, which, from their summits, seem to contemplate their land of Abruzzi with an expression of infinite love." But his sons "came to understand and love their adopted Country and to be grateful for the good things they were blessed with. Today they are pleased to enjoy a typically American kind of existence."[132]

Although the *Italamerican* feature affirmed *American*'s model of prosperity, the D'Agostino brothers' success had different meaning for the ethnic press. Patsy was again presented as an active, civic-minded executive— president of the National Association of Retail Grocers, the Yorkville Lions Club, and the New York State Food Merchants Association. But with their postwar financial windfall, the brothers also became leaders in Italian and Catholic philanthropies such as Italian Charities of America and Boys' Town of Italy. They joined a generation of successful Italian immigrants who could now model themselves as ethnic symbols because of their financial status and increased power in civic institutions.

Just as the 1950s were years of unprecedented prosperity for thousands of ethnic Americans, the decade was also a "brick and mortar" period in the history of American Catholicism.[133] For much of the nineteenth and early twentieth centuries, ethnic Catholics were typically rooted in the blue-collar neighborhoods of northern cities. Apart from machine politics, Catholics had limited influence or social power in most realms of American life. But by the mid-twentieth century, bolstered by educational opportunities and union membership, the children and grandchildren of Catholic immigrants had moved into the middle class and the professions. Meanwhile, the Catholic Church in the US became more inclusive and unified, as its ethnic rivalries began to dissolve. Flush with money and burgeoning influence, the Catholic community thus devoted itself to building its institutional power. This endeavor was realized on a literal level with the construction of hundreds of new churches, schools, and social halls, as parishes had been unable to engage in any major projects throughout the Depression and World War II. And, as the Church sought to promote its mainstream influence, it sought icons among successful Catholics.

When *Catholic Digest* featured Patsy D'Agostino in a 1956 article, it incorporated the D'Agostino mythos into a Catholic context. Reporter Lawrence Hughes covered the major points in Patsy's personal drama, but Hughes also spent significant space relating that on their 1948 visit to Italy, the D'Agostino brothers received a private audience with Pope Pius XII, that Patsy had become chairman of Catholic Charities of Greater New York (a position Nicholas would later assume), and that Patsy had raised $85,000 for Boys' Town of Italy from American retailers.[134] Hughes also proclaimed:

> Patsy still has his pushcart voice, and, when roused, may express himself stormily. But his roar is more likely to be produced by a small irritation than a real disaster. Last Lent, he promised not to raise his voice at all. He also made another promise. One of his old friends is the father of a Franciscan novice who has developed skin cancer. By way of an offering for the young man's recovery, Patsy vowed to do his best to persuade the owners of New York City's thousands of groceries to close for three hours on Good Friday.[135]

Patsy explained that although the major chain stores would not close because Good Friday was such a profitable shopping day in the very Catholic

New York of the 1950s, and independent grocers stayed open out of "self-defense" against their larger rivals, D'Agostino's closed as promised.

During this period, Patsy also began to bring in priests to christen new stores at openings, a practice that continued until his death in 1960. The store's public display of religious sentiment can be read variously. The incorporation of Catholic culture into the store's identity was emblematic of the religious and ethnic constitution of New York in the mid-1950s—where such displays might be not only accepted, but also welcomed—as well as the brothers' relationships with Monsignor John Carroll-Abbing and Francis Cardinal Spellman. These practices also showed the endurance of a broader ethnic sensibility (represented through religious ritual), even as the D'Agostino brothers achieved success and mainstream recognition.

Finally, Patsy's religious sentiments seemed to reflect his civic respectability as well as his piety. Like many Italian workingmen, Patsy and Nick had been deeply skeptical of the Church for much of their lives. The brothers had always been men of faith, but as they gained success, they immersed themselves in Church institutions. At the close of the article, *Catholic Digest* casts the brothers' accomplishments as an answered prayer, musing, "In the early days, Patsy says, 'I used to pray that God would let me earn enough money to go back to Italy, and never let me see America again. I am grateful that He did not answer.' Perhaps He did."[136]

The article also provided a snapshot of the company in the mid-1950s. The brothers still were passionate about being independent grocers, although the stores were now "Supermarkets of Distinction" rather than "Markets of Distinction." Invoking the *New Yorker* feature from the previous decade, Hughes noted that Patsy "no longer rises at 5:20 a.m., to lace his coffee with a shot of whiskey, and rush off to the Bronx Terminal market to haggle over the price of broccoli." The operation itself seemed poised for change, as many of his customers "are the married sons and daughters of people he served in his first one-man store in the East Side's Yorkville section," with Patsy surveying one store's shopping cart traffic—"a different kind of pushcart traffic than he knew as an immigrant boy 35 years ago."[137] Yet even as Patsy assured the author of his modest ambitions, the brothers were preparing to open three more stores, bringing their total to seven. Their annual sales volume had reached $8 million and, for the first time, they procured a loan—$300,000—to finance their expansion.

Queens and Kings:
Suburban Migration and the Struggle for Identity

When the D'Agostino brothers move to a bedroom community in Queens, they get an early taste of the American Dream. Despite the transition, family roots are replanted and nurtured in new soil. With a postwar migration to the posh suburbs of Westchester and Long Island, however, "Old World" affiliations recede, traditional social networks atrophy, and family life begins to founder.

When the D'Agostino and Tucciarone families arrived in New York, they first settled in the Italian enclaves of Manhattan's Lower East Side and East Harlem. Once the two families gained a measure of economic stability, they began to disperse across the city. While some family members moved to working-class communities in the Bronx and Staten Island, others went up to Yorkville, where various relatives owned groceries that served the wealthy residents of the Upper East Side. For the first two years of their marriage, Nicholas and Josephine D'Agostino shared a Yorkville apartment with Patsy and his wife. As the couples began to have children, the close quarters of this living situation put a strain on family relations. After the birth of their first son, Nicholas and Josephine (along with his father) moved to one of the new "elevator" apartments in Upper Manhattan. With a loan from an older relative, Nicholas and Josephine were then able to buy a neat, two-story brick house in the Elmhurst section of Queens. Their move, as well as Patsy and Irene D'Agostino's purchase of a property on the same block, illustrates a larger demographic and cultural shift within America's immigrant communities throughout the 1930s, '40s, and '50s. At the turn of the century, immigrants like Ignatius D'Agostino had tended to live among their ethnic familiars until they earned enough money laboring in the industrial economy to either move back to Italy or bring their families to America. Even when they began to settle permanently in the US, the older generation often lived in tenement apartments among their relatives for reasons of economy and companionship. But by the 1920s, as the next generation of immigrants started to climb the socioeconomic ladder, they could take their families out to the neighborhoods of modest single-family houses that were growing on the periphery of American cities.

As residents of working-class, ethnic enclaves, Italian Americans realized that outward migration and upward mobility were often linked. While Robert Orsi's seminal study of Italian Harlem celebrates the vibrancy of the neighborhood's religious culture, he also notes that it was "crowded, filthy, and dangerous," and when residents "improved their lot . . . they usually left."[138] In fact, by 1930, one-third of New York households with an

Italian-born head of family owned their own homes, mostly in the outer boroughs—which demonstrates both the advancement of the city's Italians and the role that communities like Queens played in their social mobility.[139] Within two decades, the exodus of thousands of Italian Americans from areas like East Harlem and the Bronx to homes in suburban New York would be catalyzed by government policies, such as the creation of the Servicemen's Readjustment Act of 1944 (a.k.a. the GI Bill) and urban renewal, which simultaneously trapped their African American and Puerto Rican neighbors in rapidly decaying ghettos.[140]

While a move to the outer boroughs meant that an immigrant family was progressing into the middle class, it could also affect their social networks and sense of identity. The migrating family was often transitioning from a close-knit ethnic neighborhood to a melting pot of fellow strivers. Migration from the hub of extended family—with its web of mutual obligations and insular social networks—to a stable, single-family home was a stride toward Americanization that might conclude in the far suburbs of Long Island or New Jersey. Even though the Italian residents of Yorkville were a definite minority in their neighborhood, they maintained a communal culture where the "Old World" family still ruled.

When the D'Agostino brothers and their families arrived in Queens, the borough was completing a period of dramatic growth. In the first two decades of the twentieth century, New York had built miles of streetcar tracks, as well as two major bridges and a railroad, which had opened thousands of acres of borough farmland for residential development. The city increased this accessibility with the opening of the Triborough (now Robert F. Kennedy) Bridge in 1936 and the Queens–Midtown Tunnel in 1940. For the many working-class strivers looking to buy their first homes, the outer boroughs had the same allure that the postwar suburbs would have for the next generation. In the period between the wars, Queens thus became one of the hottest real estate markets in the city, as its population grew from 469,000 to nearly 1.3 million between 1920 and 1940.[141]

Still, life in Queens remained urban in its design and amenities. In Elmhurst, which welcomed a spectrum of white ethnics, Nicholas and Josephine and Patsy and Irene lived with Greek, Irish, and Polish neighbors and even joined a predominantly Polish parish. The modest houses had stoops or porches that the adults used for socializing. Nicholas and Josephine's children played stickball in the streets, hung out with the kids at the corner vacant lot, and walked to the movie theater on Queens Boulevard. From Elmhurst, Josephine could still have coffee or lunch with the network of Italian relatives and neighbors who were scattered throughout

Manhattan, the Bronx, and Staten Island, or go into the city for shopping or a trip to St. Patrick's Cathedral. Despite their need to gain some distance from relatives, Nicholas and Josephine's new home was only two doors down from the house Patsy and Irene purchased that same year. Nicholas and Patsy's father lived with Nicholas's family until 1939, while their uncle moved in with Patsy's family. Before 1939, the couples did not even own separate automobiles, sharing a Dodge to drive into the city or using the store's panel truck for family outings, with the children sitting on orange crates in the back. The families celebrated every holiday, birthday, baptism, and First Holy Communion together, and Irene and Josephine had coffee with one another nearly every day.[142]

In 1943, Patsy moved to Westchester, appreciating the "old money" charm of the area, but the two families remained close.[143] Nicholas was content to remain in Queens until 1954, when he learned that the planned route for the Long Island Expressway would run directly behind the family's house, even taking out their garage. Rather than following in his older brother's footsteps to stately Westchester, Nicholas moved to Manhasset, Long Island, where he and his wife followed other "new money" émigrés, including friends from various Italian philanthropies. One might conclude that Nicholas D'Agostino's decision revealed his determination to create a life apart from his brother and his relatives. But the purchase of suburban homes also served as an expression of Nicholas and Patsy's long-simmering sibling rivalry—the brothers had shared in the work and the risks that built D'Agostino's, but Patsy had enjoyed more of the accolades. In their pursuit of domestic bliss and social status in their home purchases, Patsy and Nicholas resembled two case studies from Vance Packard's classic portrait of postwar competitive consumption, *The Status Seekers*.[144] When Nicholas attempted to build a modern dream house, complete with the latest amenities, he was poised not only to enjoy the fruits of success, but to finally outdo his older brother.

The construction of the Long Island Expressway and the mass migration to the suburbs, like the building of Stuyvesant Town and Peter Cooper Village, signaled a new epoch in the city's history.[145] As with other urban renewal projects envisioned by Robert Moses, the Long Island Expressway was meant to sustain and modernize New York, making it accessible to a white-collar labor force that was migrating to the bedroom communities of suburbia.[146] Instead, the expressway served to speed a postwar exodus, as thousands used its construction as an opportunity to move farther from the urban core. In the popular imagination, Great Neck, the area of Long Island in which Manhasset was nestled, may have once been associated with the glamour of Jay Gatsby's West Egg (even Nicholas and Josephine D'Agostino considered it a tony village beyond the reach of the city when they decamped there). But the highway building of the 1950s effectively created a series of new boroughs populated by young middle-class families and the upwardly mobile.

The 1955 move from Queens took Nicholas and his wife to a community of neocolonial houses with expansive lawns and no sidewalks. The lack of stoops, porches, street corners, and neighborhood stores in Manhasset limited the social interactions that had created relationships in the old neighborhood. For Nicholas, relocating to Long Island meant a longer commute and a more varied social circle, but his daily life remained focused on the stores in Manhattan and his colleagues in the grocery industry. The move to the suburbs may have had a greater impact on his wife, Josephine. Two of Nicholas and Josephine's children had already left home by the time of the move, and as their youngest departed for college, she was confronted with a large, empty house decorated with recently purchased antiques and furnishings that required constant cleaning. She could no longer walk down to the neighborhood stores or to the local subway stop. To shop or visit relatives in the city, she had to take a taxi to the local Long Island Railroad station, and then take the train to Penn Station, before boarding any number of subway trains.

In the historical and sociological literature examining the 1950s, one can certainly find testimonies from women who found suburban life stifling and unfulfilling. But the alienation of suburbia had a particular sting for women from ethnic-immigrant families. Women traditionally served as the keepers of culture in these families by teaching religious and social traditions and preserving ethnic foodways in their role as cooks. These women were usually the main cogs in their family's social network, maintaining a sense of kinship against the pulls of Americanization. The regular lunches and afternoon coffees that Josephine enjoyed with her sister, aunts, and cousins were primarily opportunities to socialize. Yet the gossip that they exchanged not only maintained family ties, but also served as a reservoir of history—as women reminisced about departed relatives, old friends, and the lives of previous generations. In this context, Josephine's less frequent, more arduous treks to the homes of friends and relatives in the Bronx and Manhattan took on even greater symbolism for her. She struggled to maintain her connection to a world that was slowly drifting away, even as her husband and brother-in-law further integrated themselves into New York's business community.

Nicholas and Josephine D'Agostino's migration to the suburbs also altered their existing relationships. Nicholas joined a Long Island country club and took up golf. Old friends and relatives from Yorkville, Staten Island, and the Bronx may have felt uncomfortable in the couple's new house, with its fine furnishings that carried the stamp of social legitimacy. The family's trips to Manhattan and the outer boroughs to visit relatives and old friends became less frequent, and, inevitably, the sense of kinship that had developed at Sunday dinners, afternoon coffees, shared vacations at the Jersey shore, or ethnic society dinners began to erode. Gone were the days when Josephine would pose for a photograph with one hundred of her cousins at a parish-hall wedding. Of course, the changes to these social networks were not simply the product of distance. The dynamics within the D'Agostino family were also being affected by shifts in the larger culture. In the age of television, family dinners became less frequent. Upward mobility and movement to the suburbs meant cultural dislocation; with their migration to Queens, the family had assimilated to a neighborhood that was more broadly ethnic, albeit Catholic, but Nicholas's move to Manhasset, and Patsy's move to Westchester, meant integration into communities that were predominantly WASP. Still, the achievement of great personal wealth and their corresponding exodus to the suburbs transformed, rather than erased, the markings of ethnicity for Nicholas and Patsy D'Agostino. Even as the brothers broke from the web of relationships that once defined their social and business affiliations, they sought more emblematic displays of identity in the formal societies that were collecting the Italian professionals who had been dispersed by their very success.

"The Immigrant Didn't Forget": Philanthropy, Faith, and Identity Formation

Amid postwar prosperity, the D'Agostino brothers "get religion," Italians get respectable, and ethnic strivers discover the many uses of charity. The brothers also make a grand return to their hometown, or "Bugtown" as their children label it. While Nicholas and Patsy receive a hero's welcome, their families long for indoor plumbing.

Mutual aid societies were established in the nineteenth century as informal collectives to provide desperately needed services to fellow immigrants. Within New York's Italian community these organizations initially represented regional identities, as they were founded by Abruzzesi, Calabrians, Sicilians, and so on.[147] As Donna Gabaccia has observed, "Kinship, friendship, and neighborliness rooted in the village remained important sources of social and financial security for migrants living on insecure incomes far from home."[148] Over time, the regional and neighborhood sensibility that shaped Italian associative life evolved and provided the foundation for more formal, citywide institutions such as the Society for the Protection of Italian Immigrants, the Italian Benevolent Institute, and Columbus Hospital.[149] The associative life of the D'Agostino and Tucciarone families followed a similar pattern. Soon after their arrival in the US, they found a measure of social and economic support in the Minturno Aid Society and the neighborhood Democratic Club. But by the 1930s, as Patsy and Nicholas began to prosper as entrepreneurs, they drifted from provincial societies and political clubs to merchants' organizations, including the Manhattan Grocers Cooperative and, later, the New York State Food Merchants Association. These shifting affiliations paralleled broader developments within the family and the company.

The D'Agostino brothers certainly appreciated the luxury sedans, expensive cigars, and country club memberships that accompanied their newfound wealth, even as these items served as totems of status. As they savored the trappings of postwar prosperity, however, Nicholas and Patsy also became active in various philanthropic missions. They understood an implied immigrant code that success brought obligation, and that an individual's advancement should uplift the community. At first, the brothers' aid was based in their network of family, friends, and "paesani." They became resources if relatives needed a doctor, could not pay their bills, or had an unruly son who needed counseling. They were able to use their influence to find apartments for those relations who were on the long waiting lists at Stuyvesant Town and Peter Cooper Village. And after hostilities with Italy ended, the brothers renewed ties to their homeland, committing themselves to the aid of those who had been victimized by the war. They began to sponsor dozens of relatives and friends who hoped to come to New York and become citizens. Nicholas and Patsy would typically buy their tickets, meet them when their boats docked, find them housing, and even hire them to work in their stores.

Years later, Nicholas D'Agostino's son, Stephen, would observe that the identities of successful immigrant entrepreneurs tended to follow an evolutionary pattern as they moved up the socioeconomic ladder. "In business," he remarked, "you get on, you get honest, and then you get honorable."[150] In other words, the pushcart peddlers and small-time grocers of an earlier generation were often compelled to survive by any means necessary—including adding a little heft when weighing a produce order or "mistakenly" counting an extra digit when tabulating a wealthy customer's bill. Once merchants became established, they often became respected members of the community. And if immigrant entrepreneurs achieved higher levels of success, they craved the social legitimacy that came with membership in various philanthropies, even if their primary motivation was aiding the less fortunate.

As their operation continued to thrive, the D'Agostino brothers became active in more formal ethnic charities. In the late 1940s, a high-ranking Vatican cleric, Monsignor John Carroll-Abbing, and an Italian American judge, Juvenal Marchisio, asked Nicholas and Patsy to take leading roles in a new organization to benefit Italian youth who had been orphaned by World War II. According to one estimate, there were 50,000 children left homeless or parentless by the war, many of whom slept on the street or in railroad stations and survived by stealing, shining shoes, or selling black market cigarettes.[151] The brothers became involved with Boys' Town of Italy for a multitude of reasons. They may have believed that the plight of Italian orphans represented a life of poverty and abandonment they had avoided through their good fortune in America. Working with a group that was focused on the problems of Italy also allowed them to reconnect with their native land even as their success in America carried them away from their roots. And they certainly saw an opportunity to "give back" and express a measure of gratitude for their success. Over the years, Nicholas and Patsy would become crusaders for Boys' Town, chairing numerous banquets and lobbying upwardly mobile Italians to be generous with the young people still suffering in their home country.[152]

The banquets for Boys' Town and for Italian Charities, another philanthropy the brothers became involved with, celebrated their guests' ascendancy as Americans while simultaneously providing opportunities for ethnic fellowship. At the lavish dinners for Boys' Town, Nicholas and his wife formed friendships with doctors and executives, a process that was accelerated by the couple's migration to the suburbs. At fundraisers, the brothers also met fellow immigrants who had become lawyers, judges, jewelers, interior designers, and Park Avenue art dealers, professions that defied their expected notions of Italian identity. Through Italian Charities, Nicholas and Patsy met Generoso Pope, perhaps the most powerful Italian in New York outside of Fiorello La Guardia. Pope came to the United States virtually penniless but made a fortune in the cement business during the city's construction boom in the 1920s. He then used his millions to buy a radio station and several newspapers, including the nation's premiere Italian daily—*Il Progresso Italo-Americano*. Pope's prominent position in the Italian American community and his role as owner of the paper made him a dubious public figure. In the 1930s, he had been a vocal supporter of Mussolini before denouncing the dictator in 1940. After the war, Pope was plagued by rumors that because of his work in the building industry, he had ties to the mob.[153] The D'Agostino brothers made a concerted effort to avoid the taint of organized crime, but because they were part of a generation of Italian immigrants who were enjoying their first taste of wealth and influence, and were hungry for social legitimacy, it was not uncommon for them to be in social situations with other "new money" Italians who had ties to the Mafia. Nicholas often became agitated that "hoods" were occasional guests of the same philanthropic societies he patronized.[154] And at the North Shore Country Club, which Nicholas joined after he and his wife moved to Manhasset, some of the members were rumored to be "connected." This quandary showed the immigrant's difficulty in distancing himself from the dangers and corruption of his former world even with success.

By the mid-1950s, the D'Agostinos had followed their triumph at Stuyvesant Town with a new location at 56th Street, and then opened stores at 80th Street, 72nd Street, and 65th Street in rapid succession. The brothers began to reward themselves with daily lunches at Gino's, a well-known Italian restaurant, and became friends with the owners (Gino Circiello and Gaetano Avventuriero), who were local celebrities.[155] There, they met several prominent Italians who belonged to Tiro a Segno Rifle Club, a men's lodge that boasted tenor Enrico Caruso and Mayor La Guardia as alumni; Nicholas and Patsy began to frequent Tiro a Segno as guests.[156]

Patsy D'Agostino had been active in state and national food organizations since the 1930s, emerging as a leading voice for the small businessman in newspapers and magazines and in the halls of Congress. While Patsy's heritage continued to inform his identity, his politicking brought him into social circles in which ethnic ties were secondary to his achievements as an entrepreneur. When D'Agostino's expanded across Manhattan over the next two decades, the company offered itself to a citywide clientele, rather than to folks from the neighborhood. And, as the brothers moved their families to the suburbs of Westchester and Long Island in the 1950s, they would encounter new classes of friends and associates. In time, through Boys' Town, Italian Charities, and work with the Catholic Church in Manhattan, Nicholas D'Agostino joined his brother as a person of considerable influence. In this era of heady success—both for himself and his Italian community—Nicholas became fond of remarking, "We have the finest name in New York City."[157]

In the nineteenth and early twentieth centuries, Italians had been faceless laborers on the railroads, in mines, and in construction and public works. In the years following World War II, they emerged as successful entrepreneurs, as well as lawyers, doctors, and politicians.[158] Through philanthropy, this immigrant group signaled that it now had wealth to spare on favored causes and social power that it could flex in public forums. The fundraising events for ethnic charities provided opportunities for prosperous Italians to show that their community had indeed arrived. At the same time, these events created the chance to mix with the most prominent figures in the Italian community, which generated a shared sense of ethnic pride as well as professional connections. Thus, the D'Agostino brothers gained a social network as well as a degree of visibility and acclaim from their philanthropic activities. But outside of the possibility for greater influence, the brothers' charitable efforts did represent a genuine sense of obligation, generosity, and gratitude. Like many of their compatriots, they understood that electricity, plumbing, a bountiful diet, education, and the opportunity to lift oneself out of poverty were privileges.

In the Italy of Nicholas and Patsy's youth, the formal practice of religion was primarily the province of women and children. Men often maintained the culture's long tradition of anti-clericalism and suspicion of the institutional Church while women took on the responsibility for religious education and familial piety. When they came to the US, many working men were reluctant to go to church on Sunday after a long week of manual labor and were suspicious of the Irish priests that dominated American Catholicism. As illustrated by Robert Orsi's chronicle of the festas of East Harlem, Italian immigrants did have a deep sense of Catholic spirituality, as expressed in public celebrations and devotion to patron saints, but the community did not equate church attendance with religious fidelity.[159] Yet as Italian immigrants became successful—no longer merely digging ditches, mixing concrete, or selling fruit from a cart—prominent members of their communities often "got religion."[160] As with their involvement in philanthropies, engagement with the Catholic Church provided them with an opportunity to express gratitude for life's blessings, to assert newly won cultural authority, and to acquire legitimacy in a country where religiosity was often a measure of one's civic respectability.

In their first two decades living in the US, Patsy and Nicholas D'Agostino were no exceptions to this truism, often staying home from Sunday mass and maintaining a hardened skepticism about the religious establishment. But in the postwar era, the brothers returned to the Catholic Church with renewed devotion. In the 1950s, Patsy began to attend daily mass. He then became chairman of Catholic Charities of Greater New York and made it a policy to close the stores early on Good Friday. He even invited a priest to christen new stores. Nicholas's relationship to Catholicism was more complicated. As his children grew and attended parochial school, he did begin to attend mass regularly. In 1948, he and his brother were honored with a private audience with Pope Pius XII—which Nicholas later described as a deeply religious experience. Despite his lingering suspicion of the clergy, he was appointed to Cardinal Cooke's Commission for the Laity in the 1960s and gained membership in prestigious Catholic societies the Knights of St. John Lateran and the Knights of Malta. When considering these commissions, Nicholas would express wonder that "a grease ball with a fourth-grade education" would be so honored.

Like most European countries, Italy had to literally dig itself out of the rubble in the aftermath of the Second World War. The poverty that had plagued the daily lives of its citizens continued unabated, as the Italy of Fellini's *La Dolce Vita* was still several years off. The end of hostilities meant that Italians residing in the US could return to the nation of their birth for the first time in nearly a decade, however. In the interim, many of these emigrants had prospered, and they were eager to display the money and manners they had acquired in America. One might even view their passage as a reconstituted version of the "Grand Tour" that members of the nineteenth-century Yankee elite undertook to absorb the culture of Italy.

After the war, Nicholas and Patsy returned to Italy for the first time in two decades. They took the opportunity to see their ailing mother, who had been diagnosed with severe liver problems after being bedridden since the early 1920s. Over the next five years, Nicholas took four more trips back, two with Patsy. The brothers' primary purpose in returning to Italy was to monitor their mother's health and reacquaint themselves with a host of aunts, uncles, and cousins. On these visits, however, the brothers also offered support to their native village and the nation itself. In 1946, when Nicholas went back for the first time, he not only secured a scarce plane ticket, but also commandeered an army jeep to chauffeur him around the country to meet with various persons of note. On later visits, the brothers installed indoor plumbing and electricity in their mother's home, toured Boys' Town of Italy, and had audiences at the Vatican.

While closing the family circle and rendering financial assistance, these trips also served Nicholas D'Agostino's desire to be simultaneously more Italian and more American. When he was a boy growing up in provincial squalor, Nicholas never ventured more than a few kilometers from Bugnara and, because of his lack of formal education, he had a limited perspective on his native country. Now that he had made his fortune, he claimed the glories of Italy—from Renaissance art to Roman antiquity—as his own. During a visit to his mother in 1948, Nicholas had promised that if she recovered, he would bring his wife and children over from America. In 1951, he did take his family to meet Loreta and show them the land of his birth. The six-week tour of the major sites and cities of Italy was a grand affair—the D'Agostinos first traversed the Atlantic Ocean by luxury liner and then stayed in fine hotels all over the country. Throughout the expedition, Nicholas expressed incessant pride in the artifacts of Italian culture, whether he was pointing out old Roman ruins or using a Super-8 camera to film peasant women taking in the wheat harvest. His use of the Super-8 was itself significant, as that camera would become the tourist's favored method of itemizing the narrative of travel and of ordering the world beyond America's borders—much to the annoyance of native populations everywhere.

Although he reveled in the grand history of Italy, Nicholas also loved returning to his childhood home. Going back to Bugnara not only allowed Nicholas to reconnect with his family and savor the simple pleasures of country life, but also to measure his own accomplishments. When Nicholas arrived in town, it was always an event—he had "made it" in America and copiously shared his good fortune. He would walk the dusty streets buoyed by pride, enjoying chance encounters with old acquaintances and neighbors.[161] The younger generation had a different perspective on these rural sojourns, however. While they were impressed with the art, history, and culture of Rome, Nicholas's American-born children were shocked by the poverty and grime of the provinces and nicknamed their father's village "Bugtown" because there were so many flies.[162] They were revolted by the lack of refrigeration, as all food was kept in sideboards or pantries, and not particularly fond of their meals—as country folk ate mostly pasta, tomato salad, strong homemade cheeses, and coarse bread. In the decade following the war, Italy was like a developing country. Items that American travelers took for granted, such as ice and indoor plumbing, were often scarce. But for the boy who had left home with only a few lire sewn into his clothing, bringing his family to Bugnara for a hero's welcome was an affirmation of his American dream.

D'Agostino v. D'Agostino:
A Death in the Family, A Death of the Family

Cancer strikes Patsy D'Agostino, and his untimely death leads to another family tragedy—litigation and the severing of ties between blood relatives. The ugly dispute between Patsy's heirs and his younger brother leads several family members to question the cost of doing business.

In the inside cover of *Food Marketing*, an anthology that featured Patsy D'Agostino's views on the state of the industry, he inscribed the following message, dated January 1951:

> To my dear brother Nick, May the next eighteen years be as progressive as our first, and may our business grow, so as to be, happy to turn it over to Skippy, Stevie and Nicky with pride and confidence that they will even do a better job then we where [sic] able to do. With love and affection, Patsy.[163]

Both brothers had wished that the company would endure after their deaths, with their three sons furthering the family name in the grocery business. When Nicholas's son, Stephen, joined D'Agostino's in 1955, however, they began to debate how power and responsibility within the boardroom should be apportioned. Nicholas hoped that he might bring in his sons as full partners, with Patsy taking in his son and son-in-law to create a "balance of power."[164] In 1958, Patsy's son Stephen left home to attend Boston College, but it was clear that he would soon come into the family business. With Nicholas's younger son, Nick Jr., also preparing to join the firm after college, Nicholas tried to convince his brother to institute his model for the company. But Patsy, to Nicholas's great agitation, did not want to offer a partnership to Nicholas's children or to his own, preferring to keep control in the hands of the two founders.

In 1958, when he was only fifty-three years old, Patsy was diagnosed with cancer. For months, Patsy deferred making any formal plans for the future of the organization, as he was naturally preoccupied with his own mortality. He eventually decided that he wanted his son to inherit his half of D'Agostino's, thereby making him a full working partner. (Patsy's daughters and his wife were to inherit their portion of his estate through a buyout arrangement with his son.) Nicholas was willing to accept an arrangement in which he and Patsy each matriculated their sons in as partners. He refused to grant his twenty-one-year-old nephew an equal partnership, however, especially when he would have to divide his half of the business between himself and *his* two sons. As Patsy became sicker, Nicholas became obsessed with resolving the apportionment of the business. He reasoned that a proper settlement of Patsy's affairs would help his brother "die in peace." Yet, focusing on the financial details distracted Nicholas from the reality that his beloved brother was facing an untimely death and prevented him from walking with Patsy through a painful, frightening passage.

In the summer of 1960, after two years of struggle, Patsy finally succumbed to cancer. At Patsy's wake, both floors of a funeral parlor at 82nd Street and Madison Avenue were jammed with the friends he had charmed in his many years in the food business and with ten carloads of flowers sent by well-wishers. His two-column obituary in *The New York Times* described his many positions within the grocery industry and his charitable activities, but only in the very last line did it mention "a brother, Nicholas, with whom he was associated in business."[165] In the years following Patsy's death, the two families engaged in a protracted legal dispute over ownership of the company that sabotaged their social ties while alienating many of the brothers' associates in the ethnic and business communities as they were compelled to choose sides in the dispute.

For Nicholas, the court case was not simply about money or control of the company's name and assets, though these issues were certainly factors. Rather, the battle over ownership stakes was also about validating his role in building the business. For much of the company's history, Nicholas woke at dawn to go to the meat market, and then labored for ten to twelve hours in the stores. He was rarely featured in the articles that made Patsy a media darling. Nicholas believed that the quality of the stores' meat, as well as his business acumen and vision, were crucial to the brothers' success. Perhaps a favorable resolution might vindicate his labors, while ensuring that his children would continue to steer the company to an even brighter future.[166]

The court proceedings and Nicholas's singular focus on legacy confirmed that in the case of D'Agostino's, "family history" and "business history" had become indivisible. Litigating ownership could be seen as an attempt to measure and apportion Patsy's and Nicholas's respective contributions. Yet the process of reducing their importance to mere dollars and cents revealed two competing narratives, and embedded in each was a business model—a vision of what had made the firm successful. For over twenty-five years, Patsy was the public face of the company and his story had provided its mythos. Patsy attributed its growth to the adoption of the industry's latest innovations as well as his ability to cultivate relationships— with newspaper and magazine writers, associates and fellow grocers and, most importantly, with customers. By contrast, Nicholas saw the brothers neither as executives nor as theorists, but as grocers. Nicholas believed that they owed their prosperity to a basic formula of hard, honest labor, an impeccable product, and unwavering self-belief. In the coming years, he would lecture his sons that customers came to their stores merely because they had the best meat and produce in the city. Of course, quarreling over the company's legacy only served to cement D'Agostino's identity as a multigenerational family business—as posterity became Nicholas's primary motivation. Over the next two decades, whenever his sons reconsidered their commitment to the organization, Nicholas would remind them of his efforts and their corresponding obligation to him.

The dispute over stewardship of D'Agostino's was finally resolved in 1964, as the courts upheld Nicholas's right to utilize the family name and maintain ownership of the business.[167] Unfortunately, litigation triggered years of bitterness and back-biting, the airing of private grievances in public, and payment of costly legal fees. And what was won—or lost—in the five years of internecine strife? Relationships between family members were forever strained. For extended periods in the 1930s, Patsy and Nicholas had literally lived and worked together in Yorkville. When they moved to Queens, they bought homes two doors away from one another and their families shared almost every holiday, birthday, and personal milestone. The brothers had toiled side-by-side for twenty-eight years and ate lunch together nearly every day throughout the 1950s. After the summer of 1960, the two families never regained their closeness. One might even say that a death *in* the family was followed by a death *of* the family.[168]

Was the outcome fair and just? It is not surprising that Nicholas would resist the idea of inheriting his brother's son—essentially a junior partner—as an equal after two and half decades of working to build a single grocery into a respected chain of supermarkets. He also fully compensated his brother's family for their share of the company. Yet Patsy D'Agostino's heirs were forever denied what they perceived to be their legacy, as they considered Patsy to be the true founder of the business. They saw Nicholas's maneuvers as a betrayal, motivated primarily by bitterness and jealousy.[169] The court's judgment assured Nicholas that his would be the face and the voice of the organization, a role that he took to with surprising alacrity. He proved to be a great success in his time as the undisputed head of the operation. D'Agostino's continued to expand across the city, gaining a premiere position among consumers because of its association with a high-grade product. Nicholas also ensured that his sons would lead D'Agostino's into a new era. And yet, the litigation and its aftermath illustrated the fragile balance between corporate interests and domestic harmony in family businesses. Structurally, family-owned firms lack the means to impartially address grievances, as disputes often do irreparable harm to either kin or the company.

On more than one occasion Nicholas remarked, "I'm blessed and I'm afraid to ask [Him], because God always gives me what I ask for."[170] His dispute with his brother's heirs also sowed dissension within Nicholas's own family. His oldest son, Stephen, had shared an especially close relationship with his Uncle Pat, admiring Patsy's charm, social graces, and genius for management. In his uncle, Stephen saw a kindred spirit—someone who shared his fascination for innovation and big ideas and his love for meeting new people, especially those from Manhattan's smart set. Stephen was saddened by Patsy's death and disheartened by all the infighting the court battle engendered.[171] He had once considered becoming a priest or a teacher, but his father made Stephen promise that he would give at least five years to the company upon his graduation from the College of the Holy Cross.[172] Yet when litigation concluded in 1964, Stephen threatened to quit, claiming he was "fed up" with the grocery business. Armed with a degree from a prestigious college, he found himself working behind a butcher block, surrounded by coworkers who had rarely finished high school. His father offered him a full partnership in part to placate him, but also to provide an incentive for Stephen to invest himself completely in his trade.[173] Nicholas then promised him that he would have greater latitude to participate in food and business institutes if he met his commitments to the organization.

Yet, even as Nicholas integrated his sons into leadership positions and initiated a new era in the company's history, the next chapter of this family drama was already taking shape. Like his father before him, young Nick D'Agostino Jr. was eager to learn the details of the grocery business and dedicate himself to the stores.[174] He was proving to be a talented executive in his own right and was ready to make his mark. His brother, Stephen, ranked above him in the company hierarchy and was being groomed for its presidency. Like his Uncle Pat, Stephen was drawn to industry trade groups and their discourse, as well as to the cultural life of the city. The conceptual aspects of food retailing held more attraction for Stephen than the daily operations of a store. Even though Nicholas's dreams of a family dynasty were being realized, his progeny may have questioned their price.

Figure 15. The "D'Ag Bag" (ca. 1970) was one of the company's most successful attempts at branding, becoming part of the cultural landscape of Manhattan in the 1970s and '80s. Courtesy of D'Agostino Supermarkets.

Figure 16a. "If there's no D'Agostino near you...move!" (1971). This advertisement models D'Agostino's targeting of young, upwardly mobile consumers, typically in the "Living" section of *The New York Times*. Courtesy of D'Agostino Supermarkets.

Figure 16b. "Keep New York Delicious...Shop at D'Agostino" (1972). In its appeal to the cosmopolitan lifestyle of young Manhattanites, the ad's tagline reads, "Keep New York Delicious. Catch a Flick. Cook a Treat. Shop at D'Agostino." Courtesy of D'Agostino Supermarkets.

Figure 17a. "If there's no D'Agostino near you, MOVE" (1973). With Marvin Glass's *New Yorker*–style cartoons and a slogan that promoted the quality of the D'Agostino stores by suggesting that shoppers should brave the city's notoriously tight rental market to be near one, the company used sly humor to signal its kinship with New Yorkers of a certain class. Courtesy of D'Agostino Supermarkets.

Figure 17b. "D'Agostino Love-In" (ca. 1974). In the 1970s, D'Agostino's advertising often gestured toward the popular culture of the 1970s, as seen in this Valentine's-themed promotion. Courtesy of D'Agostino Supermarkets.

Figure 18a. "If there's no D'Agostino near you... MOVE" (Central Park Zoo edition, ca. mid-1970s). Throughout the 1970s and '80s, the company sought to promote its own iconic status by incorporating landmarks such as the Central Park Zoo, the Statue of Liberty, and the Brooklyn Bridge in its advertising. Courtesy of D'Agostino Supermarkets.

Figure 18b. "If there's no D'Agostino near you... MOVE!" (Brooklyn Bridge edition, 1977). Courtesy of D'Agostino Supermarkets.

Figure 19a. The statue of St. Patrick at the Cathedral, decorated with a D'Agostino button for the Christmas season, 1975. Courtesy of *The New York Times*.

Figure 19b. "One of the Nice Things About New York" button (ca. 1970s). In its "One of the Nice Things About New York" campaign, D'Agostino's acknowledged the challenges the city faced in the 1970s while using civic boosterism as a form of branding. This drive preceded the famous "I Love New York" campaign by two years. Courtesy of D'Agostino Supermarkets.

Figure 20. "What's Hot... What's Cool... What's New York!: D'Agostino Sur L'Herbe" (1983). In the 1980s, D'Agostino's named the latest trends in art, food, fashion, and culture in ads that placed its stores at the center of Manhattan's social life. Here D'Agostino customers picnicking in Central Park are caricatured as figures in Manet's painting, Le déjeuner sur l'herbe. Courtesy of D'Agostino Supermarkets.

Figure 21a. "Men of Distinction": Patsy D'Agostino and grocery executives for Lord Calvert Whiskey (1956). Patsy is second from the right in the photograph. Public domain.

Figure 21b. Stephen D'Agostino for The Antiquary 12 Scotch Whiskey (1976). Two decades apart, Patsy D'Agostino and his nephew, Stephen D'Agostino, were featured as spokesmen for whiskey brands, illustrating both their celebrity and their company's association with aspirational consumerism. Public domain.

Figure 22a. "If the New York Times left town, we just might move" (May 1977). This ad for *The New York Times* is notable both for its inverted reference to D'Agostino's slogan and its recognition of Stephen D'Agostino's familiarity to New Yorkers in this period. Both Stephen and Nick D'Agostino Jr. understood that their participation in ad campaigns for other products also bolstered their company's reputation. Courtesy of *The New York Times*.

Figure 22b. "Would I kid you about a cookie?" (1989). With his ascent to CEO and chairman, Nick D'Agostino Jr. became the face of the company, featuring prominently in store advertising and radio spots for local institutions such as Chase-Manhattan Bank. Courtesy of D'Agostino Supermarkets.

CHAPTER 4

One of the Nice Things About New York (1960–82)

At the close of the 1950s, the grocery industry expected the wave of postwar prosperity to roll onward, lifting its fortunes to extraordinary heights in the new decade. Trade journals continued to describe the supermarket as a product of the nation's ingenuity, industrial might, and faith in free-market principles. Certainly, the industry had endured more than its share of challenges, including low profit margins, the need for constant innovation in an environment heavy with competition, and a lingering conflict between small grocers and corporate heavyweights. But most analysts believed the supermarket—which promised every consumer access to American abundance—to be the perfect embodiment of the mass market. They declared that the modern American food store had become the envy of the world and a symbol of the West's ultimate superiority over its Soviet competitors, as "the American super market star" remained "undiminished by Sputniks."[1] Vice President Richard Nixon would mirror these sentiments in his 1959 "Kitchen Debate" with Soviet Premier Nikita Khrushchev.[2] Steeped in the patriotic fervor of the Cold War, these declarations would later seem myopic given the turn the industry would take in the 1960s and '70s—as it would be beset by inflation, excess, and fragmentation (not unlike the country itself).

Commentators saw the advancement of grocers into the middle and upper classes as further confirmation that the supermarket had become a vehicle of progress. Toward the end of the 1950s, *Progressive Grocer*, a leading trade journal, published a profile of food retailers and store managers titled "The Modern Grocer: All-American Success Story." It reported that in a survey of hundreds of members of the industry, the annual income of supermarket operators fell into the top 1 percent of the nation's earners, while store managers were in the top 11 percent.[3] According to the survey, 95 percent of supermarket operators owned their own homes, as did 74 percent of store managers. The average grocer also had a higher level of education than the typical American male.[4] These findings were especially remarkable considering the number of neighborhood grocers, clerks, and pushcart peddlers who had struggled to earn a living in the decades leading up to World War II.

The expectation that the nation's good fortune would endure was not limited to the grocery trade. In February 1960, *Fortune* devoted its thirtieth-anniversary issue to New York City, which it considered the very symbol of the wonders of the American system. The magazine profiled the massive building campaign the city had initiated in the 1950s as it invested heavily in ultramodern skyscrapers, high-rise apartments, and new cultural institutions to maintain its supremacy as a center of commerce and the arts. *Fortune* reported that in a few short years, New York had witnessed the raising of the Time-Life, Chase Manhattan, and Seagram's buildings, several sleek apartment complexes, 168 schools, and the Guggenheim Museum, as well as the conception of Lincoln Center.[5] It also noted that since 1947, private enterprise had invested $2 billion for construction in Manhattan, two-thirds for offices and one-third for apartments.[6]

By 1963, New York had added almost 60 million square feet of office space since the end of the Second World War.[7] The fact that all of Manhattan's new privately funded apartments were in the upper-middle to "fabulously high" price range suggested that the business and political establishments envisioned a city dominated by a professional class "glad to trade history for . . . gleaming ultramodern apartments."[8] Noting New York's premier position as the headquarters for multimillion-dollar companies, *Fortune* declared, without irony, that further development of the white-collar economy would virtually eliminate the poor and working class from its streets. The magazine concluded that this shift would give the city unlimited resources and make Manhattan a beacon of progress and wealth:

> As the national economy burgeons during the 1960's, the number of white-collar workers in the U.S. will continue to grow faster than the number of blue-collar workers. New York City is the vanguard of this shift. Paced by the dynamic core of the headquarters companies . . .

the proportion of the city's poor should steadily decrease, and the proportion of its middle and upper-income people should as steadily increase. If so, New York will be able to afford the amenities and services it now lacks. More and more it will look and act the part of the world's most opulent city, the city that makes the decisions that count.[9]

Over the next two decades, white-collar professionals would continue to colonize Manhattan. However, when hundreds of thousands of blue-collar workers left the city with the decline of its industrial sector, they were replaced by a much poorer migrant population. At the same time, the continued flight of the middle class negatively impacted tax revenues, even as municipal government coped with an increasing demand for social services. Soon, New York would endure all the maladies that defined one of the most troubled chapters in urban history—including rising levels of violent crime, racial tension, poverty, urban decay, and debt loads so severe that the city would be on the verge of bankruptcy. By the mid-1970s, the president of the United States would abruptly dismiss New York's requests for a federal bailout, leading critics to wonder if the city was doomed. Throughout this period, Manhattan seemed a juxtaposition of two cities— the cosmopolis envisioned by *Fortune* and the urban jungle of neighborhoods like "Alphabet City" and "Hell's Kitchen."[10] This same disjuncture would be realized in the history of D'Agostino Supermarkets, a company whose founders rose from the immigrant streets but whose fortunes rested with New York's upwardly mobile clientele.

It's Good to Be the King: Reviewing the Reign of Nicholas D'Agostino

With control of the company firmly in hand, Nicholas D'Agostino authors a program of continued expansion and steady growth. Yet amid the empire building, Nicholas affirms time-honored values and methods, including his "ne plus ultra"—quality.

After 1960, when Nicholas D'Agostino Sr. assumed full control over the business he and his brother had built, he maintained many of the elements that had made their enterprise so successful. The company portrayed itself as an honorable independent toiling among larger competitors who prioritized the bottom line over a commitment to quality or service. At the opening of the first D'Agostino store in the Bronx, at the Metropolitan Life project Parkchester in October 1966, Nicholas declared:

We offer a great deal more than quality food, low prices and dependable service in a warm atmosphere. . . . We offer them [customers] moral responsibility. Before anything else, D'Agostino Bros. is a responsible company. We are responsible to our customers, always. That means we're forever trying to please them. We're willing to forgo some opportunities for profit in order to be of better service. For instance, we haven't a delicatessen section in the supermarket. Not because such a section isn't profitable. It's very profitable. But we feel that we can't do as good a job with delicatessen as we do with other departments. So we won't have such a section.[11]

While Nicholas D'Agostino's comments might be interpreted as consumer-friendly rhetoric, they reveal a great deal about his retail strategies, if not his personality. Those who knew Nicholas would not have been surprised to hear him describe his business in terms of moral responsibility. He was unambiguous in his perception of right and wrong, and completely sure of his judgment. Nicholas had a missionary fervor about the merits of produce and meat, sometimes musing that a piece of fruit was "a miracle from God." Having climbed through the ranks of the grocery trade, he was suspicious of the chatter of salesmen or self-appointed industry representatives—precisely the types of people with whom his brother Patsy had enjoyed a rapport. Despite the rapid rise of his own sons in the business world, he expressed distaste for the new generation of supermarket executives who had not sufficiently paid their dues. But a fanatical belief in the power of quality was Nicholas's defining business principle. He felt that he owed his customers the best product, and if he provided it to them, they would be loyal patrons no matter the cost. Of course, in the early days of the brothers' enormously successful 20th Street store, he had sometimes groused at customers who ordered an inferior cut of meat. And he would scoff at those shoppers foolish enough to patronize stores like the A&P, where the merchandise was "garbage."[12]

Nicholas's commitment to "moral responsibility" suggested that he would keep his operation on a scale that would allow him to monitor the merchandise, especially produce and meats. D'Agostino's business model was rooted in his experiences working on a pushcart, and he was confident that his expertise in meat, fish, and produce—developed through apprenticeships with skilled butchers and fish and produce men—would ensure a dominant share of the market. He believed that, above all, customers would be drawn to quality, not packaging or advertising. Yet his conviction assumed an older, discerning customer base—shoppers who mirrored

Nicholas's own tastes and priorities.[13] The peddler's ethos shaped Nicholas D'Agostino's strategic approach in other ways. His experience taught him an understanding of the necessity of high turnover especially in New York, where a retailer had no shelf space to waste on overstock or a line that wouldn't move. Knowing the tastes and buying habits of his customers was an essential part of this calculus, especially as they had dozens of other outlets vying for their loyalty as well as their food dollar. Under these conditions, a grocer's miscalculation of his stock could mean a product line that was decomposing before his very eyes. And Nicholas understood that for his discerning patrons, one rotten apple might not spoil the box, but it could quickly kill his store's reputation.

Nicholas D'Agostino's reverence for fruit and vegetables also had a practical application. Merchants traditionally displayed fresh produce at the front of their shops to entice customers and "class up" a store's image. Nicholas and Patsy's sense of aesthetics had been necessary for the pushcart trade, where the attractive arrangement of ripe oranges or tomatoes could mean the difference between a day's profit or loss, and they applied these talents to their operation. Nicholas would often patrol the aisles and reorder the pyramids of fruit to make them more pleasing to the eye. As a trained butcher, he was also fanatical about the appearance of the meat department at each location. One might say that he saw his stores as he saw his home and his family—as an extension of his own identity. Of course, this approach made him prone to micromanaging, which sometimes engendered the resentment of managers and employees.

One might assume from Nicholas's earnest statements about quality and his responsibility to the customer that he would be reluctant to expand. His alliance with the values of the old-fashioned grocer often clashed with his own sense of destiny, however. As a merchant, he may have been suited for a modest venture that sold only the finest merchandise, but as an entrepreneur he burned with the desire to outshine his competitors, his peers, and his brother. Building a small empire of grocery stores became his way of proving his worth, expelling the demons and grudges he had carried since childhood. And with his acute sense of competition, he wanted desperately to beat the chain stores at their own game, not merely to strike a blow for the rights of the "little guy." Nicholas thus pursued an aggressive program of expansion over the next two decades, opening ten new stores and even venturing into Brooklyn and the Bronx. Working with his two sons, he promoted the company's reputation as one of New York's elite food stores while extending its revenue streams, as sales increased twentyfold between 1952 and 1981. Nicholas thus seemed to marry vision and values—building a chain of profitable stores that offered what he thought were the choicest cuts of meat and freshest produce in the city.

Reflecting on his youth, Nicholas D'Agostino had once said that he was habitually "burning the candle at both ends and in the middle, too!" He certainly believed that he was the hardest-working man at his company, and he expected his employees to share his dedication. Yet he was intense about all aspects of life, including its many delights. If he enjoyed an especially fine meal, he would call for the chef to be brought out from the kitchen so he could shake his hand and thank him personally. Nicholas also loved tailored suits, colorful ties, and silk handkerchiefs. Even when he was a teenaged immigrant, he had tried to dress with flair, and like the fictional heroes in the stories of Horatio Alger, he understood that the right clothing could win him respect and social legitimacy. Buoyed by success, he now took to going to Finchley's (an exclusive haberdasher on Fifth Avenue) to buy his suits five at a time or ties by the dozen. Throughout their partnership, Patsy had served as the face of the company, while his younger brother had labored behind the scenes. Now that Nicholas was more secure in his position and embedded in the suburbs, he began to devote himself to more gentlemanly pursuits like golf, gardening, reading, and studying Italian and Classical history—despite his lack of formal education. After decades working on pushcarts, behind butcher blocks, and in the back of grocery stores, he also developed a longing to see the world. While he journeyed back to Italy several times to visit his relatives and reconnect with the land of his birth, Nicholas also traveled throughout Europe, the Caribbean, and Latin America in his later years.

In his early days as a grocer, Nicholas had gained a reputation as someone "paesani" could approach if they needed money to pay for hospital bills, school clothes for their children, or a job. Throughout his life in America, he received dozens of letters from little convents and seminaries in Italy asking for his aid. But over time, Nicholas's openhandedness became more formal and expansive. In the 1960s and '70s, as D'Agostino's enjoyed a windfall of profits, Nicholas redoubled his charitable endeavors. He was especially dedicated to the Catholic Church and its ancillary organizations and was asked to join the boards of Catholic Charities and the Cardinal's Committee of the Laity by New York's Francis Cardinal Spellman. He became active in international Catholic fraternities like the Knights of Malta, the Knights of the Holy Sepulchre, and the Knights of St. John Lateran.[14] Nicholas also extended his benevolence outside the familiar circles of ethnicity and religion. In this period, he became a benefactor of New York City's leading cultural institutions, including the Metropolitan Museum of Art, the New York Public Library, Lincoln Center, and the Bronx Zoo.

By the late 1960s, Nicholas had begun to win public recognition for his charitable efforts. In 1967, the Italian Executives of America feted him, and in 1969, a regional Italian society (the Columbus-ESCA Alliance) named him their "man of the year." Then, in 1971, Italian Charities of America granted him their highest honor for "his exceptional accomplishments in the world of business and for his special reverence for and commitments to the principles of charity."[15] But the former immigrant, who left his village with little money and less education, must have been stunned when, in the early 1970s, the Italian government granted him its Order of Merit of the Italian Republic for his continued work with Boys' Town and his achievements as an Italian.

For Nicholas D'Agostino, charity was an expression of his personal theology, gratitude for success, and sense of obligation to his community. Nicholas and Patsy had always shared a commitment to "giving back" and aiding those in need. Yet, the visibility of Nicholas's later efforts also suggested an evolution in his identity. While in partnership with his brother, Nicholas had groused about Patsy's frequent tours on the banquet circuit for the National Association of Retail Grocers or the New York State Food Merchants Association. Nicholas thought that Patsy's work as an industry spokesperson showed a lack of focus and an excess of self-absorption. But with his older brother's passing, Nicholas may have felt free to broaden his own social role.

As the principal leader of the company, Nicholas had to assume a more visible profile by necessity, but he soon took a liking to the spotlight as he did his share of "pressing the flesh" and consorting with influential figures. Although Nicholas never assumed his brother's persona, he may have understood that leading the business meant stewardship of its public identity. While he was not as articulate or charismatic as Patsy, Nicholas discovered that he enjoyed public speaking. His language was peppered with the aphorisms and anecdotes of a peasant, and he was not shy about sharing a bit of earned wisdom with any available audience. Nicholas also developed a particular interest in politics, which should not have been surprising, considering that he had an opinion on every subject. Becoming heavily involved in Richard Nixon's reelection campaign in New York, Nicholas secured his place as a full-fledged member of the "Silent Majority" by serving as chairman for a 1972 fundraising dinner at the Plaza Hotel at which Vice President Spiro Agnew was the guest of honor.

While Nicholas D'Agostino was now secure in his achievements, his role as a philanthropist—and the accolades that came with success—must have been tremendous sources of validation for him. As an immigrant boy, Nicholas had been anxious about his lack of education and polish, so he continuously cultivated himself. He had impeccable table manners and from his sincere love of music, developed an ear for opera. He also became an enthusiast for fine furniture, art, and landscaped gardens. In the second half of his life, he pursued pastimes that confirmed social legitimacy even as they were sources of enjoyment. Indeed, one could interpret Nicholas's attempts to become a "Renaissance Man" as symbolizing this immigrant's grand aspirations and personal evolution.

Grocers at the Ramparts: An Overview of Food Retailing in the 1960s and '70s

The sixties hit food retailing, as shoppers take to the streets and grocers scramble for a share of a shrinking pie. Over the next decade, the industry suffers its own "malaise days," with rising costs, higher prices, changing appetites, and the scourge of the "Golden Arches." Meanwhile, a new market for gourmet and natural foods develops, paving the way for a new generation of supermarkets.

As the 1960s began, the astounding productivity of agriculture and the efficiency of packaging and distribution continued to make the food industry the symbol of national abundance. *Progressive Grocer* reported that between 1959 and 1964, sales for grocery stores had increased by nearly 25 percent without a significant increase in food prices, even as the cost of housing, health care, and consumer services had begun to climb. The magazine observed that these developments were a "direct and powerful testimony to the truly competitive nature of food distribution" and "a reflection of the constant drive for more and more efficiency and greater cooperation with this biggest U.S. industry."[16]

Yet, while all chain supermarkets (national, regional, and local) had seen their sales increase by over 30 percent during this period, the volume of purchases for the larger "top 10" chains was growing at a much slower pace than that of independent and regional franchises. This trend hinted at the value of smaller chains like D'Agostino's, with their merchandising flexibility and understanding of local tastes.[17] *Progressive Grocer* warned its readership that other potential concerns might be looming on the horizon—including declining profit margins, the expansion of convenience and discount stores, and a consumer base that no longer conformed to uniform marketing strategies. Continued economic growth also meant the construction of more stores and heavier competition between food merchants, as more grocers struggled to gain a slice of the proverbial pie.

As a result of these issues, retailers considered a range of strategies to differentiate themselves from their rivals. To win new customers, supermarkets faced off in a series of ugly price wars while chain stores invested heavily in promotions, such as issuing trading stamps.[18] But by the mid-1960s, as the nation was struggling with a host of political and cultural issues, inflation and rising food prices also began to erode consumer confidence. In 1966, the annual food price index jumped 5 percent and in keeping with the charged political environment of the times, housewives organized boycotts to protest the high cost of meat and groceries. Women in over one hundred cities picketed chain supermarkets, calling for the abolition of trading stamps and the extraneous marketing that seemed to be escalating costs.[19] The culture of the 1960s enhanced consumers' growing sense of empowerment, as they began to lobby Congress for lower prices, labels that contained more extensive nutritional information, and unit price listings for all items.[20] Yet these developments were also symptomatic of a changing dynamic between grocers and shoppers in which the advantage increasingly tilted toward consumers.

As prices continued to soar, food became a national issue, with President Nixon even instituting a series of price controls.[21] In the decade that followed, as America suffered through inflation, the oil crisis, and concerns over a global food shortage, the grocery industry endured its own "malaise days." Considered a model of American ingenuity and efficiency only a few years before, the nation's system of food processing and distribution now became a primary reason for continued price hikes as labor and energy costs skyrocketed. Between 1966 and 1976, wage rates within the industry rose by 60 percent and, from 1973 to 1976, its utility bills grew by 75 percent. Meanwhile, between 1972 and 1975, food prices increased by 42 percent, and even though they stabilized in succeeding years, the cost of staples like meat caused many Americans to reevaluate their diets.[22] In the 1950s and '60s, the widespread consumption of beef had symbolized the nation's economic health; now, the prospect of meatless meals seemed to signal its decline.

The 1970s witnessed other troubling developments for grocers. Throughout the decade, families became smaller and customers more cost-conscious, and with rising wage and utility bills and shrinking margins of profit, even large retailers faced the prospect of bankruptcy or merging with competitors.[23] In the early 1960s, chain stores appeared to be entering a period of manifest destiny, controlling nearly 60 percent of the business by 1963. Another study showed that by 1971, supermarkets had captured over 75 percent of all retail grocery sales, with a sales volume of over $72 billion. But since the mid-1950s, their operating profits had actually fallen by 50 percent, as the number of food outlets decreased from 310,000 to 204,900.[24] By the mid-1970s, the supermarkets' explosive growth over the previous two and half decades would peak. By the end of the decade, industry giants such as Bohack and Food Fair would go out of business while A&P closed approximately 1,800 locations.[25]

Retailers experimented with various remedies to cure their ailing industry. The 1970s saw the introduction of several expensive new technologies that promised greater efficiency and reduced labor costs, including universal price code symbols (the barcode) on packaged material; computer systems for bookkeeping, inventory, and employee records; and price-scanning machinery at checkouts.[26] To meet competition from convenience store franchises, many supermarkets extended store hours to 11:00 p.m.[27] Yet grocers also had to reconsider the very nature of their enterprise. What was the correct business model for a marketplace in which customers were reluctant to spend their money or pledge their loyalty? Some opened discount warehouses that emphasized economy and quantity.[28] Others tried their hand at suburban-style "superstores," which provided a large margin of profit through the sale of pharmaceuticals and nonfood items.[29] But in New York City, with its spiraling rents and utility bills, most retailers resigned themselves to operating smaller stores or going out of business.[30] Even chains like A&P experimented with smaller "bring your own bag" marts that offered a limited array of nonperishable goods—a trend that harkened back to the old corner groceries and dry goods stores.[31]

These developments signaled that, like American society, the marketplace was becoming more segmented. In the 1950s and '60s, the ubiquity of the supermarket seemed to indicate the predominance of a mass market—a universal consumer to match the postwar "culture of consensus." Now, as the "Me Decade" dawned, merchants had to decipher the needs of a customer base that had become more diverse. In the 1950s, many retailers had presumed their targeted customer to be a housewife shopping for a large family. In the ensuing two decades, the market shifted toward smaller families and consumers who were single, professional, and often male. Moreover, in the social context of the late 1960s and the 1970s, shoppers wielded more power and were more notably individualistic. A range of different food stores emerged from this economic and political climate to serve an evolving marketplace.

Some observers argued that in cities like New York, a certain type of established, upscale grocery would be immune to these changes. One executive said of two of his competitors, "In Manhattan, the Sloan's and the D'Agostino's will be with us forever. They're tailored to serve a certain segment of the market."[32] At its 20th Street store in Stuyvesant Town, D'Agostino's had already served the new type of consumer that was upsetting the conventional wisdom of corporate supermarkets. At Stuyvesant Town, and the locations that followed, the stores welcomed working professionals whose busy lives made convenience a necessity, even as they demanded an upscale product line that satisfied their taste for sophistication. And while the company's urban orientation might seem to make it a national anomaly, D'Agostino's formula was, once again, a harbinger of the industry's future.

In the 1960s and '70s, in an atmosphere of heightened racial tensions, deindustrialization, and the flight of the middle class, urban groceries suffered their own decline. While stores that catered to wealthier residents of metropolitan areas like Manhattan continued to prosper, those that served more middling shoppers faced an uncertain future. Many chains were already reluctant to invest in city supermarkets because of higher built-in operational costs, the lack of available parking, and their low volume of trade. But now, small and independent retailers felt compelled to leave the communities that had sustained them for decades—another symbol of the changing face of New York.

City grocers faced a number of hurdles in this period, including high insurance rates (due to rising crime rates and the supposed threat of riots), the inability to obtain loans to make capital improvements, a customer base who bought goods in low volume, an increasingly undertrained staff of employees, greater loss of stock due to theft and mishandling, and a lack of space for expansion or parking.[33] In addition, wholesalers often refused to sell to smaller retailers because they bought in such limited quantities, which resulted in higher prices at the register. Many stores began to relocate or fail as their traditional patrons continued their exodus to the suburbs. Some merchants struggled to adapt to changing neighborhood demographics, as millions of African Americans and Latinos migrated to northern cities after World War II.

The economic struggles of cities certainly contributed to the nationwide decline of "mom and pop" groceries. Between 1967 and 1972, their overall numbers dropped from around 90,000 to just over 66,000, and by 1976, the "mom and pop" store accounted for only 15 percent of national food sales.[34] A 1977 study found that the total number of "inner-city" groceries had fallen between 28 and 56 percent since the early 1960s.[35] The combined departure of chain and neighborhood retailers forced some needy residents to shop at convenience or corner liquor stores in areas that researchers would come to label as "food deserts." The apparent demise of the neighborhood grocer provided an entrée for the next generation of ethnic entrepreneurs, however. In the 1970s, hundreds of Dominican and Puerto Rican shopkeepers would begin to earn their share of the American dream by serving communities in Manhattan, Harlem, and the Bronx.[36] And by the 1980s, newcomers from the Middle East and Asia would undertake the same path to prosperity blazed by Italian and Jewish merchants one hundred years before.

Changes in American foodways also shaped the fortunes of supermarkets in the 1960s while serving as a barometer for the evolving domestic life of the nation. In the 1950s, a revolution in production, distribution, and packaging had ushered in the era of frozen foods and TV dinners. Over the next decade, as young professionals continued to keep long hours, more women worked outside the home, and families maintained a full slate of social activities, Americans hungered for more convenience in the kitchen.[37] By the mid-1960s, sales of frozen foods totaled an annual average of $4.25 billion, double the amount of a decade before. Meanwhile, US food companies spent nearly $125 million a year to develop new products to add to the list of some 8,000 items shoppers could already find in supermarkets.[38] Manufacturers boasted about such culinary masterpieces as "Hamburger Helper," onion-flavored instant whipped potatoes, powdered nondairy creamer, and dehydrated "cup-a-soup." One industry executive claimed that "convenience foods" accounted for 70 percent of grocery purchases, as the industry poised for greater profits with the proliferation of microwave ovens.[39]

Not all sections of the supermarket were sustaining their profitability, however. With the pushcart and the corner grocery now a distant memory, the US Department of Agriculture reported that per capita consumption of fresh fruits and vegetables had declined by over 21 percent since 1948.

In 1960, *Progressive Grocer* observed that the produce department had been "put out in a kind of limbo," with this neglect reflected in cramped preparation areas, a lack of advertising and promotion, and fewer training programs for employees.[40] The magazine hoped that this trend could be reversed with increased consumer buying power, urbanization (as city people tended to buy more fresh produce than country folk), and the "wonders" of irradiation, mechanized harvesting, chemical baths, wax applications, sophisticated cold storage, and extensive use of packaging. That same year, *Modern Packaging* proposed another strategy for revitalizing the produce trade, writing that the "neglected sister" of supermarket merchandise—fresh fruits and vegetables—could blossom into a "packaging Cinderella." It suggested that "100% pre-packaging of fresh produce" would enable a more efficient, high-volume system of distribution while enabling retailers to create greater brand recognition for fruits and vegetables. *Modern Packaging* then quoted a survey that claimed most housewives preferred prepackaged produce because it was displayed more attractively, seemed more sanitary, and was more convenient to handle—even if those surveyed also admitted that bulk produce was equal or superior in quality to the prepackaged fruits and vegetables. At the time of the sample, the USDA reported that one-third of all produce was already prepackaged.[41] The consumer's romance with terminal markets and pushcart peddlers was now a distant memory.

As the supermarket industry had grown at an annual rate of 5 percent between 1955 and 1965, analysts were slow to anticipate the downturn the market would take in the 1970s.[42] One financial magazine pointed out that, in hindsight, inflation in the early 1970s had exaggerated revenues, while the stagnation of food sales was hidden by the increased sale of nonfood products. Even as the average family income rose from just under $5,000 to nearly $8,000 between 1958 and 1968, families were spending a smaller percentage of their earnings on food.[43] Critics noted that American affluence was increasingly directed toward material objects and leisure pursuits, rather than traditional domestic activities or the joy of eating.[44]

By the 1970s, grocers had to contend with the popularity of fast-food franchises like Kentucky Fried Chicken and McDonald's, as families increasingly chose to "drive-thru" rather than dine in. As with the rise of prepared foods, the popularity of fast-food restaurants arose out of Americans' desire for convenience and an increase in their disposable incomes. This development revealed a shift in the demographics and culture of the American family, as households increasingly had both parents working outside the home or were headed by a single parent. In 1965, it was reported that over 25 million women were in the labor force.[45] By 1979, over 42 million women were employed or actively looking for work—more than half the adult female population. More than 55 percent of working women in this survey were married, which often translated to households that had more income but less free time than previous generations.[46] By the late 1970s, Americans used one out of every three dollars of their food budget to dine out and spent nearly $14 billion at fast-food restaurants.[47]

In this environment, retailers had to find new ways to distinguish themselves from their competitors and still earn a profit. Many supermarkets tried to win back customers with prepared foods and heat-and-serve dinners, or by installing delicatessens and modified cafeterias in their stores. Here, it is important to note how the changing roles of women began to alter the industry's conception of consumer demographics. Once, grocery advertising had been directed mainly at housewives. In the 1970s, savvy merchants like D'Agostino's reimagined their ideal customers as active, independent career women, or even single men.[48]

Many industry observers failed to recognize that over the next thirty years, two parallel developments would transform American food culture—the growing popularity of gourmet foods and a natural foods craze that emerged from the counterculture of the 1960s. The nation's fascination with all things gourmet had initially been the product of postwar prosperity. With their new wealth and opportunities for travel, an unprecedented number of Americans went abroad during the 1950s—stimulating the demand for versions of Continental cuisine at home. And in the affluent, domestic culture of the fifties, hosts often used exotic dishes as a way of impressing neighbors and clients at cocktail and dinner parties. Meanwhile, clubs like the Wine and Food Society gained new members, *Gourmet* magazine's circulation increased by 300 percent from 1953 to 1959, and *Mastering the Art of French Cooking* repeatedly sold out at bookstores. Between 1931 and 1958, the wholesale trade in specialty foods increased from $39 million to $70 million, while over a third of supermarkets began to carry these items by the end of the 1950s.[49] By the mid-1960s, as figures such as Julia Child became cultural icons, knowledge of gastronomy became a mark of sophistication for young professionals.[50]

Curiously, the same economic and cultural factors that helped drive the fast-food revolution and throw the supermarket industry into chaos also turned a segment of the population into aspiring "foodies." As prices soared in the early 1970s, some Americans began to reconsider their taste for convenience foods, especially for items that they could prepare more cheaply at home. In this period, sales of flour, cheese, and fresh produce would steadily rise, while those of canned soups, TV dinners, frozen pies, and "Snack Pack" puddings plunged.[51] American eaters were still motivated by expedience, but they often satisfied this need by dining out. And as they returned to their kitchens, a segment of the public discovered that they could create meals that were wholesome, nutritious, and inexpensive. This countervailing trend had major consequences for food retailing. The heads of large distribution companies and supermarket chains were anxious about the rejection of convenience foods because processed, ready-made products carried such high margins of profit. They were also wary of consumers' growing skepticism and social power. One Pillsbury executive remarked that the food business was now "a tougher sell. Today's consumer is asking 'why' all the time."[52] Shoppers began to develop an awareness of health and nutritional issues in their purchases, holding the industry accountable for the frequent use of artificial flavors and food dyes. At least one influential critic posited that the growing popularity of home cooking was a rebellion against the ready-made products that had been food companies' biggest moneymakers in the previous decade.[53]

The gourmet movement that developed in the late 1960s and the 1970s aimed to bring the gospel of gastronomy to a wider audience. Here, rising food prices in the '70s had a serendipitous effect. While the high cost of shopping had already brought many Americans back into the kitchen, some middle-class consumers also opted to buy more high-end merchandise—figuring that price variations between classes of items were now relative while the differences in quality were clear. And by the late '70s, as more Americans gained a taste for food that was both sophisticated and pure, small cheese shops and fruit and vegetable stands began to reappear in cities like New York.[54]

Young professionals were the fastest-growing segment of the new culinary movement, in contrast to predecessors who viewed the kitchen as the province of the old-fashioned, the ethnic, and the effete. In the 1940s, some educated women saw cooking as belittling them, while in the 1950s, many of their daughters aspired to become "modern mothers" who drew their identity from social and community activities, rather than traditional domestic duties. When fixing meals, these women often opted for the expediency of prepared and frozen foods. One might think that the politics of the 1960s, especially as related to the women's liberation movement, would have further devalued the role of cooking among the young. Yet the culture of the sixties seemed to make food fashionable among "baby boomers" who viewed it as a form of self-expression and creativity, as well as a mark of cultural distinction.[55] Soon, hip couples were investing in

KitchenAid mixers and expensive cutlery, while treating the kitchen as the social center of their homes.[56]

The era's progressive politics also reshaped the country's eating habits, as health food stores, "natural" and "organic" labels, and "hippie" staples like granola and herbal teas came into vogue. Previously, health food had been rooted in a few mom-and-pop shops that served cultists and senior citizens. In the 1960s, however, a younger, more politicized population brought this niche market visibility and profits. Between 1970 and 1972, annual sales of health food soared from $100 million to nearly $400 million.[57] Over the course of the decade, health food sales would continue to trend upward, even though the rest of the grocery industry was suffering from a recession and soaring prices. "Natural foods" were reaching a broader market, as the general population became concerned about the health risks of standard supermarket fare.[58] *The New York Times* reported that "suspicions about the established major food producers in the United States run so deep among a core of middle-class consumers that they are willing to continue paying high prices for what they consider to be purer and more nutritious food even when times are hard."[59]

While the popularity of "health food" would ebb in the late 1970s, the public's desire for more wholesome fare rebounded in the early 1980s—especially with growing concerns over the role diet plays in cancer, cholesterol, and heart disease. In 1983, Americans ate about seventy-nine pounds of beef per person, down from ninety-four pounds per capita in 1976.[60] One survey in 1984 found that over the previous decade, the annual consumption of fresh fruit and vegetables had increased by about 8 percent, while the intake of canned fruit and vegetables had decreased by nearly 30 percent and 10 percent, respectively.[61] By the 1980s, these changing consumer habits would lead *The New York Times* to comment, "With millions of Americans getting 'into nutrition,' the nation's food producers and purveyors are undergoing the greatest upheaval since the advent of frozen and fast foods in the 1950s and the 60s."[62]

This culinary "green revolution" was spurred largely by tastemakers who would become the targeted customers for high-end retailers like D'Agostino's. Vegetarianism became fashionable, winning over countless musicians, artists, and actors.[63] Children of the sixties, including California's Alice Waters, opened restaurants that emphasized locally grown produce and other regional ingredients, and simple, rustic dishes. The philosophies of Waters and her cohort revived the demand for seasonal produce and unfamiliar varieties of greens among urban consumers—making the pushcart peddlers' art relevant again even as agribusiness tried to tighten its grip on the marketplace. In the disciples of Julia Child and Alice Waters, the supermarket industry would begin to realize opportunities for those who could appeal to gourmet sensibilities, even symbolically, while presenting a stock of the freshest produce.

Many retailers seemed mystified by the contradictory desires of consumers. On the surface, the decade of the 1970s was defined by a troubled economic climate, the primacy of convenience, and the explosive popularity of "fast food." But executives also heard the public calling for more fresh vegetables and wholesome fare, and higher nutritional standards, even as they devoured Big Macs. Retailers saw frozen dinners continue to win significant sales while gastronomy was all the rage.[64] The marketplace was, in fact, becoming more segmented—a development that was not apparent to all analysts. The popularity of gourmet foods and celebrity chefs in the 1960s and '70s indicated consumers' growing dissatisfaction with the American diet and the assumptions of the mass market. Moreover, the vogue of whole foods and vegetarianism began to diversify the marketplace and suggest a return to the bygone era of greengrocers. A 1980 survey of buyers and merchandisers revealed that produce's share of stores' total sales was at a ten-year high, with *Progressive Grocer* even discussing a "Renaissance of the Fresh."[65] With the rise of gourmet and healthful eating, fresh vegetables and fruits and fine cuts of meat once again became signature products for upscale grocers.

By the early 1980s, cities like New York witnessed a new wave of food stores that were both chic and profitable. In 1981, *Business Week* reported that so-called prestige grocers were enjoying sales gains of 20 percent a year. As New Yorkers flocked to Zabar's and Dean & DeLuca, the president of one supermarket chain observed that shopping at gourmet groceries had become "the 'in' thing to do."[66] Retailers attempted to capture or co-opt these customers with exclusive product lines. Chains such as New York's Shopwell began to create upscale alternatives like their highly successful Food Emporium stores, which offered posh produce, salad bars, fresh fish, and service meat counters.[67] These markets, by necessity, were more labor intensive and required more knowledgeable, presentable, and service-oriented employees—which meant higher operating costs for retailers.[68] Gourmet groceries thus needed to generate a higher volume of sales to offset costs, as well as the expense of their merchandise. So, they turned to a time-honored formula—relying on "high-turnover, perishable products" to make their profits and stay competitive.[69] Naturally, these innovations—from the service-oriented staff to the presence of butchers proffering cut-to-order meat and fresh fish, to the reliance on fancy fruits and vegetables to build profit margins—mimicked the strategies of high-end, urban markets like D'Agostino's.

Yet, as in the 1950s, so-called fancy foods also presented middle-class shoppers with the opportunity for a taste of luxury amid the conspicuous consumption of the 1980s.[70] Here, the industry witnessed the rise of an aspirational food consumer allied with emergent "Yuppie" culture. In the eighties, mineral water, Brie cheese, fresh pasta, and gourmet ice cream became signifiers of status for young urban professionals.[71] As "foodie" culture became popularized, one business journal noted, consumers "may not be able to afford a new car, but they can plunge for fresh spinach noodles at $2.25 a lb."[72] *Progressive Grocer* even observed that "gourmet food" was now "one of the few remaining affordable luxuries." It reported that the 1980s would be the "Decade of the Gourmet" since fancy foods had "not only become more palatable—they've gained mass appeal." The article listed D'Agostino's among the chains seeking to incorporate new gourmet items into their stores with the "Democratization of Fine Foods."[73]

In this new era of merchandising, D'Agostino Supermarkets combined two facets of its identity—the "Old World" grocer and the elite supermarket—to continue building its prestige and its market share, as management saw the rise of the "gourmet grocery" as an affirmation of its own history and strategies. To some degree, D'Agostino's had always stood apart from its rivals. In the 1930s and '40s, Patsy and Nicholas D'Agostino had achieved success, despite difficult historical circumstances, because of their innovative, "all-in-one" retailing model and their ability to serve an affluent clientele in Yorkville. In the 1950s, the brothers had become wealthy because their 20th Street store had a virtual monopoly on the vast market of middle-class strivers in Stuyvesant Town while offering a higher grade of meat and produce. As these customers prospered, moved uptown, and became "upscale," their favorite grocery was there to share the journey. Throughout the 1960s and much of the 1970s, D'Agostino's believed that it stood alone as a "class" chain. Stephen D'Agostino would recall that in this period, the company had limited competition from A&P, Gristede's, and Sloan's, but never felt that these stores threatened its position.

The company's organizational structure did give it a notable advantage over its larger rivals. In the 1970s, industry executives had begun to worry about "overstandardization." The growth of chain supermarkets had been enabled by the ready application of a single prototype—the "standard store." Now, chains were having difficulty serving an increasingly disparate and diverse spectrum of customers, while independents and smaller chains were able to create a more flexible model that could adapt to the specifics of a neighborhood. As a New York City merchant, D'Agostino's had already developed the capacity for matching the shifts in local demographics and trends. With the gentrification of Chelsea, Greenwich Village, and the Upper West Side, for example, the company was able to appeal to the tastes of a new elite. Moreover, D'Agostino's was actually one of the first supermarkets to anticipate the gourmet trends of the early 1980s because it developed the practice of surveying its customer base.[74] Stephen and his brother, Nicholas D'Agostino Jr., thus began to install fresh-fish counters, high-end delis, and bakeries that served croissants and artisan breads, while reorienting the stores' meat and produce departments. They even began to redesign their stores to match the feel of shops like Zabar's. Unbeknownst to Stephen and Nick Jr., however, competitors like the Food Emporium chain were adopting similar strategies. With the rise of the new gourmet grocery, D'Agostino's would increasingly have to fight for its share of the market.

"Please Don't Kiss the Butcher": Stephen D'Agostino and the "New" D'Agostino's

Under Stephen D'Agostino's leadership, the business adopts the latest innovations to stay ahead of the competition. Advertising becomes an effective means of fashioning its brand and its identity, as once again, the company's personality is made in the image of its president.

Stephen D'Agostino's memories of working in the family business began during World War II, when on Saturdays he would sit in the back of parked delivery trucks to make sure that no one stole the merchandise. When Stephen was a little older, he was also given a few odd jobs around the stores. He later recalled that one Sunday morning, when the men were inside his great-uncle's market on 85th Street playing cards, he was given the duty of sweeping the steps. The boy swept the bottom step and then continued to the step above when he was approached by an old Italian gentleman, who with a heavy accent passed on this bit of wisdom: "There's one thing you gotta know. In most things in life you start from the bottom up, except sweeping the steps."[75]

Though his father had determined that Stephen would one day succeed him in the family business, he also was adamant that his son have some experience with its proverbial "bottom step." Every morning of his summer breaks from the College of the Holy Cross, Stephen would take a bus from his house in Elmhurst to a subway stop, take the subway into Manhattan, and then ride the Third Avenue "El" up to the Bronx, where he would then walk several blocks to the Buy-Low Grocery Company—the cooperative warehouse that D'Agostino's owned and used to supply independent merchants throughout the city. Through stifling heat, Stephen worked alongside the warehouse's regular crew as they loaded and stacked crates and boxes by hand, as forklifts were not yet used.

Stephen officially joined the family business in 1955, as a twenty-one-year-old college graduate armed with a business degree and a labored sense of duty to his father. Nicholas had promised Stephen a secure future with the company, including a chance at the helm, but had also emphasized his son's obligations. And as a man who believed the five-day workweek was "soft," Nicholas thought his son should learn the business from the bottom up, just as he had. He started him in the produce department, training under his uncle, Marty Tucciarone. After a brief stay in produce, Stephen's father moved him behind the butcher block so he could learn the basics of the meat trade.

In order to advance in his apprenticeship, Stephen, like all aspiring butchers, had to learn how to clean chickens—which was a nasty chore, by any measure. He remembered that it was "a demeaning kind of a job for a so-called 'liberal arts graduate' from Holy Cross." He added that to "move up," he had to clean a crate of twenty-four to thirty birds in thirty minutes, a task which included "taking the head off, the skin off the neck, cleaning it inside and out, and you'd stink. You'd absolutely, absolutely stink when you went home. I don't know how my wife put up with me."[76] Once Stephen graduated from cleaning the chickens, his next task was to go into the refrigerator and learn how to "break down" whole sides of beef by hand. This was an especially demanding task because Nicholas D'Agostino wanted his stores to feature premium cuts of meats from the animal's hindquarters.

As he made his way through this apprenticeship, Stephen also had to adjust to the social challenges of the workplace. At Holy Cross, Stephen had acquired a dose of intellectual and social polish, but now he found himself working with a collection of former immigrants, crusty relatives, and blue-collar guys who likely saw him as a wet-behind-the-ears college boy. Still, Stephen worked hard at his new trade, even as he was unsure whether he had found his life's vocation. After a few months, Nicholas D'Agostino announced to his son that he was going over to Europe for a month to visit his mother, leaving his son in charge of meat buying. Since D'Agostino's was making its reputation on its steaks, roasts, and chops, this was a daunting task for young Stephen. His father sent him to the city's notorious meatpacking district (which has since become one of its trendiest neighborhoods) to meet a few veterans of the trade, and then left Stephen to his own devices—"a meat buyer with all the credentials of a four-year-old who's driving a cab in New York City."[77]

Stephen's new assignment would lead him to discover his true talents in the grocery business and enable him to lead the company into a new decade. When Stephen asked his father how to price the meat, he realized that his father had a system that seemed crude by the standards of any modern business curriculum. Nicholas instructed his son that whatever beef or lamb cost at the market, he should simply double the price for retail. While this system had suited Nicholas and Patsy—especially since the company specialized in pricey cuts of meat—it left Stephen in a bind when, in his father's absence, the price of lamb began a steady climb. Stephen was sure that if he kept doubling its price, no right-minded customer would purchase it. To meet this challenge, Stephen applied two strategies that would serve him well over the next three decades—he asked a lot of questions and then improvised his own plan. He first asked salesmen how he should price meat and they, in turn, talked to their connections within the industry. These men then provided Stephen with pricing formulas and other modern methods of estimating the quality and cost of meat. He was initially unsure of his own calculations and mathematical expertise, but after weeks and months of "doing the percentages" in the context of the marketplace, through instinct and effort, he became a skilled meat buyer.

Stephen later remarked that his father, like most of the merchants of his generation, had little concept of "productivity"—that his father's "concept of a profit was people working hard, no waste . . . buy low, sell high." But Stephen sensed that the company needed to become more efficient, so he instituted another simple but important innovation. With the stench of freshly slaughtered chickens still fresh in his mind, Stephen began to purchase eviscerated poultry for the stores. This decision meant a steeper initial cost, but, in the long run, stores saw their profits increase because of the savings in time and labor costs. By the 1960s, D'Agostino's would offer its clientele a full line of packaged steaks, chops, and hamburger, though it maintained skilled butchers on its staff.[78]

In the succeeding months, Stephen, who had a young family at home, discovered how taxing a grocer's life could be. He found himself working six days a week, usually until 7:00 p.m., while on Mondays he would have to go to the market at 4:00 in the morning. Stephen was still convinced that he had no idea what he was doing when his father returned from Italy. In looking over the financial statements, however, Nicholas D'Agostino discovered not only that three stores had produced a nice profit in his absence, but also that the meat operation was making more money under his son's watch. Stephen recalled that rather than patting him on the back, his father was completely "flabbergasted" by his son's feat. Stephen later mused that while his father was "shrewd," Nicholas lacked a sophisticated understanding of how the larger economy worked. In describing a generational divide in their worldviews, Stephen mused that his father "had the mental capacity of a pure peasant in the mountains or in the vineyards. I think the big problem [was], I don't think he could synthesize . . . [to] tie it all together."[79]

While Stephen's assessment of his father's mentality might seem unduly harsh, Patsy and Nicholas had once shared similar views of their elders Ignatius D'Agostino, Frank Tucciarone, and the generation of "Old World" Italians that preceded them in the grocery business. Patsy and Nicholas D'Agostino's personal and public narratives include several anecdotes about their frustrations with their predecessors' inability to see the developments that were poised to transform food retailing—including innovations like the incorporation of butchers, produce men, and grocers into a single entity. Patsy recalled how his father had scoffed at his aspiration to graduate from the pushcart to a higher-status position as a clerk. And Nicholas remembered how Ignatius discouraged him from learning the butcher's art, while his father-in-law, Frank Tucciarone, had cried that the "independent was finished" when he was forced to sell his store. The brothers' own venture rebelled against the unassimilated, conservative business culture of an older generation of immigrants. By the time Stephen D'Agostino was rising through the ranks of the organization, many of his father's ideas seemed antiquated. Yet Stephen was a businessman of his time—a would-be executive with the managerial aptitude, intellectual sophistication, and ambition to enlarge D'Agostino's legacy—just as Nicholas and Patsy had been part of a new generation of entrepreneurs whose skills and vision allowed them to outshine the modest achievements of their forebearers.

Nonetheless, from that point forward, Stephen went to work as a meat buyer under his father's supervision. Over the next few years, as D'Agostino's continued to prosper, he advanced from a meat buyer to the supervisor of its meat departments. Even as his father promised him a partnership and a seemingly golden future, Stephen questioned whether he should stay with the company; he sometimes wondered if, with the grueling hours, he was "wasting his youth." He found working for his father to be a tremendous challenge, and he saw the world of the grocery business as coarse and somewhat limiting.

Stephen was also drawn into his father and uncle's social circle, as they shared daily lunches at Gino's (their favorite Italian restaurant) and introduced him to "people who were *true* New Yorkers—doctors, lawyers, jetsetters." In taking his nephew under his wing, Patsy D'Agostino also initiated Stephen into a side of Manhattan that he grew to love—a city of color and cocktail parties, of big ideas and outsized personalities. Stephen recalled that in the late 1950s, Patsy invited him to the prestigious Union League Club of New York to meet several people associated with the supermarket industry. He remembered being in awe of his surroundings (knowing "you don't belong there as soon as you walk in the door"), as he watched the men laughing and exchanging ideas around an immense table. For young Stephen, the experience reinforced the differences between his father and his uncle, as his father "would never have been invited into that crowd." In retrospect, Stephen believed that his uncle was preparing him for the life of a modern executive—trying to get him "to see the world differently" through his associations with people of a different class and intellectual mindset.[80] Patsy also introduced his nephew to trade organizations that would stimulate his mind and shape his business philosophies. Because of Patsy's membership in the National Association of Retail Grocers, Stephen would join the organization and, many years later, he, too, would become its chairman. For Stephen, involvement in these organizations enabled him to endure the drudgery of the grocery trade and cultivate his own set of talents.

Stephen was deeply saddened by Patsy's death in 1960, as he lost his favorite uncle as well as a valuable mentor and ally. He also resented the protracted litigation that split apart the two families. Yet, in 1964, after the courts settled the D'Agostino case and his father again filled his ear with notions of duty, Stephen agreed to become a full partner in the business, with a few stipulations. Nicholas D'Agostino granted his eldest son time away to pursue membership in organizations like the New York State Food Merchants Association. Crucially, Nicholas also allowed him to incorporate new retail strategies into the firm's daily operations. Over the next several years, Stephen worked toward a position of leadership while bringing his own sensibility to the partnership. Then, in 1972, Nicholas D'Agostino named himself chairman of the company while appointing Stephen its president and chief executive officer and his younger son, Nick Jr., its executive vice president. In 1978, Stephen would rise to the position of chairman and CEO of D'Agostino Supermarkets, with Nick Jr. assuming its presidency.[81]

Under Stephen D'Agostino's leadership, at his father's urging, the operation expanded across Manhattan—including the rapidly gentrifying

Upper West Side—and then to Brooklyn and the Bronx. But Stephen also preached modernization within the boardroom. He first sought to limit the ethnic cronyism that had typified employment practices within the business for the past three decades. D'Agostino's had been the product of New York's network of Italian peddlers, clerks, and grocery store owners. For much of its early history, D'Agostino employees were typically Italian, and many were related to the brothers personally or to existing members of their workforce. Any time one of their "paesani" migrated to America, Nicholas and Patsy would fill out their staff (and meet their ethnic obligations) by giving them a job. Stephen wanted to distance the company from these traditional customs. He expanded its labor pool, especially at the top levels and, throughout the 1970s, sought the input of experts in the fields of management and advertising.[82] He also tried to limit the nepotism that had influenced hiring, promotion, and the delegation of responsibilities (which was ironic, considering his own pathway to the top), while instituting a culture of meritocracy.[83]

Like his uncle before him, Stephen D'Agostino developed a feel for the latest innovations within food retailing. In his quest to create a more progressive business model, he expanded D'Agostino's membership in national grocery organizations and developed relationships with CEOs and operational managers throughout the country. He joined the Super Market Institute and the National Association of Food Chains, where he met the heads of major food distribution companies and national grocery chains. Through these associations, Stephen was able to pick the brains of the "big boys" of the industry—giving his company access to a sophisticated level of discourse despite its modest size.[84]

Stephen soon imported more corporate methods into D'Agostino's business model. He called for updated accounting practices and filing systems, and for the introduction of computers. As a result of his experiences at seminars, Stephen got "caught up trying to understand information systems, [but] realized we had no information." When he started in the grocery business, the warehouse would supply individual stores based on their managers' handwritten orders. This scheme not only forced the managers to spend hours writing out every line of their requisitions but left D'Agostino's exposed to the fallible estimates of its staff when determining supply and demand. Stephen first tried to implement an information-gathering system using IBM punch cards. He also instructed the warehouse to send out inventory that central management determined the stores needed, based on the sales histories of each location. This strategy was not completely successful, as past sales were not necessarily a determinant of what would sell under current circumstances. Moreover, the old guard of managers resented Stephen's impositions. He recalled visiting one store where an older Italian manager had stashed boxes of inventory in the back. When Stephen asked him to explain this, he responded, "It was your fucking idea, not mine." The company then adopted an early IBM computer model, which had little memory, but allowed them to begin to implement a system of recordkeeping and supply that was comprehensive and adaptable to the latest market developments.[85] But Stephen found that older buyers and managers—many of them immigrants who had come up through the ranks like his father and his uncle—stubbornly resisted adopting these reforms.

Stephen's father was initially skeptical of his son's new methods. Over his son's protests, every week Nicholas D'Agostino signed some four hundred to five hundred employees' checks by hand and then delivered them to all the stores. As a merchant weaned in a different time, he did not want to delegate this responsibility to a service, a machine, or even other employees because he feared the potential for graft. From Stephen's perspective, his father still suffered from the mentality of the struggling immigrant who "never stopped trying to get on" and thought that every day he had to monitor all aspects of his operation. Stephen often wearied of the demands of a family-owned business, where it was not unusual "for siblings to fight the boss, and then the siblings to fight each other, and [then] to fight the cousins." In addition, Stephen felt that his father and his peers focused too often on the day's receipts and maintaining a steady stream of profits, rather than cultivating the company's long-term growth and development—"counting profit in their pocket rather than the value of their business in the open market."[86]

Management's program of modernization was mainly the product of trial and error, not some grand design. And not every innovation the company instituted was a winner. For example, Stephen brought in a comptroller to tighten up the company's accounting, and it had a negligible effect on the bottom line. Yet D'Agostino's modest size helped it stay on the leading edge of the industry because, as Stephen recalled, "we were willing as a small company to experiment."[87] Among the most valuable lessons he learned from his dialogue with corporate heavyweights was that D'Agostino's could not do daily battle with its competitors, especially based on price; rather, it had to stake out its own share of the marketplace. Over time, this tactic complemented the company's promotion of its public image, as it attempted to establish a unique place among the city's grocers.

In a 1981 *New York Times* article, Stephen detailed his plan to make D'Agostino Supermarkets the "dominant name" among the city's food retailers.[88] Stephen admitted that he was not seeking control of the grocery trade in terms of volume. At the time of the article, D'Agostino's had seventeen stores (fifteen in Manhattan, one in the Bronx, and one in Westchester County), while competitors (which the *Times* characterized as "class chains") such as Sloan's and Gristedes had thirty-nine and sixty, respectively. D'Agostino's $100 million in sales represented only 3 percent of the New York market. Instead, the company sought the "perception of dominance" by becoming "the dominant retailer in the borough, not so much in volume as in recognition" and "the subject of the consumers' principal perception as their food store in quality, price, value, and honesty."[89] In other words, the company would use reputation and image to project an identity as New York's premier grocery store.

Stephen D'Agostino also hoped the business could earn its "perception of dominance" through a concentration on "motivation and management." By the late 1960s, Nicholas D'Agostino and his sons had moved the company well beyond its early image as an earnest underdog. Still, one must recall Patsy D'Agostino's statement in the 1952 edition of *American Magazine* that "since we started being successful I have had a dread of becoming too big. Once I begin to forget the names of any of my employees, I no longer want to grow. I might get careless and start putting numbers on them."[90] As he modernized the operation, Stephen confronted the depersonalization Patsy feared, instituting a management strategy that could be viewed as paradoxical. He had the director of human resources, his cousin Stephen D'Agostino, create a comprehensive database that could store the "personal background, needs, education, and ambition" of his now eight hundred employees "in an effort to develop their potential" and match their talents "with the company's present and future requirements."[91]

Another major strategy Stephen D'Agostino detailed in the *New York Times* article was the "maximization" of the stores' small retail spaces, as the urban markets were only about 8,500 square feet, between one-third and one-half the space of their suburban competitors. The company embarked on a campaign to raise counters, build shelves close to ceilings, and install triple-deck cases in freezers.[92] As a result, the number of products sold increased by 20 percent in some stores. After wrestling with the older generation of store managers in the 1960s and '70s, Stephen urged them to now become more "efficient" and "avail" the stores of technological advances such as optical scanning and computer-to-computer ordering. This new focus contrasted with Patsy D'Agostino's aversion to the corporate obsession with efficiency he had encountered at the First National chain store in Boston, when he quit his job as a manager because he was tired of being treated "like a number."

Stephen coupled this "maximization" strategy with an aggressive blueprint for growth throughout New York City. He announced plans to expand further into the "core" of Manhattan with four new locations, as well as one for Queens and another for Brooklyn. At the time of the story's publication, D'Agostino's continued to be one of the most profitable stores in the New York area, with a net profit of 1 percent, against an industry average of eight-tenths of 1 percent. Yet, at the close of the article, Stephen called the supermarket industry a "scramble" and "over-stored"—a glutted industry of supermarkets, warehouses, convenience stores, and specialty stores. In this extremely competitive environment, the company needed to distinguish itself from the opposition. Thus, under Stephen's leadership, D'Agostino Supermarkets undertook a series of hip advertising campaigns that would soon become a key part of its brand.

When D'Agostino's was a fledgling business, Patsy D'Agostino's outgoing, charismatic persona was more effective than any advertising the company could purchase.[93] But this personality-as-advertising also presumed the existence of close neighborhood ties in Manhattan, as local relationships made major promotional campaigns unnecessary. When grocers advertised, they tended to emphasize lower prices or specials; older newspaper ads were full of information but lacking in graphics or character. However, in the postwar era, as D'Agostino Supermarkets expanded across the city from its neighborhood base in Yorkville, the brothers encountered a more anonymous marketplace. In this context, advertising was a way of introducing the merchant to the customer and of providing some type of quality assurance.[94]

Previous generations of shoppers trusted the expertise of their corner grocer largely because of their personal connection to him. In introducing themselves to a new customer base, the D'Agostino brothers had to essentially put a human face on the operation, if only symbolically. The magazine articles that told the life stories of Patsy and Nicholas were a form of promotion and a means of creating a distinctive identity for their stores. In the 1940s and '50s, D'Agostino's immigrant origins were the centerpiece of published accounts that made the brothers public figures while promoting their business. When Nick Jr. became head of the company in 1982, he would revive its heritage as family-owned and firmly rooted in the community. This mantle as New York's neighborhood grocer helped affirm the organization's familiar ties to the city in an era of urban anomie.

In each of these cases, D'Agostino's corporate personality was a projection of the identity of its presidents.

For decades, supermarket advertising, while common, typically consisted of spots in the newspaper that listed promoted items and their corresponding prices. These ads were so lacking in sophistication and visual attractiveness that they earned the nicknames the "obituary notices" or the "telephone listings."[95] Vendors also relied on cooperative agreements with major brands to provide advertising; thus, their ads were often unoriginal, pitched at a broad customer base and, by necessity, packed with as many listings as possible.[96] As the growth rate for supermarkets slowed and competition thickened, however, retailers sought innovations to differentiate their stores. Most tried to compete on the level of price, which presented the greatest challenge for sustaining a long-term advantage in a competitive marketplace. Independent grocers and smaller chains began to experiment with new forms of advertising to create a "personality" that could set them apart from chain supermarkets.[97] The most forward-looking among them even hired ad agencies to handle this task.

Since his early days in the grocery business, Stephen D'Agostino had been intrigued by the possibilities of marketing. As junior executives, he and his brother, Nick Jr., had persuaded their father that as part of developing a more modern identity, "D'Agostino Brothers" should be rebranded as "D'Agostino" (or, more formally, "D'Agostino Supermarkets") because the former name sounded "old-fashioned" and connoted "smallness."[98] Now, Stephen became convinced that the company needed an ambitious advertising campaign to appeal to a new generation of customers—urbane young professionals, just like him. He understood that this strategy was not necessarily cost effective, nor could its results be charted in specific dollar amounts. Rather, it reflected a belief in the power of image, and for that image to make an impact in a marketplace as vast as New York's, it would have to be "ubiquitous."[99] With the intention of becoming the most visible supermarket in the city, D'Agostino's made a significant financial commitment to this venture. In 1968, Stephen hired Jo Foxworth, a rising star on Madison Avenue, to head the new initiative—which would include both print and radio ads—but he also possessed his own untapped flair for advertising and soon became Foxworth's collaborator.

Jo Foxworth was a bold choice to craft a public image for a family of Italian American grocers. She grew up in an isolated Mississippi town, which by her own admission could have been the setting for a Carson McCullers novel. As a young woman, she had earned a degree from the prestigious University of Missouri School of Journalism and managed advertising for a number of department stores in Southern towns, before ambition drew her to the bright lights of the North.[100] After working as a copywriter and executive at two prestigious New York ad agencies and winning her share of accolades—including Advertising Woman of the Year and the presidency of the Advertising Women of New York—Foxworth decided to strike out on her own. D'Agostino's was her first client, even providing her with an "office" (a stockroom overlooking the floor at the store at 83rd Street and Lexington Avenue). While Nicholas or Patsy might have been reluctant to give a single woman from the South the power to define their identity, Stephen developed an immediate rapport with Foxworth. Both he and Foxworth were determined, witty, outspoken, and ready to challenge the accepted wisdom of their respective professions.[101]

Foxworth viewed the standard practices of her industry as stale and heavy-handed. "For at least twenty years customers everywhere have been trying to tell everybody who sells anything that they are bored with most of the advertising that bombards them and unconvinced by the corporate chest thumps about caring and saving," she explained. "I agree with their plaint and try to practice another kind of advertising."[102] Foxworth's style was literate, wry, and subtle—a perfect match with the mindset of D'Agostino's desired Manhattan clientele. Foxworth and Stephen D'Agostino's first campaign, "Please Don't Kiss the Butcher," depicted an old-time butcher winning the affection of housewives because of the quality of the store's meat.[103] According to Foxworth, the winking "Please Don't" theme was so successful that it bred many imitators, including one toilet paper company's "Please Don't Squeeze the Charmin" commercials.[104]

Foxworth also initiated one of the company's signature promotions— large white shopping bags (nicknamed "D'Ag Bags") emblazoned with images of produce and other merchandise in the style of pop art (see fig. 15).[105] Throughout the 1970s, these items became trendy accessories for New Yorkers of a certain class. A 1981 *New York Times* article noted that the "stores have already gained wide public exposure with the company's 'Dag Bags,' extra-large plastic shopping bags first issued in 1970 to help create an awareness of the supermarket chain. Since then . . . more than two million have been distributed. Fashion models, particularly, are said to like them because of their size, using them to carry extra shoes, clothes and makeup."[106] Their iconic status even led Nicholas D'Agostino Jr. to comment, "D'Ag bags are a status symbol in this city."[107] This association with Manhattan chic was later evidenced in a 1984 issue of *Rolling Stone* magazine, which showed singer Debbie Harry, of the pop-punk band Blondie, dressed in haute couture, armed with her "D'Ag Bag." This company "swag" also appeared in *Modern Bride* in 1984 and *Lei* (the Italian edition of *Glamour*) in 1983, as well as later issues of *Vogue*.

In a 1981 profile on Jo Foxworth, *The New York Times* commented on the unique spirit of D'Agostino's advertising, noting that the ads and their taglines had become as well known as the stores themselves:

> You people who live around here but who don't know D'Agostino Supermarkets at least know D'Agostino Supermarkets advertising. It's got a light touch and a spirit one doesn't generally associate with that genre of advertising, either in newspapers or on radio. "If there's no D'Agostino near you . . . move," in print. "Please, Mr. D'Agostino, move closer to me," set to music, on radio.[108]

Foxworth mused that the key to the company's advertising was its self-deprecating wit: "We believe you shouldn't take yourself too seriously. Take the business seriously, but not the message."[109] The ads' particular brand of humor assumed that their intended audience was literate and discerning. As referenced by the *New York Times* feature, in the late 1960s, the company had introduced its popular "If there's no D'Agostino near you . . . move!" campaign with a series of ads that showed a wholesome-looking but hip couple enjoying the simple pleasures of shopping at its stores (see fig. 16a). Because D'Agostino's had relatively few locations, most of which were in Manhattan, it could not advertise its convenience. Instead, the tagline was a tongue-in-cheek reference to the near impossibility of finding an apartment in Manhattan and the obvious merits of the stores if patrons would relocate just to be near one. Foxworth would later twist the premise of this slogan to create a signature radio jingle for the company in which a hopeful customer begged, "Please, Mr. D'Agostino, move closer to me." The company's radio spots featuring this catchphrase would become a staple of the New York airwaves in the 1970s and '80s.

According to one consumer advocate, a central problem with traditional supermarket advertising was that it focused on the housewife figure as its ideal customer even as the shopping population was becoming younger, more professional, and more diverse in its ethnicity, gender, and marital status.[110] Foxworth and D'Agostino, however, often made Manhattan's youthful cosmopolitans—as well as their concerns and pastimes—the stars of their campaigns. While this approach reflected the store's targeted customer base, as well as the distinctive character of New York's population, it also anticipated the changing demographics of the American marketplace. In the early 1970s, D'Agostino Supermarkets became one of the first retailers in the city to employ an African American model (Jane Hoffman) in its advertising. The resulting ad appealed to the lifestyle and lingo of cultured, ultramodern New Yorkers with the slogan "Keep New York Delicious. Catch A Flick. Cook A Treat. Shop At D'Agostino" (see fig. 16b). The tagline was a play on the antilittering slogan "Keep America Beautiful," while adding grocery shopping at D'Agostino's to the favored hobbies of urban sophisticates—a list that by implication included cooking (no longer the sole province of housewives after the period's culinary revolution) and attending films. The ad's text also allied D'Agostino's with the lifestyle of "those in the know" with some mild suggestion, at it announced, "New Star in Town. Delicious Jane Hoffman. Model and film actress—paints a little, writes a little, cooks cozy little dinners. Shops—where else?—D'Agostino."

In 1971, Foxworth made the crucial decision to hire Marvin Glass, a well-known illustrator of children's books. Glass's caricatures would help define the company's image for the next two decades. The novelty of the visual style and sly New York–based humor of the company's advertising was the subject of a feature in the May 1980 issue of *Supermarket News*: "D'Agostino Has Fresh Ad Approach." The article commented that while most stores had made "boldly printed prices" the focus of their promotions, D'Agostino's weekly ads in *The New York Times* devoted much of their space to cartoons "illustrating the company's latest theme." D'Agostino's proffering of iconography over information distinguished it from competitors who relied on a more conventional approach. *Supermarket News* quoted Joseph Burns, an advertising manager for D'Agostino's, as claiming that the ads helped brand the stores themselves:

> We try to communicate the difference of what we offer in the store by communicating differently. . . . If our store is different, then the fact our newspaper and radio ads are different will help communicate that. . . . I suppose what we try to communicate is that we're kind of New York. We really like to position ourselves as the consumer's agent in this gigantic industry. The New York consumer is kind of a special person. We try to reflect that specialness and provide the kinds of service New York expects.[111]

The print ads' reliance on visual humor indicated their sophistication, as did their weekly placement in *The New York Times*.[112] While Glass's caricatures associated D'Agostino Supermarkets with the pleasures of urban living, they maintained undertones of self-parody to deflate arrogance or snobbery, perhaps reflecting their intended customers' own self-consciousness. Foxworth and Glass also filled the ads with "in" jokes about life in the city, directed at New Yorkers of a certain class. Applying the familiar tagline, "If there's no D'Agostino near you . . . MOVE!," one of Glass's early efforts showed a fashionable young mother tackling the impossible task of moving the contents of her apartment—including child, dog, and "D'Ag Bag"—to a neighborhood with a D'Agostino's market (see fig. 17a). The absence of an automobile in this portrait spoke to the particulars of living in Manhattan. A 1974 Valentine's Day promotion winked at the decade's sexual culture, as it urged customers to "Hurry in to the big D'Agostino Love-In" (see fig. 17b). Glass's use of self-referential humor, set against a background of New York landmarks, reinforced the sense of Manhattan as a community (especially for those "in the know"), despite its anonymity and magnitude.

Marvin Glass's work also evoked the iconic cartoons of another urban institution—*The New Yorker* magazine. As previously discussed, both D'Agostino Supermarkets and *The New Yorker* appealed to patrons by picturing Manhattan as a village of literate, cultured individuals, and then offering them membership.[113] This parallel was more than a coincidence, as both D'Agostino Supermarkets and *The New Yorker* sought the same audience—urbane consumers whose identity was related to their consumption of the right foods, liquors, and clothes, as well as their familiarity with the city's art galleries, bookstores, concert halls, and theaters. Historian Mary Corey wrote that advertising in *The New Yorker* "offered . . . to guide this status-conscious audience through the marketplace by suggesting that their choices could set them above the common herd (the rest of the middle class), who bought poorly made, cheap, and tasteless objects." Corey added that the magazine's critical content was a check on its promotion of materialism, increasing "its credibility with a class of consumers who scorned the vulgarities of the mass market" while playing to the intelligence of its readership.[114] Similarly, the self-deprecating, droll style of the D'Agostino ads in the 1970s leavened the company's claims to elite status, while acknowledging its patrons' sophistication and sense of humor. The very act of drawing attention to its own commercial efforts helped D'Agostino's win customers' affections.

In the mid-1970s, Glass initiated a run of advertisements that paired D'Agostino's with the Central Park Zoo, the Statue of Liberty, and the Brooklyn Bridge (see figs. 18a and 18b). This motif satisfied multiple objectives, as D'Agostino Supermarkets appealed to its customers through a shared sense of civic pride while burnishing its image as an authentic New York business. Stephen and Nick Jr., like their father and uncle before them, carried a deep affection for their hometown. But by associating itself with the city's familiar landmarks, these ads implied that the company's status was, in its own small way, historic and monumental. In the early 1980s, Glass would push the notion that D'Agostino's was a cultural barometer with a series that announced, "What's Hot . . . What's Cool . . . What's New York!" The resulting ads listed the week's hottest fashions, foods, lifestyle trends, and social events while placing D'Agostino's at the center of "the good life." The self-aware pretension of the campaign was deflated by images that teased customers and tweaked the latest art show or play. Of course, these jokes assumed a working knowledge of high culture. One example from 1983 named as "hot" "Manet at the Metropolitan Museum . . . the resurgence of white for bed, bath and well dressed tables . . . nighttime fashions, a-glitter again . . . Sirloin D'Agostino!" The corresponding illustration was itself a parody of Manet's painting *Le Déjeuner sur l'herbe*, which showed the store's grocers and customers settling down to a lovely picnic in Central Park (see fig. 20).[115]

Yet, even as D'Agostino's continued to celebrate the joy of urban living in its ads, New York's own fortunes began to wane. By the mid-1970s, with a growing reputation for crime, crumbling infrastructure, racial turmoil, and pollution, the city had become a symbol of national decline.

As the company increasingly became known for its media savvy, its president, Stephen D'Agostino, emerged as a prominent public figure around New York City and in food retailing. His likeness was familiar enough to New Yorkers of a certain class that it was used in print advertisements for Antiquary Scotch (just as Patsy D'Agostino had once been featured in a promotion for Lord Calvert whiskey) and *The New York Times* (figs. 21a and 21b). The ad for the *Times* even played off of the D'Agostino slogan, quoting Stephen as claiming: "If the New York Times Left Town We Just Might Move" (fig. 22a). Antiquary and the *Times* capitalized on the upscale reputation that the supermarket had cultivated, while affirming their own associations with the culture of Manhattan.[116] Meanwhile, Stephen earned greater name recognition for the company through his appearances, but it was a measure of his renown that he could be associated as much with the life of New York as his own business.

As his uncle Patsy had hoped, Stephen had also become a respected figure within industry circles. Following his uncle's lead, he had used his charisma and the force of his ideas to achieve the presidency of the New

York State Food Merchants Association, and the chairmanship of both the National Association of Retail Grocers and the Food Marketing Institute (another major trade association). He became so recognizable to his peers that he was used to advertise trade publications such as the *Food Merchants Advocate* (the organ of the NYSFMA) and *Chain Store Age*. Stephen's celebrity was confirmed when he was one of sixteen executives invited to the White House in 1979 to meet with President Jimmy Carter to discuss the rising cost of groceries. From the 1930s through the 1960s, D'Agostino's was made in the image of Patsy and Nicholas—as it evolved from an "Old World" corner grocery with "New World" ideas to a modern "Supermarket of Distinction." Now, as its CEO, Stephen D'Agostino—well dressed, articulate, cultured in his ideas and tastes—was the embodiment of the company's identity as well as its model customer.

"Bite the Big Apple": The Fall and Rise of New York City

In the 1970s, New York becomes a symbol of American decline, as crime, pollution, poverty, and racial tension swell. As its problems mount, the nation's financial capital faces economic collapse and bankruptcy. Amid this urban crisis, D'Agostino's works to promote the "nice things about New York." Even as a million New Yorkers receive some form of welfare, a new gentry seeks to revive the cosmopolitan life of the city.

In the 1950s, it appeared as if New York's ambitious plan of redevelopment had minimized the damage caused by the postwar flight of thousands of residents to bedroom communities in the suburbs. In the next decade, as the city unveiled impressive new office towers and apartment buildings, commentators continued to praise New York as a model for the new urban economy. Yet the fanfare surrounding the city's reimagined skyline masked the damage caused by the erosion of its industrial base. As historian Joshua Freeman has documented, New York's midcentury prosperity was also the product of its vibrant manufacturing and port economies, which provided full employment for its legions of unionized workers. Between 1950 and 1970, New York lost about 300,000 manufacturing jobs, spurring the migration of thousands of blue-collar and clerical workers to the outer boroughs and the suburbs.[117]

As its established middle- and working-class populations departed, the city attracted hundreds of thousands of migrants from the Caribbean and the American South. Between 1940 and 1960, New York's African American population grew to over one million, while its Puerto Rican population increased to over 600,000.[118] Immigration from Cuba, Haiti, and the

Dominican Republic in succeeding decades would continue to diversify the city's demographics. These new arrivals stabilized New York's population figures, offsetting the massive flight from the city. However, by the 1980 census, New York's population still had declined by several hundred thousand to just over seven million, with Black and Latino residents now making up almost half of its population.[119]

Unlike previous generations of migrants, these newcomers no longer had access to the manufacturing jobs that had typically offered a path to middle-class respectability. As many of them were indigent, their arrival, combined with the decline of Lyndon Johnson's "Great Society" programs, made municipal government responsible for expanding necessary social aid at a time of declining tax revenue. By the end of the 1960s, one million New Yorkers received some form of welfare.[120] Moreover, the city's shifting identity and lingering inequalities stirred racial tensions, as New York endured several contentious episodes—including rioting in Harlem in 1964 after police shot a Black teenager, protests over housing segregation, and a face-off between white teachers and Black parents for control of Brooklyn schools in 1968. Several commentators wondered if New York was losing the social glue that had allowed a city with such a diverse ethnic and socioeconomic composition to achieve its glorious history.

The quality of life for New Yorkers also began to erode. For decades, the city had provided a network of public schools, libraries, hospitals, parks, transportation, and services that was the envy of mayors around the country. This commitment had been supported by the federal government's urban initiatives as well as by the city's robust economy. But as national politics grew more conservative and local sources of revenue evaporated, New York struggled to fix its decaying infrastructure and meet its financial obligations. By the late 1960s, national publications began to see it as a harbinger of the calamities facing all American cities in the decade to come. In bold headlines, *U.S. News* called New York a "disaster area," *Business Week* labeled it the "crucible of the urban crisis," and *Look* asked if the city was a "bust."[121] At the same time, New York endured a series of bitter labor disputes that resulted in a garbage strike, a transit strike, a newspaper blackout, and a dock strike. Public officials also squared off against the police and firemen's unions over wages and pensions, resulting in several costly settlements. Even New York's vaunted place as America's corporate headquarters was in dispute, as Pepsi-Cola, IBM, General Foods, Shell Oil, and dozens of other companies left the city to escape its high taxes, strong labor unions, rising rates of crime, and municipal dysfunction. Several firms reported that midlevel executives were no longer willing to move their families to such a hostile environment. Another executive cited New York's declining reputation as the reason for his company's move, remarking, "We originally set up headquarters in New York because we thought we needed a prestige address. Finally we came to realize that nobody thought any better of us for being in New York City."[122]

This corporate flight compounded the city's fiscal issues, as it meant a serious loss of tax revenue. By 1975, New York's woes culminated in a budget crisis so severe that the city, once America's economic engine, was some $13 billion in debt and on the verge of insolvency. As the crisis reached its nadir, the national press asked if this was New York's "last gasp."[123] Groaning under the weight of its annual public expenditures and desperate for funds, the mayor's office begged for federal relief, only to be summarily rejected. This ignominious episode was immortalized in the 1975 *New York Daily News* headline: "Ford to City: Drop Dead."[124] The federal government did eventually acquiesce, granting $2.3 billion in direct loan guarantees on a "seasonal basis," and by 1981 the city's finances were again solid. However, the threat of bankruptcy and the vexed federal reaction resulted in a series of austerity measures that continued under the new mayoral administration of Ed Koch. These culminated in severe cuts to the city's once-vaunted system of public health, education, recreation, and transportation, while social welfare and the municipal labor force were also slashed.

Meanwhile, "white flight," the malignant neglect of absentee landlords, vandalism, and arson reduced thousands of buildings in Harlem and the Bronx to rubble-strewn lots.[125] The city's rate of violent crime became a national scandal, with anxieties about the dangers of urban living reaching a fever pitch in the summer of 1977 with the bizarre "Son of Sam" murders and the looting that followed a power blackout on July 13.[126] By the end of the 1970s, New York seemed to have become a two-tiered society. The city's economy became increasingly reliant on white-collar professionals and tourism, rather than manufacturing and the trades, while the raft of public services and amenities that had been a democratic equalizer began to dissipate. As the ranks of the city's poor continued to grow, this "other half" struggled to acquire the requisite skills for employment in the burgeoning white-collar sector, especially given the deteriorating condition of public schools and libraries.

New York's apparent demise became a major theme in American popular culture in the seventies—from films like Charles Bronson's *Death Wish* and Martin Scorsese's *Taxi Driver* to television programs like *Barney*

Miller—making the city a lightning rod for debates about a larger American decline.[127] In response, in 1977 the New York State Department of Commerce, in concert with the prominent advertising agency Wells Rich Greene, embarked on a multimillion-dollar marketing campaign to promote New York City as a glamorous destination for tourism and business. The resulting "I Love New York" campaign—which included a series of successful television commercials, a ubiquitous jingle, and designer Milton Glaser's iconic logo featuring a red heart emblem—helped rehabilitate the city's image as a center of culture and commerce, as tourism became its second-biggest industry by the end of the 1970s.[128]

In this same spirit, D'Agostino Supermarkets sought to bolster local morale by promoting the positive aspects of living in New York—with D'Agostino's topping that list. Nicholas D'Agostino Jr. remembered, "We've always considered ourselves 'New York' and people do see us as a New York institution.... During the 1970s when the city was feeling down, we featured some of the high points of the city on buttons saying 'One of the nice things about New York' and we handed them out to our customers."[129] Through its boosterism, the company was able to remind its patrons that, unlike its competitors, it truly was a part of their community. Yet the campaign also signaled D'Agostino's genuine affection for its hometown, a love that would also be expressed in numerous philanthropic ventures. The slogan "One of the nice things about New York" soon became part of the local lexicon (preceding the celebrated "I Love New York" advertisements by two years), with even the statue of St. Patrick wearing a version of the button at the cathedral during Christmas of 1975 (fig. 19a).

New York had a long history of welcoming bohemians to its fallen residential and commercial districts, as neighborhoods like Greenwich Village had provided cheap apartments, studio space, and cultural access to generations of aspiring musicians, painters, and writers. Throughout the 1960s and '70s, SoHo and the East Village welcomed a new generation of avant-garde painters, performance artists, and punk rockers, as urban pioneers congregated in areas abandoned by industry and older ethnic communities. In many cases, young professionals followed in their wake, snapping up lofts and apartments in these now "trendy" districts. Still, many observers were shocked by the parade of would-be Wall Street financiers, advertising executives, lawyers, and white-collar workers who began to reclaim aging apartments and townhouses in fallen neighborhoods in Yorkville, Chelsea, and the Village. For an older generation who believed cities like New York had no future, the return of a young professional class with education, ambition, and money was a startling development. In 1979, *The New York Times Magazine* snidely reported:

> People often snicker when they first hear of it. A renaissance in New York City? The rich moving in and the poor moving out? The mind boggles at the very notion. After all, what about the graffiti, the abandoned buildings, the chronic fiscal crisis? Hard as it is to believe, however, New York and other cities in the American Northeast are beginning to enjoy a revival as they undergo a gradual process known by the curious name of "gentrification." . . . Indeed, the evidence of the late 70's suggests that the New York of the 80's and 90's will no longer be a magnet for the poor and the homeless, but a city primarily for the ambitious and educated—an urban elite.[130]

Some young people returned to the city because single-family homes in the suburbs had become too expensive and too distant from their places of employment. Many of the aspiring stockbrokers, ad execs, and corporate lawyers saw a migration to Manhattan as an opportunity to excel at the highest ranks of their respective professions. But this "new elite," drawn to the color and culture of the city, also seemed to be rebelling against their parents' postwar, suburban lifestyles. In the late 1950s and the 1960s, many young executives had been reluctant to move to the city, preferring Westchester, Connecticut, or Long Island to New York City because the big backyards and placid streets of suburbia seemed to offer opportunities for domestic bliss. Yet the new generation of professionals—often composed of single men *and* women, or couples with double incomes—were willing to hazard cramped, aging apartments and dangerous streets to experience the buzz of SoHo and TriBeCa. And, as they began to achieve a degree of wealth and status, the new gentry often bought and refurbished aging brownstones in once-prosperous neighborhoods—buildings that had often been victims of the "redlining" practices of the 1950s and '60s.[131]

This professional class fueled the growth of the top tiers of the city's economy. In 1978, New York experienced its first net job growth since 1969, with banking, real estate, law, and medicine becoming prime areas of economic expansion.[132] Yet the new urban gentry also contributed to commerce and culture in their role as trend-setting consumers. One publication even labeled this cohort the "hippoisie," and claimed that they had become the "true rulers" of the city not through their "production role," but through the power of consumption—as they made Szechuan food, designer jeans, gourmet cooking utensils, *The Village Voice*, *The New York Review of Books*, and the back sections of *The New York Times* emblems of urban style.¹³³ Amid the notorious scenes of strife and decay, it seemed as if New York in the 1970s was also defined by Studio 54, Zabar's, chic boutiques, exclusive restaurants, and elite department stores (as between 1973 to 1979, Bloomingdale's doubled its sales).

By the end of the decade, the city had juxtaposed two separate visions of the urban experience. And while D'Agostino's declared its love for New York, it sought to affiliate itself with its upwardly mobile residents. In 1973, commenting on the company's expansion to Manhattan's West Side, then vice president and future chairman Nicholas D'Agostino Jr. explained that it had to be selective about its locations since "politicians are in office for a term, and residents can always move, but when we move into a neighborhood, we have a long-term lease, and costly improvements." Nick Jr. shared that, as the city suffered from decaying resources and a shrinking population, D'Agostino's ideally would "try to appeal to that part of New York City which is going up.... We're concerned about the people in the neighborhood.... If the people are looking to leave, it's not for us."¹³⁴ Throughout the 1980s, as the city continued to gentrify, one article declared, "As new areas in Manhattan succumb to yuppiehood, D'Agostino's will be there.... Indeed, a D'Agostino's supermarket is now an indication that a neighborhood is changing."¹³⁵

No One's Godfather: D'Agostino's and the Ethnic Revival

Amid the racial politics of the 1960s, Italians seek totems of their own ethnic heritage. This drive begins with campaigns against such popular stereotypes as the Italian mobster, but eventually blooms into a cultural renaissance. Unaffected by this nascent "ethnic revival," D'Agostino's appeals to a different type of customer.

After World War II, in an era defined by suburbanization and consensus, Italian Americans became the focus of scholarship regarding class, mobility, and assimilation. Sociologist William Foote Whyte's *Street Corner Society: The Social Structure of an Italian Slum* and Herbert J. Gans's *The Urban Villagers: Group and Class in the Life of Italian-Americans* were the most prominent of these studies. Whyte and Gans characterized the Italians who populated northern cities as tribal, suspicious of change, undereducated, and almost pathologically dedicated to family and neighborhood above all other concerns.¹³⁶ Into the 1960s, the Italian American population remained rooted in the blue-collar neighborhoods of the Northeast. Their collective successes were often modest—as they continued to advance in construction and the trades, as municipal workers, police officers and firefighters, and as owners of butcher shops, grocery stores, and restaurants.[137] And while Italians signified the traditional values of family, religiosity, localism, and loyalty, pundits highlighted their mistrust of public institutions, conservatism, and insularity.

By the 1950s, however, a growing number of Italian businessmen and professionals had earned wealth and social respectability, becoming emblems of the American dream in the process. Their achievements exemplified their brethren's ability to prosper and assimilate.[138] More broadly, the community enjoyed greater access to higher education, as the number of Italian American college students increased fivefold between 1940 and 1970.[139] In the postwar period, a growing segment of the Italian population also migrated out to Long Island and New Jersey—seeming to cement their membership in the white, suburban middle class.[140]

These divergent demographic and societal trends would be reflected in the community's engagement with the ethnic revival that was emerging in the 1960s and '70s. Toward the end of the 1960s, many Italians began to agitate for greater recognition in American society. Like other groups of white ethnics, they witnessed the civil rights movement and adopted some of its rhetoric, if not its objectives. Part of this new activism stemmed from their resentment of the federal government's intrusive urban renewal programs and its attempts to integrate local public schools and housing (antipathy that was often directed against the African American community).[141] Their militancy could also be read as a backlash against the liberalism of the sixties and an expression of their economic anxieties.[142] In addition, many Italians saw in the era's racial politics a language for expressing their frustrations with the historic discrimination they had suffered.

This new brand of ethnic politicking often focused on symbolic issues—such as commemorating Italians' contribution to American society and condemning anti-Italian stereotypes. From a contemporary perspective, these efforts might seem cynical, even a bit ludicrous. In 1967, Frank Sinatra became chairman of the new American Italian Anti-Defamation League—which had as its mission to "inveigh upon publishers, editors, writers of books, magazines, and all other publishers of printed matter to halt the practice of producing fictional material that harms the reputation and dignity of American Italians."[143] Over the next decade, the group devoted much of its energy to fighting the Italians-as-Mafia stereotype, thus making Sinatra a curious choice to lead this effort. In July 1970, after the son of a reputed Mafia don was arrested, 100,000 Italians rallied in Columbus Circle to protest law enforcement's assumed link between Italians and organized crime.[144] The campaign against stereotypes became particularly active in the 1970s, with the popularity of "mob dramas" like the novels of Mario Puzo and the *Godfather* films of Francis Ford Coppola. Of course, the Mafia chic that followed from *The Godfather*, and continued with *The Sopranos*, also became a source of identity and pride to a segment of the Italian American population.[145]

Yet as historian Matthew Jacobson has documented, over the course of the 1970s, the so-called ethnic revival evolved beyond the reactionary activism of blue-collar descendants of European immigrants. Throughout the seventies, middle-class Americans disenchanted with the materialism and homogeneity of contemporary culture began to take renewed interest in their heritage—particularly in the food, language, and music of their ancestors—while films and novels with immigrant themes (including *The Godfather* and *Fiddler on the Roof*) captured the popular imagination. This burgeoning movement led Italians, and other European-descended groups, to a new appreciation of their history and caused them to rethink their identity—as white ethnics became "hyphenated Americans."[146] Meanwhile, Italian Americans would take a more prominent role in academia in the 1970s and '80s, as a new generation of scholars began to examine the legacy of their heritage and place in American society. In the coming decades, the ethnic revival also would inspire Italian Americans to rediscover numerous expressions of their cultural identity, especially as related to food. Eventually, this renaissance not only reached upwardly mobile Italians who had been hesitant to embrace their ethnicity, but also attracted thousands of other Americans who were taken with the romance of Italian food, language, music, and culture. By the 1980s, tourists and urban professionals were flocking to the quaint shops and restaurants of the "Little Italies" of New York, San Francisco, Boston, and St. Louis.

Nicholas D'Agostino was not completely aloof from the activism of New York's Italian community, even if he never became one of its partisans. In 1971, several of his associates from Italian Charities met with the New York State Division of Human Rights to discuss issues of Italian civil rights—including the community's lack of social mobility, its underrepresentation in public education, and the spread of anti-Italian stereotypes in popular culture.[147] When one of his acquaintances solicited Nicholas's financial support for the antidefamation cause, he complied. But in the 1960s and '70s, as D'Agostino's tailored its image to fit a customer base who could appreciate the finer things the city had to offer, its leadership fell out of step with the type of identity politics that were in vogue with America's white ethnics. As Italians sought expressions of their ethnic pride, D'Agostino Supermarkets continued to cultivate a cosmopolitan image that appealed to young professionals, not the denizens of Little Italy. Stephen D'Agostino's vision of New York was the city not of immigrants and laborers, but of the executives, doctors, lawyers, artists, and socialites who mingled at Manhattan cocktail parties and the hottest new restaurants. Stephen's company would not be defined by ethnic cronyism and the stratagems of the pushcart, nor would his stores carry the markings of the Old World.[148]

The Saga Continues: Family Business and the Final Acts of Nicholas and Stephen D'Agostino

In which the cycle of family history repeats itself, as the battle for control and credit within the business causes a choosing of sides, the assumption of old roles, and an impending breakup. Citing a need to grow beyond the confines of the company, Stephen D'Agostino departs. Meanwhile, Nicholas D'Agostino receives a final honor, the "Horatio Alger Distinguished American Award." Nicholas views this as the ultimate validation of his labors, though his presenters see him as another symbol of Reagan's America.

In 1982, D'Agostino Supermarkets was enjoying a half century of prosperity in the world's toughest marketplace. Through depression, war, and the straining of family ties, the business had endured, achieving new levels of success with each decade. D'Agostino's had secured a prominent place among the city's retailers and seemed poised to expand its reach and reputation. Yet once again, tensions within the family left the company's future in doubt. By the year's end, Stephen D'Agostino would resign to take an executive position with the JTL Corporation (then an independent bottler for Coca-Cola), leaving his younger brother, Nicholas Jr., to direct the operation as the company's CEO. Stephen's departure revived many of the same issues that had been at the heart of the dispute between Nicholas and Patsy D'Agostino two decades earlier.

The conflicts between Stephen D'Agostino and his father, and between Stephen and his brother, Nick Jr., showed eerie parallels to the clashes between Nicholas D'Agostino Sr., *his* father Ignatius, and *his* brother Patsy. Like his uncle before him, Stephen D'Agostino seemed to derive greater satisfaction from his engagement with the business community than he did from managing the day-to-day operations of a grocery store. Like Patsy, Stephen was elected to positions of leadership in trade associations even though he represented a relatively small enterprise.[149] Like Patsy, Stephen had remarkable instincts for predicting looming shifts in the industry and a sophisticated understanding of the latest innovations in the food trade. Like Patsy, Stephen was able to use his charisma to secure partnerships and win allies and, like Patsy, he was enchanted by the personalities and the buzz of Manhattan. Stephen D'Agostino would remember his uncle with great fondness, crediting Patsy with introducing him to what he termed "true New Yorkers."[150]

Nick D'Agostino Jr., the youngest of three siblings, had briefly considered going to law school after he graduated from the College of the Holy Cross. But once Nick decided to work for D'Agostino's, he gave himself completely to the business; in his early years, he sometimes found himself logging seventy hours a week in the same manner his father had. As Nick worked under his father and his older brother, he may have wondered about the recognition and clout he might have in an organization whose hierarchy seemed determined by the Old World model of primogeniture. He had become a vice president in his thirties but continued to serve in a junior position. Additionally, both sons had a challenging relationship with Nicholas Sr., and although Stephen and Nick were well compensated, they struggled with their father's demands. Because he saw the company as a projection of himself, Nicholas D'Agostino Sr. was an overbearing, scrupulous manager. He sometimes made unannounced visits to stores, and he would begin to rearrange cans or critique sloppy fruit displays to stockboys and managers alike. Nicholas treasured his sons' success but could not disengage from the business, or separate Stephen and Nick's accomplishments from his own sense of self. Stephen D'Agostino once said of his father, "He always wanted what was best for you. The problem was that he always thought he knew what that was."[151]

As the heads of a family business, D'Agostino's principals had to constantly negotiate roles, responsibilities, and even strategies, and this process could be exhausting for all concerned. Stephen D'Agostino later surmised that while it was the obligation of a leader to set a company's "vision," "if you have to negotiate that vision with members of the team, then you're never going to get there."[152] The underlying friction between Stephen and Nick Jr. came to a head during a meeting in 1982, when a quarrel over the details of store design escalated into an argument over the brothers' respective input into management decisions. In the weeks that followed, Stephen decided that it was time for him to strike out on his own. In September 1982, at the apparent height of his success, he publicly announced his resignation after more than a quarter century with the business. At the time of his exit, D'Agostino's was considered one of the top supermarket chains in New York.[153] In interviews, Stephen explained his departure as an opportunity to expand his horizons: "I have felt for a long time that there are other things to do in the world. I wanted to get into another field for my own personal growth and for a new, exciting challenge."[154] Both brothers strongly denied that family tensions were at the heart of Stephen's departure. Meanwhile, in *The New York Times*, Nick D'Agostino Jr. was asked about the pressure of taking the helm from his brother. He mused, "We've discussed Steve's ultimate departure from the company for a long time . . . so that the reality comes as no surprise. Over the years, he and I have shifted our duties around so that I am as prepared as I will ever be. And who knows, maybe I can do an even better job?"[155]

Nicholas D'Agostino Sr. had believed that the grocery business would provide a comfortable living for his children and grandchildren and create a legacy that would continue long after he had retired, with the name on the store marquees suggesting a small measure of immortality. Nicholas and his wife, Josephine, were shocked and hurt by their son's decision to resign, a tragedy that was compounded by Stephen moving his family to Tennessee as a condition of his new position with JTL/Coke. Still, as Stephen negotiated his departure, all parties hoped to avoid the acrimony that nearly ruined the business after Patsy D'Agostino died in 1960. While the principals in the settlement were outwardly satisfied with its parameters, the breakup did take an emotional toll. Stephen's three sons had anticipated careers running the company and had tailored their education and their professional development toward a mastery of the various aspects of food retailing, from meat buying to financing. As they reevaluated their futures, Stephen's sons may have felt a sense of betrayal, while their cousins—Nick Jr.'s three sons—would inherit the D'Agostino legacy.[156] Despite its ostensibly peaceful resolution, several family members emerged from the episode with emotional scars.

In May 1982 in Dallas, Texas, the Horatio Alger Association honored Nicholas D'Agostino Sr. with one of its annual "Distinguished American" awards.[157] In the weeks leading up to the ceremony, the Alger Association sent him a folder of materials that included a calendar of related festivities and a mission statement. Two documents in the packet also outlined the organization's commercial and political objectives. The first was an advertisement for *Only in America: Opportunity Still Knocks*, a collective biography of the previous honorees intended to show high school and college students that "Horatio Alger still lives—in the life stories of America's top men and women who have pulled themselves up by their bootstraps and achieved great success." The ad proclaimed that *Only in America* "stands ready to inspire and motivate America's young people. . . . These true stories are living proof that the American free enterprise system continues to work!"[158]

Also included in the folder was a reprint of a *Reader's Digest* article entitled "Free to Choose." Labeled as a review, the piece by Ralph Kinney Bennett celebrated economist Milton Friedman's book and PBS television series on the glories of the free market. Its introduction read, "In our desire to 'let the government do it,' America has departed from her promises and premises. Now, an important new book and television series shows us the path back to our heritage."[159] Since the 1960s, Milton Friedman's extreme doctrine of free-market capitalism had moved from the wilderness of American thought to its mainstream. His faith in the powers of enterprise was matched only by his cynicism about the government's ability to enact effective, ethical policy. Yet the genius of American conservatism in the 1980s was its ability to marry the rationale of the marketplace to sentimental pieties about traditional American virtues. Taken collectively, the documents from the Horatio Alger Association merged a belief in unfettered capitalism with nostalgia for the culture that had been pushed aside by the 1960s—making it a perfect emblem of Ronald Reagan's America.[160]

The Horatio Alger Association was pleased to add Nicholas D'Agostino to a roster that already included such conservative icons as Bob Hope, Norman Vincent Peale, Tom Landry, and David Thomas of the Wendy's fast-food chain. These honorees were steeped in the cultural values of the 1940s and '50s and could affirm the foundation's brand of politics. But Nicholas saw the award as the ultimate confirmation of his life's work, and he relished his place among other exemplary strivers. For the awards dinner, he had to submit a personal biography and make a speech about his struggles as a teenaged immigrant, laboring on his father's pushcart. For this ceremony that honored his coronation as an American icon—and his incorporation as a symbol of the market philosophies of Milton Friedman—Nicholas began to compose his life story in simple Italian, a language in which his formal instruction had ended in the fourth grade. In trying to sum up his life in the sincerest terms, Nicholas returned to his native tongue to commit to paper his story of American glory.

Nicholas's wife and family were anxious about his speech, since he often attempted grandiloquent statements on solemn occasions. But that evening, he chose to express his sincere gratitude to God, his mother, his wife, and his family. In closing, he turned to the audience and thanked *them*, and then asked his wife, children, and seventeen grandchildren to stand up. He declared to the audience, "I am blessed, but these are my real blessings. They're beautiful, aren't they?" He would later remember the Horatio Alger reception as one of the most moving moments of his life.[161] The evening seemed the ultimate affirmation of the labors and ambitions that had defined his passage from a dusty mountain village in Italy to celebrated success in one of the most cosmopolitan, competitive cities in the world. It must have provided some validation for a man who hungered for the world's respect. And yet, as he drifted from the daily struggles of running the company, Nicholas increasingly became a character in his own "rags-to-riches" story—the incarnation of the D'Agostino legend.

In his final years, Nicholas delighted in the quiet pleasures of retirement. He took considerable pride in his family and labeled them his proudest achievement. He loved nothing more than playing cards with his grandchildren or counseling them about their responsibilities in the world. Although Nicholas struggled with health issues toward the end of his days, his great appetite for life continued to tug at him. During moments of reflection, he would recall one of his favorite peasant aphorisms—"When I was young, I had the teeth and not the meat. Now I have the meat and not the teeth." He must also have pondered the limitations of his grand vision, as the business passed to another generation.

Figure 23. "Hello, Young Lovers!" (1996). In this ad, D'Agostino's sought to affirm its identity as a family business with historic roots in New York's Italian immigrant community. Courtesy of D'Agostino Supermarkets.

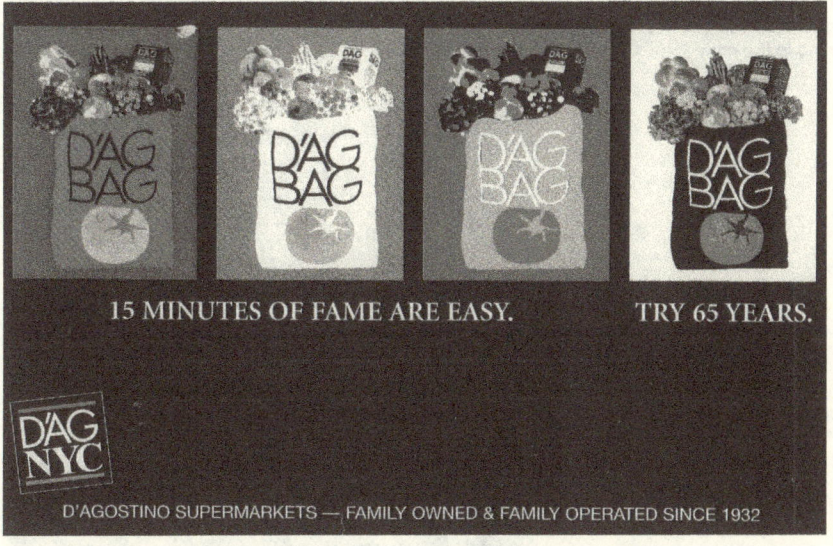

Figure 24. "Fifteen minutes of fame are easy. Try 65 years." (1997). By playing off Andy Warhol's aesthetics and his famous claim about the nature of fame, D'Agostino's again used subtle wit to appeal to the cultural sophistication of its intended customers. Courtesy of D'Agostino Supermarkets.

Figure 25a. The next generation, parts one and two. Nicholas D'Agostino Sr. (*second from left*) with his younger son, Nick Jr. (*far left*), nephew Stephen, and elder son, Stephen (*far right*), at a store opening in the early 1960s. Personal collection of the author.

Figure 25b. Nicholas D'Agostino Jr. poses with his sons Walter (*far left*), Nicholas III, and David (*far right*) in 1998. Courtesy of D'Agostino Supermarkets.

CHAPTER 5

New York's Family Grocer (1982–2025)

When Nick D'Agostino Jr. became chief executive officer of D'Agostino Supermarkets in 1982, New York was entering a new age of affluence. After a decade as a symbol of urban decay, it once again claimed the mantle of economic and cultural leadership for the nation. In the wake of the city's fiscal crisis, the administration of Mayor Ed Koch offered generous tax incentives and abatements to developers and private corporations to stimulate the construction of office buildings and luxury housing. In his quest to renew New York's position as a "global city," Mayor Koch sought to make it more amenable to corporations, international business, and tourism.[1] Although it had lost over 800,000 residents in the 1970s, by 1980 New York's "gross city product" reached $100 billion and its retail sales soared to an unprecedented $25 billion. Embarking on an aggressive program of austerity, Koch retired the city's federal loans and reestablished its fiscal solvency by the mid-1980s. Wall Street and the financial sectors also lifted New York's fortunes, as throughout the decade, its tax revenue, income, and rates of job creation rose faster than the national averages.[2] The boom on Wall Street shaped the city's image as well as its economy. While New York became the favored destination of young urban professionals, notorious figures like Michael Milken and Donald Trump merged with the fictive villains of *Wall Street* and *American Psycho* in the public consciousness, embodying the conspicuous consumption and feverish enterprise that defined the 1980s.[3] The flush times for the city's white-collar classes proved a boon for D'Agostino's, as the company endeavored to serve a population for whom food had become a status symbol.[4]

When the Dow Jones Industrial Average fell by more than 500 points on October 16, 1987, losing 22 percent of its value, New York's prospects seemed to darken. A national recession at the end of the decade exacerbated the city's financial difficulties, but within a couple of years, it became apparent that New York was beginning another renaissance. As advances in computer and information technology drove a surging stock market, New York became the hub for a potent "new economy." In this atmosphere of abundance, the city built new skyscrapers and amusement centers, renovated libraries, parks, and historic theaters, and remade "fallen" spaces like Times Square as tourist attractions. New Yorkers began to use their public institutions—from museums to Central Park and the maligned subway system—at a rate unseen since the 1950s. New York's renaissance led one policy analyst to label it the first American city in three decades to have a major success in reversing urban blight.[5] In the mid-1990s, under Mayor Rudolph Giuliani, New York's crime rate also fell to its lowest level in three decades, including steep drops in the rates of murder, robbery, and theft.[6] Giuliani's strategy for reversing the city's ugly reputation included a well-publicized plan for combating the "quality of life" offenses—such as graffiti, littering, aggressive panhandling, and turnstile jumping at the subways—that had given the city an air of lawlessness. New York's apparent safety, cleanliness, and affluence helped boost tourism to unprecedented levels, as the city received over 31 million visitors in 1996—a figure that would double within three decades.[7]

While pundits were quick to celebrate the impact of Wall Street and Mayor Giuliani's "law and order" posturing, they tended to overlook the crucial role that new immigration played in New York City's recovery. In the decades after the passage of the Immigration and Nationality Act of 1965, millions of émigrés from Asia, Latin America, Africa, Eastern Europe, and the Caribbean poured into the Five Boroughs to stem population losses and further revive the city's economy through their labor and entrepreneurship. At the same time, as the forces of gentrification took hold, legions of young hipsters colonized aging neighborhoods in Lower Manhattan and Brooklyn in search of culture and inexpensive apartments.[8]

New York's urban renaissance seemed to bolster the ranks of D'Agostino's customers. Throughout the 1980s and the early 1990s, it retained its favored place among the city's food retailers. New president Nick D'Agostino Jr. continued to expand the company's sales as well as its footprint in Manhattan and Brooklyn. Like his predecessors, he would also cast D'Agostino's in his own image—branding the firm as a contemporary version of the traditional family business through advertising, philanthropy, and a renewed corporate culture. And as someone who treasured his own connection to the city, Nick affirmed D'Agostino Supermarkets' commitment to the community. In 1993, one observer wrote that the "upscale D'Agostino stores have become an integral part of the life in New York City, helping to define the city's character just as some of the city's large department stores have in the past."[9] Yet, throughout the 1990s, the company struggled to defend its market share from a host of new contenders—including Korean greengrocers and gourmet supermarkets—who mimicked its marketing formula, as well as its image. In the face of this renewed competition, D'Agostino's sought new technologies and innovations that could reestablish its influence. By the end of the decade, D'Agostino Supermarkets would see its reputation slip, especially with the next generation of urban sophisticates. It would begin the new millennium with an uncertain future, as food retailing—and New York City itself—continued to evolve and grow.

Nick D'Agostino Jr. and the Romance of Family Business

Nick D'Agostino Jr. begins his reign as company CEO as New York enters a decade of excess and enterprise. While he maintains the company's commitment to modernization, Nick preaches the gospel of family, tradition, and community to a new generation of customers. Then, after a brief period of recession at the end of the decade, a Wall Street boom and gentrification launch New York into another Gilded Age. Nick and the company endeavor to match the tenor of the times.

When Stephen D'Agostino resigned from the family business in 1982, industry insiders questioned whether his brother Nick would be able to maintain D'Agostino's lofty position among New York's supermarkets. Under Stephen's stewardship, the company had achieved $100 million in annual sales and expanded to eighteen locations. Moreover, Stephen's understanding of marketing and promotion had made the D'Agostino name ubiquitous, with its reputation gaining an additional boost from his involvement in industry trade associations. Some commentators speculated that Nick might be too reserved or conservative to sustain the company's growth and name recognition.[10] In the 1960s, critics had similarly wondered whether Nicholas D'Agostino Sr. would continue to grow the operation after his older brother's death, especially since Patsy's social charm and understanding of the food industry had been vital to D'Agostino's postwar success. But, once he had control of the company, Nicholas surprised his critics with his vision, ambition, and willingness to become a public figure after years of working in the shadows. Like his father before him, Nick D'Agostino Jr. seized the opportunity to lead. By 1990, D'Agostino Supermarkets had doubled its annual sales to $200 million and expanded to twenty-four locations.[11] And also like his father, Nick soon became a public figure in his own right, even succeeding his brother as president of the New York State Food Merchants Association.[12] He cultivated relationships with New Yorkers of all types while showcasing his own ideas for expansion and innovation.

Yet Nick D'Agostino Jr.'s leadership style and management strategies were distinct from those of his older brother. In interviews, Nick indicated that he originally had little desire to become a grocer. Growing up, he "role-modeled after the Jesuits in high school" and briefly joined the seminary. After graduating from Holy Cross with a degree in English, he considered becoming a lawyer.[13] But when Nick married, he fully committed himself to a career in food retailing. His father, of course, was unsurprised—"I don't think he ever considered that there was an alternative," Nick admitted.[14] Despite his initial reluctance, Nick recognized that the family business had been a formative part of his youth, whether he was sharing holidays with the many relatives affiliated with D'Agostino's or working as a cashier on breaks from college. "So, even though I came into the company after college, I was familiar with a lot of the people, store managers and various associates who worked in the company, through just social experiences as part of the family," he recalled.[15]

Once in the business, Nick served an intensive apprenticeship. He began as an assistant store manager, where he trained in the essential aspects of running a supermarket—such as managing the "front end" of the store, learning how to order groceries, and observing the workings of the produce, meat, and dairy operations. Whenever D'Agostino's opened a new location, Nick helped to establish and merchandise the store, and then became its assistant manager. Within a couple of years, he had moved "upstairs," assisting the company's chief dairy and frozen foods buyer, before eventually filling this role himself. He then became the director of store operations before serving as director of merchandising. Yet Nick's recollections of his training give some clue to his own personality as an executive, as he remembered that in his early career at D'Agostino's, his "greatest experience came in managing stores. . . . That's the most fun because you're dealing with associates, you're dealing with customers, you're dealing with issues."[16]

By the mid-1960s, Nick D'Agostino Jr. had assumed the title of vice president—essentially the third in command, under his father and his older brother. Like his father before him, Nick was heavily involved in the daily operations of the stores, while his older brother assumed a more visible profile. Over the next decade, he worked alongside Stephen to implement many of the organization's innovations while awaiting a greater role in management, accepting the role of company president in 1978 when his brother became its chairman. When Nick became CEO in 1982, he built on these reforms, even expanding the operation's use of technology. But Nick also sought to renew D'Agostino's commitment to the ideals of family and tradition. He returned some of the "old guard" to positions of prominence, while expressing hope that his sons would follow him into the business. Early in his tenure, he remarked that while he wanted them to make their own decisions, he "would consider allowing one or all of my children the opportunity to enter the family business as one of my most exciting and most rewarding accomplishments."[17]

In published interviews, Nick cited the paradigm of the traditional family business as the primary source for D'Agostino's corporate culture and public image. One profile began with him talking about the lessons his father taught him, "lessons he is passing on to his five children, some or all of whom will eventually become involved in the family business. Foremost, he says, is personal integrity and business ethics. Standing for something. Backing your word. And hard work."[18] In another article, he allied himself with his father's "old-school" ethic, musing: "I learned about the business by working in it, but what you learn from your parents are values—the whole issue of integrity. I was taught that if you did the right thing and worked hard you'd be as good and probably better than your competition."[19]

Throughout Nick D'Agostino Jr.'s tenure leading the company,* philanthropy became a favored method of communicating this corporate culture to the city of New York. D'Agostino's already had a tradition of charitable giving that extended back almost fifty years. But while Nicholas and Patsy focused their efforts on immigrant societies and Italian charities, Nick recalled that one of his principal decisions "was to put more effort into supporting charities that impacted the lives of our customers."[20] Like his uncle and his father, Nick became active in the Archdiocese of New York, serving on the Cardinal's Committee, while holding key positions in the United Way of New York, the Madison Square Boys and Girls Club, and several

---

* In 1986, Nick was elected chairman of D'Agostino Supermarkets by its board of directors but would retain his title as CEO. He subsequently named Ron Nevers company president and chief operating officer. Nevers would remain in that position until 1997.

hospitals. Providing health care for the city's needy residents also became one of Nick's favorite causes. St. Clare's Hospital and Health Center, a facility that served the elderly and indigent on Manhattan's West Side, was in bankruptcy when the Archdiocese of New York took control in 1982. The archdiocese named Nick the hospital's chairman of the board soon thereafter. By the mid-1980s, he had reorganized the hospital's finances and overseen the renovation of its facilities, including its emergency room. In 1985, under Nick's leadership, St. Clare's implemented a comprehensive program of caring for patients infected with HIV and AIDS that transformed the hospital into the largest "dedicated AIDS-care facility" in the US.[21] In 1989 the United Hospital Fund—a charitable and research organization dedicated to health care—awarded Nick their Distinguished Community Service Award for his efforts.[22]

In 1989, an editorial in *The New York Times* praised the company for an innovative project in which D'Agostino's customers were asked to "round up" their grocery bills to the next dime or dollar at the checkout and donate that extra amount to Citymeals-on-Wheels, which delivered hot meals to the homebound elderly.[23] The initiative collected around $10,000 of "spare change" in its first week while anticipating a now-common charitable practice. Over the course of his chairmanship, Nick would subsequently raise hundreds of thousands of dollars for Citymeals-on-Wheels and the United Way from his business associates, well-heeled customers, and employees. The company also supported New York's public schools through a program in which students exchanged grocery receipt tapes for personal computers.[24]

Nick recognized that philanthropy was an invaluable tool for affirming the company's commitment to New York City, as civic engagement reflected its social conscience. In one interview, he shared, "We have always felt that we have a responsibility to give back to the community in which we make our living."[25] In another, he remarked, "We support our local block associations and contribute to the city's poverty and feeding programs. . . . We want to give back to Manhattan something of what we get out of it."[26] As a result of these efforts, journalists often used Nick's commitment to charity to identify him to their readership. When he became the chairman of the New York State Food Merchants Association in 1982, the organization ran a profile titled "Nick D'Agostino, Jr.: Dedicated to Improving the Quality of Life for All New York." It begins:

> Nicholas J. D'Agostino, Jr. has made a lot of money selling food to New York City consumers. For many men, that would be the

beginning and end of the story. But Nicholas J. D'Agostino, Jr. is a special man. He cares about the city—the people with whom he lives and works. In fact, he's dedicated a great deal of time and energy, as well as money, to improving the quality of life for all New Yorkers—not just for his customers.[27]

In an article titled "D'Agostino: Innovation, Sensitivity: Success," an employee described the organization's charitable endeavors as both a "trademark" and an extension of its chairman's benevolence: "Nick is especially eager for D'Agostino Supermarkets to help community groups that serve the city. He has enormous compassion for people and for New York City."[28]

This community spirit also emerged out of D'Agostino's need to brand itself in an increasingly crowded marketplace. In a 1993 interview, Nick named the "family culture" of D'Agostino Supermarkets as necessary to distinguish his company from rivals such as Gristede's and Food Emporium (which had been purchased and bankrolled by A&P).[29] With the cost of advertising becoming more prohibitive, Nick remarked that how "to differentiate yourself in today's environment is by really trying to become part of a neighborhood; supporting local charities, you always try to hire local people . . . trying to be part of the community as much as we can so that the consumer sees us as a part of their neighborhood and wants to support us for that reason."[30] Nick D'Agostino Jr. earned plaudits for his ability to weave effective management strategies with social responsibility. For both his record as chairman and his efforts in the community, he was named one of *Crain's New York Business*'s four "business all-stars" for 1990.

Nick D'Agostino Jr.'s stated allegiance to family and community extended to his relationship with employees. As president, Nick used "family" as an organizing principle to maintain the loyalty of a workforce that had grown increasingly more anonymous and temporary. In the 1930s, when Patsy and Nicholas D'Agostino were building their business, they relied on a network of relatives and coethnics as their labor pool. For the next three decades, their employees were predominantly Italian American, and many of the clerks and managers were personally known or related to Patsy and Nicholas. The workers thus had a natural kinship with management and could identify with their cultural values. And for previous generations, the grocery business was akin to learning a trade—as many immigrants rose from the pushcarts to positions as clerks, produce men, or butchers, on up to store managers and owners. At each rank in this hierarchy, they acquired skills and built relationships, with their career development often depending on the prosperity of the stores that employed them. This mutual dependency, along with a common culture, had encouraged employees to share a vision of success with their supervisors. Nick remembered that even when he entered the business in 1960, "six of the managers were Italian, one was Irish." He recalled:

> All the meat managers were Italian; most of the deli managers were Italian. And in fact, the company attracted a lot of young American Italians who were looking for job entry as teenagers from the Italian areas of Harlem and Westchester and they would see D'Agostino's as a place that they idolize, a place that they saw they could make advancement from and where they would get their first jobs while they were going to high school, college, and going on to other careers as well as careers in the food industry.[31]

Yet by the 1960s, shoppers no longer needed experienced clerks to help them choose cuts of meat or fresh vegetables or to retrieve their orders, owing to the growing popularity of self-service and frozen and processed foods. At the same time, the jobs within supermarkets required less expertise and experience. Management was thus able to pay workers less and could afford higher turnover. Over time, their staff became an assortment of high school and college students holding part-time jobs or working-class adults struggling to gain an economic foothold. Fifty years earlier, entry-level staff had a reasonable hope of matriculating into positions as clerks and managers. Now, supermarkets barely paid a living wage, and few employees stayed long enough to gain a promotion or learn the trade.

The organization also grappled with demographic shifts that reflected the city's evolving identity. As D'Agostino Supermarkets expanded to two dozen locations, its workforce became more anonymous and diverse and less connected to the company or its history. Reflecting on the difficulties of maintaining a qualified staff, Stephen D'Agostino wondered, "Why would an employee want to work . . . for $15 an hour in a grocery store when they could make $15 an hour in something else that's more clean?"[32] And with the high cost of housing in Manhattan, employees often had to take long train and bus rides to jobs that were still demanding, if less promising than in previous decades. For these reasons, in the 1970s and

'80s, management had to put more effort into getting workers to connect with the company's mission.

This situation became particularly difficult for upscale grocers who aspired to provide consumers with a higher grade of service and product. As D'Agostino's and its competitors began to add bakeries and lines of exotic produce, imported cheeses and custom-cut meats, they needed personnel who could handle and present these items with skill and care. The type of customer who sought ingredients for the latest recipes from *Gourmet* or *Bon Appétit* demanded more service at a time when management was less able to provide it.[33] When Nick D'Agostino Jr. became CEO of the company in 1982, he understood that his staff was a key element in maintaining the stores' reputation and identity. One industry publication stated, "Customer service is Nick D'Agostino's bridge from the future to the past."[34] But early in Nick's tenure, he also acknowledged the difficulty of finding quality employees ("as bright, pleasant and attractive as his stores") suited for working in Manhattan: "It's one of the greatest challenges for a retailer in New York today. You've got to constantly upgrade and develop people from the surrounding area who are up to the task of dealing with the upscale New York City consumer."[35] In his comments, Nick appeared to recognize the role of class in the relationship between his workers and his customers, admitting that D'Agostino's was essentially employing one side of New York to serve the other.

In response to these challenges, Nick declared that D'Agostino Supermarkets "works hard at maintaining its upscale image" through its human resource policies. For example, while competitors obtained delivery people from an employment service pool, D'Agostino's "hires its own people and pays them benefits in order to motivate better service."[36] Nick also hoped the ethos of "family business" would assure prospective employees that they would be stakeholders. He declared, "I believe we tend to be more concerned with them as human beings than as just people who work for the company."[37] He argued that at D'Agostino's, "the family culture gives opportunities for success that the big chains and corporations will never have" since team members would be offered a path to rise through the company ranks.[38] Nick encouraged associates to complete their educations, even instituting GED programs for those who had not received high school diplomas. He established profit-sharing plans for his entire workforce, from management to delivery staff, and expanded trainee programs for those who wanted to improve their positions. In 1990, the company founded the "Career in Focus" initiative, which provided team members with instruction in math, critical thinking, GED preparation, and English as a second language at Marymount Manhattan College.[39]

Nick claimed that D'Agostino's "family culture" gave it an advantage over its rivals because it built "employee morale throughout the organization" while providing a sense of community.[40] Under his direction, D'Agostino's founded bowling and softball teams and began to publish an in-store newsletter, the "D'AG Bagazette," which profiled the lives of employees and provided snapshots of company events and awards dinners, including an elaborate annual Christmas party. To give his staff greater access to the boss, Nick began to offer "Lunch with the President" days in which he would often dine with cashiers, clerks, and delivery boys. And to recognize those who had earned some seniority within the organization, D'Agostino's began to give pins to those associates who had at least five years of service. In an act of fellowship, he proudly wore a twenty-five-year service pin on the lapel of his own jacket.

Nick also used charity drives to promote the company's values among its workforce. He stated that as New Yorkers, every team member held "a responsibility to give back to the community in which we make our living."[41] He thus encouraged their participation in campaigns such as a program in which employees contributed $20,000 to the United Way by donating portions of their paychecks.[42] At the same time, Nick concluded that they should see that D'Agostino's corporate giving "also went to their own environment to improve their quality of life," reasoning that "if we improve the lives of our associates, it makes them happier.... This, in turn, makes them more comfortable dealing with our customers."[43] By the 1990s, D'Agostino Supermarkets was thus supporting initiatives in the neighborhoods of its employees—such as the building of affordable housing in the Bronx—that Nick hoped would secure their loyalty.

Like his father before him, Nick D'Agostino Jr. saw himself as the embodiment of the company—a patriarch for modern times. He made a point of visiting each location on a regular basis and had frequent meetings with his managers to determine "how we can make each store more successful." His engagement led one member of his management team to remark that Nick "is an owner who truly cares for this family business. His leadership inspires employees at all levels."[44] Yet Nick also epitomized the managerial principles of the 1980s and '90s, just as his brother, father, and uncle had represented the business culture of their own respective eras. A 1987 article from *Progressive Grocer*, titled "Tyranny Is Out, Teamwork Is In," featured executives from the food industry calling for more democratic, team-oriented leadership following the decade's corporate scandals. One consultant talked about the need for "horizontal arrangements, not command leadership," and another discussed the ideal model not as "the military, but like a symphony orchestra where there is only one conductor."[45] Still another industry representative defined an effective leader as someone who set "the strategy" but asked employees "how best to accomplish it," while a Harvard business professor counseled that an executive should establish a "culture of pride" throughout the organization.[46] In interviews, Nick D'Agostino was careful to refer to his employees as "associates"—a gesture that reflected the conventions of contemporary business culture. He also shared that he allowed his management team latitude to make decisions while concentrating on setting the company's culture: "We emphasize the independence of our store managers. . . . We also involve our employees in problem solving. Managers often come up with excellent solutions. Certainly, they follow through on a change they suggest better than if we just dictated it to them."[47] In 1990, one writer even called Nick an "unassuming executive" with a "laissez-faire style of management" who was generous in giving credit to others. He quoted Nick as stating, "I'm there as the leader. I don't have to tell people what to do, but they can ask me and I have an opinion."[48]

In his relationships, as well as his corporate policies, Nick tried to foster a sense of community, signaling to customers and associates that he was "one of them." As Nick was naturally friendly and approachable, the notion that he was an average New Yorker became a part of his persona. Company-issued literature observed:

> Nick D'Agostino is among the more prominent business executives in New York City, equally at ease with the famous and anonymous, the politically connected and the obscure. Which is sometimes a mixed blessing. When he rides the bus or subway, strangers feel no hesitation . . . telling him what they think about his family's stores, or other matters of apparent burning interest.[49]

In interviews, Nick made a point of mentioning that he had chosen to live and work in the city, and that his family attended its schools (albeit private ones), patronized its shops and cultural institutions, and rooted for its sports teams. He claimed that the organization shared its customers' worldview because "we actually lived in the neighborhoods where there was a D'Agostino. We actually lived in the community where our customers lived. Our children went to school with our customers' children."[50] He later recalled that it was "easy" for his company "to say we were 'New York's Grocer' because we *were* New York's grocer."[51] For example, in a feature titled "D'AG's Is New York," one trade journal noted that Nick's "household shopping is done at the D'Agostino supermarket at 74th Street and Broadway in Manhattan—just around the corner from his residence. Being a Manhattan resident keeps the company chairman closely involved with the city that his stores serve."[52] In another profile, he declared, "I've lived in Manhattan for 24 years with my wife and five children. I could live someplace else, but I don't want to, let alone work anyplace else. New York has more of everything, good and bad. It's an exciting place. When you're good in New York, you get rewarded very well."[53]

The company's success in associating itself with the culture of the city during Nick's presidency was noted by an interviewer who observed that "the D'Agostino name is a household word in New York City."[54] Nick and Jo Foxworth continued to use media and marketing to brand D'Agostino Supermarkets "as" New York. In the 1990s, management even began to emblazon bags, stationery, and its ads with a "D'AG/NYC" crest that implied a seamless relationship between the two entities.

In this era, D'Agostino's ability to make its name an emblem for the city was also reflected in the number of television programs and feature films that used its stores to establish an "authentic" New York setting. Shows such as *Mad About You*, *Will and Grace*, and *Friends* and movies like *As Good as It Gets* and *Spiderman 2* featured its shopping bags, decor, and awnings, as well as exterior shots of the stores themselves, to give their productions a Manhattan flavor—a remarkable accomplishment for a relatively small enterprise. One might attribute the visibility of D'Agostino's in popular culture to the large numbers of ex–New Yorkers scattered throughout the country. (Nick himself claimed, "It's rare that I travel anywhere that I don't meet a D'Agostino customer."[55]) Yet Nick and his staff actively cultivated relationships with film and television companies. While its competitors often requested fees or royalties from studios for use of their names, images, or merchandise, management presented interested directors and producers with free "D'Ag Bags" and company "swag" upon request. D'Agostino's thus developed a reputation in the entertainment industry for its obliging attitude. Through this version of "product placement," it broadcast itself as a virtual logo for New York.

By the 1980s, growing competition at all levels of the industry left retailers searching for new methods of identifying their stores to the buying public. One insider recommended that retailers create "a perception that you and your people care about the community, care about service and about giving value." *Progressive Grocer* concluded that retailers should replace their usual marketing with ads "that emphasize the people who make up the company."⁵⁶ In the 1970s, Stephen D'Agostino had become so recognizable to a segment of consumers that he could promote *The New York Times* and a brand of whiskey in ads that winked at D'Agostino's high-end image. When Nick D'Agostino Jr. became CEO, he literally made himself the public face of the company to connect with his customers, especially those of a certain class (see fig. 22b). One article observed, "Nick reflects the D'Agostino image. It's an image that places the store in the higher quality category of New York supermarkets. He wears three-piece suits, is articulate and knows the food business and the New York market."⁵⁷ In the 1990s, the "familiar face of the company chairman" appeared in D'Agostino's weekly ads in *The New York Times*, and his voice was used in a radio spot for Chase Manhattan Bank that discussed the two companies' shared affection for their hometown. These advertisements suggested a genuine affinity between "Mr. D'Agostino" and his customers. Nick explained to one interviewer, "I think appearing in advertising and talking on the radio helps give the company a more human identity in the city."⁵⁸

Nick D'Agostino Jr. was also quoted as claiming that "the success of the company may in part be due to the company's ability to offer a feeling of 'family.'"⁵⁹ In the 1990s, Nick and Jo Foxworth made D'Agostino's historical origins a defining theme of its advertising and its brand. Nick even commissioned a slogan—"family owned and family operated since 1932"—that celebrated the stores' eminent place in the city, while invoking the sentimental attachment Americans have for family firms.⁶⁰ D'Agostino's sought to project a sense of trustworthiness and tradition, and to connect with their fellow New Yorkers with an advertising campaign that showcased classic portraits of the family. Just as familiar images of Nick D'Agostino Jr. had given the company "a more human identity in the city"—allowing shoppers to view the chairman as their friendly neighborhood grocer—depictions of the D'Agostino family encouraged New Yorkers to associate them with their own family histories. In its 1994 Easter circular, D'Agostino's ran a full-page reprint of Nicholas Sr. and Josephine's wedding photo with the caption:

> From our family to yours, loving wishes for a Joyous Easter. This is our 64th Easter in New York and we celebrate it with a proud tribute to our founder, Nick D'Agostino, Sr. shown here with his bride Josephine Tucciarone on their wedding day in 1932—a vintage year for Nick. That was the year that the 21-year-old immigrant, with his brother "Patsy," opened the small grocery store that grew into the famous D'Agostino Supermarkets.

The characterization of Nicholas D'Agostino Sr. as the business's "founder" reinforced the notion that D'Agostino's was a venerable institution while the text, with its evocation of Nicholas's "vintage year," invited readers to share in its nostalgia. These sentiments were recreated using the same wedding photo in an ad from the July 1996 edition of the highbrow New York magazine *Avenue* (fig. 23), although with a slightly different narrative:

> Hello, Young Lovers! More we could not wish you than the happiness of Nicholas D'Agostino Sr. and his bride, Josephine (Tucciarone) photographed here on their wedding day August 14, 1932 at St. Raymond Church in the Bronx.
>
> The D'Agostino Supermarkets, founded that same year by the 21-year-old bridegroom and his brother, have grown from one small store into the citywide chain that is now New York's primary source of "food for life."
>
> Our 1932 lovers, now married for 64 years, invite this year's brides and their husbands to learn about a lifetime of healthy nutrition at the famous D'AG Supermarkets—originators of environment-protective Earth Goods.

The ad presented itself as a window into the past—both in its remembrance of that "one small store" that grew into a citywide chain and in its vision of an Italian bride and groom wed at one of New York's hallowed immigrant churches. It also represented a paradigm shift for D'Agostino Supermarkets and its desired customers. In the 1960s and '70s, D'Agostino's appealed to the city's middle- and upper-income consumers by presenting its stores as part of the "good life" of a modern cosmopolis. The new campaign portrayed "true" New Yorkers as people who treasured their family and heritage, as well as their allegiance to their hometown. It is noteworthy that the second version of the advertisement ran in a magazine with an upscale clientele. As both the marketplace and society itself had grown more changeable and anonymous, history, ethnicity, and authenticity had become prized commodities for discriminating consumers.

The marketing of its history also revealed the company's anxieties about the new cohort of professionals who were moving into Manhattan. Jo Foxworth was asked to account for this shift in advertising strategy and shared that D'Agostino's hoped its venerable status would lure younger customers who might be unaware of the stores' pedigree. She explained, "I was making a particular effort to go for the youth because . . . the last research showed that our customers were mainly in their forties and fifties. You know, the kids didn't shop with us. So, we made a big effort to go for them," adding, "the emphasis on New York really comes from the fact that . . . the company is established. It's very much an icon in the city."[61] Foxworth's assessment was supported by the tagline of the second ad, which called out "Hello, Young Lovers!" It also tried to tap into the younger generation's regard for healthy eating by allying the bloom of the matrimonial season with D'Agostino's new line of organic vegetables, invoking Nicholas and Patsy's origins as fruit and vegetable vendors in the process.

The company again tried to make its history "hip" to savvy consumers in a 1997 advertisement featuring a series of lithographs that recalled Andy Warhol's *Campbell's Soup Cans* (fig. 24). The ad showed four brightly tinted images of D'Agostino shopping bags, overstuffed with a bounty of produce and groceries, above the caption "15 Minutes of Fame Are Easy. Try 65 Years." Jo Foxworth's playful allusion to Warhol's themes achieved another layer of meaning when one considers D'Agostino's origins, and the marketing of its own saga for public consumption.

Finally, D'Agostino's advertising in the mid-1990s was notable for invoking the figure of the immigrant. Nick D'Agostino Jr. maintained that his firm based its identity on notions of family and community, rather than ethnicity. But because ethnicity figures so prominently in American culture's representation of traditional families and urban history, the company necessarily made references to its Italian identity as part of its promotional strategy.[62] Moreover, in these ads D'Agostino's recognized that its tale of the immigrant "making good" once again resonated with consumers. This incarnation of D'Agostino's identity represented the completion of a curious cycle.

In the 1943 profile in *The New Yorker*, Patsy D'Agostino had been characterized as the prototypical ethnic merchant ("a vigorous fellow of thirty-eight, with big shoulders, crisp black hair, glittering black eyes, and an energetic and confident manner") who drank black coffee laced with whiskey. In the 1950s, Patsy D'Agostino's identity began to shift from greengrocer to the grocer in the gray flannel suit—a figure of successful assimilation. In the 1960s and '70s, Stephen D'Agostino, with his ads for scotch and *The New York Times*, was more suited for the boardroom than the Bronx Terminal Market. Stephen pushed the company away from its ethnic roots to achieve a more sophisticated character. Now the company had returned to its origins, with its historic identity serving as a seal of quality and craft.

Perhaps the ultimate merging of the personal and the public, of the historical and the mercantile, occurred in the 1995 circular that paired a full-page reproduction of Nicholas Sr.'s face with text that placed D'Agostino Supermarkets among the city's most esteemed monuments (see fig. 1). Beneath Nicholas's patriarchal gaze ran the following caption:

Only in New York

> New York is the world's dream factory. Like everything else dreams are bigger here and some of them do come true. Ours began in 1932 when 21-year old Nick D'Agostino, Sr. sold his pushcart and, with his brother, opened the small grocery store that grew into today's unique chain of **D'Agostino Supermarkets**. This is our 63rd birthday and we celebrate it in the shadow of imposing neighbors who this year are observing milestone anniversaries: **The New York Public Library** celebrates its 100th birthday and so does the **Wildlife Conservation Society**. Also, the **Motion Picture Industry** which was in New York before Hollywood was born. **The Metropolitan Museum of Art** observes its 125th anniversary and so do the **American Museum of Natural History** and **Hunter College**. Finally, the **United Nations**, with its great human goals of peace, justice and prosperity, celebrates 50 years of global achievement. **D'Agostino** is proud to stand in this august company, grateful to the city that gave an immigrant boy a chance to build his dream. Dreams come true, as this one did, only in New York.

In building a "unique chain" of supermarkets from humble beginnings on the city's pushcarts, the D'Agostino family had achieved a remarkable success. Certainly, the company had every right to do a little bragging, especially when its history could win the trust and respect of consumers. Patsy and Nicholas's "rags-to-riches" legend had resonated with generations of New Yorkers. But the company could also adapt its narrative to promote a range of agendas, some of which had nothing to do with its founders' own convictions. In 2001, Nick D'Agostino Jr. applied it for political ends, as he partnered with the Food Marketing Institute to promote the abolition of the Estate Tax.[63] FMI used D'Agostino's history, as well as its unique corporate culture, as the centerpiece of political literature that it distributed to legislators.

FMI's mailer followed a formula meant to exploit Americans' reverence for family-owned firms. It began by invoking the company's origins ("a story Hollywood scriptwriters could not have done any better. Two kids—just teenagers—named Nicola and Pasquale D'Agostino set out from their home in L'Aquila, Italy in the mid-1920s to seek their fortunes in the

United States") and followed with an overview of the brothers' climb from the pushcarts and butcher shops of New York to the opening of their first store at 83rd Street and Lexington Avenue.[64] The pamphlet explained how the business initially won customers with its novel idea of offering produce, meat, and dry goods in the same location, with its reputation continuing to grow over the seventy years, as it became "New York's Grocer." This modified version of the D'Agostino "saga"—"a perfect marriage of name, setting, and story line"—highlighted the neighborhood outreach and employment opportunities the stores provided, before reflecting on how their survival was threatened by the dreaded "death tax." The text claimed that with a workforce that embodied "the polyglot world of a major global city; the company makes a special effort to recruit young African American, Hispanic and Latino youngsters for entry-level positions. Many times, it is their first job and the best chance they'll have for a better life."[65]

As the document made clear, under Nick's stewardship, D'Agostino's had made "family" its primary brand, even to the point of merging the form of family with the function of business. It declared, "'Legacy' is an important word in Nick D'Agostino's vocabulary. It is impossible for him to separate the pride he feels about the success of his business from the deeply rooted affection for his family, which includes five children—the third generation of D'Agostinos—all of whom are part of the business." Later, Nick became sentimental as he detailed the many sacrifices that had been undertaken to keep the business alive: "The family is what makes it all worthwhile—the hours, the crises, the constant pressure, the expectations. . . . I just hope we can keep it going." The pamphlet's final paragraphs tried to maximize the reader's sympathies:

> Like most family patriarchs, he [Nick] has created an estate plan to shield his heirs from the potentially devastating effect of the federal estate tax. Trust planning, insurance, legal bills have cost $300,000–350,000, he estimates, to preserve and extend the D'Agostino legacy to future generations. . . . If something were to happen to him, suddenly, Nick D'Agostino wonders what might happen, despite the estate plans he has put in place.[66]

For three decades, D'Agostino's advertising had been quite innovative, seeming to anticipate shifts in the public mood as well as the marketplace. But using Patsy and Nicholas Sr.'s tale of immigrant striving to foreground the business's identity also meant the commodification of private lives for public consumption. While Nicholas, Patsy, and their children took an active role in creating and promoting the company mythology, this strategy was somewhat problematic—as the line between public and private identities became increasingly blurred. The story of their lives had often been adapted for commercial purposes, even after their deaths. Whether advertising scotch, *The New York Times*, or fresh vegetables and prime meats, the use of the grocer's image tried to address cultured tastes even as it spoke of family or ethnicity. Yet had the family narrative become a product as well?

"An Idea Before Its Time": Technology and the Innovation Trap

> For two generations, D'Agostino Supermarket's culture of innovation had allowed it to outfox corporate giants. In the 1980s, as the competition between New York supermarkets intensifies, Nick D'Agostino uses technology to best his rivals. Alas, his vision brings his company into the twenty-first century a decade too soon, as the fashion of "Old World" markets and gourmet groceries wins the day. By the 1990s, the company's efforts to set itself apart may have, instead, set it adrift.

Nick D'Agostino Jr.'s leadership was the subject of a 1982 feature in *Chain Store Age* titled "The American Dream: A Second Generation." The article announced that the "American Dream is alive and well at New York's D'Agostino Supermarkets, and now it's Nicholas D'Agostino's turn to be its guardian."[67] Throughout its history, the company had been able to adopt the latest innovations to fend off larger predators, as its image as a family business often cloaked the progressive nature of its business model. The magazine analyzed how Nick would advance the vision of his father and uncle as he merged their principles with the most modern technology:

> The American Dream that Nick has inherited began 50 years ago, almost at the dawn of the supermarket age itself. His father, Nicholas, and uncle, Pasquale, shared with other innovative grocers a vision that would revolutionize the way customers shopped for food. As former pushcart peddlers and butchers, they knew the routine—women would go from butcher shop to greengrocer to bakery. . . . Riding the supermarket wave to success, the two Italian immigrants captured the American Dream.

The article then described Nick's own version of the next revolution in retailing, which included smaller stores that specialized in gourmet foods and the theory that the "shopper of the 21st century may stay at home in front of a personal computer that's tied directly into a D'Agostino's central distribution center." It concluded with a discussion of telephone tie-ins, personal computers, and cable television as alternatives to the traditional grocery store. *Chain Store Age* declared these innovations have "laid the groundwork for a food-buying revolution as dramatic as the D'Agostinos faced 50 years ago."[68]

Nick was prescient in his comments about the future of New York supermarkets. In the next decade, while superstores like Costco and Walmart would dominate a large segment of the market out in the suburbs, smaller operations that offered fresh produce and gourmet items would win favor with Manhattan consumers. And shopping from a personal computer would become the great retailing advancement of the new millennium (although not in food). But translating these intuitions about the industry's future into tangible, profitable strategies would be one of the great challenges of Nick D'Agostino's career—proving that in business, successful innovation is ultimately dependent on execution and timing.

As CEO, Nick tried to continue the culture of invention that his predecessors had established. The company's decision to invest in computerized and telephone shopping served as another example of how D'Agostino's modest scale, as well as the intimacy of its boardroom, allowed it the flexibility and creative freedom that larger competitors lacked. At a family firm, revolutionary ideas did not have to be filtered through an unwieldy management bureaucracy. And at D'Agostino's, the principals had generally shared a vision of the organization's future, even if they angled for control of it. Moreover, the company's powers of anticipation and its commitment to new ideas had been necessary to its survival in one of the most predatory markets in the country. The adoption of these new technologies also stemmed from the need to cope with the escalating cost of real estate in Manhattan. Reflecting on the quandary of the urban retailer, Nick remarked, "A big concern of mine is how we'll be selling food 20 years from now. . . . Today in Manhattan it takes 10,000 sq. ft. to generate a decent profit. But as real estate and installation costs keep increasing, particularly in densely populated affluent neighborhoods, it becomes impractical to have a store that size."[69] For the next three decades, real estate prices in Manhattan would soar and D'Agostino Supermarkets would grapple with strategies for achieving maximum profitability.

Nick seemed convinced that the incorporation of computer technology into food retailing would elevate the company above its competitors, proclaiming to one interviewer, "Computerized shopping will be here in our lifetime." The integration of barcodes and scanning systems at the checkout lines had already allowed retailers to track the buying habits of their customers even as these innovations had made shopping faster and easier. With the founding of online retailers like Amazon still a decade away, he explained how, in the near future, technology could allow D'Agostino's to fill phone orders out of a central warehouse (at one-tenth the rental cost of a Manhattan store), before delivering them to a shopper's doorstep on a Saturday morning. He suggested that this would signal a return to an earlier era of merchandising: "Food retailers would have come full circle from the day grocers delivered a customer's order."[70]

By the mid-1980s, D'Agostino Supermarkets had launched TeleDag, its own computerized shopping service. With TeleDag, customers would call operators at a switchboard; the operators would then forward their orders via computer to a warehouse in the Bronx. The warehouse would fill orders and send a fleet of delivery vans into Manhattan, and within four hours, the customers would receive their groceries. While the company made expensive capital outlays for the vans and computers, it was projecting significant savings on the costs of real estate, rents and utilities, store design, labor, and packaging.[71] D'Agostino's was careful in its implementation of the program, serving only the Riverdale section of the Bronx before expanding into Upper Manhattan. Each order carried a $5 service charge. Since the orders averaged about $50, the financial success of TeleDag was ultimately dependent on attaining a high volume of orders. Soon after its launch, TeleDag was filling nearly one thousand orders a week—a respectable number—but demand never increased enough to justify the expense of running the service. By the 1990s, TeleDag was deemed a failure and shut down.[72]

When considering the role of computerized shopping in the industry's future, Nick D'Agostino Jr. had explained that a dose of caution was necessary: "You don't want to be 100% ahead of your competition—only about 10%. Too far ahead of one's time is as devastating as too far behind because people have difficulty accepting an idea before its time."[73] One possible explanation for the ultimate failure of TeleDag was that it was a model whose cultural moment had not yet arrived. Though it was technically a phone-ordering service, TeleDag anticipated the advent of online shopping. But internet commerce would not become a common practice in American homes for another decade, and virtual shopping was still primitive. Customers had difficulty with the limitations of the ordering system, as they had to choose their groceries out of a catalog, order them by number and, if buying meat or produce, guess the weight of their order. Operators could only estimate the customer's total grocery bill, leaving the final price to be determined upon delivery.

This type of "blind shopping" was problematic for all shoppers, but especially for those of an older generation. One D'Agostino employee recalled: "One time a woman ordered a sirloin steak and the operator asked her to be more specific, in terms of size, thickness or pounds. She insisted that she wanted the same kind of steak that she always buys."[74] This apparent problem of habit and convenience also suggested the unique psychology of grocery shopping. While most consumers have a list or mental inventory of the basic foodstuffs they need, they tend to select individual pieces of fruit based on their color, smell, heft, and feel. They often pick a steak or a cut of salmon based on the appearance of the meat or fish counter and the item's apparent freshness. Customers may even make impulse buys based on the vibrancy of a store's atmosphere, the appeal of its displays, or the beauty of its interior.

The "revolution" in virtual grocery services was limited by the visceral pleasure consumers derived from doing their own shopping. And as a high-end retailer, D'Agostino's claimed to have customers who were best able to *see* the quality of their produce, meats, and fish. Despite Nick D'Agostino Jr.'s prediction that computerized shopping was the wave of the future, stores that emphasized rustic design features—such as open floor plans, displays of produce in wooden crates, and carts of handcrafted cheeses—that recalled the terminal markets and corner stores of the early twentieth century became the vogue in the 1980s and '90s. Ironically, sophisticated shoppers began to frequent Korean fruit markets and high-end groceries that put them in touch with "Old World" food culture, rather than the abstractions of cyberspace.

In the 1980s, business analysts continued to praise the technologies that had allowed for greater efficiency in food distribution while creating a corresponding decline in prices. Americans now spent only about 14 percent of their disposable income on food (versus 40 percent at the turn of the twentieth century). But while supermarkets offered shoppers nearly 17,000 items, retailers typically made little more than a penny on each dollar of sales.[75] And after the supermarket experienced annual growth in sales of 5 percent for most of the 1980s, this figure slowed to 2 percent by the end of the decade.[76] Companies were further imperiled by a wave of mergers and takeovers (which left surviving retailers with significant debt)

and increased competition from superstores and hypermarkets.[77] When Walmart entered the business in 1988, it instantly became the world's biggest grocer.[78]

Throughout the 1990s, retailers sought technological innovations to increase narrowing profit margins, including in-store satellite radio (which allowed stores to air programming and radio ads targeted at their customers), "cashless" shopping (with the increasing acceptance of credit and debit cards), electronic coupons issued at checkout, and computer ordering systems that easily matched retailers with their suppliers.[79] One of D'Agostino's shrewdest applications of technology occurred in 1990, when it became the first major chain in New York City to incorporate debit cards into the checkout lanes of all twenty-three of its stores.[80] The checkout scanner, viewed as a labor-saving device when it was introduced in the 1970s, allowed retailers to track what customers were buying—information that was especially valuable with the continued segmentation of the marketplace. This technology then enabled the introduction of "smart cards," which rewarded shoppers for their loyalty while providing D'Agostino's with a record of their purchases.[81]

Commentators also began to promote online shopping as the next great innovation in the supermarket industry, arguing that it was far more efficient and about thirty times less expensive to maintain than the phone-ordering systems (such as TeleDag) that had been introduced in the 1980s.[82] They also claimed that online shopping, which required high-volume purchases, would mean larger sales. And as mass marketing became outdated, online retailing would allow grocers a system of "one-to-one marketing" in which they could easily and efficiently document customers' buying habits and send them ads tailored to their demographic profile. One analyst even referred to online shopping as an "electronic mom and pop" store in which supermarkets could reestablish the close relationships they once had with customers while gaining the flexibility to react quickly to changing tastes.[83]

But by the early 2000s, Kozmo, HomeRuns, and Webvan—three of the most highly touted online grocery services—were considered failures while Peapod had achieved only modest success. As with predecessors like TeleDag, these online retailers were unable to attract enough business to recover the costs of building warehouses, purchasing vans and equipment, and maintaining an efficient delivery service. Shoppers were still reluctant to relinquish the immediate, visceral experience of in-store shopping to purchase groceries online. And like many of the era's failed dot-com ventures, online vendors fell into the trap of rapid overexpansion and foolish stock offerings. Yet grocers continued to search for the secret to unlocking the burgeoning tech economy. D'Agostino's, under the influence of Nick's sons Nick III and David, seemed to believe that computer technology would allow the company to maintain its esteemed position among the city's retailers even as it struggled with new competitors. As early as 1989, the company had negotiated with Prodigy Services (a joint venture of IBM and Sears) to establish a personal-computer shopping service, but D'Agostino's eventually scrapped the electronic-ordering plan because of a lack of interest from shoppers.[84] Then, in 1999, D'Agostino's became one of 1,200 stores to join the WebHouse Club network, a division of Priceline.com, a system in which customers would "bid" for grocery staples in an attempt to get the lowest price possible, and then purchase them at the agreed-upon price at their local retailer.[85] However, amid the financial turmoil of the dot.com bubble bursting in 2000, Priceline's value plummeted, leading the company to shut down WebHouse Club.

D'Agostino's made another foray into online retailing in 2001, when it announced a relationship with MyWebGrocer.com.[86] Shoppers in Manhattan would log on to the D'Agostino website, which "plugged into" MyWebGrocer, and order their groceries. They would then pick up their order at their local D'Agostino's or have it delivered for a small fee. The company hoped to correct their previous mistakes with "virtual" shopping ventures by avoiding expensive capital outlays (like central warehouses) and expanding the service on a store-by-store basis.[87] The company argued that this localized version of online shopping was a return to the practice of phone ordering and delivery—once an expected service of New York groceries.[88]

By the mid-2000s, electronic grocery shopping again seemed poised to upend food retailing in Manhattan, as the e-commerce site FreshDirect produced more than $100 million in sales and had more than 250,000 customers in Manhattan, Queens, and Brooklyn.[89] More significantly, 52 percent of New Yorkers surveyed by Zagat claimed that they had ordered groceries online, as opposed to 16 percent the previous year. Some analysts predicted that because of the city's density, its busy residents, and its heavy internet use, New York would soon lead the online food shopping revolution. Still, in 2005, internet sales were only 0.4 percent of the $570 billion grocery business.[90] Many New Yorkers continued to choose the convenience and accessibility offered by the city's many neighborhood stores, preferring to physically select their own apples, tomatoes, and cuts of meat. They also could not afford the space in their relatively small apartments to store the large purchases or packaging often typical of an online grocery service. Meanwhile, city residents continued to complain about the noise and pollution from delivery trucks. Consequently, the fabled revolution in online food shopping would not be actualized for at least another decade.

With the encouragement of Nick's three sons, D'Agostino Supermarkets continued to attempt to harness technology to distance itself from its rivals. As the competition in food retailing intensified, grocers were forced to look for any possible boost in revenues and profit margins. In 2002, to create a more effective system of pricing inventory, the company incorporated a "demand-based management system" with price-optimization software into its operations. Previously, shopkeepers had to estimate the degree to which raising prices would increase profits and affect consumer behavior, based on experience, intuition, and the traditional formula of straight percentage over cost. Most retailers had a relatively limited inventory that allowed this method to be effective. But the new software used algorithms and computer modeling techniques to find "optimum" prices (considering such factors as competitor pricing, location, and product availability) depending on whether a retailer wanted to increase unit sales, dollar sales, or profit margins. With the software, a company like D'Agostino's could predict the elasticity of demand for particular goods at a given store while changing prices on up to a thousand products on a weekly basis.[91] While the adaptation of computer programs to effectively monitor and forecast consumer demand was a logical evolution from the systems that forward-looking companies such as D'Agostino's had been developing since the 1960s, they also meant a continuing shift in the nature of food retailing. Merchants were becoming more cognizant of the desires and habits of their consumers—another indication that old assumptions about mass marketing and the pliability of shoppers were no longer relevant.

The industry itself was continuing to place more stock in data and technology, and less in relationships, unlike the days when Patsy D'Agostino used friendships with dozens of suppliers and salesmen to ensure fair prices, the correct mix of inventory, and recommendations on new products.[92] For D'Agostino's, the adoption of pricing software may have also indicated a shift in philosophies. In previous decades, the company had asserted that its higher prices were a sign of the quality and prestige of D'Agostino stores. Now the company was figuring how it could beat the competition based on elaborate, price-determined calculations.

The Global Apple: New Immigrants and the Ethnic Revival

As immigration transforms the city and the nation once again, a new generation of entrepreneurs become inheritors of the American dream. The earnest labor of Korean grocers wins the admiration of journalists and the loyalty of discerning shoppers. Meanwhile, Italian food and fashion signify high style for young urban professionals, and ethnicity becomes an expression of cultural sophistication, causing Italian Americans to reconsider their own assimilation.

New York's revitalization—especially in the areas of commerce and neighborhood redevelopment—was fueled by the millions who came to the US from Asia, Latin America, the Caribbean, Eastern Europe, and Africa in the wake of the Immigration and Nationality Act of 1965.[93] About one million New Yorkers left the city in the 1970s and '80s, leading demographers to make dire predictions about its future. But over 1.6 million immigrants came to New York during the same period, and by the 1990 census, the population of the nation's largest city had risen to over 7.3 million residents.[94] In the decades that followed, newcomers from the Dominican Republic, Haiti, Korea, India, and China repopulated areas like Washington Heights and Flushing, while reviving the city's working-class neighborhoods and their institutions. In other instances, European émigrés—Irish, Poles, Russians, Ukrainians, and Greeks—invigorated communities by affirming their established character. Astoundingly, by 2010 one in three New Yorkers had been born outside the United States.[95]

These new immigrants effectively changed the face of New York, as well as the nation. By 1990, New Yorkers of European origin were less than half the city's population while immigrants from the Dominican Republic became the city's largest "foreign born" population.[96] Meanwhile, Queens became the most ethnically and racially diverse county in the US, with its Number 7 subway train earning the nickname "the International Express." Of the community where Patsy and Nicholas D'Agostino had bought their first homes, sociologist Nancy Foner wrote, "Elmhurst . . . is a true ethnic mélange, with large numbers of Chinese, Colombians, Koreans, Mexicans, Filipinos, Asian Indians, Dominicans, and Ecuadorians."[97]

While they rehabilitated aging housing stock and resuscitated public and retail spaces, immigrants also gave a massive boost to the city's economy, making up 45 percent of its labor force by the early 2000s. While their contributions were typically in the areas of construction, food service, maintenance, health care, and childcare, this new cohort had much higher levels of education and professional skills than their predecessors, owing to provisions in the US immigration policy (including the establishment of H-1B visas in 1990). As a result, nearly half of New York's immigrants worked in white-collar jobs, including in administrative, finance, and technical positions.[98] Moreover, they applied their sweat equity and ingenuity as entrepreneurs; by the early 2000s, nearly half of the small business owners in New York City were immigrants, predominating in areas such as newsstands, dry cleaners, beauty salons, and small groceries.[99] By the 1990s, Puerto Ricans and Dominicans ran the majority of the city's "bodega" markets, and Koreans became its principal produce dealers. *The Economist* reported that New York was witnessing "the emergence of a new immigrant 'middle class'" that paid taxes and earned solid incomes, leading to the conclusion, "News-stands and bodegas may seem humble, but they are still the stuff from which immigrants' dreams are made."[100]

As with their predecessors, this "new wave" used familiar avenues of commerce to achieve social respectability as well as upward mobility. Their pursuit of the American dream through food retailing echoed the story of the city's Italian population—especially as Latino and Korean grocers were lionized in the press and popular culture. In a 1978 feature, *The New York Times* mused, "All sorts of dreams and contentions revolve around the bodega, the Hispanic grocery store that should be studied as a measure of the long-sought new middle class for the city. The bodega is as rich in mom-and-pop notions of free enterprise as it is in pinto beans, pigeon peas and green bananas."[101] In the 1980s, however, Korean shopkeepers became the most applauded figures of immigrant striving, much like Patsy and Nicholas D'Agostino four decades earlier.[102] The parallels between the Korean and Italian grocers are instructive for a couple of reasons. The revival of the immigrant merchant as a symbol for the virtues of American business—presented in the same metaphorical language as forty years earlier—showed the continued potency of this narrative within the larger culture. At the same time, the shrewd tactics and sheer exertion of ethnic grocers again put the complacency of American society in sharp relief.

The majority of New York's Korean population arrived after 1968, and the community numbered a modest 100,000 by the mid-1980s.[103] But in that time, Korean grocers came to dominate the selling of fresh produce in New York City, which had become a $500 million business.[104] *Money* magazine wrote that along Broadway, from 72nd Street to 116th Street, a fruit stand had been opened on almost every block, leading one sociologist to label the movement a "Korean gold rush."[105] How did the Korean community achieve success with a business model that seemed a relic of a bygone era? Korean merchants, like their Italian predecessors, did have some notable assets, including a pool of relatives and coethnics who could help staff their operations. Extended families were often employed in all aspects of these cramped stores, from purchasing produce at the terminal market at Hunts Point to cleaning and arranging the day's stock of vegetables. The grocers' need for workers in a labor-intensive profession helped create a pipeline that could provide employment for other newcomers. And when the time came for immigrants to open their own shops, they often relied on these same relatives and associates for financial aid. Thus, the network of Korean merchants—like that of the "old wave" of ethnic grocers—became self-propagating, as it doubled and redoubled in size in a few short years.

Journalists depicted Korean shopkeepers as family oriented and industrious. A 1977 article in *The New Yorker* noted that their operations "are often family affairs, and the family often has ten, twenty, or more members."[106] It described the immigrants as "clean" and "thrifty," with an inexhaustible capacity for labor, tending "their goods fastidiously, sorting and arranging them, washing everything washable—there are sinks visible in the back of most stores, and props like hoses and watering cans." The magazine related that they usually visited Hunts Point in the predawn hours to choose the day's offerings. One grocer mused that he did not think the fruit business "would be hard as described . . . Or so heavy physically. But it is steady, and we like the steady."[107]

Because of these apparent virtues, the business press also took a particular interest in the achievements of Korean merchants. *American Magazine* had anointed Patsy D'Agostino a symbol of pure enterprise amid the contented masses of the 1950s in the article "I Found $5,000,000 in a Pushcart." In the late 1970s, conservative pundits routinely criticized the nation's workers for their lack of commitment and lamented the inefficiencies of American industry and government. As Korean grocers began to prosper, some critics anointed them the incarnation of an entrepreneurial spirit that could lift the US out of its malaise—as suggested by the title of one article from *Forbes*, "Breathing New Life into Small Business." *Forbes* reported that through their ambition and enterprise, Koreans had come to own two-thirds of the city's small fruit and vegetable stands by the end of the 1970s, after decades in which "it seemed every produce stand in New York was run by 'Tony.'"[108] *Forbes* depicted the struggles of Jae Ok Kim, a twenty-nine-year-old immigrant with a degree in chemical engineering, who worked sixteen-hour days in the hopes of building a vibrant business.

In the article, Kim displayed the hunger for success that seemed to be lacking in his American-born counterparts, and the ingenuity that defied the corporate mentality of the supermarket industry. While chain supermarkets bought their produce in bulk and were thus focused on the durability of their wares, Korean shopkeepers—the prototypical "little guy"—would buy small batches of overripe fruits and vegetables and then labor to clean and assemble them into attractive arrangements, like greengrocers fifty years before. *Forbes* reported:

> The chain stores feel their impact. "You can literally smell the bargains [at Hunts Point]," says a jealous A&P produce manager—"the almost overripe tomatoes, the bursting peppers that large grocery stores can't use. The Koreans can buy for next to nothing and they have the time to fix them up. You see the old lady in the back of the store scrubbing each carrot."
>
> Sure enough, there in the back of Kim's store you find his mother at the sink, ankle deep in discarded vegetables, picking, peeling, paring, washing to prepare Kim's beautiful displays—pyramids of perfect red apples, ordered rows of carefully moistened spinach and celery and watercress, tempting heaps of basil, dill, mint, and more.[109]

The theme of Korean immigrants as models for Reagan-era America was continued by *Money* magazine: "To native-born Americans discouraged by a languishing economy, the newcomers' success serves as a reminder that the nation's upward-mobility machinery still works—that in neglected backwaters of commerce, hard work and entrepreneurial spirit can pay off." Korean grocers were an anomaly compared with their older counterparts, as an estimated 40 percent had at least a college degree when they arrived in the United States. But many of these newcomers discovered that their credentials did not translate into professional jobs because of discrimination and the language barrier. In an America that valued hard work and earned wealth, but was suspicious of eggheaded intellectuals, one Korean vendor mused, "I threw my Ph.D. in the garbage can and started in the fruit and vegetable business. . . . I had to make money because in America money is everything."[110] Later in the article, Korean merchants became symbols for a type of gladitorial capitalism. *Money* catalogued their tribulations when buying fruit in the early morning hours at the Hunts Point market, from the discriminatory practices of white merchants to the danger of petty criminals lurking in the "dark no-man's land" between loading docks. Despite the beatings and muggings endured by his countrymen, one grocer declared, "Only we Koreans are tough enough to do this business."[111]

Many Koreans made their living selling groceries in the city's underserved, low-income neighborhoods.[112] Yet those merchants who served the city's young, upwardly mobile professionals became fixtures on Manhattan street corners, just as the Tucciarone and D'Agostino families had once ingratiated themselves into the fashionable neighborhoods of Yorkville and the Upper East Side. These groceries were ideal for the city, where consumers lacked cars and adequate living space, and thus shopped daily at their corner stores. The grocers also seemed to anticipate the changing appetites of American food culture, as *Money* magazine wrote that before the advent of the Korean greengrocer, New Yorkers "had resigned themselves to bruised, unburnished apples and artificially ripened tomatoes."[113] Discerning shoppers had tired of standardized, tasteless produce and the anomie of the modern supermarket. Korean grocers—with their meticulous cleaning and trimming of fruits and vegetables, their attractive displays, and their desire to cater to the most nuanced tastes of their customers—represented a return to service. Their markets were ideal for a new generation of "foodies," who were drawn to their selection of fresh and often exotic ingredients, including herbs and vegetables that were essential to Asian cooking.[114] As healthful eating became a priority for many Americans, its adherents were drawn to ethnic cuisines that emphasized vegetables in their dishes, and Korean shopkeepers offered a wide array of ingredients like tofu, sprouts, and Chinese cabbage.

In the stores, customers also had free rein to handle and choose the best tomatoes or pears. For many patrons, the towers of fresh vegetables that were a hallmark of these groceries seemed the very picture of health. For this reason, one must recognize the fundamental role of aesthetics in their success. Their interiors—featuring a colorful array of produce nestled in a spartan, "Old World" setting—had surprising charm for consumers. Consider how *Money* described the markets as sanctuaries—"warm, well-lit, oases in New York City's mean streets," in which entire families "worked together, washing and polishing apples, oranges, eggplants, mangoes and squashes, trimming and refreshing the green and stacking the produce in tempting pyramids on wooden bins that crowded out onto the sidewalk."[115] According to this typification, Korean groceries served as bucolic havens amid the steel and concrete of the city. Using pastoral metaphors to describe their emergence became commonplace, as in a 1977 column from *The New Yorker* which observed that seemingly overnight, "someone sprinkled them over Manhattan" like vegetable seeds, resulting in a "flowering of the Korean greengrocers . . . from a dozen or so, hardly visible, to three hundred strong."[116]

The New Yorker's mawkish portrayal recalled the romanticizing of Italian peddlers earlier in the twentieth century. In the 1943 *New Yorker* profile of Patsy D'Agostino, Mark Murphy had written that the "intimacy" that the men at the Bronx Terminal Market had with fruits and vegetables gave them "a profound respect for things that grow in the earth." He depicted the market itself as a place where the organic mixed with the urban, and then introduced Patsy as a keeper of a premodern ethos through a transcription of his shopping inventory. A partial sampling of Patsy's list read:

> Two boxes artichokes, half bushel Jerusalem artichokes, two boxes extra-select asparagus, two boxes jumbo asparagus, a bushel Lima beans, three bushels string beans, a bushel wax beans, a box celery, cabbage (Chinese), a basket red cabbage, a bushel green cabbage, a crate California carrots ... a basket yellow squash, a basket zucchini squash, five boxes repacked tomatoes, a basket white turnips, two bags yellow turnips, a bushel beet tops, a crate beets, two crates broccoli, a crate cauliflower, a basket chicory, a dozen eggplants, a box endive, a basket escarole, five pounds garlic, five pounds root horseradish, three bunches leeks, a bundle mushrooms (six baskets), a box parsley, a bushel parsnips, six bunches oyster plants, three bushels California peas, a quarter box green peppers (expensive), dozen bunches hothouse radishes, a box rhubarb, four bushels spinach, six bunches scallions, a bunch dill, a crate strawberries, a box red grapes.[117]

In a passage from its 1977 feature, the magazine makes a similar index of the bountiful produce tendered by the Korean shopkeepers:

> Tiers of bushel baskets, cartons, and crude green wooden bins on legs, within the store and as far out in front as the law permits, already held, in no particular order, celery knobs, bundles of leeks, baby carrots, asparagus, snow peas, okra, bean sprouts, endive, hot red peppers, brussels sprouts, rhubarb, parsnips, artichokes, peas, beans, watercress, zucchini, yellow squash, cucumbers (regular, seedless, and pickling), leaf lettuce, Italian parsley, curly parsley, spinach, chicory, escarole, romaine, Boston lettuce, mustard greens, Texas scallions, new potatoes, baking potatoes, mangoes, citrus fruits, peaches, plums, strawberries, cherries, melons, grapes, peanuts, walnuts, and almonds. The artichokes were fat, like those in France; the leeks were thin, also like those in France. The sheaves of lettuce were still wet. All the colors were clear and radiant.[118]

This use of the literary catalog suggested that, by proxy, the grocers themselves were vessels of nature, above the cynicism of modern civilization and the avarice of capitalism.

Korean grocers fit an established pattern for immigrant entrepreneurs—drawn to small business because of barriers to entry in other fields (including their uncertain command of English and lack of capital), and reliant on a network of family and coethnics for employment, labor, and financing. Their story was a notable example of the "American dream" being realized through hard work, sacrifice, and communality. Here, entrepreneurship not only enabled upward mobility, but became a form of cultural assimilation, as evidenced by *Money* magazine's declaration that their achievements illustrated that Lady Liberty's "lamp still burns bright besides the Golden Door."[119] As with their Italian predecessors, mastery of the free market validated Korean merchants' compatibility with American values.

Yet the case of the Korean grocers in the 1970s and '80s also revived a particular image of the immigrant that had faded with time and assimilation. One must recognize the writers' inclusion of the immigrant family, laboring at an honest trade, at the center of this sentimental portrait. Many New Yorkers are on a constant quest to find the "real thing"—perhaps a hidden neighborhood bakery or an obscure restaurant that is untouched by the hype or the fashion that rules the city. For some consumers, the immigrant families that staffed these groceries may have made their establishments seem both authentic and exotic, even if the grocers themselves were sweating away for a few hundred dollars a week. One might even wonder if the figure of the immigrant was part of the sale, for shoppers who had trouble separating the merchant from the merchandise.

In a 1989 interview Nick D'Agostino Jr. outlined the company's plan for holding onto "middle- to upper-income" consumers in an increasingly competitive marketplace that included Korean produce markets, "gourmet groceries," and larger competitors like Food Emporium. Nick promoted the stores' new fresh pastas, craft bakeries, and the high-end packaged goods from the "private label" President's Choice—additions that he hoped would match new developments in the industry.[120] He emphasized that D'Agostino's could also show New Yorkers "what an urban store can be like. Stores don't have to be dirty, and the people can be polite."[121] Nick then discussed his decision to open a series of smaller groceries, called "Fresh Markets," as part of an "attempt to freshen up his stores' appeal." The reporter noted that although D'Agostino Supermarkets had enjoyed a $130 million increase in sales over the previous decade, it felt the "pressure to find new ways of attracting its traditionally upscale customer" who had "the option of shopping at the growing number of Food Emporiums in the city."[122] At the same time, the cost of doing business in New York had caused the closure of several supermarkets while preventing further expansion by established food retailers.[123]

With ventures like the Fresh Market stores, D'Agostino's attempted to rejuvenate the urban supermarket by going "back to the future"—merging aspects of the old-fashioned corner grocery with an evolving food culture. The first Fresh Market—a 5,000-square-foot venture at 30th Street and Second Avenue—eliminated most aisles and gondolas, and placed produce at the center of the store, rather than at its perimeter.[124] One observer compared it to an "overgrown Korean green grocer," remarking, "Fruits and vegetables are displayed in their original crates and cases and the usual aisles are abandoned for a more random arrangement. The entire back area is reserved for a bakery and a butcher counter that sells fresh chickens and homemade sausages. Staple grocery items are thinly stocked."[125] Nick explained that New Yorkers were now "more interested in a store where shopping is easier. They want an emphasis on fresh cut meats, fish and produce, as opposed to half the store being devoted to canned goods and cereals—half of which they don't buy anyway" (because of space limitations in their apartments).[126] D'Agostino's business plan for the Fresh Market concept was to locate the stores in the path of white-collar workers returning from the office. Nick hoped that it could function like the city's delicatessens or bodegas in "underserved neighborhoods." But the Fresh Market model had only a two-year lease in which to endear itself to customers. Nick expressed some doubt about the venture's future, admitting, "we don't even know if we know how to do it. It demands a much higher level of service. And that isn't easy."[127] Within a few years, D'Agostino's did, in fact, scrap the Fresh Market concept.

By Nick D'Agostino's admission, the Korean groceries had pushed his operation to become "more aggressive with its produce merchandising" and to reevaluate its business model.[128] But why had D'Agostino's Fresh Market stores ultimately failed, especially since the company's founders had formative experience with similar formats? It is possible that

D'Agostino's could not match the hours, attention, or care that the immigrant merchants put into their stores—ventures that could essentially make or break their futures in America. Some observers noted that in the hands of D'Agostino's, the spartan greengrocery seemed grim and uninviting, without the anticipated look and feel of a D'Agostino's supermarket. This explanation suggests another reason for the model's failure—D'Agostino's traditional customers rejected the Fresh Markets because they contradicted their expectation of a high-end supermarket. But the issue of expectations points to another potential theory: The hip New York shoppers who viewed Korean grocers as stewards of fresh produce may have viewed D'Agostino Fresh Markets as imitations that lacked authenticity. Despite their roots, the D'Agostinos could not replicate a successful model of the "Old World" immigrant-grocery because they were no longer "Old World" nor immigrants.

While millions of immigrants streamed into cities like New York in the 1980s and '90s, Americans continued to experience the "ethnic revival" that had blossomed in the 1970s. These cultural expressions contradicted accepted wisdom about assimilation, identity, and class in the US. Before the 1960s, many pundits had assumed that, over time, descendants of European immigrants would no longer identify themselves by their heritage as they assimilated into the middle class. As the ethnic revival unfolded among groups such as Irish, Polish, Greek, and Italian Americans, scholars reasoned that it was mainly a reaction against the civil rights movement and federally mandated integration, as well as expressions of anxiety over urban decay, the flagging economy, and the decline of industry. But over the final two decades of the twentieth century, ethnicity increasingly became the province of the educated and the prosperous, as well as the working-class and the immigrant. Middle- and upper-class Americans immersed themselves in the language, culture, and history of their ancestors through movies, food, tourism, music, language, and genealogy.[129] Meanwhile, as ethnic studies programs multiplied on college campuses, some critics wondered if the ethnic renaissance was primarily symbolic, contingent, and based in the pleasures of consumption.[130]

By the 1980s, Italian Americans had climbed into the upper echelon of American society in significant numbers. Publications such as *The New*

York Times decreed "Italian-Americans: Coming into Their Own," trumpeting the success of figures such as Lee Iacocca and Geraldine Ferraro at the highest levels of public life.[131] These pronouncements recalled the media's heralding of figures like Patsy D'Agostino as respectable members of the middle class in the 1950s. In New York, the continued ascension of Italian Americans was visible in finance and corporate management, the legal profession, politics, and academia. In the 1980s, two of New York's largest banks had Italian vice chairmen and, in 1974 and 1991, two of the city's colleges named Italian American presidents. This development culminated in Mario Cuomo's election as governor of New York and Rudolph Giuliani's reign as mayor of New York City from 1993 to 2002.[132]

A century before, social critics had caricatured Italian immigrants as backward and maladjusted to modern society. But by the 1980s, Italian culture became synonymous with style and sophistication—as Italian cuisine, furnishings, and fashion gained favor with upscale consumers while gelato shops, bistros, and pasta-makers became part of yuppie fashion. This rebranding of Italian identity began in the 1960s, when the confluence of postwar Western aid, the Italian government's investment in infrastructure and public welfare, and the emergence of consumer society among young people transformed Italy's economy and made it an exporter of consumer technology, fashion, and film.[133] Soon thereafter, products like Vespa scooters and the films of Federico Fellini became icons of the modern aesthetic. For the next two decades, the fashion of Italy continued to spread across the global landscape. In the late 1970s, *Time* reported on the vogue of Italian boutiques along Manhattan's fashionable Fifth Avenue, which was labeled "La Quinta Strada" by one retailer. According to the article, there were eleven Italian shops along one stretch of the avenue, each earning between a half million and five million dollars in annual profits from sales of designer dresses, shoes, sportswear, handbags, and furnishings.[134] Meanwhile, in the 1980s "Made in Italy" became a privileged label for high-end retailers like Bloomingdale's and Barney's, while Armani suits became the favored uniform for the city's young, upwardly mobile professionals.[135] Historian Donna Gabaccia even posited the presence of a global Italian culture, which she labeled "civiltà italiana," signified by "Milan's sofas or menswear, the leatherware of Fendi, fine Tuscan food, or a generally romantic and hedonistic zest for living. It is a modern, and corporate, version of the urban pleasures of the Italian 'style' of the Renaissance."[136]

A 1988 feature in *The New York Times* sought to explain the vogue of Italian culture in the city, observing that while the US had always been a "magnet for Italians," their influence had recently become "far more pronounced." Examining the scope of Americans' interest in Italy, the *Times* noted that the "deepening awareness of all things Italian is partly a consequence of the travel boom" that had been fueled by the decade's new wealth.[137] But this chic version of Italian culture was also fueled by a new class of émigrés who, according to scholar Lydio Tomasi, were "more educated . . . have more money and . . . a different value system" than the Italians who had come to America between 1880 and 1930. With the continued growth of the global economy, Manhattan had welcomed an expatriate class of businesspeople who created a market for Italian newspapers and magazines, cafes, and restaurants. The Italian Trade Commission reported that the number of Italian companies with offices in New York had doubled since the late 1970s. This cohort was joined by significant numbers of Italian professionals looking to make their fortunes in the US. The *Times* concluded that the city thus remained the center of the "Italianization of America." Journalists had once anxiously described the exoticism of the Italian quarters of Lower Manhattan. Now, as the number of Italian-themed retailers proliferated, one representative of an Italian trade association crowed, "You walk on Madison Avenue and it's like walking on an Italian street."[138]

In a decade in which Americans seemed fixated on wealth and consumerism, Italian culture thus came to signify the "Good Life." Would-be sophisticates were falling in love with Italian furniture, housewares, shoes, and clothing from Benetton, Versace, and Armani. Between 1983 and 1987, the total exports from Italy to the United States doubled from $5.8 billion to $11.7 billion. The *Times* noted, "The Italian people and their way of life have come to epitomize style."[139] The most prominent symbol of the status of Italian culture was the popularity of its gastronomy. On a retail level, it had become common practice for supermarkets to carry olive oil and fresh mozzarella, while a growing legion of Italian specialty shops sold an array of products to more adventurous consumers. Italian food had also emerged as the most popular ethnic cuisine among the nation's "restaurant-goers," but the version that took hold in the 1980s was decidedly European in nature, as critics labeled it the new "haute cuisine."[140] Restaurants were introducing dishes like risotto and tiramisu, while American cooks were discovering sun-dried tomatoes and balsamic vinegar. In still another piece on the burgeoning Italian restaurant scene in New York City, the *Times* reported that many proprietors believed that the vogue of Italian fashion was making their food fashionable. One owner claimed,

"If you look at the whole Italian restaurant boom, it grew along with the popularity of Armani and designers like him. They gave a better image, a chic image, to all things Italian."[141]

In the 1980s and '90s, D'Agostino's tried to offset competition from the next wave of immigrant entrepreneurs—the Korean grocers—with an upgraded version of the produce mart. In advertising for these "Fresh Markets," the company had referenced its origins in the business. However, in an era in which Italian culture was suddenly in vogue, D'Agostino Supermarkets never fully capitalized on its ethnicity nor fashioned itself as an Italian grocery. In appealing to consumers' desire for the authenticity and artisanship of the Old World, the company did inevitably play into the ethnic revival. But management tried to communicate a sense of family and connection to New York, rather than trumpet their Italian identity. While D'Agostino's may have referenced its history in creating a public image, its heritage did not influence its business practices—it did not promote itself as a vendor of Italian products such as olive oil, imported cheeses, sausages, or homemade pastas, although its stores offered many of these specialties because of their popularity with high-end shoppers.

How does one account for the muting of ethnicity at D'Agostino's? The chief architect of the company's advertising, Jo Foxworth, asserted that despite their history as immigrants, the D'Agostinos "never positioned themselves as ethnic at all," adding, "New York has been the focus of everything they have done."[142] Stephen D'Agostino was critical of the notion that the ethnic or family business had any cachet with customers: "I think you better give the customer what the customer wants and expects. Give to them in the best possible way, the fairest price, consistently over time and then that person doesn't care if you have two heads, if you sleep with dogs and cats."[143]

Nick D'Agostino Jr. gave a more nuanced view of the Italian question, particularly as his administration put the company's history at the forefront of its public identity. He mused, "I think the family culture was much more important than the Italian culture. Now, someone might say, 'Yeah, well Italians are very family oriented.' In that sense . . . you can never divorce things totally one from the other. But I think the family culture was more important to us than the Italian background." He attributed his generation's reluctance to capitalize on ethnicity to choices his parents made, raising their family in a "melting pot" neighborhood: "They [his parents] affiliated with a lot of Italians but never *just* with Italians. . . . They never lived in an Italian ghetto and when we were brought up we were brought up in Queens. . . . We had Irish, Polish, Italian, Russian, Greek, all living on the same block, all kids playing with each other."[144] Over the course of generations, members of the family would continue to assimilate themselves into the suburbs of New York and Connecticut.

The theme of Italians' integration into the middle and upper classes, after decades of trailing other immigrant groups in educational and professional achievement, has been featured in studies by academics such as Nancy Foner and Richard Alba.[145] Alba wrote that the "ultimate test of assimilation" for any ethnic group was their rate of intermarriage, and by this measure "the growing integration of Italians with the American mainstream is beyond question." He added that while only about one-quarter of Italian Americans born before World War II had "mixed ancestry," most young Italians were now growing up in "ethnically mixed families" "outside of ethnic communities."[146] Yet as Alba examined the decline of the traditional structures (neighborhood, ethnic societies, religion) that once defined cultural identity, he noted the continued resilience of ethnic expressions in the contemporary lives of Italians. Alba, along with scholars Mary Waters, Micaela di Leonardo, Peter Kivisto, and Donald Tricarico, described how ethnicity has become malleable to circumstance, often private and symbolic while remaining crucial for identity formation for middle-class Americans.[147]

From this perspective, D'Agostino Supermarkets was trading in reconstituted ethnic symbols through its narrative and its identification with family and the city. This sublimated version of ethnic commerce was part of the company's appeal. When Patsy and Nicholas D'Agostino shared their tale of immigrant struggle with journalists, they were incorporated into a larger narrative of American opportunity. When Nick D'Agostino Jr. and Jo Foxworth used the family's history in advertising, they were offering a sense of authenticity and expertise to an increasingly skeptical buying public in a changing city. Yet in venerating their "founder" Nicholas D'Agostino Sr. and in celebrating his journey as an immigrant, one had to consider whether the company could reference its ethnicity because its principal ethnics had passed on. Moreover, one might wonder if D'Agostino's failed to acknowledge that in late twentieth-century New York, Italian culture, style, and food had come to represent the height of sophistication because it had come so far from its humble origins.

"Whole Paycheck": New York in the Age of the High-End Supermarket

In the final decade of the twentieth century, D'Agostino's struggles with a new breed of competitor who threatens the company's lofty reputation. Market trends and a more demanding shopper force many supermarkets to go upscale or go out of business. The most successful operations merge the sensibilities of gourmet shops, natural foods co-ops, and "Old World" groceries. Primary among these is the Whole Foods chain, which becomes the industry leader and new bully on the block.

At a party in the 1960s, when Stephen D'Agostino was asked to name his company's main competition, he answered it was "ourselves." Throughout the 1960s and '70s, D'Agostino Supermarkets was able to stay above such high-end rivals as Sloan's, Bohack, and Gristede's, as well as larger chains like A&P and Shopwell, because of the quality of its inventory and the magnitude of its reputation. By the late 1980s, D'Agostino's began to lose customers to gourmet challengers like Food Emporium and Citarella, which recognized the growing dissatisfaction with traditional food retailers. While these upstarts forced the company to reevaluate its retailing strategy, most were modest operations and thus did not endanger its market share. But soon D'Agostino's found itself facing competition from across the economic spectrum—as a new wave of elite supermarkets threatened to annex its upscale customer base while the arrival of "big-box" superstores cut into its profits.

New Yorkers, particularly those in Manhattan, had long enjoyed a reputation as the most discerning and demanding shoppers in the US. Throughout the 1980s and '90s, the contest between New York's food retailers grew even more cutthroat.[148] Smaller "gourmet groceries" like Dean & DeLuca, Balducci's, and Citarella tested D'Agostino's claim on upscale consumers with their array of fine produce and expensive packaged and prepared foods.[149] In the mid-1990s, independents Morton Williams, a nine-store upscale "co-op," and Fairway joined this fray.[150] Fairway soon emerged as a premier retailer in the city, first with its 10,000-square-foot store on West 74th Street and Broadway and then with a 35,000-square-foot warehouse at West 133rd Street in Harlem. One of the owners of Fairway called it "a new breed of food retailing entrepreneur who wants to go back to the basics."[151] Once a modest produce shop, Fairway now offered a premium selection of fruits, vegetables, cheeses, coffees, pastas, and fresh bread for relatively low prices—which attracted legions of food lovers and bargain hunters throughout the New York area. *The New*

York Times called Fairway a "larger and more price-conscious" version of a fancy foods store.[152]

The owners of Fairway consciously rejected the conventional supermarket model by devoting 70 percent of its space to fresh food and 30 percent to dry goods—the opposite of the traditional "supers." Taking a dig at his neighbor on Broadway, Fairway's Joe Fedele commented, "Since we're not a full-line supermarket, D'Agostino's is basically left to sell what we don't carry."[153] By design, Fairway provided a "marketplace atmosphere" in a warehouse that it crowded with open bins and pyramids of produce—comparable to an "urban farm stand."[154] Echoing sentiments once expressed by Patsy and Nicholas D'Agostino, one of the store owners explained, "A pile of fresh oranges is a beautiful thing in and of itself. We don't put dollars into frills or showy displays like some of the downtown markets."[155] In the 1990s, the appeal of this rustic aesthetic was also signaled by the proliferation of open-air farmers' markets throughout the city, leading *The New York Times* to muse, "The biggest ones, at Union Square, Grand Army Plaza in Brooklyn and the World Trade Center, seem as permanent as skyscrapers." These "greenmarkets," which allowed about two hundred farmers to sell their wares directly to shoppers, were especially popular with chefs, one of whom remarked that at the markets "you can feel the purity. There is no commercial marketing. It's all from the gut."[156]

Even as smaller, high-end groceries gained popularity in New York, the city began to welcome a new generation of large retailers. Traditionally, the inherent difficulties of doing business in Manhattan—including high rents and the lack of available retail space—had protected the city's established merchants from chain stores. One consultant commented, "New York has always been a sort of poison pill. The barriers to entry here are so high that you really have to look long and hard at the bottom line." Even into the late 1990s, Nick D'Agostino Jr. expressed confidence that the localism of the New York marketplace would continue for the foreseeable future, remarking, "I don't think the big guys want to come in and waste their time."[157] While New Yorkers enjoyed a wide selection of epicurean delights at specialty shops like Zabar's, they did not have access to big-box discounters like Walmart or Costco.

Throughout the 1990s, however, chains such as Tower Records; Bed, Bath & Beyond; Virgin Records; Staples; T.J. Maxx; and Barnes & Noble (and, later, Target and Home Depot) opened superstores that threatened the city's established book and record shops, clothiers, and department stores.[158] Why, after decades of failing to conquer New York, were big-box outlets successfully "invading" the city? By the 1990s, suburban mall development had slowed because of rising rents and a lack of vacant land, while American cities were enjoying a renaissance as millions of young professionals returned to the neighborhoods their parents had once rejected. Retailers also saw New York as an untapped market that could provide their companies with instant name recognition from consumers and Wall Street investors. Mayor Rudolph Giuliani, who saw national chains as a means of ensuring long-term economic stability, began to lobby for changes to zoning laws to make it easier for big-box operations to conduct business in the city. *New York* magazine speculated that the mayor's prodevelopment campaign could either "revolutionize the way the city does business" or "destroy the mom-and-pop urban élan that distinguishes New York from so much of the rest of the country."[159] Within a decade, both would come to pass, despite the proposal's defeat.

The emergence of retail superstores throughout New York helped pave the way for a new wave of deluxe supermarkets, such as Whole Foods' 58,000-square-foot complex at Columbus Circle. Its impact led *New York* magazine to declare that the city had entered the "Age of the High-End Supermarket Chain."[160] Executives who had once believed that the "suburban" model was ill suited for the city now saw the success of Whole Foods as "proof that you can plop down a 50,000-square-foot store in Manhattan and be successful."[161] Whereas a 10,000-square-foot space had once been the norm for local groceries, the "megastore" became the latest trend in food retailing, often corresponding to neighborhood gentrification. It seemed as if those transplants who had deserted the cul-de-sac for the dynamism of urban living had infected the city with suburban notions of scale and space. As new lofts and mixed-use housing developments emerged downtown and in the decaying commercial districts of Lower Manhattan, retailers took advantage of cheap rents and plentiful space to open several new supermarkets, leading *The New York Times* to remark that downtown "seemingly overnight [has] become a mecca for food shopping."[162] On the heels of its other Manhattan successes, Whole Foods built a three-story, 50,000-square-foot shopping center on 14th Street in Union Square, a spot that had been notorious for illegal drugs in the 1970s. Trader Joe's—a grocery chain whose private label products earned it a devoted following—also planted a large outlet in Lower Manhattan, in an area that had once been dominated by industry.[163]

Some observers worried that the supermarket business was suffering the same fate as the city's book trade, wherein Barnes & Noble and Borders used their massive selection of titles and their cafes to sweep away established booksellers (before suffering their own decline at the hands of online retailers).[164] It did seem plausible that local groceries would survive, since New Yorkers were ruled by issues of time and convenience, did most of their shopping on foot, and were extremely loyal to neighborhood shopkeepers. One analyst speculated that D'Agostino's and its peers could "co-exist" with the new megastores because their locations, product mixes, and prices appealed to traditional customers.[165] High rents and bureaucracy were also likely to limit the ultimate "suburbanization" of the city's food retailing. But as New York's established merchants struggled with competition from ethnic and gourmet groceries, as well as from the new high-end superstores, critics began to question the fundamental assumptions of the traditional supermarket. Since the 1940s, most retailers had placed their faith in "all-in-one" self-service operations that offered brand-name packaged goods, frozen foods, prewrapped produce and meat, and a limited stock of cleaning products and toiletries. The conventional "super" found its embodiment in "Mrs. Consumer," an icon of the 1950s and '60s who signified the belief that the American shopper had singular needs and desires—all of which could be met by the supermarket. One industry publication mused, "It used to be simple. Grocery marketers, like all retailers, held fast to the notion that success meant being 'all things to all people.' This weary axiom also implied that consumers' needs were basic and predictable, and could be easily satisfied without much imagination on the retailers' part."[166]

Since the 1960s, cultural diversity and changing lifestyles had gradually called the wisdom of mass marketing into question. One analyst declared, "There's no longer a creature called 'the typical consumer.'"[167] Ryan Mathews, a prominent business journalist, opined, "One-stop shopping was a revolutionary weapon, but the lesson of war is that one generation's weapon is another generation's folly."[168] Mathews later extended this argument, musing that "For nearly five decades, the supermarket flourished, fueled by the creation of an artificial demand for branded products on the part of a diverse consumer base that yearned desperately for the veneer of homogeneity."[169] By the 1980s and '90s, however, consumers demanded a much wider selection of products, from types of mustards and olive oils to brands of soft drinks. Nick D'Agostino Jr. remarked that previously "you didn't have Diet Coke let alone the fifteen different varieties of Coca-Cola that you could buy . . . it was the question of what size bottle you would buy, not whether you were going to buy a different variety."[170] Within twenty years, larger supermarkets would routinely stock forty thousand to fifty thousand items.[171]

But variations in the habits and expectations of shoppers also challenged retailers like D'Agostino's, as established formulas no longer matched the lives of contemporary Americans. As working professionals grappled with demanding schedules and irregular mealtimes, the number of families who opted for "take-out" over home-cooked meals continued to rise.[172] D'Agostino's had built its reputation as the store for New Yorkers who enjoyed cooking, especially if their menus included a choice steak or roast. In the 1990s, traditional supermarkets discovered that their primary competition was often from restaurants rather than other retailers. One critic observed that the supermarket was "becoming more like a takeout restaurant,"[173] while another declared, "Home cooking may be on the verge of obsolescence."[174] Upscale supermarkets like Whole Foods began to offer food halls and restaurant-style kitchens, staffed by chefs—renovations that were difficult for the urban retailer to match.

In the last two decades of the twentieth century, retailers struggled to serve the multiplicity of classes, tastes, ages, and ethnic groups that now populated the marketplace.[175] Analysts speculated that the food trade seemed to be evolving into two basic formats that were each distinguished by their physical design.[176] Volume dealers like Walmart and Sam's Club began to take over the rural and suburban regions with low-priced superstores that offered a wide array of home and dry goods in a department store setting.[177] Meanwhile, upscale gourmet markets became preeminent in more prosperous urban neighborhoods.[178] The separation of food retailing into two ruling models implied a larger divide within American society, with the vaunted middle-class losing numbers and authority. One executive observed, "There is a two-tier market today, with the middle-income group being decimated. There are people who want variety and quality and will pay for it and those who are interested primarily in price."[179] Even if conventional supermarkets continued to be a presence in American cities, they were no longer the leaders in terms of influence or visibility. Meanwhile, their decline highlighted the difficulties of poorer residents, who were notoriously underserved by the industry. In 1997, *The New York Times* reported that the city "has one of the country's widest disparities in supermarket availability between affluent and poor neighborhoods."[180]

In the 1990s, D'Agostino Supermarkets began to grapple with the changing demographics of the city and the evolving demands of the marketplace. According to Nick D'Agostino Jr., in the 1960s and '70s, the company shared the "top of the pyramid" with Gristede's, while A&P and Sloan's catered to the next level of customers with "low-priced, moderate quality stores." Nick recalled that neighborhoods like the Upper West Side once included many "moderate-income people" like firemen and teachers, but "buildings have been renovated [and] gentrification has taken place." He observed that in contemporary New York, the "middle- to lower-income segment . . . no longer exists," and that there were "no low-priced supermarkets in the city of New York."[181] He related that with the high cost of real estate, heavy competition, and "different distribution of the business," merchants had been forced to pursue the "high-priced market area." D'Agostino's had few competitors for the "prestige" segment of the market for much of its history, and thus had "an easy way of differentiating ourselves in the past." Nick lamented that with most of New York's major retailers targeting high-end consumers, it was increasingly difficult for a supermarket to "differentiate itself" and that his stores no longer had the same assumed "sophistication."[182]

The segmentation of the market and the vogue of the gourmet grocery pointed to a growing counterrevolutionary trend in food retailing—a return to the pre-supermarket past. One analyst claimed that the future of the business seemed to reside in the strategies of the prewar era: low-priced superstores resembled the discount warehouses that preceded the modern supermarket while smaller, high-end shops offered nonpackaged produce, bulk foods, service meat and fish counters, and bakeries in the fashion of the old corner markets.[183] Another journalist observed that some retailers "are looking back to a time before conventional stores became the norm, when customers were loyal to small neighborhood grocery stores that put a high priority on service."[184] In New York, many consumers were even dividing their shopping tasks—purchasing soap, paper products, and canned goods at traditional supermarkets, produce and meat at gourmet groceries, and the evening meal at Whole Foods.[185]

Rising consumer expectations also frustrated D'Agostino's ability to compete in this evolving marketplace, as the company's proven strategies seemed to lose their effectiveness. Nick observed that the "specialty store" (i.e., Food Emporium, Citarella, Fairway) had begun to assume the role of supermarkets. When price had been more of a "competitive issue" and supermarkets dominated the economic landscape, a high-end grocery like D'Agostino's could charge their customers a premium in exchange for promises of better quality and service. By the 1990s, a growing segment of New Yorkers began to assume a distinction between specialty stores and traditional supermarkets. According to Nick, consumers began to see D'Agostino's "as a supermarket not a specialty store" and, despite its previous reputation, "not having as fresh a product, not having as sophisticated a product."[186] But as a supermarket, D'Agostino's was also supposed to have a full stock of meat, produce, canned goods, and household items such as toilet paper at a fair price. As management attempted to upgrade its merchandise, its traditional customers often expected the same convenience, pricing, and variety as a conventional super—all of which moderated D'Agostino's ability to compete with its high-end rivals. Nick admitted that its main challenge was to get the shoppers who "come to my store for the soap and the toilet paper" to buy more premium merchandise. Nick also lamented that contemporary food retailing had become "a struggle," as D'Agostino's was caught between shoppers' contradictory demands.[187]

Even as upscale independents won the loyalty of discerning shoppers, many of New York's local groceries were threatened by the arrival of the Whole Foods Market chain. The prominence and profitability of Whole Foods represented a cultural moment, as well as the advent of a successful business model. One major shift that retailers had to address was consumers' growing appetite for fresh fruit and vegetables, which more than doubled between the late 1960s and the early 1990s (to 300 pounds per capita).[188] When Nicholas and Patsy D'Agostino were making their fortunes in the 1950s and '60s, meat had been the most significant category in the supermarket; now shoppers of a certain class were indicating that a produce section that offered quality and diversity was a "primary consideration" in their choosing a place to shop.[189] One leading retailer argued that perishables and produce were becoming the best means of "differentiating" a store from its competitors, especially as health and convenience became customers' two leading objectives in food purchases.[190] By the mid-1990s, many stores carried over three hundred different produce items, even as annual employee turnover in that department neared 30 percent.[191]

Retailers also had to engage customers who were better educated about the nutritional content and risks of the food sold by supermarkets. Shoppers could access much more information—via labeling, government and academic studies, and online research—than their predecessors, and they had grown up in an era in which it was socially acceptable to question authority. Contemporary consumers were thus likely to hold grocers accountable for environmental, health, or safety issues. One D'Agostino employee related that the "biggest concerns of D'Agostino customers are nutrition and health," adding that shoppers believed that they had the power to control these factors.[192] The demand for better produce also stimulated the organic food movement, leading farmers to refine their methods and management to allot greater shelf space for organics. Reflecting on the "mainstreaming" of organic produce from its origins in the counterculture, Nick D'Agostino Jr. commented that in the past "it was normally of a very poor quality, very ugly looking, little availability, and then very expensive." He concluded that the consumer "almost had to be an extremist to want to eat these things," but as "demand for this product increased, more and more people committed their farms to growing better foods, more and more manufacturers recognized that they had to use less preservatives, less additives."[193]

By the 1990s, stores that displayed a "green" ethic became fashionable. Offering a wide variety of organic and exotic produce, hormone-free dairy, free-range cattle and poultry, Whole Foods Markets represented both the culmination and the commercialization of the movement for pure food. With its successful marketing and acquisition strategies, Whole Foods became the brand equivalent of virtuous shopping for many middle- and upper-class Americans. But the company offset its version of the health food diet with a banquet of imported cheeses, choice meats, and rich desserts—thus rejecting the asceticism that seemed to marginalize the macrobiotic co-ops and health food shops of the 1970s. As a result, it was able to capture the gourmet food movement that had been growing in American kitchens since the early 1960s. Part of the genius of Whole Foods was the chain's ability to weave together these two strands—the natural and the epicurean—in a format that was appealing to the middle and upper tiers of the market.

The original Whole Foods had been founded in Austin, Texas, in 1978 by John Mackey, a twenty-five-year-old college dropout, and a handful of his socially conscious friends as a modest health food store. Over the next decade, the Austin-based company became a regional power. But Whole Foods was not the only retailer to recognize the developing market for natural and gourmet foods, as Bread & Circus and Fresh Fields emerged in the Northeast, Mrs. Gooch surfaced in the South, and Andronico's gained prominence in the West. Mackey gradually bought out his competition and by 2005, Whole Foods had amassed 166 stores with $4 billion in annual revenues.[194] Whole Foods was thus able to make itself the preeminent brand for natural foods and gourmet shopping, while becoming a symbol for an entire development in American food culture.

In an industry in which most major retailers—with the notable exception of Walmart—were facing shrinking profits and stagnant growth, Whole Foods posted impressive financial numbers. In the new millennium, Americans were spending well over $400 billion a year for food at nearly 35,000 supermarkets. But since the mid-twentieth century, the real cost of food had fallen by two-thirds, and Americans were spending only 6 percent of their total income on groceries (a decrease of 11 percent from the 1950s). The grocery industry had traditionally suffered slender profit margins, but contemporary grocers were now making less than a penny of profit on every dollar spent. In the mid-2000s, Whole Foods' profit margin was triple that figure, and its stores' annual sales-per-square-foot figures were double the industry average.[195] The company specialized in prepared meals, which had now become socially acceptable for busy professionals to serve. With its successful marketing of perishables and prepared foods (which made up two-thirds of its sales) and organic produce (which carried prices that were between 40 and 175 percent more than comparable items), Whole Foods reaped the benefits of selling inventory that carried a far higher premium than its competitors' stock.[196]

A major component of Whole Foods' success was its ability to sell the image of pure food through skilled marketing and in-store design. Displays of the stores' organic produce, for example, often contained biographies and photos of friendly local farmers, while wedges of cheese and handmade pastas were accompanied by histories of the traditional European artisans who had crafted the products. Whole Foods also incorporated and distilled the aesthetic of the pushcart and Korean markets for a mass audience, as produce was often stacked in four-foot-high pyramids, "suggesting an abundance so rich that a farmers' market must have just parked at the store for the day." One critic remarked that the stores' use of dramatic lighting "illuminates heirloom tomatoes as if they were heirloom diamonds."[197]

At the beginning of the new millennium, Whole Foods targeted New York as its next frontier—a move that had grave consequences for retailers like D'Agostino's. Whole Foods opened its first location in the Chelsea neighborhood in 2001, before opening a glamorous superstore at Columbus Circle (a venture that was soon making $1 million in weekly revenues). The grand opening of the D'Agostino's on 20th Street, at the middle-class housing developments of Stuyvesant Town and Peter Cooper Village, had signified its rising fortunes in the postwar era. Now, Adam Gopnik of *The New Yorker* asserted that the new Whole Foods superstore was an icon of "our own time and place" in an environment "where organic prepared foods and organic raw foods are laid out in an abundance that puts every other food hall in this city (or any other) to shame."[198] Gopnik noted how Whole Foods embodied both the politics and the fashion of contemporary Manhattan, as the store's offerings were all "insistently virtuous. Farm-raised, 'naturally fed,' uncaged, honest, healthy."[199]

In March 2005, Whole Foods opened its third store, a three-story 53,000-square-foot model at Manhattan's Union Square. The company also broke ground on stores in trendy TriBeca (Manhattan) and Park Slope (Brooklyn) and had plans for a 66,000-square-foot complex in the East Village.[200] The company's successes led Dave Lannon, the president of Whole Foods' North Atlantic region, to boast, "There's a vacuum. The regular supermarkets in New York are pretty crappy. And the gourmet sector is dead. . . . There's the legends, like Zabar's, which still has great prices for cheese, and Citarella does a great job. But there's not a lot of growth there. With our store and Fairway now, why would you overpay for the same product in a small gourmet store?"[201]

In 2005, *The New York Times* observed that "Legions of New Yorkers" were "paying higher prices and traveling greater distances to shop at Whole Foods, Citarella, Fairway, and other high-end groceries throughout the city, shunning traditional supermarkets that they regard as dirty, drab and limited in their offerings."[202] The *Times* noted that chains like D'Agostino Supermarkets and Gristedes* were suffering from declining sales and losing shares of the market, leading one retailer to speculate that "specialty stores" had cost New York's established supermarkets almost one-third of their business over the past several years.[203] Meanwhile, D'Agostino's ability to maintain the allegiance of local shoppers was being hindered by the issue of choice. Not only could consumers now buy their groceries at a range of outlets, from drugstores to hypermarkets, but they had also become more mobile. A 1997 report from the Manhattan borough president's office reported that 23 percent of New Yorkers shopped for food outside the city.[204] Nick D'Agostino Jr. related that in the past "if a guy opened a store near you, he was a competitor, if he opened it fifteen blocks away it didn't make any difference. That's not as true anymore." Now, New Yorkers were more likely to drive to 40,000-square-foot superstores outside the city and bring home products like detergent and toilet paper. According to Nick, this situation was exacerbated by consumers who no longer wanted "to go to the store when the store is open, they want to go to the store when they feel like it."[205] The customer's ability to transcend local geography, along with expectations of convenience and immediate gratification, would only intensify with the rise of cybershopping.

New York's traditional supermarkets certainly suffered from the continued escalation of rents and the stigma of being undesirable tenants for residential properties. But changes in consumer behavior seemed to play the most significant role in the flagging status of the "super." The

---

* The chain eliminated the apostrophe from its name in the 1990s as part of a rebranding campaign.

Times noted that as New Yorkers placed a higher value on healthier lifestyles—"changing their eating habits from processed and prepackaged foods to organic produce and meats and fresh ingredients"—they were shopping less at "traditional supermarkets."[206] One executive claimed that the grocers' failure to anticipate consumers' desire for natural foods and organics had resulted in a marketplace "littered" with smaller, independent retailers. And as consumers "in the know" became devotees of local produce markets, butcher shops, and bakeries, as well as gourmet groceries, established supermarkets struggled with their own fallen reputation. Celebrated journalist and "foodie" Bill Buford remarked, "The virtue of being in a city like New York is that it's a market city, and you can get the best of anything. The supermarkets here are constrained by space and by the unspoken understanding that the only people who go there are losers."[207]

At the end of the millennium, D'Agostino Supermarkets faced an identity crisis, as management wondered how the stores could recoup their status and market share. In the 1950s and '60s, D'Agostino's had become a preeminent name with New York shoppers because of its association with fine meats—the central component of upscale food culture in that period. Now the company chased rivals that had mastered the essentials of the new "foodie" ethos—which included natural, gourmet, and ethnic foods. By the late 1990s, D'Agostino's also had the oldest customer base in New York City. It desperately needed to win over a new generation of consumers, including the many young professionals who were coming to Manhattan to make their fortunes.

In the postwar era, middle-class strivers and their young families had fueled the business's growth. In the 1960s and '70s, D'Agostino's had capitalized on the city's growing cohort of white-collar professionals who were as enamored with life in Manhattan as the company was. In the 1980s, D'Agostino's had made itself synonymous with the city's yuppie culture and nascent gentrification. Although the latest cohort of consumers seemed similar in class and kind, it differed in its expectations and attitudes. With gentrification and the economic climate of the 1990s and early 2000s, D'Agostino's confronted a New Yorker who was "paying a lot of money to live there. A lot more than they paid in the past," who therefore carried a healthy sense of entitlement. Nick admitted that "you have new generations moving into the city and . . . many of them don't appreciate how long you've been around and what commitments you've made to the city."[208]

In the past, D'Agostino Supermarkets had capitalized on its sterling reputation; now Nick D'Agostino Jr. complained about the "mystique" of newer, high-end competition. Whereas customers might come into his stores with a shopping list looking for necessities, the clientele at Whole Foods were saying, "Okay, what are you going to sell me? And I'll buy that!" Shopping thus became "a field trip, something exciting they're doing. So, one is shopping for necessities and the other is shopping for luxuries." For a previous generation of consumers, Nick added, luxury meant "better quality for a few more cents," and D'Agostino's had put this calculus at the center of its business model. Yet as suppliers and distributors had become more adept at providing retailers with good produce and meats on a consistent basis, they effectively leveled the playing field on quality. Thus, for D'Agostino's, it became "much more difficult to say, 'I'm selling a head of lettuce that's better than somebody else's piece of lettuce.'" Nick claimed that their smaller size gave the specialty grocers an advantage because they could more easily introduce unique items while a chain like D'Agostino's had to supply several stores and educate a large customer base. This was an ironic turnabout, as once D'Agostino's had used its own flexibility to gain an advantage over chain behemoths.

As issues of quality evened out, "uniqueness" became the shopper's primary means of distinguishing between competitors. Nick D'Agostino Jr. argued that even if his stores had the same offerings as the new breed of high-end retailers or the city's popular "Greenmarkets," customers believed that these other retailers had a better product because of image. Many consumers assumed that the produce sold at farmers' markets was superior because of their rustic atmosphere. But in many cases, D'Agostino's had gotten its fruits and vegetables from the same suppliers. Nick complained that "the mystique of being able to buy from a guy on the stand is still there," and even if that vendor was selling inferior merchandise at a higher price, "the customer will be overjoyed with it . . . they'll buy it like crazy. . . . The consumer perceives it to be fresher, the consumer perceives it to be higher quality even though it isn't." He also intimated that New York shoppers of the new generation were more susceptible to the aura of gourmet retailers than their parents and grandparents had been. He observed:

> They want to go into a store where they can smell the coffee beans being roasted and then ground for them. Now, are they any better coffee beans than the ones we sell? Probably not. . . . But the customer, [with] the smell of the coffee beans, buys that coffee. Now that they've paid twice as much for that coffee in the specialty store as they spent in our store, you've got to believe that's going to taste better because they can't afford to have it not taste better.[209]

As the company's prestige began to flag, it experimented with several strategies to regain its stature. In addition to its experiments with technological and online shopping services, D'Agostino's tried to capitalize on some of the latest innovations in food retailing. With the recent explosion of urban cafes, several supermarkets had installed coffee bars in their stores to create a chic atmosphere and boost sales of higher-margin coffee products.[210] In 1996, D'Agostino's opened its first "Coffee Works" at one of its Manhattan locations.[211] Despite the company's high hopes (and a large capital investment), its version of the coffee bar concept failed—as New Yorkers stayed loyal to their neighborhood cafes. To compete with more prestigious rivals, it also added gourmet prepared meals, a greater variety of produce, and an upgraded private label program. Yet even as it adapted to evolving tastes, D'Agostino Supermarkets continued to suffer from diminished status. Despite management's best efforts, upscale consumers seemed unconvinced of the comparable quality and stature of its stores, leaving Nick to conclude: "They're not going to believe it, so we just leave it alone."[212]

D'Agostino's also hoped that its new internet shopping service would attract busy young professionals, especially those with families. But even this investment in online retailing seemed to represent a surrendering of the city's upscale consumers. Instead, Nick D'Agostino Jr. intimated that the business now sought price-conscious customers who would buy in large volume and who valued convenience above everything else: "I think what we're trying to do is attract that customer who is a larger buyer. . . . We're trying to attract younger people, families and recognizing that our quality and our pricing is competitive." Once, company advertising had confidently advised: "If there's no D'Agostino near you, move." Now, Nick observed that New Yorkers who wanted to go to specialty stores were welcome to take on the inconvenience of long bus or car trips and bringing their haul across town, while D'Agostino's provided "neighborhood service—we deliver it to your house, we're there to take care of you, we're there when you want to be there and you don't have to plan to spend half a day to go shopping."[213]

By the late 1990s, one of the hallmarks of D'Agostino's identity—its skilled use of advertising—fell into disuse. The company's leadership in marketing had begun to diminish over the previous decade, as other supermarkets adopted "slick, creative" images that resembled "consumer product ads."[214] Once corporations like Dole or Swanson had dictated the style and content of grocery ads, which resulted in copy that was focused on price and information. But as retailers gained independence from vendors and competed for customers who were media savvy and ruled by choice, more of them began to hire marketing and ad agencies to craft creative messages.[215] Industry analysts called this approach to advertising "an indication" of a "decidedly sophisticated turn" in the "romance between consumers and their grocers." D'Agostino's peers thus devoted more of their resources to electronic media, color, and photo art, and "image-building campaigns."[216] Even the fabled "D'Ag Bag" was no longer a unique concept, as dozens of New York City retailers now produced branded shopping bags for their customers.

Meanwhile, a major shift in D'Agostino's marketing strategy occurred in the 1990s, during Ron Nevers's tenure as company president. Nevers phased out Marvin Glass's playful renderings of New York life because he believed that the caricatures were not "dignified."[217] Nevers's decision earned him the acrimony of Jo Foxworth, the organization's creative genius. Soon after, D'Agostino's introduced the series of popular ads that utilized historic photographs to emphasize the company's long-standing connection to its fellow New Yorkers and to capitalize on the public's affection for family businesses. According to Foxworth, management "began to play very big on the family angle," hoping that customers would realize that "they are dealing with human beings . . . not huge corporations" and understand that "D'Agostinos are on the job there, every day. And that they live in New York."[218] But Nick D'Agostino Jr. admitted that the cost of advertising—whether it be on radio, on television, or in print media—had "become extremely hard to bear." He explained, "It's very hard to get that message across in today's environment. . . . We're just not doing that much advertising as we were in the past. . . . We try to do it with product presentation but it's not the same as it was in the past."[219] Thus, in the new millennium, D'Agostino's ceased most of its print and radio campaigns—arguing that the cost no longer justified the return.[220] The company's commitment to innovative and ubiquitous promotion—despite considerations of cost, efficiency, or thrift—had once reflected its chairman's desire to be the city's number one retailer in terms of "visibility." Now, in measuring the cost-benefit of advertising, D'Agostino's was acknowledging the limits of its own ambitions as well as of its celebrity.

D'Agostino's did have one apparent success, as it experimented with a host of strategies for reestablishing its prestige. In 2002, the company opened a new outlet that merged the sensibility of the traditional immigrant grocery with the vision and the amenities of a high-end Manhattan supermarket. The store, in the Westchester suburb of Rye Brook, was spacious and attractive, but its most celebrated feature was its "Marketta"—an open, European-style market that featured a bakery and patisserie, a pizzeria, a sushi counter, a "rotisserie," and a gourmet coffee stand. The new location, according to advertisements, also offered a "custom cut" butcher shop with prime beef "aged on site," an abundant selection of organic foods, fruits, and vegetables, over twenty thousand grocery products, an assortment of gourmet cheeses, and the region's biggest selection of microbrewed beers. The produce department at the store featured a section called the "City Market," which had wooden stands and gondolas that resembled a bucolic farmers' market. D'Agostino's even promoted its new operation with a small campaign that alluded to the company's origins in the produce business. One local magazine described the latest iteration of D'Agostino's as the perfect marriage of an upscale supermarket and the prototypical family business, thus making it "a 25,000-square-foot paradigm of 21st-century marketing" while giving "a whole new meaning to the term mom-and-pop market."[221] Although the Rye Brook store seemed to indicate that D'Agostino's understood the contemporary formula for winning an elite following, it would abruptly close in 2015, a victim of the organization's growing financial struggles.

The Store That Would Be King's: D'Agostino's and the Future of Family Business

In the new millennium, D'Agostino's struggles with its identity and vision, and the shifting demands of the marketplace. The company floats several strategies to remain vital, including the purchase of a suburban chain. Meanwhile, its future is clouded by squabbles inherent to the family business, leading to uncertainty about the ultimate survival of this New York institution.

Throughout his career as CEO and company chairman, Nick D'Agostino Jr. maintained a sincere commitment to the concept of family business. In several interviews, he defended the family firm as an operational model, claiming that it enjoyed a significant advantage over its competitors because its management team tended to have a unified sense of mission. He argued that a family business often had more stability than its corporate peers because its chief personnel was part of a multigenerational legacy and thus willing to defer short-term profits for long-term growth. Nick claimed that with smaller management teams, companies like D'Agostino's had the flexibility to react quickly to changes in the market. And, of course, in press releases, interviews, and advertising, Nick explained to his fellow New Yorkers that businesses like his own were more likely to be "good citizens" because of their enduring relationships with their hometowns.

In the 1980s, reports of mergers, hostile takeovers, and leveraged buyouts dominated the news. In 1985 alone, there were twenty-four mergers of food companies involving assets of more than $1 billion, while coverage of R.J. Reynolds's purchase of Nabisco and Philip Morris's takeover of General Foods filled the financial pages in 1986.[222] As the supermarket industry experienced limited growth, management viewed these strategies as necessary for keeping their businesses vibrant in a crowded marketplace. Over the next several years, the ability of large chains to swallow smaller competitors led analysts to speculate that midsize companies were an endangered species.[223]

The rise in mergers and acquisitions was particularly threatening to the older generation of family-owned establishments, as corporations offered huge paydays to those who were willing to trade their stakes for an early retirement. In this context, Nick D'Agostino Jr. began to voice concern for the future of the family business. In addition to defending the social and economic value of family firms, he would confront his peers about their responsibilities as stewards and caretakers. He made it clear that he felt accountable to his workforce, even speculating that if D'Agostino Supermarkets were to be sold (a possibility he denied), he would have to give his employees the opportunity to buy into the company: "When management wants to cash in, it has responsibilities to employees. There are no guarantees in life, but you have to explore ways of selling out without hurting your people. You shouldn't just sell to the highest bidder or work out a deal at a cocktail party." In his critique of the period's economic climate, Nick advocated for looking beyond immediate profits to historic legacies. He commented that while management preached loyalty to its employees, "too often when we want to get our piece of the pie we say, 'screw them.'" He expressed particular concern that with all the sales and mergers, ownership was jeopardizing the very stability of their businesses and risking the unique "company cultures" that they had spent decades cultivating.[224]

Like his brother Stephen, Nick D'Agostino Jr.'s perspective on these issues was shaped by his relatives' bruising struggle for ownership of the business following the death of his uncle, Patsy D'Agostino. Nick warned other family retailers that it was an owner's obligation to develop a new line of succession "even if he spends the last five years of his working life with the company doing nothing else." He expressed confidence that he had built a team capable of guiding D'Agostino Supermarkets into the next generation, relating, "They're not my clones, but they can run the business along the same lines that it is being conducted now."[225] Yet Nick also hinted that he would be a presence in the company even after he had stepped aside. He related that the entrepreneur "considers himself the father of his family while the business is growing, but often doesn't feel that way after he gets out. My part in the play doesn't end because I sold my business."[226] In another interview, he remembered that after the settlement of Patsy's estate, his father "reorganized the business and took his value in preferred stock. We split up the common stock between three of us. We were equal partners except he had all the votes."[227]

Nick viewed the continued expansion of D'Agostino Supermarkets—in terms of financial health, status, and operational scale—as his ultimate goal. In a 1993 feature, Nick was asked about his greatest career accomplishment, and the reporter related that "he said it was assuming the role of CEO and building a management team and organization that could grow the business. 'I think D'Agostino's has always had an excellent reputation, and I think my accomplishment has been in maintaining that reputation as we grow.'"[228] But like his father before him, Nick envisioned the business as a family legacy that would extend across generations. In various articles, he made clear that while he might not try to pressure them, he would "like nothing better than to see his offspring holding key roles in D'Agostino's."[229] An interviewer observed that as Nick's two eldest sons made their way up the corporate ladder, "If Mr. D'Agostino has his way, yet another D'Agostino will be running the store after he retires." Nick seemed ready to uphold the convention of primogeniture—a curious position, considering that he only became head of the company once his older brother resigned. As one writer explained:

> Nicholas D'Agostino, Jr. believes in tradition. To this day he still doesn't question the assumption that the eldest son should be heir to a family business. In Mr. D'Agostino's case, that meant his older brother Stephen was handed the reins to D'Agostino Supermarkets. But fortunately for him, tradition was broken when Stephen announced on his 49th birthday in 1982 that he was leaving the enterprise after 27 years.[230]

The issue of succession at D'Agostino's was complicated by the fact that Nick had three sons who were candidates to head the operation. At the first meeting he had with his two older sons to discuss the future of the organization, he asked them about their career objectives, and as Nick recalled, "One guy said he wanted to be president of the company someday. The other guy said he wanted to be president of the company. I said, 'Wait a minute. It might have to be another company.'"[231] In addition to the issue of entitlement, Nick also had to consider the respective talents and the credentials of his children. Were they ultimately qualified to run a supermarket chain? He remarked that he would "love to see them take over management of the organization," yet he did not think "their success has to come out of being chief executive or chief operating officer of the company." He proposed that his children might retain ownership, but appoint a president to manage the operation, reasoning, "Ownership is responsible for getting the best people. Management's job is to make a profit. Ownership is much more important."[232]

In the late 1980s, Nick D'Agostino Jr.'s concern for the beleaguered state of the family business in America had led him to cofound a consulting firm to advise his peers on issues such as transfers of assets, ownership, and control.[233] As his sons Nicholas III and Walter worked their way up the company ladder, Nick shared that as a consultant, he was interested in "the emotionally troubling aspects of the situation, such as the distribution of wealth among the members of the family who do and do not work in the family business, and choosing who should run the business without negatively affecting family members."[234] His comments seemed to reflect both the trauma the family and the business experienced in the early 1960s—when Nicholas D'Agostino Sr. fought his brother's heirs for control of the operation—and Nick's own anxieties over the future distribution of power.[235] As he faced additional questions about a potential sale of the company, Nick repeated his allegiance to the principles of stewardship and fairness:

> I have a responsibility to the people who have worked for me for 20 or 30 years. There's more to the sale of your equity than improving stock prices or getting cash. There should be more, even in the real world. I have the right to cash in my chips. But does it matter if I take it all at once, or over a period of time from employees? I have two sons in the business. I couldn't say to them, "Here's a few million dollars; I've sold the business." And if I couldn't do it to my sons I couldn't do it to my other employees.[236]

Late in his career, Nick D'Agostino Jr. reflected on the decline of family firms throughout his time in food retailing. When Nick became a grocer in the early 1960s, D'Agostino's had several family-run competitors; by the early 2000s, however, it was the only family-owned supermarket chain left in the city. He concluded that over time, as management continually welcomed family members into the business, these organizations tended to stagnate and lose focus. Nick was philosophical about this development, however, as he mused that the "truth of the matter is, most family businesses don't make it to the second generation. Those that make it to the second generation, only about thirty percent make it to the third generation. . . . Between the loss of direction and the dilution of talent it's not an easy challenge—and that's life."[237] As to the legacy of the D'Agostino brand, Nick disclosed that if he was starting a company, he would not use "the family name as the title of the business" because "it puts undue pressure on all the family members" who are "always affiliated as 'the business.'" He confided that even he had felt the burden of carrying the company name, occasionally thinking, "Oh Jesus, I'd like to be able to go someplace and not have somebody say to me, 'Mr. D'Agostino, I want to tell you about your stores.'" He added, "I don't think that I should challenge the children to say that you're only going to be successful if you can now pass this business on to the next generation. . . . That's a decision they must make based upon their own lifestyles."[238]

Domestic politics tended to complicate the long-term viability of most family businesses. Nick D'Agostino Jr. observed that oftentimes, an older sibling thinks "he has authority over the younger one just because he happens to be older" while the parent often takes his authority for granted because "they're the parent, not because they're the Boss." Moreover, the natural rivalries and tensions experienced by any company might be played out at Sunday dinners or holiday celebrations, since there are few boundaries between work and family. Nick mused, "I can't go home and complain to my wife about my brother or my children in their work habits because she's either their mother or their sister-in-law . . . and it can create a lot of friction within the family."[239] According to Stephen D'Agostino, the "boss-worker relationship" often dominates the social life of a family, as the family dinner "becomes a business reinforcement of who the boss is."[240] And as siblings vie for positions of power, they may be tempted to flaunt the fruits of success—such as salaries, houses, and cars—at backyard cookouts or birthday celebrations.

Nick D'Agostino Jr. continued the dinner table metaphor when discussing the inherent conflict between hierarchy and harmony within a family-owned company. He asserted, "If there are several children involved, there is always going to be natural sibling rivalry. These are the same two people who will yell at each other across the dinner table and that relationship can be carried over to the business."[241] At the same time, younger siblings limited to junior management positions might feel marginalized, as they wonder when they will have opportunities to showcase their talents and leadership. But even if family members become disenchanted and want to resign, they might be dissuaded by a case of "golden handcuffs"—a situation in which associates will not leave the company because they are drawing handsome salaries and have job security, and thus are essentially "trapped" with little power and little chance for advancement.

As D'Agostino Supermarkets reached its eighth decade in business, Nick began to sense the uncertainty of its future. He remarked that "if we don't develop some way of differentiating ourselves from the competition," D'Agostino's would "merge with another company, acquire another company or sell the company and to become less and less of a family-controlled and operated business." As far as its line of succession, Nick observed, "If the talent within the organization can't keep the business successful and growing, it's going to have to cede to other talent in order to maintain its integrity." He also acknowledged that his children might have "different expectations" about the company's future—whether to keep it in the family or sell to the highest bidder and divide the shares. But he placed ultimate responsibility on his sons, who had all been in management for at least a decade, arguing that "they are the ones who will make the decision. I don't have a vision because I really think it has to be *their* vision."[242]

In the mid-2000s, as Nick D'Agostino Jr. began to drift from the day-to-day operations of the business, his three sons jockeyed for position as his successor. To maintain the peace, he gave each of them executive status with titles, offices, and generous salaries.[243] Nick maintained ultimate control of the company while retaining some direct involvement in its management.[244] He explained that if an executive "divorces himself from the day-to-day operations of his business completely, things tend to lose control. I still have to go into the stores, I have to be there, and I have to give feedback to the executives that work for me.... You have to listen to the customers, you have to listen to the associates, you have to look with your eyes; intuition still has a lot to do with what you're doing."[245] Then, in 2002, Walter D'Agostino decided to sever ties with the business in a dispute over its direction and his future role. Walter's departure—which occurred as D'Agostino's was prepared to acquire a New Jersey grocery chain—was explained as "typical management philosophy differences."[246] In 2005, Nick finally named his eldest son, Nicholas D'Agostino III, as president and chief operating officer—positions that had been vacant since Ron Nevers's departure in 1997. It appeared that the company was poised to begin a new chapter in its history.[247]

As it entered the new millennium, D'Agostino Supermarkets was at a crossroads. How would it meet the next generation of competitors and continue as a viable, dynamic enterprise? How would it maintain its character, especially after Nick D'Agostino Jr. retired? In the 1980s, Nick had concluded, "Growth is part of our strategic plan. . . . I don't see us rivaling the size of a major national chain, but I do see us going from 25 to 50 stores in the coming decades."[248] A member of his management team declared: "Nick has accomplished what most family-run businesses have been unable to accomplish—namely, to expand upon the company's past successes."[249] One might argue that the ultimate mark of success during Nick D'Agostino Jr.'s tenure was his ability to combine a program of corporate growth with the values and the visage of a traditional family business. By the mid-1990s, D'Agostino's was operating twenty-four stores (including nineteen in Manhattan, one in the Bronx, two in Brooklyn, and two in Westchester County) and had annual sales of over $200 million.

Nick D'Agostino Jr.'s comments about the organization's future described a modest plan for expansion that complemented the firm's traditional identity. Yet Nick may have harbored even greater aspirations for D'Agostino's commercial footprint in the mid-1980s as he transitioned into his role as chairman and CEO.[250] He first targeted Westchester County as the new locus of operational growth.[251] In interviews, he related that D'Agostino Supermarkets could have up to a dozen Westchester stores within a decade, hinting that the business might even locate a majority of its stores outside the city sometime in the future.[252] And as D'Agostino's was threatened by flashy new rivals, it twice tried to remake itself through mergers and acquisitions, which had become accepted methods of expansion in the increasingly prohibitive New York real estate market. In 1990, D'Agostino's tried to buy out Sloan's, formerly one of its main challengers—a move that would have given the company more than seventy stores. But a New York district court ruled against the bid, arguing that D'Agostino's would have gained an illegal monopoly through the sale.[253] Then, in 2001, management sought to acquire King's, a large New Jersey supermarket chain, for $160 million, from England's Marks and Spencer. The purchase of the King's chain was a financial gamble, but, more significantly, it would have transformed the culture of D'Agostino's.

D'Agostino's hoped to reap $700 million in combined sales from the acquisition. On the surface, King's also seemed to be a perfect partner—as the chain had twenty-seven modest-sized stores as well as a reputation for gourmet quality among its loyal, prosperous customer base. The outgoing president of King's even spoke of a "cultural overlap" between the two companies.[254] Yet D'Agostino Supermarkets had built its name serving the distinct needs of New Yorkers. With the purchase of King's, the company would have directed its resources and intellectual energy into dozens of suburban superstores. D'Agostino's even made plans to move its corporate offices to New Jersey. The sale of King's to D'Agostino's ultimately fell through when Nick and his management team failed to procure sufficient financing for the purchase, but the proposed deal signaled a crisis of identity within the company. In the second half of the twentieth century, D'Agostino's had anticipated the gentrification and growth of neighborhoods like Chelsea, Greenwich Village, and the Upper West Side, and effectively tied its destiny to the city's redevelopment. Now, with the emergence of Whole Foods and its ilk, D'Agostino's was no longer a bellwether for rising fortunes in New York.

Throughout the twentieth century, the grocery business was shaped by a dialogue between consumer and merchant, which one might characterize as the "call and response" of the marketplace. Each decade, shoppers demanded new products and services because of changes in their lifestyles and patterns of settlement. Shifting desires and demographics forced retailers to constantly innovate their commercial strategies and product lines or risk obsolescence. Meanwhile, enabled by the latest technologies and the relentless need to differentiate themselves from the competition, retailers stimulated revolutions in consumption. Neither party had ultimate power in this conversation; rather, consumer and merchant constantly remade each other.

For much of its history, D'Agostino Supermarkets was one of the most prominent retailers in New York not because of capital resources or size, but because its management had the vision and the flexibility to anticipate and adopt the newest commercial paradigms. In the 1930s, Patsy and Nicholas D'Agostino sensed the transition from the corner grocery to the "all-in-one" combination stores that preceded the supermarket revolution. In the 1950s, the brothers offered the city's finest selection of meats and produce, as well as the markings of status, when many Americans were enjoying their first taste of the "good life" following years of war and economic deprivation. In the 1960s and '70s, Stephen D'Agostino instituted corporate reforms and image-driven advertising to bring an atmosphere of modernity and class to the operation, at a time in which consumers were increasingly discontented with the traditional supermarket. In the 1980s and 1990s, under the leadership of Nicholas D'Agostino Jr., the company continued to experiment with commercial technology while also responding to gourmet trends in its merchandising. In this period, as the city underwent another shift in its identity, D'Agostino's also used the concept of the family business to reconnect with its associates and the urban gentry.

For more than eight decades, D'Agostino Supermarkets witnessed the evolution of New York's economy, population, and identity, demonstrating a keen instinct for anticipating looming economic and cultural shifts. Perhaps each generation of management could sense changes in the city's character because these intuitions stemmed from their own experiences as New Yorkers. Although Patsy and Nicholas D'Agostino were immigrants raised on the city's pushcarts, they were part of a cohort who were climbing from blue-collar trades into the professions. When the company made its fortune serving the middle-class strivers of Stuyvesant Town and Peter Cooper Village, Patsy and Nicholas shared their customers' experience of upward mobility and connection to the American mythos. When Stephen D'Agostino became president, he was part of a generation who viewed New York as a "world city" based in its professional classes and cultural institutions. In the 1970s, when New York suffered through one of its darkest periods, Stephen and his brother, Nick Jr., launched advertising campaigns that expressed their civic loyalties as well as their own urbane sensibilities. And in the last two decades of the twentieth century, Nick D'Agostino Jr. used the business's heritage to speak to a city whose identity was being remade by gentrification and immigration.

In each era of its history, the company also had the managerial acumen to match the tenor of the times. Patsy and Nicholas D'Agostino were versed in all the elements—meat, produce, groceries, merchandising—for mastering the supermarket paradigm. Stephen D'Agostino understood modern marketing and management strategies, which allowed the company to gain celebrity despite its modest size. Nick D'Agostino Jr. applied the concept of the family-owned business, as well as his understanding of the changing nature of food culture, to attract a new legion of shoppers. In addition to their executive skills, these individuals also grasped the impact of image and narrative on the marketplace. Whether it was the recounting of Patsy and Nicholas's "rags-to-riches" tale by popular magazines, the sophisticated wit of the *New Yorker*-style cartoons commissioned by Stephen D'Agostino, or Nick D'Agostino Jr.'s utilization of family and history, the company's ability to market its own identity was nearly as vital to its success as any product line or business plan. The history of D'Agostino Supermarkets demonstrated how narrative could become a valuable form of capital—as well as a method of self-representation—especially as the business established its legacy. The family's fascination with its own legend certainly illustrated this point.

Yet D'Agostino's branding strategy also reflected the personas of its protagonists. Patsy's charisma, Nicholas's drive, Stephen's sophistication, and Nick's fellowship all brought the company's image to life. These figures were literally the face of the business—giving D'Agostino's a distinct identity while making it a familiar part of the culture of New York. One could argue that during its periods of greatest success, D'Agostino's had an authentic connection to the city, becoming an extension of New York's unique character.

Matters of personality and personnel embody the principal issues facing family-owned businesses, however. In a family enterprise, each generation of management must further the company's core vision while devising new formulas for keeping the operation viable. In the new millennium, D'Agostino's mission was complicated by the decline of the supermarket paradigm, the rise of new forms of commerce, and the success of competitors like Whole Foods and Fairway—which usurped its formula of quality meats and produce and gourmet dry goods, pitched at New York's sophisticated consumers. Balancing a sense of tradition and a culture of innovation is particularly challenging for a company with such a long history. How would D'Agostino Supermarkets maintain its identity while, by necessity, modernizing its retailing strategies? Most family businesses also struggle to maintain talented management teams because they draw on such a small pool of candidates. As organizations that are often dependent on the genius of leadership, questions of managerial quality and succession typically plague family firms. Would D'Agostino's be able to foster another ambitious, skilled crop of executives to extend the family legend into the twenty-first century? Could the company continue its love affair with the city that spawned its founders' dreams?

By 2020, D'Agostino Supermarkets was operating only eleven stores, less than half the number it maintained in the early 1990s, when the company seemed to be at its peak in terms of prosperity and prominence. With declining sales, a shrinking footprint in Manhattan, and a diminished reputation among New York's savvy consumers, the company was struggling for its very survival. Where had D'Agostino Supermarkets gone wrong?

In the twenty-first century, the company has been battered by competition from Whole Foods, Fairway, and even Trader Joe's. As a business, D'Agostino's had come of age when retailing in New York was dominated by neighborhood shops and corner groceries. As discussed in chapter 2, in the 1930s and '40s, the A&P chain may have represented a formidable threat to local merchants, but Patsy and Nicholas D'Agostino carved a profitable niche for their enterprise by offering their middle- and upper-class clientele a distinctive mix of products and services—including quality meats, fish, and produce—at a time when the supermarket concept was still relatively young. They assumed that their customers would discern that A&P offered an inferior product. In the 1950s and '60s, as the company emerged as one of New York's premier food retailers, D'Agostino's profited from its ability to maximize revenue in the cramped commercial spaces of Manhattan as well as from its understanding of the tastes and aspirations of its customers. In the 1970s and '80s, the company continued to promote itself as part of the cosmopolitan life of the city.

For much of the twentieth century, New York had been a hostile environment for large retailers and chain stores owing to the city's high rents, stifling traffic patterns, web of regulations, and local corruption. In addition, New Yorkers had distinctive tastes and purchasing habits—often dictated by their small apartments and local loyalties. But in the 1990s, the Giuliani administration and commercial landlords enabled big-box stores and high-end chains to operate more easily and profitably in New York, and these operations transformed the city's retail landscape. In the succeeding decades, neighborhood commerce was supplanted by well-financed national retailers, including a Costco at 117th Street and a Wegmans gourmet superstore in the Brooklyn Navy Yard complex.[255] The reach of the city's high-end supermarkets was further elevated in 2017 when online giant Amazon purchased Whole Foods for $13 billion. These developments culminated in Wegmans opening an 82,000-square-foot supermarket at the site of a former department store in Lower Manhattan in 2023.[256]

Members of the media mourned the disappearance of local groceries, as one *New York Times* writer observed:

> Corner markets and grocery stores have closed in neighborhoods across the city—forcing many New Yorkers to rethink their daily routines and in some cases changing the very tenor of a neighborhood.... Supermarkets of suburban proportions, like Whole Foods, are making their mark on the city.... But while these stores have distinctive—and sometimes pricier—offerings like artisanal cheese and artichoke ravioli, they cannot replace the labyrinthine corner market, a linchpin for any neighborhood.[257]

In addition to competition from upscale supermarkets, the city's established retailers faced rising rents, falling profit margins, and the proliferation of drugstores like Duane Reade, whose ubiquity and growing food inventory made them a convenient choice for consumers.[258] Real estate developers also seemed to prefer chain drugstores as tenants because they were cleaner and less intrusive than traditional supermarkets. One industry analyst lamented, "The greengrocers that New Yorkers grew up with have become more a thing of the past." The *Times* concluded, "In a city of eight million, the shops on the corner are the ones that make New York feel like a small town. Without them, a neighborhood can feel less like home."[259]

In the new millennium, D'Agostino Supermarkets has also struggled with its identity. For much of its history, the company appealed to New York's middle- and upper-income shoppers with a promise of quality and cachet. But by the mid-1990s, the contradictory needs of consumers began to cloud its mission. D'Agostino's traditional patrons wanted the stores to offer staple items at reasonable prices, along with the same assortment of dry goods and drugstore necessities one would find in a conventional supermarket. Meanwhile, the customers that it most wanted to attract—upwardly mobile "foodies" who were populating Lower Manhattan and, increasingly, Brooklyn—were drawn to Whole Foods or Fairway for their wide array of fresh and organic produce, gourmet cheeses and meats, and their association with a lifestyle that was both ethical and indulgent.[260]

Increasingly, younger consumers were opting out of the supermarket model altogether. The more adventurous sought out the city's vibrant network of ethnic and farmers' markets. And in the digital age, a growing number were choosing to buy their groceries online and have them delivered through services like FreshDirect or Instacart—a bitter irony for D'Agostino's, given the large sums it had sunk into "TeleDag" in the 1980s.[261] To many New Yorkers, especially the newer generation of customers, the remaining D'Agostino stores may have seemed cramped and outmoded compared to their upscale competitors. Meanwhile, according to the executive director of a leading restaurant trade association, 2015 was the first year that Americans spent more money dining out than on groceries.[262]

How much of D'Agostino's demise could be attributed to changes in the size and shape of the American household? In the 1980s and '90s, much of the D'Agostino narrative—both real and adapted—was centered on notions of family, particularly the lore of the family business. Through its advertising, the company had claimed kinship with consumers based on a shared sense of community and its roots as New York's family grocer (or "New York's Grocer," as promoted by its established branding), thus invoking a deeper sense of place and values. However, in the new millennium, this motif reflected neither the reality nor the aspirations of many urban Americans. In cities like New York, households populated by singles and nonmarried couples became the new norm—especially among the young—while the "traditional" nuclear family seemed outdated. At the same time, while younger consumers were less beholden to established supermarkets, D'Agostino's customer base was increasingly older and of more modest means.

D'Agostino Supermarkets had once elevated its name and reputation with New York City shoppers through ingenious, nearly ubiquitous print and radio advertisements. In the 1970s and '80s, the company engaged in several high-profile marketing campaigns while its shopping bags—emblazoned with colorful images of fruit and the "D'Ag Bag" logo—became artifacts of Manhattan culture. As discussed in chapter 4, in the 1970s "D'Ag Bags" were often favored by aspiring dancers and models as affordable fashion statements and a convenient way to carry shoes and makeup. In the 1980s and '90s, the bags were sometimes used by television and movie directors to establish a sense of authenticity for productions set in New York. Acclaimed works of literature like Alison Bechdel's graphic memoir *Fun Home* (2007) even featured D'Agostino grocery bags to recapture New York in another era, a nostalgic glance at a city now altered by gentrification.[263] In recent years, however, the company has limited its marketing mainly to emails, circulars, and its website, and even discontinued the use of the stylized grocery bags—which signified its limited resources and lowered horizons.[264]

In the twenty-first century, New York and cities around the country have enjoyed renewed prosperity and prestige, driven by real estate development, a resurgent white-collar economy, the tech boom, and gentrification, as young, college-educated professionals colonized the working-class neighborhoods of the urban core. The impact of gentrification has been evident in the city's restored brownstones and public spaces, vibrant street life, and bustling restaurants and bars, despite being paused during the COVID-19 pandemic.[265] The new urban gentry were often "foodies" who drew their cultural identity from literal acts of consumption. Once upon a time, this group would have been D'Agostino's targeted demographic. But the company's inability to connect with young tastemakers—many of whom preferred Brooklyn over Manhattan, seeing the borough as a buzzword and a brand, as well as a destination—would have profound consequences for its reputation and profit margins.

Here the demise of D'Agostino Supermarkets also corresponded to changes in New York City itself. Gentrification can mean urban revitalization, buzzing nightlife, a resurgent restaurant and food scene, and improved city services and public safety. But, of course, gentrification also initiates rising rents and displacement. New York, like San Francisco and Boston, has largely become a city of "haves" and "have-nots" in the twenty-first century—increasingly populated by the wealthy and the poor as the middle class and families with children have dispersed. This has had a deleterious effect on D'Agostino's and other established retailers. Many New Yorkers have wondered if the city, rife with social divisions, is losing its sense of place and history. Looking at landmarks from Patsy and Nicholas D'Agostino's own narrative, Stuyvesant Town and Peter Cooper Village—MetLife's middle-class housing development that hosted D'Agostino's flagship 20th Street store—were sold to Tishman Speyer and BlackRock Realty in 2006 for $5.4 billion. The developers had plans to convert the complex's rent-stabilized apartments to market-rate properties before they were slowed by legal challenges and bankruptcy.[266] Meanwhile, Gino's Restaurant—where Nicholas and Patsy regularly toasted their success with a lunchtime bottle of wine—closed in 2010. This New York institution, founded by Neapolitan immigrant Gino Circiello, and favored by such luminaries as Gay Talese and I. M. Pei, was replaced by a high-end cupcake shop.[267]

The growing affluence of New York has brought other dissatisfactions. The proliferation of big-box and chain stores and the relative lack of conspicuous dirt and disorder has led many New Yorkers to complain that the city has lost its soul and edginess. With rising rents, gentrification, and seeming "Disney-fication" of areas like Times Square, a wave of nostalgia for New York in the 1970s has emerged in popular culture—romanticizing the seventies as a time in which the menace of city living was balanced by a sense of adventure and creative ferment. For revisionists, the New York of this era is remembered not so much for the city's bankruptcy, the "Son of Sam" murders, the Blackout of '77, or the arson that ravaged the Bronx, but as the decade that gave birth to punk rock and CBGB's, MC'ing and hip-hop, graffiti art, SoHo, and the downtown art scene. This longing for a grittier, more colorful New York—a city that was affordable and wide open to creatives—has been evidenced by literary touchstones such as Patti Smith's memoir *Just Kids* (2010) and Garth Risk Hallberg's 900-page (2016) debut novel *City on Fire* (which earned him a $2 million advance from his publisher).

Finally, in the last ten years, D'Agostino Supermarkets has endured a series of financial and organizational challenges that have jeopardized its future. While traditional supermarkets throughout the country had difficulty staying afloat in the 2010s, D'Agostino's situation became particularly dire. As Whole Foods, Fairway, Trader Joe's, and even the drugstore chain

Duane Reade ate into its market share, the company struggled to meet the rising costs of Manhattan real estate and its unionized workforce—leading to the closure of multiple locations. D'Agostino's unsettled finances also had a corresponding effect on the quality and quantity of its merchandise, which further eroded its reputation with consumers. By 2015, management's inability to pay its suppliers on time resulted in half-empty shelves in many of its stores.[268] In the months that followed, it was rumored that D'Agostino's was looking for a buyer, with interest from the Key Food Stores Co-operative.[269]

To stave off bankruptcy and revive his remaining outlets, Nicholas D'Agostino III forged an agreement with billionaire John Catsimatidis of Gristedes, formerly one of the company's main competitors. Catsimatidis had originally made his fortune as owner of the Red Apple grocery chain before buying Gristede's and Sloan's in the 1980s and '90s. He leveraged his ownership of these supermarkets into vast real estate, energy, and media holdings under the umbrella of the Red Apple Group conglomerate. In 2016, Catsimatidis set up a revolving credit line for D'Agostino's so that his former rival could continue to fill its inventory and pay its suppliers, with the expectation that the two companies would eventually agree on a joint venture that could withstand the pressure from Whole Foods, Trader Joe's, and other well-financed entrants.[270] Catsimatidis explained, "Almost every supermarket company has gone bankrupt. But the D'Agostino name deserves to survive."[271]

While industry analysts assumed that Gristedes and D'Agostino's would eventually merge, the arrangement was slow in coming.[272] Then, in 2019, Catsimatidis suddenly announced that he and the Red Apple Group had taken controlling ownership of the D'Agostino chain, with D'Agostino's and Gristedes each maintaining their brands but operating collectively as the New York Food Group.[273] Even as Catsimatidis created the largest supermarket chain in New York City, the stores represented less than 2 percent of the Red Apple Group's assets. Catsimatidis indicated that real estate would continue to be his primary focus, telling an interviewer, "Retail is dying by the dozen. Supermarkets are dying faster."[274]

As part of this new arrangement, Nicholas D'Agostino III remained as president and COO of D'Agostino Supermarkets, although it appeared to customers that the product lines, food offerings, and pricing of the two companies had begun to meld.[275] Under pressure from ownership, Nicholas—the last member of the family serving in a managerial capacity—quietly stepped down in 2021, accepting a position as vice chairman of D'Agostino's.[276] Going forward, he would have less involvement in its daily operations, instead overseeing real estate and special projects while serving as a consultant for the New York Food Group. In 2022, John Catsimatidis appointed veteran food executive Joe Parisi as the new president and chief operating officer of Gristedes and D'Agostino Supermarkets.[277] For the first time in nine decades, no D'Agostino would head the institution that Patsy and Nicholas had built from a modest grocery in Upper Manhattan, nor were there any heirs waiting in the wings. Over the course of the twentieth century, companies far more successful or socially significant than D'Agostino Supermarkets had once seemed indomitable, looming over their respective cultures, before declining or fading away. In the end, these businesses aged and atrophied; like the visionaries who founded them, they proved to be merely mortal.

ACKNOWLEDGMENTS

I would like to first thank Marilyn Halter, Bruce Schulman, and Susan Mizruchi at Boston University and Regina Blaszczyk of the University of Leeds for their expert guidance and mentorship, which nurtured my development as a scholar and a writer. I am forever indebted to Kandice Hauf, Blake Pattridge, and Stephen Deets at Babson College for their advocacy and encouragement as I struggled to complete this project. Thanks also to Beth Wynstra, Kerry Rourke, Sandra Graham, Marjorie Feld, and Jenny Rademacher and my other wonderful colleagues in the Arts and Humanities/History and Society Divisions at Babson for their friendship and insights throughout the writing process.

The benevolent support of the Tariq Farid Franchise Institute and the Arthur M. Blank School for Entrepreneurial Leadership's Faculty Research Angel Fund helped make this book possible. I am especially grateful to Ab Igram, the Executive Director of the Tariq Farid Franchise Institute; Donna Levin, the CEO of the Blank School for Entrepreneurial Leadership; Sandra Castaldini of Babson's Office of Sponsored Research; and Lauren Beitelspacher of the Babson College Marketing Division.

The generous cooperation of members of the D'Agostino and Tucciarone families also enabled this book to become a reality. Stephen D'Agostino and Nicholas D'Agostino Jr. offered their candid reflections on the development of the grocery business and the history of the family, as well as access to numerous company documents. I have gained a new appreciation for their brilliance as executives and their great affection for the city of New York. Nick D'Agostino III and Frank Tucciarone contributed their thoughtful perspectives on the complexities of business and family, which furthered my understanding of the contemporary challenges of food retailing. This book's treatment of advertising owes much to the testimony of Jo Foxworth—a talented, delightful woman who is missed by all who knew her.

My deepest appreciation to Fredric Nachbaur of Fordham University Press and Lisa Regan at TextFormations, LLC for their kind and careful editing as this project reached its final stages. Robert Alvis at St. Meinrad's Seminary and School of Theology and Stephen Pitti of Yale University were always discerning and wise in their commentary and criticisms.

I am also obliged to several members of my family. Matthew, Anne, and Martha Schmitz and Kevin Murphy gave able assistance in various research and editing tasks, as well as moral support and counsel. My late mother and father, Loretta and Dennis Schmitz, provided intellectual direction, historical perspective, and a well of love and encouragement. This book is a testimony to their talents as writers, thinkers, and parents. Finally, I would like to thank my lovely wife, Rebecca, who offered an unlimited supply of emotional, intellectual, and technical support. Without her love and fortitude, I would never have been able to finish my journey.

NOTES

1. Italian Immigration and the Currency of the Ethnic Merchant

1. D'Agostino Supermarkets, *D'AGs Consumer Newsletter*, September/October 1982, 1. The original source of the story is *The New York Times*, January 10, 1979.

2. Federal Writers' Project, *The Italians of New York* (1938; Arno, 1969), 2.

3. Nancy Foner, *From Ellis Island to JFK: New York's Two Great Waves of Immigration* (Yale University Press, 2000), 6 and 10.

4. Carlo Levi, *Christ Stopped at Eboli: The Story of a Year*, trans. Frances Frenaye (1947; Farrar, Straus, and Giroux, 1980), 123.

5. Rollin Lynde Hartt, "Made in Italy," *The Independent*, July 23, 1921, 19. The nation's Italian population was, itself, transformed by the thousands of immigrants who began arriving in the latter third of the nineteenth century. Before 1880, the US's Italian community was fed by a slow trickle of émigrés, mainly from that country's northern region. These immigrants usually sought permanent residency in the US, and tended to have higher levels of income and education than those who followed. Between 1820 and 1850, fewer than 4,500 Italians came to the United States. From 1850 to 1870, the pace of Italian immigration climbed to over 21,000. By 1890, however, the nation's Italian population reached 180,000, and by 1900, it had risen to almost a half million. In the first decade of the twentieth century, Italians continued to arrive in startling numbers. Between 1900 and 1914, more than three million Italians came to this country—almost 60 percent of the total Italian immigration over the course of US history. While the Great War slowed this tide, several thousand Italians came to the US once hostilities ended, until the Immigration Act of 1924 virtually ended new immigration from Italy. For more on the patterns of Italian immigration to the US, see Robert F. Foerster, *The Italian Emigration of Our Times* (Harvard University Press, 1919), 323–27; Richard Alba, "Italian Americans: A Century of Ethnic Change," in *Origins and Destinies: Immigration, Race, and Ethnicity in America*, ed. Silvia Pedraza and Rubén G. Rumbaut (Wadsworth, 1996), 172–73; Maddalena Tirabassi, "Why Italians Left Italy: The Physics and Politics of Migration," in *The Routledge*

History of Italian Americans, ed. William J. Connell and Stanislao G. Pugliese (Routledge, 2018), 117–31; and Laura Buonanno and Michael Buonanno, *Remembering Italian America: Memory, Migration, and Identity* (Routledge, 2021), 44–61.

6. It is estimated that 80 percent of the Italians who immigrated to the US between 1876 and 1930 were from the southern regions (Foner, *From Ellis Island to JFK*, 19).

7. For more on the occupational history of Italian immigrants in their native country, see Thomas Kessner, *The Golden Door: Italian and Jewish Immigrant Mobility in New York City, 1880–1915* (Oxford University Press, 1977), 32–41; and Tirabassi, "Why Italians Left Italy," 117–31.

8. Foerster, *Italian Emigration of Our Times*, 343. The immigrants' status as laborers would continue years after their initial passage to America. A survey made in 1905, for example, found that approximately 60 percent of Italians could be classified as unskilled or semiskilled laborers, 20 percent could be classified as skilled blue-collar workers, and only about 20 percent could be labeled as "lower white-collar workers"—a category that included shopkeepers and merchants (Alba, "Italian Americans: A Century," 173).

9. Foner, *From Ellis Island to JFK*, 110. Such were the needs of America's growing industrial economy that US companies would sometimes hire "padroni" (or "bosses") to recruit and import pools of Italian workers and direct them to jobs. A "padrone" would pay for the immigrants' passage, as well as their room, board, clothing, and tools, while keeping them in virtual indentured servitude until they could pay off their debts. The 1885 Contract Labor Law would eventually make this system illegal. By the early twentieth century, the immigrants' own personal networks were responsible for delivering Italians to sources of employment. For more on the padrone system, see Humbert S. Nelli, *From Immigrants to Ethnics: The Italian Americans* (Oxford University Press, 1983), 73–95, and Foerster, *Italian Emigration of Our Times*, 324–27.

10. Foerster, *Italian Emigration of Our Times*, 374.

11. Foner, *From Ellis Island to JFK*, 174.

12. For a thorough examination of the transnational condition of Italian immigrants, see Donna Gabaccia, *Italy's Many Diasporas* (University of Washington Press, 2000), 14–128. Gabaccia proposes that throughout the nineteenth and twentieth centuries, an Italian diaspora created a global collectivity—"civiltà italiana"—that then drew its sense of identity and homeland from "il paese," or the local community. Gabaccia argues that this notion of homeland was both portable and adaptable, sustaining Italians in countries as diverse as Argentina, Brazil, and the US—as captured in the proverb "tutto il mondo è paese" (all the world is home).

13. For a discussion of how Italian families adapted to modern conditions, while maintaining Old World cultural traditions, see Virginia Yans-McLaughlin's *Family and Community: Italian Immigrants in Buffalo, 1880–1930* (Cornell University Press, 1977). Yans-McLaughlin argues that ethnic families helped immigrants adjust to the demands of urban life by providing economic security, a means of socialization, and the preservation of historic customs and rituals.

14. World War I, the anti-immigrant legislation of 1924, and the Great Depression also helped create a more cohesive Italian American community, as the dearth of new arrivals and the end of transatlantic migration affected provincial loyalties. For more on the evolution of Italian identity in America, see Stefano Luconi, *From Paesani to White Ethnics: The Italian Experience in Philadelphia* (State University of New York Press, 2001).

15. Some Italian immigrants did successfully practice trades in the US—shoemakers and barbers, for example, integrated themselves seamlessly into the American marketplace. Other notable exceptions to the labor category included merchants and shopkeepers who served the immigrant communities.

16. Foerster, *Italian Emigration of Our Times*, 354, and Foner, *From Ellis Island to JFK*, 81. This estimate was made by the Inspector of Public Works.

17. Foner, *From Ellis Island to JFK*, 81.

18. Frederick M. Binder and David M. Reimers, *All the Nations Under Heaven: An Ethnic and Racial History of New York City* (Columbia University Press, 1995), 140.

19. Binder and Reimers, *All the Nations Under Heaven*, 141. Young women also commonly labored in candy, tobacco, and box factories. For more on immigrant women's work, see Elizabeth Ewen, *Immigrant Women in the Land of Dollars: Life and Culture on the Lower East Side, 1890–1925* (Monthly Review Press, 1985), 24–26, 121–26, and 246–62; and Donna Gabaccia, *From the Other Side: Women, Gender, and Immigrant Life in the U.S., 1820–1990* (Indiana University Press, 1994), 46–52.

20. Foner, *From Ellis Island to JFK*, 82.

21. Kessner, *Golden Door*, 136.

22. Foner, *From Ellis Island to JFK*, 39.

23. Richard Alba notes that at the turn of the century, Manhattan was home to 150 different mutual aid societies ("Italian Americans: A Century," 174). Alba adds that by the 1920s, as legislation stifled new immigration, Italians began to form more unitary organizations like the Sons of Italy. For a discussion of how diverse immigrant cultures fused through a shared urban-industrial experience, but in the setting of Tampa, Florida, see George E. Pozzetta and Gary R. Mormino, *The Immigrant World of Ybor City: Italians and Their Latin American Neighbors in Tampa, 1885–1985* (University of Illinois Press, 1990), 97–142 and 175–209.

24. Those Italian immigrants who arrived in the US between 1899 and 1910 also had the lowest literacy rates of all European groups. Nancy Foner notes that 47 percent of Italians over the age of fourteen who arrived in this period could neither read nor write (*From Ellis Island to JFK*, 72). Richard Alba writes that even by 1930, Italians "ranked at or near the top among immigrant groups in the percentages who did not speak English and who were not citizens" ("Italian Americans: A Century," 173).

25. The Italian community's political apathy also stemmed from its historic distrust of government, and from Irish domination of New York City politics. While Tammany Hall made some overtures toward Italian immigrants, the community's indifference was slow to dissipate. By the time of the Great Depression and Fiorello La Guardia's election as mayor in 1933, however, Italians had begun to become more active in civic affairs. For more on Italian politics, see Nelli, *From Immigrants to Ethnics*, 96–113. The Italian immigrants' relationship to the Catholic Church was more curious. One would expect that Italians would suffer discrimination from America's Protestant majority, like the Catholic immigrants who preceded them. But Italian immigrants were also marginalized within an American Catholic establishment dominated by the Irish clergy. The Catholic hierarchy was suspicious of the immigrants' religious practices—which, in southern Italy, had often incorporated traditional folk beliefs. Moreover, the Italian immigrants came from a culture that had a long tradition of anticlericalism and considered church attendance a woman's province. Male immigrants were thus skeptical of the authority of the Church and the priesthood. Because of these attitudes, and their relative poverty, Italian families were the least likely of all Catholic immigrant groups to send their children to parochial schools. The Italian communities did have vibrant expressions of faith with their neighborhood "festas"—annual public festivals dedicated to particular patron saints. These celebrations served as expressions of both community (as the saints often had an association with the home regions in Italy) and religious faith—what one scholar called "a sacred theater" of neighborhoods like East Harlem. See Robert Orsi, *The Madonna of 115th Street: Faith and*

Community in Italian Harlem, 1880–1950 (Yale University Press, 1985), 1–13 and 163–218. For more on the Italian immigrants' religious practices and their relationship with the institutions of Catholicism, see Charles Morris, *American Catholic: The Saints and Sinners Who Built America's Most Powerful Church* (Vintage Books, 1997), 50–51 and 128–31; Richard Alba, "Social Assimilation Among American Catholic National-Origin Groups," *American Sociological Review* 41, no. 6 (December 1976): 1030–46; and Silvano M. Tomasi, "The Ethnic Church and the Integration of Italian Immigrants in the United States," in *The Italian Experience in the United States*, ed. Silvano M. Tomasi and Madeline H. Engel (Center for Migration Studies, 1970).

26. Binder and Reimers, *All the Nations Under Heaven*, 195. The survey was carried out by the US Immigration Commission, for children aged six to fifteen.

27. See Gabaccia, *Italy's Many Diasporas*, 181; James R. Barrett and David Roediger, "Inbetween Peoples: Race, Nationality and the 'New Immigrant' Working Class," *Journal of American Ethnic History* 16, no. 3 (Spring 1997): 3–44; and Matthew Frye Jacobson, *Whiteness of a Different Color: European Immigrants and the Alchemy of Race* (Harvard University Press, 1998). For other perspectives on the subject of Italian Americans and race, see Jennifer Guglielmo and Salvatore Salerno, *Are Italians White? How Race Is Made in America* (Routledge, 2003); David A. J. Richards, *Italian American: The Racializing of an Ethnic Identity* (New York University Press, 1999); and David R. Roediger, *Working Toward Whiteness: How America's Immigrants Became White* (Basic Books, 2005).

28. Barrett and Roediger, "Inbetween Peoples," 8–9.

29. Frank Marshall White, "To Rid This Country of Foreign Criminals," *Harper's Weekly*, June 27, 1908, 16, and "Black Hand Holds Sway in Italian New York," *Literary Digest*, August 30, 1913, 308–9. White also authored "The Black Hand in Control in Italian New York," *Outlook*, August 16, 1913, 857–65.

30. The Immigration Act of 1924 limited migration to the United States from outside the Western Hemisphere to 165,000 a year, while establishing a quota was based on 2 percent of each nationality living in the US in 1890. The law thus allotted most of the annual visas to immigrants from Great Britain, Ireland, Germany, and Scandinavia while giving Italy fewer than 6,000 slots per year.

31. Jacobson, *Whiteness of a Different Color*, 6.

32. Thomas A. Guglielmo, *White on Arrival: Italians, Race, Color, and Power in Chicago, 1890–1945* (Oxford University Press, 2003), 9.

33. See Luconi, *From Paesani to White Ethnics*.

34. John Foster Carr, "The Coming of the Italian," *Outlook*, February 24, 1906, 419.

35. G. E. DiPalma Castiglione, "Immigrants in Cities," from "Italian Immigration into the United States, 1901–4," *American Journal of Sociology*, September 1905, as reprinted in *A Documentary History of the Italian Americans*, ed. Wayne Moquin (Praeger, 1974), 55–56.

36. Foerster, *Italian Emigration of Our Times*, 415.

37. Federal Writers' Project, *Italians of New York*, 62–63.

38. Binder and Reimers, *All the Nations Under Heaven*, 143. See also Kessner, *Golden Door*, 115–26.

39. Foner, *From Ellis Island to JFK*, 42, and Binder and Reimers, *All the Nations Under Heaven*, 153.

40. Federal Writers' Project, *Italians of New York*, 21; Binder and Reimers, *All the Nations Under Heaven*, 158; and Simone Cinotto, *The Italian American Table: Food, Family, and Community in New York City* (University of Illinois Press, 2013), 9.

41. Charlotte Adams, "Italian Life in New York," *Harper's Magazine*, April 1881, 676–84, as reprinted in *A Documentary History of the Italian Americans*, ed. Wayne Moquin (Praeger, 1974), 40.

42. Foerster, *Italian Emigration of Our Times*, 395.

43. Foerster, *Italian Emigration of Our Times*, 337.

44. For a prime example of the sentimentalization of Italian immigrants, see Caroline Singer, "An Italian Saturday," *The Century*, March 1921, 591–97. Singer gives her readers a tour of Little Italy on market day—the "gayest place in the city." She introduces her audience to such characters as the "blind flutist, who pipes 'Il Travatore' through the markets," a wandering fortune-teller, and the ubiquitous organ-grinder, who nestles between "mounds of tomatoes and green peppers" to play his ancient music to balconies of "Madonna-faced women" and frolicking urchins. Even as Italian Americans assimilated themselves into the larger community of white ethnics, many of these stereotypes maintained a remarkable resilience. The 1938 Federal Writers' Project study *The Italians of New York* described the city's Italian neighborhoods as hosting "picturesquely dressed peasants from the warm Italian southland, with their swarthy complexions, fierce mustaches and antique headgear" who could be "easily mistaken for bandits from Sardinia—bandits come to life on New York streets" (1).

45. Adams, "Italian Life in New York," 41.

46. Foerster, *Italian Emigration of Our Times*, 436.

47. Lilian Brandt, "A Transplanted Birthright: The Development of the Second Generation of the Italians in an American Environment," *Charities*, May 7, 1904, 497.

48. For two elucidating studies of the primary role that food and food retailing played in the making of Italian identity and community in American cities, see Hasia Diner, *Hungering for America: Italian, Irish, and Jewish Foodways in the Age of Migration* (Harvard University Press, 2001), and Cinotto, *Italian American Table*. Diner argues that food enabled a disparate collection of migrants to experience the abundance of the US while also allowing them to assert a sense of "Italian" culture in their adopted country (albeit one that responded to an American context) (48–83). Cinotto affirms the role that food played in the construction of Italian identity among immigrants to New York, in terms of both habits of consumption and the ethnic food trade. Cinotto characterizes food as "a toolkit that helped New York Italians, immigrant and New York-born, work their own way through the realities of class, gender, race, and nation" (16).

49. Brandt, "Transplanted Birthright," 495.

50. Foerster, *Italian Emigration of Our Times*, 434.

51. The peddlers' lack of overhead and their ability to buy overripe, wholesale produce in small quantities made their low prices possible. In the mid-1920s, fruit peddlers made $126 a week while paying out only $9.22 in overhead costs—approximately one-third of that of a neighborhood grocer. See "New York Pushcarts Do $35,000,000 Trade," *New York Times*, May 25, 1925, 30. The peddlers' ability to turn over mature produce also allowed them to salvage a large quantity of fruits and vegetables that retail markets had rejected, thus limiting waste and price fluctuation. See "More Pushcarts to Vanish," *New York Times*, September 20, 1936, 10; and Florence Brobeck, "Outdoor Food Markets Are Moving Indoors," *New York Times*, October 11, 1936, sec. 7, 16.

52. "Farewell to the Pushcarts," *New York Times*, July 23, 1937, 18.

53. "New York Pushcarts Do $35,000,000 Trade," 30.

54. "New York's Many Miles of Pushcarts," *New York Times*, November 30, 1924, sec. 4, 4. The figures come from a survey conducted by the City Department of Markets and the Federal Department of Agriculture.

55. "New York Pushcarts Do $35,000,000 Trade," 30.

56. "Raid Pushcart Peddlers," *New York Times*, December 24, 1910, 2. It was not uncommon for police to disperse the informal gatherings of peddlers that served as "de facto" markets, to the chagrin of the vendors and their customers. See "Want the Pushcarts Back," *New York Times*, June 14, 1912, 6.

57. See "To Regulate Peddlers," *New York Times*, April 16, 1910, 10, and "Pushcart Men's Problems," *New York Times*, June 18, 1912, 22.

58. "Pushcart Market Planned," *New York Times*, June 16, 1912, 15; "Pushcart Markets," *New York Times*, November 21, 1912, 12; "Pushcart Markets Now," *New York Times*, December 10, 1912, 14; and "The Pushcart Markets," *New York Times*, April 1, 1913, 10.

59. "More Pushcarts to Vanish," 10.

60. "New York's Many Miles of Pushcarts," IV: 4.

61. "All Peddlers Barred from Midtown Area," *New York Times*, July 10, 1929, 18.

62. "Pushcart Markets Found Insanitary," *New York Times*, February 27, 1930, 25.

63. Some officials merely called for stricter licensing of peddlers to eliminate those who dealt on the margins of the law. Others—including officials in the New York Department of Markets—actively campaigned for the pushcarts' total elimination. See "Seeks to Curb Peddlers," *New York Times*, February 10, 1935, sec. 2, 2; and "Opening Anti-Pushcart Drive," *New York Times*, February 28, 1935, 5.

64. Brobeck, "Outdoor Food Markets Are Moving Indoors," 16.

65. "Mayor Forecasts 'Four More Years,'" *New York Times*, July 22, 1937, 14.

66. "Mayor Orders Curb on Pushcarts Permits," *New York Times*, November 13, 1934, 4.

67. "Mayor Forecasts 'Four More Years,'" 14.

68. "Pushcarts Losing Ground," *New York Times*, August 25, 1935, IV, 10. This figure represented a gradual decline in peddlers' numbers. In 1930, there had been 8,000 licensed pushcarts in the city. See "A Thriving Business," *New York Times*, August 3, 1930, sec. 11, 7.

69. "Farewell to the Pushcarts," 18.

70. "Farewell to the Pushcarts," 18.

71. Food Industry Alliance of New York State, "FIA Celebrates 100 Years," *Food Advocate / Griffin's Modern Grocer*, 2000, 16.

72. Marc Levinson, *The Great A&P and the Struggle for Small Business in America* (Hill and Wang, 2011), 124.

73. Levinson, *Great A&P*, 125–26.

74. Ryan Mathews, "Special Report: Social Change and the Supermarket," *Progressive Grocer*, December 1996, 42 and 47.

75. For more on the early history of the supermarket, see Richard S. Tedlow, *New and Improved: The Story of Mass Marketing in America* (Basic Books, 1990), 182–258; James M. Mayo, *The American Grocery Store: The Business Evolution of an Architectural Space* (Greenwood, 1993), 81–155; Michael Ruhlman, *Grocery: The Buying and Selling of Food in America* (Abrams, 2017), 29–46; Levinson, *Great A&P*, 23–85; Mathews, "Special Report," 29–54; Food Industry Alliance of New York State, "FIA Celebrates 100 Years," 2–13; and J. Tevere MacFadyen, "The Rise of the Supermarket," *American Heritage*, October/November 1985, 22–32.

76. Tracey Deutsch, *Building a Housewife's Paradise: Gender, Politics, and American Grocery Stores in the Twentieth Century* (University of North Carolina Press, 2010), 4.

77. Donna Gabaccia, *We Are What We Eat: Ethnic Food and the Making of Americans* (Harvard University Press, 1998), 132–33.

78. Federal Writers' Project, *Italians of New York*, 72.
79. Binder and Reimers, *All the Nations Under Heaven*, 171.

2. Immigrant Grocers and American Dreams (1880–1946)

1. Mark Murphy, "If Trouble Can Be Avoid," *New Yorker*, May 15, 1943, 34.
2. Murphy, "If Trouble Can Be Avoid," 25. In the quote, Murphy refers to the system of rationing in which the government classified car owners as A, B, C, or X and then provided coupon books for particular allotments of gasoline. As a food distributor (and thus essential to the war effort), Patsy was entitled to a B card and an extra ration of gas because he used his auto for work purposes. See Richard R. Lingeman, "Remembrance of Rationing Past," *New York Times Magazine*, September 9, 1973, 108–9.
3. Murphy, "If Trouble Can Be Avoid," 29.
4. Corey posits that these ethnic portraits addressed the readership's anxieties about the "morally corrosive effects" of mass consumption, technological development, and affluence, especially in a post–World War II context. See Mary F. Corey, *The World Through a Monocle: "The New Yorker" at Midcentury* (Harvard University Press, 1999), 102. Corey also analyzes the composition of *The New Yorker*'s community of readers in the 1940s and 1950s, concluding that the newly affluent middle class drove the magazine's success in this period. This same demographic became the engine of D'Agostino's postwar expansion.
5. Murphy, "If Trouble Can Be Avoid," 28.
6. Murphy, "If Trouble Can Be Avoid," 26 and 28.
7. When he began working on the pushcart, Patsy was the prototypical immigrant "greenhorn." He was still known by his given name—Pasquale—and spoke little English. But he worked alongside "Patsy" Tucciarone (the brother of his future partner and the uncle of his future sister-in-law), who gave him an Americanized nickname, and taught him essential English vocabulary: "potato," "tomato," "string beans," and "celery."
8. Murphy, "If Trouble Can Be Avoid," 31.
9. Murphy, "If Trouble Can Be Avoid," 30.
10. Murphy, "If Trouble Can Be Avoid," 31.
11. Murphy, "If Trouble Can Be Avoid," 33.
12. Murphy, "If Trouble Can Be Avoid," 35.
13. While the brothers' father and several relatives (including the family of Nicholas's wife) hailed from Tufo di Minturno, in the province of Latina in southern Lazio, Patsy and Nicholas claimed Abruzzi as their ancestral home due to the serendipitous circumstances of immigrant marriage. Ignatius D'Agostino, Patsy and Nicholas's father, was working on a railroad crew in Ohio when a "paesan," Tony D'Espinosa, showed him a photograph of his sister, Loreta. Of course, D'Espinosa advertised his sister's charms, and after a courtship by mail, Ignatius went back to Bugnara to win her hand. The couple did marry, but after a brief sojourn in New York, Loreta went home—despite being pregnant with her second child—never to return to America.
14. Thomas Ashby, *Some Italian Scenes and Festivals* (E. P. Dutton, 1929), 89.
15. Ashby, *Some Italian Scenes and Festivals*, 89 and 109. In his portrait of Abruzzi, Ashby incorrectly translates the region's motto as "brave, but gentle."
16. One missionary observed that in southern Italian villages, the streets "give one the impression of chicken runs. Life is at the door, with babies, pigs, chickens and household operations indescribably mingled." See Philip M. Rose, *The Italians in America* (George H. Doran, 1922), 35–36.

17. The brothers would install electricity and the town's first private bathroom with working plumbing in their boyhood home after they had "made it."

18. Loretta D'Agostino Schmitz, unpublished personal journal, collection of the author, 2001.

19. Robert F. Foerster, *The Italian Emigration of Our Times* (Harvard University Press, 1919), 450.

20. Foerster, *Italian Emigration of Our Times*, 468.

21. For more on how socioeconomic conditions in Italy served as a catalyst for immigration, see Maddalena Tirabassi, "Why Italians Left Italy: The Physics and Politics of Migration," in *The Routledge History of Italian Americans*, ed. William J. Connell and Stanislao G. Pugliese (Routledge, 2018), 117–31; Laura Buonanno and Michael Buonanno, *Remembering Italian America: Memory, Migration, and Identity* (Routledge, 2021), 44–61; John W. Briggs, *An Italian Passage: Immigrants to Three American Cities, 1890–1930* (Yale University Press, 1978), 1–14; Dino Cinel, *From Italy to San Francisco: The Immigrant Experience* (Stanford University Press, 1982), 15–70; Federal Writers' Project, *The Italians of New York* (1938; Arno Press, 1969), 36–50; Donna Gabaccia, *Italy's Many Diasporas* (University of Washington Press, 2000), 35–57; and Foerster, *Italian Emigration of Our Times*, 23–43 and 51–105.

22. Gabaccia, *Italy's Many Diasporas*, 83–90.

23. Gabaccia, *Italy's Many Diasporas*, 84.

24. The autobiography was titled "The Four Seasons of Nicholas D'Agostino" and consisted of three chapters: "Loreta's Son" (on his childhood), "Stephen's Son" (on his early days in America and in the food business), and "Josephine's Husband" (on his courtship and marriage to Josephine Tucciarone).

25. Nicholas D'Agostino, "Loreta's Son" in "The Four Seasons of Nicholas D'Agostino," unpublished manuscript, collection of the author, 1982, 2.

26. N. D'Agostino, "Loreta's Son," 2–3.

27. N. D'Agostino, "Loreta's Son," 3.

28. Donna Gabaccia argues that because domestic life in America severely limited women's social interactions, it often became a target for their general discontent. See *From Sicily to Elizabeth Street: Housing and Social Change Among Italian Immigrants, 1880–1930* (State University of New York Press, 1984), 99.

29. Nancy Foner, *From Ellis Island to JFK: New York's Two Great Waves of Immigration* (Yale University Press, 2000), 122–23. Italian women also had to deal with the added burden of American standards of domestic cleanliness, as propagated by social workers and settlement houses. In rural Italy, it was not uncommon for women to wash the interior of their stone or stucco houses once a month; in New York they learned that a proper home should have curtains and blinds and be washed at least once a week. See also Elizabeth Ewen, *Immigrant Women in the Land of Dollars: Life and Culture on the Lower East Side, 1890–1925* (Monthly Review Press, 1985), 148–52.

30. Patsy D'Agostino, *How I Made a Million*, ed. Noah Sarlat (1955; Paperback Library, 1961), 82.

31. N. D'Agostino, "Loreta's Son," 3.

32. N. D'Agostino, "Loreta's Son," 3.

33. N. D'Agostino, "Loreta's Son," 7.

34. N. D'Agostino, "Loreta's Son," 11.

35. N. D'Agostino, "Loreta's Son," 12.

36. N. D'Agostino, "Loreta's Son," 13.

37. Patsy D'Agostino, "I Found $5,000,000 in a Pushcart," *American Magazine*, September 1952, 107.

38. P. D'Agostino, "I Found $5,000,000 in a Pushcart," 15.

39. Frank and Ignatius had known each other since childhood. Moreover, the marriage of Nicholas D'Agostino to Josephine Tucciarone was not the first union between the families; according to one family member, in Tufo the D'Agostinos and Tucciarones had been marrying one another for generations (Loretta D'Agostino Schmitz, unpublished personal journal, 2001).

40. Loretta D'Agostino Schmitz, unpublished personal journal, 2001.

41. Loretta D'Agostino Schmitz, unpublished personal journal, 2001.

42. The practice of buying on the margins meant that the would-be investor used the promise of a stock's future profitability to purchase more shares. It was a common strategy in the 1920s, as thousands of speculators, inspired by the era's atmosphere of easy wealth, jumped into the market without sufficient capital. Of course, this tactic was one of the principal causes of the market's downward spiral.

43. Loretta D'Agostino Schmitz, unpublished personal journal, 2001.

44. Nancy Foner cites one 1905 study which estimated that 62 percent of single Italian-born women in New York City were wage earners (111). For more on the work lives of Italian women in America, see Foner, *From Ellis Island to JFK*, 108–41; Donna Gabaccia, *From the Other Side: Women, Gender, and Immigrant Life in the U.S., 1820–1990* (Indiana University Press, 1994), 45–60; and Ewen, *Immigrant Women in the Land of Dollars*, 93–110.

45. For more on the social habits of the children of immigrants, especially in relation to modern mass culture and courtship rituals, see Ewen, *Immigrant Women in the Land of Dollars*, 185–240, and Foner, *From Ellis Island to JFK*, 111–15.

46. Loretta D'Agostino Schmitz, unpublished personal journal, 2001.

47. N. D'Agostino, "Stephen's Son," 3.

48. N. D'Agostino, "Stephen's Son," 3.

49. Simone Cinotto, *The Italian American Table: Food, Family, and Community in New York City* (University of Illinois Press, 2013), 52.

50. N. D'Agostino, "Stephen's Son," 4.

51. N. D'Agostino, "Stephen's Son," 4.

52. N. D'Agostino, "Stephen's Son," 5. The healthy wages the merchants paid to cousins and acquaintances illustrates how this close-knit community spread the wealth among its members (and was prone to competitive, self-aggrandizing acts of generosity).

53. N. D'Agostino, "Stephen's Son," 5.

54. N. D'Agostino, "Stephen's Son," 6. Nicholas's story illustrated how those grocery men who "made it," whether through talent, fortune, or capturing a prime customer base, could be as prosperous as many white-collar workers, even during the Great Depression. Meanwhile, the rest of the Italian American population was particularly affected by the Depression, since so many of its wage earners were laborers. For example, in 1930, over 16 percent of the families in Little Italy had no adult wage earner; by 1932, that figure had risen to nearly 48 percent (Frederick M. Binder and David M. Reimers, *All the Nations Under Heaven: An Ethnic and Racial History of New York City* [Columbia University Press, 1995], 178).

55. N. D'Agostino, "Stephen's Son," 7.

56. N. D'Agostino, "Stephen's Son," 9.

57. N. D'Agostino, "Stephen's Son," 9.

58. P. D'Agostino, "I Found $5,000,000 in a Pushcart," 108.

59. How did Nicholas meet his future bride? The genesis of their partnership is unknown, though it likely can be traced to the closeness of the Italian community in New York—not only did the couple's fathers know one another, they also had several friends and relatives in common. Soon after Nicholas's arrival in the US, he was even invited to Josephine's "sweet sixteen" birthday party. His cousin asked him to carry in some phonograph records, which were wrapped in paper, and when he arrived at the door, Josephine thanked the immigrant "greenhorn" for what she thought was a gift, exclaiming, "Oh, Nick! You shouldn't have" (N. D'Agostino, "Josephine's Husband," 2). Though the episode would eventually be a great source of amusement for the couple, it would be five years before they began dating.

60. N. D'Agostino, "Josephine's Husband," 2.

61. N. D'Agostino, "Josephine's Husband," 2.

62. N. D'Agostino, "Josephine's Husband," 6.

63. N. D'Agostino, "Josephine's Husband," 4 and 9. While Patsy did buy Adolf Tucciarone's stake in the grocery for $4,000, it seems possible that Nicholas may have mischaracterized the size of Tony D'Espinosa's loan to his nephew.

64. N. D'Agostino, "Stephen's Son," 9–10.

65. N. D'Agostino, "Stephen's Son," 11.

66. Loretta D'Agostino Schmitz, unpublished personal journal, 2001.

67. Stephen D'Agostino, interview by author, August 9, 2001.

68. At the time of the article, the Third Avenue store was now called the Yorkville Food Shop, the second store was known as the Yorkville Food Store, and the Mount Vernon store, which the company closed within a few years, was called D'Agostino Brothers. The symbolic issues regarding the naming of the company's stores will be analyzed in greater detail in the next chapter.

69. Murphy, "If Trouble Can Be Avoid," 33–34.

70. Food Industry Alliance of New York, "FIA Celebrates 100 Years," *Food Advocate/Griffin's Modern Grocer*, 2000, 6.

71. Food Industry Alliance of New York, "FIA Celebrates 100 Years," 7. Certain figures in the trade, including the editor of the *Progressive Grocer*, argued that restrictions on gas and travel actually helped the independent retailers because consumers were coerced into shopping locally (7). Of course, this benefit was less applicable to urban merchants like the D'Agostinos. Historian James Mayo has argued that while the war forestalled the supermarket's conquest of the buying public, wartime conditions did help the supermarket model establish itself. The lack of personnel, for example, forced store owners to speed their conversion to self-service, and the lack of canned goods (as they were shipped abroad, or the tin was used in the war effort) encouraged the sale of frozen foods. See James M. Mayo, *The American Grocery Store: The Business Evolution of an Architectural Space* (Greenwood, 1993), 158–61.

72. Loretta D'Agostino Schmitz, unpublished personal journal, 2001.

73. Loretta D'Agostino Schmitz, unpublished personal journal, 2001.

74. For more on this evolving identity, see Stefano Luconi, *From Paesani to White Ethnics: The Italian Experience in Philadelphia* (State University of New York Press, 2001), 39–94.

75. Gabaccia, *Italy's Many Diasporas*, 129–31.

76. Gabaccia, *Italy's Many Diasporas*, 144–52; Binder and Reimers, *All the Nations Under Heaven*, 190; and Danielle Battisti, *Whom We Shall Welcome: Italian Americans and Immigration Reform, 1945–1965* (Fordham University Press), 20–25.

77. "FIA Celebrates 100 Years," 9.

78. Gabaccia, *Italy's Many Diasporas*, 148.

79. For more on the treatment of Italians during the war, see Stanislao G. Pugliese, "Fascism and Anti-Fascism in Italian America" and Dominic Candeloro, "World War II Changed Everything," in *The Routledge History of Italian Americans*, ed. William J. Connell and Stanislao G. Pugliese (Routledge, 2018), 349–84.

80. Loretta D'Agostino Schmitz, unpublished personal journal, 2001.

81. Murphy, "If Trouble Can Be Avoid," 25.

82. For more examples of Patsy D'Agostino's public commentary regarding food policy, see "Poultry Shortage Feared by Dealers," *New York Times*, March 6, 1943, 10; "Food Stores Urged to Close Full Day," *New York Times*, March 12, 1943, 11; "New Ceilings Set for 7 Vegetables to Restore Supply," *New York Times*, March 14, 1943, 1; "Adverse Effect on Food Shops Seen in Point Rationing System," *New York Times*, March 20, 1943, 18; "Sausages Spoiling, Retailers Assert," *New York Times*, April 20, 1943, 1; "Point-Cutting War on Rationed Food in the City Is Begun," *New York Times*, April 4, 1943, 1; "Early Shortage of Meat for Army as Result of OPA Rules Predicted," *New York Times*, May 2, 1943, 1; "Draft Exemption Sought," *New York Times*, April 23, 1944, sec. 3, 3; "Food Black Market Costs $1,200,000, Bowles Declares," *New York Times*, March 1, 1944, 1; "Cigarettes Hoarded," *New York Times*, October 5, 1944, 25; "Holiday Prospects for Turkey Vanish," *New York Times*, October 28, 1944, 17; "'Oleo' Now Harder to Get Than Butter, Stores Find," *New York Times*, November 30, 1944, 20; "Grocers, Tired of Abuse, Drop Cigarette Sales," *New York Times*, February 2, 1945, 21; "Little Meat Here Again This Week," *New York Times*, May 26, 1945, 12; "Cake Production to Be Cut Again," *New York Times*, June 12, 1945, 16; "Orange Prices Rise on Black Market," *New York Times*, June 17, 1945, 20; Marshall Newton, "Fear Meat Costs Will Soar Dims Relief of Housewives," *New York Times*, October 15, 1946, 1; and "Food Trade Is Told to Put House in Order," *New York Times*, November 20, 1946, 49.

83. Meg Jacobs, *Pocketbook Politics: Economic Citizenship in Twentieth-Century America* (Princeton University Press, 2005), 179–80.

84. Murphy, "If Trouble Can Be Avoid," 25.

85. While Patsy defended the government's rationing of coffee and sugar, he criticized the OPA's lack of understanding of the realities of the local marketplace as it set prices. He saved particular scorn for its confusing system of "point rationing" in which the OPA categorized food by type and assigned them each a point value, and then allotted consumers a certain number of points with which to "shop." "The people was not educated to point rationing," he declared (Murphy, "If Trouble Can Be Avoid," 30). In the 1930s and '40s, food retailing also became highly politicized, as indicated by Patsy's crusading. It is important to note, however, that the politicization of shopping extended to the female consumers who populated his stores. Patsy was perhaps dismissive of some of his female customers who, as Tracey Deutsch explains, viewed the marketplace as a place of advocacy and empowerment in this period. In their domestic roles as providers for their families, women were obliged to negotiate with and contest the authority of male shopkeepers like Patsy. For more on this dynamic, see Tracey Deutsch, *Building a Housewife's Paradise: Gender, Politics, and American Grocery Stores in the Twentieth Century* (University of North Carolina Press, 2010).

86. For more on rationing and the system of price control, see Jacobs, *Pocketbook Politics*, 179–220; Deutsch, *Building a Housewife's Paradise*, 155–82; and Barbara McLean Ward, ed., *Produce and Conserve, Share and Play Square: The Grocer and the Consumer on the Home-Front Battlefield During World War II* (Strawberry Banke, 1994). For a sampling of contemporary magazine and newspaper articles on the OPA, see D. Clark, "Hard-Hitting Boss of Prices," *New York Times Magazine*, April 27, 1941, 6; R. Robey, "OPACS: The New

Price Control Organization," *Newsweek*, April 21, 1941, 48; "OPA's Police Job," *Business Week*, March 28, 1942, 19–20+; L. Huston, "GHQ For Our Daily Life: Leon Henderson's OPA Headquarters," *New York Times Magazine*, May 10, 1942, 4–5+; "Price Education: OPA Trying to Educate the Retailer," *Business Week*, May 23, 1942: 66+; M. Straight, "Why Henderson Goes," *New Republic*, December 28, 1942, 847–49; F. A. Baughn, "We're Going to Be Closed Up Anyway: O.P.A. Driving Retailers Out of Business," *Nation's Business*, January 1943, 18+; C. Wilcox, "In Defense of Price Control," *New York Times Magazine*, October 10, 1943, 12+; D. Lang, "Menus, Nylons, Wiping Cloths and Abdullahs," *New Yorker*, July 14, 1945, 36+; "Farewell to Price Control," *Fortune*, August 1946, 3; "Final Showdown on OPA," *Nation*, June 22, 1946, 736–37; and "How They Killed O.P.A.," *New Republic*, September 23, 1946, 378+.

87. Murphy, "If Trouble Can Be Avoid," 30.

88. For more on the political battle between independent merchants and chain retailers such as A&P, see Nancy Beck Young, *Wright Patman: Populism, Liberalism, and the American Dream* (Southern Methodist University Press, 2000), and Marc Levinson, *The Great A&P and the Struggle for Small Business in America* (Hill and Wang, 2011), 220–46.

89. U.S. Congress, Select Committee to Conduct a Study and Investigation of the National Defense Program in its Relation to Small Business in the United States, *Hearings on Small Business*, 78th Cong., 1st Sess., June 7, 1943, 871–969 (testimony of Patsy D'Agostino). On July 11, 1947, Congress would again call Patsy D'Agostino to testify. This time, however, he spoke about unionization and its effect on the food industry, as Fred A. Hartley, George McKinnon, Richard Nixon, John F. Kennedy, and Adam Clayton Powell and the other members of a special subcommittee listened and took notes. See U.S. Congress, Special Subcommittee on Education and Labor, *Hearings on Labor Practices in the Food Industry*, 80th Cong., 1st Sess., July 11, 1947, 62–65.

90. Under OPA legislation, stores were given numeric classifications based on the size of their inventory, their prices, and the range of services they offered. Most independent grocers were designated as "class 1" or "class 2" stores, while larger operations such as the chain retailers were classified as "3" or "4." The OPA labeled D'Agostino's as a "class 2" store.

91. P. D'Agostino, Congressional Testimony, June 7, 1943, 959.

92. P. D'Agostino, Congressional Testimony, June 7, 1943, 960–61.

93. P. D'Agostino, Congressional Testimony, June 7, 1943, 961.

94. Independents often had to charge higher prices and carry more restricted inventories because of their lack of capital and limited access to the supply chain. Larger retailers also had the ability to make deals with their suppliers to get certain items that were unavailable to smaller grocers.

95. P. D'Agostino, Congressional Testimony, June 7, 1943, 964 and 966.

96. P. D'Agostino, Congressional Testimony, June 7, 1943, 964.

97. P. D'Agostino, Congressional Testimony, June 7, 1943, 966.

98. P. D'Agostino, Congressional Testimony, June 7, 1943, 968.

99. Foerster, *Italian Emigration of Our Times*, 415.

100. Murphy, "If Trouble Can Be Avoid," 30.

101. Cinotto, *Italian American Table*, 134.

3. The Grocer in the Gray Flannel Suit (1946–60)

1. "A Triumph and an Obligation," *Life*, January 3, 1955, 2. This introductory essay includes several statistics that indicate just how unprecedented the levels of food production

and consumption were in the 1950s. Despite the fact that the population had increased by 50 percent in the previous three decades, and the acreage of available farmland had remained relatively stable, America harvested so much food that it had a $6.6 billion surplus stored in government warehouses. The advances in food production had also reduced the share of income that each individual spent on food from 45 percent to 25 percent.

2. "Shopper's Delight," *Life*, January 3, 1955, 39.

3. The article noted that the city consumed one-twelfth of all the food in the United States ("Biggest Appetite," *Life*, January 3, 1955, 22).

4. Nicholas D'Agostino, "The Four Seasons of Nicholas D'Agostino," unpublished manuscript, collection of the author, 1982, 1. This tale was also featured in several official company publications.

5. As a spokesman for the interests of independent grocers and a favorite source among reporters, Patsy was frequently quoted by *The New York Times* on these postwar concerns, just as he was during World War II. For examples of his opinions, refer to "Sees Food Pipeline No Longer Clogged," *New York Times*, February 4, 1947, 35; "Grocers' Group Head Urges Lower Prices," *New York Times*, April 28, 1947, 33; "Details Problems of Retail Grocers," *New York Times*, June 23, 1947, 27; "For Study Abroad: Retail Grocers Ask Truman to Send Experts to Europe," *New York Times*, September 23, 1947, 8; "Meat, Butter, Eggs Take Another Dip," *New York Times*, September 23, 1947, 1; "Sales of Meat Drop Little On 1st 'Meatless' Tuesday," *New York Times*, October 8, 1947, sec. 1, 6; "Grocers Say Cost Cuts Their Profit," *New York Times*, November 3, 1947, 37; Charles Grutzner, "City's Food Buying Normal; Consumers' 'Sense' Praised," *New York Times*, May 11, 1948, sec. 1, 6; "Grocers Demand Fair Opportunity," *New York Times*, June 21, 1948, 29; and "Meat Prices Seen Remaining at Peak," *New York Times*, August 8, 1951, 33.

6. At this time, the industry defined a supermarket as a store that did approximately $250,000 worth of business, had at least four departments—meat, produce, dairy, and grocery—and relied on self-service. By 1952, a leading trade journal, *Super Market Merchandising*, defined a supermarket as having a minimum of $375,000 worth of business, giving some indication of the rapid growth of the grocery business—at least in scale—throughout the 1950s (Rebecca Franklin, "From Soup to Nuts to Art," *New York Times Magazine*, September 24, 1950, 25).

7. See "Co-Ops Spring Up," *Business Week*, November 20, 1943, 70, and "Local Supermarkets' Business Is Growing," *Business Week*, July 17, 1948, 65. For a scholarly perspective on how the war delayed the supermarket's hegemony, see James M. Mayo, *The American Grocery Store: The Business Evolution of an Architectural Space* (Greenwood, 1993), 157–61.

8. "Denies Misuse of Ad Allowance," *New York Times*, June 16, 1948, 50. The 1947 antitrust case against A&P, which limited the volume discounts chains could receive from suppliers and the advertising allowances they would receive from newspapers, did provide independents with some relief.

9. Food Industry Alliance of New York State, "FIA Celebrates 100 Years," *Food Advocate/Griffin's Modern Grocer*, 2000, 19. These statistics are drawn from a survey conducted by the A. C. Nielsen Company between 1948 and 1951.

10. Food Industry Alliance of New York State, "FIA Celebrates 100 Years," 15. For more on A&P's conquest of the retail market, see Richard S. Tedlow, *New and Improved: The Story of Mass Marketing in America* (Basic Books, 1990), 182–258, and Marc Levinson, *The Great A&P and the Struggle for Small Business in America* (Hill and Wang, 2011), 206–19 and

235–46. Tedlow argues that even as A&P became the nation's preeminent food store, it was already sowing the seeds of its own demise—as its operation became increasingly unwieldy, its management structure ossified, and its marketing strategies out of touch with the new desires of postwar consumers (*New and Improved*, 246–54). For perspective on the legislative efforts to limit the chain's expansion, see Nancy Beck Young, *Wright Patman: Populism, Liberalism, and the American Dream* (Southern Methodist University Press, 2000), 92–98, and Levinson, *The Great A&P*, 220–34.

11. "Grocer Horns In on Druggist," *Business Week*, February 16, 1952, 158. The trade journal *Progressive Grocer* defined regional and local chains as having from four to ninety-nine stores under one ownership, and the smaller independents as having three or fewer stores. In the 1950s, D'Agostino's was slowly ascending from the bottom to the middle category.

12. "Grocers Demand Fair Opportunity," *New York Times*, June 21, 1948, 29.

13. Marcel Martino, "The Family Grocer," *New York Times*, May 23, 1951, 34.

14. "Co-Ops Spring Up," 70. As the article detailed, many grocers had once considered the meat counter to be a financial drain. But with the proliferation of self-service refrigerator cases and the availability of precut, packaged meats from Armour and Swift, grocers no longer had to staff their stores with the expert butchers of Nicholas D'Agostino's youth.

15. "Retail Self-Service Urged," *New York Times*, October 8, 1948, 38.

16. "Food Markets Discussed," *New York Times*, February 16, 1949, 43.

17. "Food Independent Has Bulk of Sales," *New York Times*, June 24, 1952, 48.

18. John Stuart, "'Old Time' Store Passing Swiftly," *New York Times*, February 17, 1952, sec. 3, 7.

19. "Today's Food Stores Cost 12 Times 1940's," *New York Times*, April 26, 1953, sec. 3, 7.

20. "Super Markets Planning Outlay of $375,000,000," *New York Times*, May 18, 1951, 43.

21. "Never Say Die," *New York Times*, March 3, 1955, 39. The survey was conducted by the trade journal *Super Market Merchandising*, which defined a "smaller chain" as one that operated twenty-five units or less.

22. "'Superette' Held Answer to Chains," *New York Times*, March 13, 1950, 26. The trade journal *Progressive Grocer* later defined the distinction between supermarket and superette in economic terms. It asserted that supermarkets did more than $300,000 worth of business; a superette did a volume of business between $100,000 and $299,999; smaller grocery stores did less than $100,000 worth of business. See "Grocer Horns In on Druggist," 158–59.

23. While wholesale cooperatives and voluntary chains had first been founded in the 1920s to combat the growth of chain stores, between 1948 and 1958 the volume of sales for retailer-owned cooperatives had expanded by over 200 percent and those of voluntary chains had increased by nearly 100 percent. When several retailers banded together to purchase from the same larger wholesaler and used a shared store name, this arrangement was known as a "voluntary chain," of which IGA Supermarkets is a prime example. See "The Smaller Food Chains Come Up Fast," *Business Week*, May 20, 1950, 66, and James Nagle, "Small Grocers Keep a Foothold," *New York Times*, March 16, 1958, sec. 3, 8.

24. "Small Grocers Fight Back," *Business Week*, April 12, 1947, 70.

25. "A Gospel for Independent Grocers," *Business Week*, October 27, 1951, 86.

26. "Smaller Food Chains Coming Up Fast," 65.

27. "Local Supermarkets' Business Is Growing," *Business Week*, July 17, 1948, 65.

28. *Business Week* was one of the publications that held that the development of the supermarket benefited larger independent operations while damaging the prospects of "mom and pop" groceries. In 1951, five thousand of these smaller stores went out of business, while

independents with more than $100,000 in annual revenues continued to build their share of the market—earning nearly half of all national independent sales. By 1956, one financial executive, Morris Volper of Credit Executives Association, even claimed that the traditional family grocer, with few exceptions, "had reached the end of its existence" because of chain and supermarket competition. The executive claimed that those independent merchants that had survived had been able to adapt the strategies of their larger competitors, replicating their buying power by forming "cooperative chains" or merging with their peers. In 1958, *The New York Times* reported that independent grocers affiliated with retailer cooperatives and voluntary chains accounted for 44 percent of national food sales. The *Times* reporter noted that "corporate chains of four or more stores" accounted for 38 percent of national sales, while unaffiliated independents accounted for only 18 percent of national sales. See "The Supermarket: The Revolution in Retailing," *Business Week*, June 28, 1952, 44; "Credit Failures Remain Stable," *New York Times*, January 3, 1956, 52; and Nagle, "Small Grocers Keep a Foothold," sec. 3, 8.

29. "The Supermarket: The Revolution in Retailing," 44.

30. Paul Sayres, "The World's Biggest Business," in *Food Marketing: Twenty-Two Leaders of the Food Industry Tell How the Nation's Biggest and Most Complex Business Works—and Why*, ed. Paul Sayres (McGraw-Hill, 1950), 6.

31. Patsy D'Agostino, "Independents on the Band Wagon," in Sayres, *Food Marketing*, 30.

32. P. D'Agostino, "Independents on the Band Wagon," 30. D'Agostino explained that in this listing "every organization with four or more units is counted as a chain. This is significant because quite a few owners of small groups of stores, up to ten or fifteen units, think of themselves as independent merchants." Of course, under this definition, D'Agostino's was considered a chain retailer, despite its independent image.

33. P. D'Agostino, "Independents on the Band Wagon," 33. By 1953, 80 percent of groceries had converted to the self-service model. See "Supermarket Study," *New York Times*, January 13, 1953, 40.

34. P. D'Agostino, "Independents on the Band Wagon," 33–34.

35. P. D'Agostino, "Independents on the Band Wagon," 35.

36. P. D'Agostino, "Independents on the Band Wagon," 36–37.

37. Mark Murphy, "If Trouble Can Be Avoid," *New Yorker*, May 15, 1943, 35.

38. P. D'Agostino, "Independents on the Band Wagon," 37–38.

39. "Gospel for Independent Grocers," 81. The brothers' one Westchester store, in Mount Vernon, closed at the end of the 1940s.

40. Leonard Wallock, "New York City: Capital of the Twentieth Century," in *New York: Culture Capital of the World, 1940–65*, ed. Leonard Wallock (Rizzoli International, 1988), 9–29.

41. Arthur Simon, *Stuyvesant Town, U.S.A.: Pattern for Two Americas* (New York University Press, 1970), 17.

42. From the mid-1930s to the 1970s, Robert Moses lorded over New York's plan of urban renewal in a variety of positions. Moses directed the establishment of scores of new public parks, an expansive system of expressways, and the New York City Housing Authority's construction of seventeen low- and middle-income housing projects. Yet despite his accomplishments, Moses became an infamous figure in urban politics. As chairman of the Mayor's Committee on Slum Clearance, Moses advocated a "bulldozer approach" to redevelopment, displacing thousands of mainly poor and ethnic citizens in the cause of constructing dozens of new apartment buildings, hospitals, and university buildings. And with his espousal of superhighways, and his heavy-handed use of eminent domain to fracture city neighborhoods, Moses actually enabled

the urban blight he was seeking to prevent. For more on Moses's influence on New York's redevelopment and city politics, see Robert Caro, *The Power Broker: Robert Moses and the Fall of New York* (Knopf, 1974); Joel Schwartz, *The New York Approach: Robert Moses, Urban Liberals, and Redevelopment of the Inner City* (Ohio State University Press, 1993); George J. Lankevich, *American Metropolis: A History of New York City* (New York University Press, 1998), 164–90; and Wallock, "New York City," 26–50.

43. Metropolitan Life had first become involved in housing investments in the 1920s when the city faced a postwar housing shortage, and the New York state legislature contracted with them to build affordable housing in exchange for tax breaks. The Parkchester development was the result of legislation that allowed insurance companies to invest in affordable housing, but without any tax breaks. With over 35,000 residents, Parkchester was the largest development in the world until Co-op City was built in 1972. Metropolitan followed Parkchester's design and scale, but it was a private venture. See Schwartz, *New York Approach*, 26–50, and Simon, *Stuyvesant Town*, 17–21.

44. In 1943, the New York State Legislature passed the Hampton-Mitchell bill, which liberalized the provisions of an urban redevelopment law to permit agreements for slum clearance between insurance companies and municipalities (See "Calls for Unity in Housing Aims," *New York Times*, May 2, 1943, sec. 8, 1). This was the first law in the country designed to attract private enterprise for the rebuilding of cities. The city government also took the unprecedented step of helping Met Life acquire the real estate, and provided significant tax exemptions for twenty-five years. See Schwartz, *New York Approach*, 90–95, and Simon, *Stuyvesant Town*, 21–22.

45. "East Side 'Suburb in City' to House 30,000 After War," *New York Times*, April 19, 1943, 9.

46. Simon, *Stuyvesant Town*, 8.

47. Boyden Sparkes, "Can the Cities Come Back?," *Saturday Evening Post*, November 4, 1944, 28.

48. "East Side 'Suburb in City,'" 1.

49. "Housing Plan Seen as a 'Walled City,'" *New York Times*, May 20, 1943, 23.

50. "East Side 'Suburb in City,'" 1.

51. "Housing Plan Seen as a 'Walled City,'" 23. See also "Housing Plan Disapproved," *New York Times*, June 1, 1943, 22. Arthur Simon argued that Stuyvesant Town, like the suburbs, offered its residents "the comfort of white, middle-class neighborhoods" with "a shelter from the poor and the black" (Simon, *Stuyvesant Town*, 15). Some of Stuyvesant Town's notoriety stemmed from several high-profile campaigns conducted by New York's civil rights community in the 1950s. While Stuyvesant Town and Peter Cooper Village attracted a wide sampling of New York's post-immigrant middle class, it originally excluded African Americans. After World War II, the city's African American population was poised for greater personal success, enjoying the benefits of greater educational and professional opportunity. But for the most part, the community was restricted to Harlem and its limited housing stock, regardless of wealth or education. The Metropolitan Life Insurance Company maintained a strict policy of segregation in all of its housing developments, and insisted on the power to screen and choose its prospective tenants. Met Life president Frederick Ecker was quoted as claiming, "Negroes and whites do not mix." (See "Stuyvesant Town Approved by Board," *New York Times*, June 4, 1943, 23.) The projects were protected from antidiscrimination legislation because they were ostensibly private, and Robert Moses and other city leaders expressed concern that any political wrangling by the city might lead Met Life to scrap its proposed developments, with

no other suitors willing to invest private capital in such a significant development project (see "Stuyvesant Town Defended," *New York Times*, June 3, 1943, 20). Met Life did eventually allow a few African American tenants to reside at Stuyvesant Town and Peter Cooper Village to placate activists, but it was not until 1968 that the city government charged the company with discrimination and moved to open the projects to people of color. For more on this issue see Schwartz, *New York Approach*; Caro, *Power Broker*; and Simon, *Stuyvesant Town*.

52. The project also offered its residents on-site parking garages.

53. Simon, *Stuyvesant Town*, 27.

54. For more on the architectural and design details of Stuyvesant Town and Peter Cooper Village, see Richard Plunz, *A History of Housing in New York City: Dwelling Type and Social Change in the American Metropolis* (Columbia University Press, 1990), 253–59.

55. Simon, *Stuyvesant Town*, 51. Peter Cooper Village was built just north of Stuyvesant Town on the former "gashouse district," which was a notorious nest of crime in the nineteenth century. See "Gardens to Bloom on 'Gas House' Site, *New York Times*, January 4, 1945, 21.

56. Murray Schumach, "The East River Shore Regains Its Glory," *New York Times Magazine*, January 19, 1947, 8.

57. "Housing 'Slicks Up' East Side's Stores," *New York Times*, January 24, 1950, 21.

58. "Gospel for Independent Grocers," 78.

59. Jim Williams, "We Gain New $200 Stop," *Arnold Bakers Breadwinner*, March 2, 1950, 5. Tex McCrary and Jinx Falkenberg were two radio stars of the period, Arlene Francis and Jack Sterling were actors of some renown, and John Reed King was a host of early television game shows.

60. Nicholas and Patsy's failed Mount Vernon grocery was the first location to carry the "D'Agostino Brothers" name. As the organization continued to evolve, so did its self-image—in the 1960s, Nicholas's sons, Stephen and Nick, convinced him to change the name of the company's stores to "D'Agostino" (officially "D'Agostino Supermarkets") because it sounded more modern and sophisticated (Stephen D'Agostino, interview by author, August 9, 2001, and Nicholas D'Agostino Jr., interview by author, May 15, 2001). Of course, with the death of Patsy D'Agostino in 1960, the company's former name was no longer accurate.

61. "From Pushcart to Super-Market," *Town & Village*, February 23, 1950, 15. The ad then gave a couple of additional sentences on Patsy and Nicholas's history in the food trade, before describing the wonders of the new store. One should note that even at this early date, the public recollection of the brothers' story has some flaws (e.g., Nicholas did not come to the US until 1924).

62. "Gospel for Independent Grocers," 78. According to Patsy's nephew, Stephen D'Agostino, the store did well over a million dollars' worth of business annually in succeeding years (Stephen D'Agostino, interview by author, August 9, 2001).

63. Nicholas D'Agostino Jr., interview by author, May 15, 2001.

64. The widespread adoption of self-service meat departments in the 1950s was, in and of itself, a stunning development for the grocery trade. In 1950, only 2,750 stores in America offered full self-service meat; by the end of the decade, that figure had risen to 22,500. See "The Classic Years," *Progressive Grocer*, December 1988, 136.

65. Jane Holt, "The Post-War Store," *New York Times Magazine*, April 1, 1945, 30, and Franklin, "From Soup to Nuts to Art," 44.

66. "Supermarket: The Revolution in Retailing," 45.

67. Sidney Margolius, "Super Business of Supermarkets," *New York Times Magazine*, March 29, 1959, 23.

68. Nicholas D'Agostino Jr., interview by author, May 15, 2001.

69. For years, canned food had been a standard offering at grocery stores, though the rationing of tin during the war had limited its production. With the end of the war, mass-produced canned foods proceeded to conquer the nation's cupboards and pantries. One concerned representative of the Western Growers Association even warned "most of the country's 6,000,000 married veterans were eating out of cans because 'hardly any' of their wives know how to cook." Ironically, the spokesman advised his fellow growers to make more prepackaged vegetables available to shoppers as a way of addressing this problem. See "Fears Rise in Canned Food Use," *New York Times*, November 23, 1946, 18.

70. "Classic Years," 72.

71. Stephen D'Agostino, interview by author, August 9, 2001.

72. Patsy noted that in 1958, frozen foods made up 8 percent of the company's total volume of sales, an increase of some 30 to 40 percent since the early 1950s. This figure was especially notable when one considers the lack of retail space in the brothers' stores. He cautioned his peers, "Your frozen food operation must be handled by a specialist. It must not be the orphan of fresh meat and produce." See Patsy D'Agostino, "Stop Treating Frozen as Stepchild, Promote Quality," *Quick Frozen Foods*, June 1958, 92.

73. As Harvey Levenstein explains, "In 1957 twenty-two million women were working full-time—32 percent of the labor force—and over half of them, twelve million, were married. By 1960 there were twice as many working wives as there had been in 1950. . . . Most important, whereas before the war the vast majority of working mothers had been working class, by the mid-1950s about one-half were middle class. Food processors recognized that these women represent an excellent market for convenience foods." See Levenstein, *Paradox of Plenty: A Social History of Eating in Modern America* (Oxford University Press, 1993), 105.

74. The president of the Grand Union supermarket chain declared that with its lack of adequate parking facilities, New York had not a single "really modern supermarket" and that the city was "suffering from the anemia that results when the life blood of commerce can no longer flow freely through its arteries." Merchants scrambled to utilize any large retail space in the city, with some retailers even converting old movie houses in Upper Manhattan to supermarkets. See "Markets Here Not Super?," *New York Times*, December 2, 1954, 40, and Thomas Ennis, "Unused Theaters Become Markets," *New York Times*, October 21, 1956, sec. 8, 1.

75. "Supermarket: The Revolution in Retailing," 41–42.

76. Franklin, "From Soup to Nuts to Art," 26. Of course, in a corresponding development, department stores were becoming more like supermarkets—as they increasingly adopted the practices of self-service and trimmed their army of clerks and salespeople ("The Supermarket: The Revolution in Retailing," 47). For more on the evolution of the department store, see Vicki Howard, *From Main Street to Mall: The Rise and Fall of the American Department Store* (University of Pennsylvania Press, 2015).

77. "From Pushcart to Super-Market," 15.

78. Lawrence M. Hughes, "Patsy D'Agostino: Neighborly Grocer," *Catholic Digest*, May 1956, 15.

79. The president of the Independent Grocers' Alliance even claimed that the supermarket of the future would resemble the old-fashioned general store. See "Supermarkets Plus," *Business Week*, October 12, 1946, 69.

80. *Super Market Merchandising*, an industry trade magazine, conducted the survey. The New York State Food Merchants Association reported that its independent grocer members were compelled to stock new lines that might produce greater profits than food. Meanwhile,

The New York Times reported that in a climate of increased competition and lowered profits, it was essential that retailers take "full advantage of all the traffic" in their stores. See "Expanding Supers," *Business Week*, July 12, 1947, 70, and "Retailers Moving to Diversify Lines," *New York Times*, October 9, 1949, sec. 3, 7.

81. For more on how mass marketing became a projection of the democratic ideals of the 1950s, see Lizabeth Cohen, *A Consumers' Republic: The Politics of Mass Consumption in Postwar America* (Alfred A. Knopf, 2003), 112–65.

82. Margolius, "Super Business of Supermarkets," 26.

83. Levenstein, *Paradox of Plenty*, 102.

84. Mary F. Corey, *The World Through a Monocle: "The New Yorker" at Midcentury* (Harvard University Press, 1999), 197 and 202–3.

85. Stephen D'Agostino, interview by author, August 9, 2001. Stephen added that as these strivers continued to prosper, and moved from Stuyvesant Town and Peter Cooper Village to the Upper East Side, there were already D'Agostino stores in their new neighborhoods to serve them. In the 1960s and 1970s, Stephen and his brother, Nick, would also expand to the Upper West Side to serve a new generation of upwardly mobile residents.

86. Coincidentally, Corey uses Calvert Whiskey's ad campaign, "Men of Distinction," as her principal example for "discriminating consumption" (197–204). Calvert's ads were placed primarily in *The New Yorker* and *Life*, and appealed to the upper-class desires of the new middle class. They depicted minor celebrities and businessmen in various aristocratic poses (around the fireplace, at their stables, etc.), sipping Calvert. It is unknown if D'Agostino's tagline "markets of distinction" was inspired by the distiller's. But in 1956, Patsy D'Agostino did pose with other grocery executives for a Calvert whiskey ad (see fig. 21a).

87. Nicholas D'Agostino Jr., interview by author, May 15, 2001.

88. "Meat Situation," *Life*, January 3, 1955, 75.

89. According to one account, Nicholas D'Agostino did have some difficulty adjusting to the changing tastes of his postwar customers. He was initially offended by the notion that shoppers might prefer London broil when he was offering a fine T-bone steak. Yet, eventually, the retailer and the customer met in the middle—D'Agostino's offered the busy families of Stuyvesant Town more boneless cuts of meat while the shoppers appreciated the notion of quality proffered by the company (Stephen D'Agostino, interview by author, August 9, 2001).

90. "Housing 'Slicks Up' East Side's Stores," *New York Times*, January 24, 1950, 21.

91. In an atmosphere of new wealth and social mobility, *Fortune* reported that the 1958 sales of gourmet foods had doubled since mid-decade, and were close to $200 million for the year. Katherine Hamill, "Caviar in the Supermarket," *Fortune*, January 1959, 101.

92. Hamill, "Caviar in the Supermarket," 102.

93. Hamill, "Caviar in the Supermarket," 102–3.

94. Hamill, "Caviar in the Supermarket," 133.

95. In an address to his fellow grocers at the 1947 National Association of Retail Grocers convention, Patsy D'Agostino—the champion of the "little guy"—proclaimed that in order to help its members beat the chains, the organization must teach the independent to become "a good merchandiser, salesman, promotion and advertising man, and a top notch business man, all rolled into one." See "Details Problems of Retail Grocers," *New York Times*, June 23, 1947, 27.

96. "Supermarket: The Revolution in Retailing," 50. Of course, in New York, these developments were mediated by the limitations of the urban market, as the lack of space and the cost of real estate prohibited the building of "superstores." Cigar stores and corner newsstands would remain part of the city's charm, even as their numbers began to decline.

97. "Supermarket Study," *New York Times*, January 13, 1953, 40.

98. "Congressional Focus on Food Marketing," *Business Week*, October 19, 1957, 146.

99. "Closing of Pushcart Markets to Be Urged in Economy Drive," *New York Times*, January 14, 1958, 35.

100. Margolius, "Super Business of Supermarkets," 28.

101. The title of the article, "A Gospel for Independent Grocers" (*Business Week*, October 27, 1951), is taken from a comment that Patsy made about his speeches for grocers' organizations, in which he proselytizes for the ways of independent merchants. Early in the article, Patsy jokes, "Like the Gospel, it is worth it if one speech saves one life" (78).

102. "Gospel for Independent Grocers," 78.

103. "Gospel for Independent Grocers," 84. It is worth noting that some of his advice contradicted the company's earlier policies (as the wealthy residents of Yorkville expected credit and prompt delivery of their groceries) and some of its future strategies (as when in the 1980s they relied on high-end private label merchandise and vibrant presentation to attract affluent shoppers).

104. "Gospel for Independent Grocers," 86.

105. "Gospel for Independent Grocers," 86.

106. "Gospel for Independent Grocers," 78 and 86.

107. "Gospel for Independent Grocers," 86.

108. Patsy D'Agostino, "I Found $5,000,000 in a Pushcart," *American Magazine*, September 1952. It is unclear whether Patsy's colorful, sometimes coarse English was edited by a company employee or an editor from the publication. However, the rendering of Patsy's voice in clear, correct English not only made his narrative more lucid, but affirmed his assimilation.

109. P. D'Agostino, "I Found $5,000,000 in a Pushcart," 15.

110. P. D'Agostino, "I Found $5,000,000 in a Pushcart," 15.

111. P. D'Agostino, "I Found $5,000,000 in a Pushcart," 107.

112. P. D'Agostino, "I Found $5,000,000 in a Pushcart," 107.

113. In this regard, the episode recalls the earlier discussion of Italian merchants' reluctance to advertise their ethnicity to WASP customers, as with the Yorkville Food Shoppe, the Butterfield Market, and the Florence Market. Even though Murphy's article in *The New Yorker* appeared to acknowledge that the Italian grocer was a recognizable symbol for the American public, the notion that a merchant would market the ethnicity of their operation was still undeveloped. Over time, as Italians integrated themselves into the larger culture, their identity could be sold to consumers in a more forthright manner.

114. P. D'Agostino, "I Found $5,000,000 in a Pushcart," 107–8.

115. P. D'Agostino, "I Found $5,000,000 in a Pushcart," 108.

116. P. D'Agostino, "I Found $5,000,000 in a Pushcart," 108.

117. P. D'Agostino, "I Found $5,000,000 in a Pushcart," 108.

118. P. D'Agostino, "I Found $5,000,000 in a Pushcart," 108.

119. This concept comes from William H. Whyte's 1956 examination of postwar business culture, *The Organization Man*. Whyte's critique of America's corporate mentality clearly spoke to a nation anxious about conformity and a loss of individuality in the 1950s, as the book became a runaway bestseller. See William H. Whyte Jr., *The Organization Man* (Simon and Schuster, 1956).

120. Sidney Fields, "The Immigrant Didn't Forget," *New York Daily Mirror*, May 20, 1949, 30.

121. P. D'Agostino, "I Found $5,000,000 in a Pushcart," 111. As noted in the previous chapter, there was another side to this story. According to accounts in Nicholas D'Agostino's autobiography, Frank Tucciarone was deep in debt, and if someone did not buy his half of the business and the store went into receivership, Patsy too would have lost his original investment. Mr. Tucciarone's daughter Josephine knew the store's value, and she and Patsy begged Nicholas to buy Frank's share—which he did, for $5,000 (N. D'Agostino, "Stephen's Son," in "The Four Seasons of Nicholas D'Agostino," 10–11).

122. P. D'Agostino, "I Found $5,000,000 in a Pushcart," 111. Again, one must recall Nicholas D'Agostino's account of his origins in the food business. Before becoming his brother's partner, Nicholas had several jobs in the trade, including pushcart vendor, grocery clerk, fish man, and butcher. He claimed that he had learned the meat and fish business of his *own* volition, and against the wishes of his father, even taking a pay cut to gain an apprenticeship.

123. The introduction to the eponymous chapter on Patsy D'Agostino read, "When they call him 'Professor' at City College where he gives a weekly lecture on the grocery business, Patsy knows you don't need a diploma to know economics. Further proof comes from the credit side of his grocery chain's ledger—the gross was over five million last year" (Patsy D'Agostino, "Patsy D'Agostino," in *How I Made a Million*, ed. Noah Sarlat [1955; Paperback Library, 1961], 81).

124. P. D'Agostino, *How I Made a Million*, 88–89.

125. P. D'Agostino, *How I Made a Million*, 84.

126. P. D'Agostino, *How I Made a Million*, 86 and 90.

127. *Italamerican* was a monthly bilingual lifestyle magazine published out of New York. In addition to profiles on prominent Italian Americans, it featured restaurant and fashion reviews, an entertainment section, advice columns, and an abundance of ads for cheeses, liquors, restaurants, cruise lines, and travel services.

128. Vittorio de Fiori and Enrica Laglia, "The D'Agostino Brothers," *Italamerican*, October 1954, 5.

129. De Fiori and Laglia, "D'Agostino Brothers," 6.

130. De Fiori and Laglia, "D'Agostino Brothers," 8. This was one of the many instances in which *ItalAmerican* shares the conclusions of *American Magazine*, with De Fiori and Laglia appearing to "crib" from another magazine's work.

131. De Fiori and Laglia, "D'Agostino Brothers," 9.

132. De Fiori and Laglia, "D'Agostino Brothers," 10.

133. For more on the institution building and growing social power of the American Catholic Church in the 1950s, see Charles Morris, *American Catholic: The Saints and Sinners Who Built America's Most Powerful Church* (Vintage Books, 1997), 141–95, and John T. McGreevy, *Parish Boundaries: The Catholic Encounter with Race in the Twentieth-Century Urban North* (University of Chicago Press, 1996), 79–154.

134. Hughes, "Patsy D'Agostino: Neighborly Grocer," 14.

135. Hughes, "Patsy D'Agostino: Neighborly Grocer," 16.

136. Hughes, "Patsy D'Agostino: Neighborly Grocer," 17.

137. Hughes, "Patsy D'Agostino: Neighborly Grocer," 15.

138. Robert A. Orsi, *The Madonna of 115th Street: Faith and Community in Italian Harlem, 1880–1950* (Yale University Press, 1985), 45.

139. Simone Cinotto, *The Italian American Table: Food, Family, and Community in New York City* (University of Illinois Press, 2013), 10.

140. As scholars such as Stefano Luconi and Thomas Guglielmo have argued, housing, schooling, and neighborhood boundaries were principal sources of tension between Italians and Black and Puerto Rican residents of urban communities. When the federal government became involved in offering home loans with reasonable down payments and low interest rates through the creation of the Federal Housing Administration in the 1930s and the GI Bill in 1944—often at the exclusion of applicants of color—Italian Americans realized how whiteness might grant them access to better neighborhoods and public schools, thus reinforcing its value. Luconi and Guglielmo conclude that Italian Americans, like their European-descended peers, exploited their whiteness to seize opportunities to move into the middle-class suburbs that were being built throughout the country in the 1940s and '50s. See Stefano Luconi, *From Paesani to White Ethnics: The Italian Experience in Philadelphia* (State University of New York Press, 2001), 119–57, and Thomas A. Guglielmo, *White on Arrival: Italians, Race, Color, and Power in Chicago, 1890–1945* (Oxford University Press, 2003), 146–76.

141. Frederick M. Binder and David M. Reimers, *All the Nations Under Heaven: An Ethnic and Racial History of New York City* (Columbia University Press, 1995), 154. The two bridges in question were the Queensboro Bridge and the Hell Gate Bridge (between Queens and Manhattan), which opened in 1909 and 1917, respectively.

142. Loretta D'Agostino Schmitz, unpublished personal journal, collection of the author, 2001.

143. Patsy D'Agostino's new house in Westchester was not palatial, however, despite the cachet of the area. In the late 1950s, after his children had grown, he and his wife sold their house and acquired an apartment in Manhattan (Stephen D'Agostino, interview by author, August 9, 2001).

144. See Vance Packard, *The Status Seekers* (David McKay, 1959; reprinted in *American Social Classes in the 1950s: Selections from Vance Packard's "The Status Seekers,"* ed. Daniel Horowitz [Bedford/St. Martin's, 1995]). Packard argues that as the prosperity of the 1950s brought the masses into the middle class, Americans continued to seek outward markers of status to distinguish them from their neighbors, particularly through such "big-ticket" purchases as houses in the suburbs.

145. On a national level, the federal government effectively subsidized the building of new postwar suburbs with the generous loans it offered to veterans through the Servicemen's Readjustment Act of 1944 and the 1956 Federal-Aid Highway Act. The Servicemen's Readjustment Act of 1944, more commonly known as the GI Bill, provided returning veterans with affordable mortgages, low-interest loans to purchase homes and start businesses, and tuition money for college. Meanwhile, the Federal-Aid Highway Act of 1956 provided $25 billion to build 41,000 miles of interstate highways.

146. Public officials began to contemplate the future of New York's transportation network in the 1920s, and in 1929 the Russell Sage Foundation published a ten-volume survey—the Regional Plan for New York—that would become the blueprint for the city's expansion. The city's new Regional Plan Association (RPA) advocated for a plan of industrial and residential decentralization and regional development that relied on a network of highways and rail lines circling and radiating from Manhattan. Under the direction of Robert Moses, the city began work on more than 1,400 miles of highway between 1929 and 1941, including the Midtown Tunnel; the Triborough Bridge; parkways through Long Island, Westchester, and the Bronx; the Henry Hudson Bridge; and the West Side Highway. After World War II, under Moses's direction, the RPA embarked on an even more ambitious plan of highway construction, building the Cross Bronx, Bruckner, and Major Deegan Expressways in the Bronx; the Van Wyck

Expressway across Queens; the Brooklyn-Battery Tunnel to Manhattan; the Verrazzano-Narrows Bridge from Staten Island to Manhattan, and the Cross County Parkway in Westchester. Robert Moses believed that the dispersal of the city's commercial and population centers would "conserve" New York's infrastructure and eradicate blight, and through the 1940s the regional plan seemed to feed the city's economy. Yet Moses ignored any mandate to invest in public or rail transportation, and the new expressways destroyed several neighborhoods, especially in blue-collar and ethnic communities. Moreover, the regional concept of development actually enabled the popular and industrial flight to New York's and New Jersey's suburban communities. For example, in Long Island's Nassau County, where Nicholas and Josephine D'Agostino settled, the population grew from 400,000 to 1.3 million between 1940 and 1960. Moses's critics argue that the model he instituted ultimately paved the way for the urban blight that ravaged New York in the late 1960s and the 1970s. For more on Robert Moses and his execution of the regional model of transportation and development, see Caro, *Power Broker*, 895–919; Wallock, "New York City: Capital of the Twentieth Century," 26–40; and Lankevich, *American Metropolis*, 173 and 177.

147. By 1912, there were 258 Italian societies in New York alone. See Antonio Mangano, "The Associated Life of the Italians in New York City," *Charities*, May 7, 1904, 479.

148. Donna Gabaccia, *Italy's Many Diasporas* (University of Washington Press, 2000), 104.

149. Federal Writers' Project, *The Italians of New York* (1938; Arno, 1969), 107–13.

150. Stephen D'Agostino, interview by author, August 9, 2001.

151. Monsignor Carroll-Abbing founded the first Boys' Town at the close of World War II, after he witnessed Italian children lining up outside a GI mess hall to beg for leftovers. Monsignor collected $85 from some American sailors to open the first home in a bombed-out house. He opened seven more homes in the succeeding years, each modeled after Father Flanagan's Boys' Town—with young men learning vocational training as part of their education and practicing a limited degree of self-government (Fields, 30). Marchisio and Boys' Town were part of a larger effort to expand Italians' political and social power while lobbying for changes to the nation's immigration policies. Boys' Town of Italy became a popular charity among donors who supported the construction of orphanages and education programs as Italy sought to rebuild from the ravages of war. Beyond helping to uplift the young victims of the war, these acts of generosity signified the growing influence of an upwardly mobile class of Italian Americans. On a geopolitical level, the work of charities like Boys' Town brought greater stability to Italy at the onset of the Cold War while signaling the abundance of postwar America. In the years to come, Juvenal Marchisio's mission would evolve. Dismayed by the 1952 McCarran-Walter Act—which purported to reform immigration laws but maintained discriminatory national origins quotas—leaders in the US Catholic Church encouraged Marchisio to form the American Committee on Italian Migration (ACIM). Under Marchisio, ACIM would function as both an aid organization and a political action group that would pressure the federal government to liberalize its restrictive policies. As national chairman of ACIM, Marchisio would harness the community's frustrations with the low number of visas offered to Italians and the quotas that seemed to affirm their inferior status. ACIM and Marchisio not only offered practical assistance to immigrants and their American sponsors but built support for the larger cause of reform. In this regard, Marchisio and the thousands of members of ACIM played a key role in the eventual passage of the landmark Hart-Cellar Act, also known as the Immigration and Nationality Act of 1965. For more on this topic, see Danielle Battisti, *Whom We Shall Welcome: Italian Americans and Immigration Reform, 1945–1965* (Fordham University Press, 2019), and Maddalena Marinari, "'In the Name of God . . . and in the Interest of Our Country': The Cold War, Foreign

Policy, and Italian Americans' Mobilization Against Immigration Restriction," in *New Italian Migrations to the United States*, ed. Laura E. Ruberto and Joseph Sciorra (University of Illinois Press, 2017), 59–79.

152. For examples of these efforts, see "Food Industry to Aid Boys Town in Italy," *New York Times*, May 26, 1948, 27, and "A Boys Town Immigrant; Italian, 15, Flies Here to Live with New Rochelle Family," *New York Times*, November 9, 1952, 88.

153. For more on Pope's life and exploits, see Paul David Pope, *The Deeds of My Fathers: How My Grandfather and Father Built New York and Created the Tabloid World of Today* (Rowan & Littlefield, 2010).

154. In fact, in 1952, the New York State Crime Commission investigated a couple of politicians with ties to Italian Charities (Nathan Glazer and Daniel P. Moynihan, *Beyond the Melting Pot: The Negroes, Puerto Ricans, Jews, Italians, and Irish of New York City* [MIT Press, 1963], 210–13).

155. Known for its menu of Italian standards and the loyalty of patrons such as the writer Gay Talese, Gino's would remain a beloved Manhattan institution until its closing in 2010. For more on Gino's history, see Gay Talese, "Basta," *New Yorker*, May 31, 2010, 22–23.

156. Founded in 1888 as a hunting club, Tiro a Segno (which translates as "Fire at the Target") evolved into a philanthropy and meeting place for Italian American doctors, lawyers, businessmen, politicians, and persons of note. At Tiro's clubhouse in Greenwich Village, members and guests could dine at its fine restaurant, have coffee and play bocce, and revel in their common ethnic identity and all-American success. Boys' Town of Italy was one of the principal recipients of the club's charity. See Douglas Martin, "For 100 Years, Providing a Tie to Italian Culture," *New York Times*, December 21, 1988, sec. 2, 1, and Calvin Trillin, "The Italian Thing," *New Yorker*, November 19, 1990, 107–18. Trillin's article focused on the battle between older and younger members over the renovation of Tiro's facilities in the late 1980s, which he viewed as symptomatic of a larger tension in the Italian American community over assimilation and changing identity.

157. Loretta D'Agostino Schmitz, unpublished personal journal, 2002.

158. Though Fiorello La Guardia had been a successful mayor, Italian Americans only truly became a factor in New York City politics after World War II. Figures such as old-school "pols" Edward Corsi and Carmine DeSapio in the 1940s, and smooth, middle-class types like Vincent Impelliteri and Lawrence Gerosa in the 1950s, embodied the political evolution of the Italian community. See Glazer and Moynihan, *Beyond the Melting Pot*, 208–16, and Binder and Reimers, *All the Nations Under Heaven*, 201–3.

159. In *The Madonna of 115th Street*, Orsi distinguishes between the grassroots Catholicism of the Italian community—which he labels a "religion of the streets"—and the dogma of the Church. While Church officials "criticized Italian religiosity for being exotic and pagan" (lviii), "Italian Harlem continually made a distinction between religion and church. A person could be a good man or a good woman . . . in other words, could be religious without this having anything to do with how often he or she went to church" (lxi).

160. One must also note the vital influence of parochial schools in bringing Italian American men back into the fold. As Italian immigrants integrated themselves into the institutional life of the Catholic Church, they began to send their children to parish schools. Catholic education mandated that parents play an active role in their children's religious training and attend mass themselves.

161. One may recall the story from the previous chapter about Baron D'Agostino, a local noble. When Nicholas was a boy, the Baron had asked his mother, Loreta, to change their

family name to avoid "confusion" after the Baron had mistakenly received some of Ignatius D'Agostino's letters from the US. Upon Nicholas's return in 1946, the Baron's nephew—who had no knowledge of the incident—hosted his prosperous American namesake at his estate, in fact treating him like New World royalty (N. D'Agostino, "Loreta's Son," 11).

162. Stephen D'Agostino, interview by author, August 9, 2001.

163. "Skippy" and "Nicky" refer to Nicholas's two sons, while "Stevie" refers to Patsy's son.

164. Although Patsy had two daughters and Nicholas had one daughter, there was never any discussion of bringing in any of these three women as working partners.

165. "Pasquale D'Agostino, 55, Dies; Supermarket-Chain President," *New York Times*, July 27, 1960, 29.

166. Loretta D'Agostino Schmitz, letter to the author, March 15, 2004.

167. For more details of the case and the court's decision, see *John Foley et al., as executors of Patsy D'Agostino, Deceased v. Nicholas D'Agostino et al., Defendants*, 21 A.D. 2d 60; 248 N.Y.S. 2d 121, Supreme Court of New York, Appellate Division, First Department, 1964.

168. Despite the acrimonious litigation, Patsy's son Stephen continued to work in a minor management position within the company for years afterward.

169. Joan Lowman, letter to Loretta D'Agostino Schmitz, August 2001.

170. Loretta D'Agostino Schmitz, unpublished personal journal, 2002.

171. Years after his retirement from the company, Stephen D'Agostino admitted that he considered walking away from the family business as a way of resolving the conflict. "Part of my big mistake was not just quitting," he remarked. "I think if I would have left the business based on the unfriendly behavior of other parties, my father would have nothing to fight for" (Stephen D'Agostino, interview by author, August 9, 2001).

172. Loretta D'Agostino Schmitz, unpublished personal journal, 2002.

173. Loretta D'Agostino Schmitz, unpublished personal journal, 2002.

174. Loretta D'Agostino Schmitz, telephone interview with the author, February 7, 2004.

4. One of the Nice Things About New York (1960–82)

1. "The Modern Grocer: All-American Success Story," *Progressive Grocer*, June 1958, 64.

2. In 1959, the United States and the USSR agreed to hold exhibitions in each other's countries as a form of cultural exchange. Vice President Nixon journeyed to Moscow to lead Premier Khrushchev on a tour of the US exposition, which included a wealth of consumer goods and technologies. In a model kitchen, Nixon used the exhibit's dishwasher, stove, and refrigerator as evidence of the consumer abundance available to all Americans under the capitalist system.

3. "Modern Grocer," 66. The magazine reports that while the average American family earned $5,300, the average supermarket operator earned over $25,000, and store managers earned about $7,200.

4. "Modern Grocer," 71. The average American male over the age of twenty-five had approximately ten years of education, while supermarket and superette operators, and store managers, averaged approximately twelve years of education. While these statistics might suggest that supermarket leadership had begun to assume an elite character, other figures revealed that there remained an older, traditional ethos among grocers. The magazine found that most of those surveyed continued to work long hours (about sixty hours a week) and had apprenticeships of between eighteen and twenty years in the food business. The survey of the average retailer's level of education also revealed that "college boys" such as Stephen and Nick

Jr. were still anomalies in the food business. Among the supermarket operators surveyed, only 35 percent had ultimately graduated from high school, while only 50 percent of store managers had finished their secondary education. These educational statistics also highlight Nicholas D'Agostino's rare accomplishment in becoming the president of a successful grocery chain despite his fourth-grade education—only 4 percent of supermarket operators surveyed had only a grammar school education.

5. "The New City," *Fortune*, February 1960, 102–17. See also Carol Herselle Krinsky, "Architecture in New York City," in *New York: Culture Capital of the World, 1940–65*, ed. Leonard Wallock (Rizzoli, 1988), 89–116.

6. John McDonald, "The $2-Billion Building Boom," *Fortune*, February 1960, 119.

7. George J. Lankevich, *American Metropolis: A History of New York City* (New York University Press, 1998), 192.

8. McDonald, "$2-Billion Building Boom," 106 and 119. Another *Fortune* article from the same series argued that middle-class flight from New York in this period was overstated, with the city having 44 percent of its households in the middle-income bracket ($4,000 to $7,500), as compared to 31 percent in the upper-income bracket (over $7,500) and only 23 percent in the lower-income bracket (under $4,000). See Charles E. Silberman, "The Home of the Middle Class," *Fortune*, February 1960, 269–70.

9. Gilbert Burck, "Headquarters Town," *Fortune*, February 1960, 266.

10. Several notable texts analyze New York City's urban crisis. Jeanne R. Lowe's *Cities in a Race with Time: Progress and Poverty in America's Renewing Cities* (Random House, 1967) considers the looming economic, social, and racial problems facing American cities in the 1960s. Joel Schwartz's *The New York Approach: Robert Moses, Urban Liberals, and Redevelopment of the Inner City* (Ohio State University Press, 1993) explains how the failed policies of urban renewal contributed to the deindustrialization and decay of the late 1960s and the 1970s just as Robert Fitch's *The Assassination of New York* (Verso, 1993) focuses on the role of financial elites and real estate brokers in the decline of the city's neighborhoods and industry. Joshua B. Freeman's *Working-Class New York: Life and Labor Since World War II* (New Press, 2000) provides a comprehensive portrait of the city's laboring classes and the rise and fall of its industrial economy in the postwar era, which shaped its civic culture. Ken Auletta's *The Streets Were Paved with Gold* (Random House, 1979) offers meticulous analysis of New York's fiscal crisis, while Kim Phillips-Fein, *Fear City: New York's Fiscal Crisis and the Rise of Austerity Politics* (Metropolitan Books, 2017) argues that the resulting austerity measures signaled a larger backlash against liberalism and the public sector. For a study of how segregation, job loss, and urban renewal fueled the city's gang problem, see Eric C. Schneider, *Vampires, Dragons, and Egyptian Kings: Youth Gangs in Postwar New York* (Princeton University Press, 1999). For a broader discussion of the period's racial politics, especially as related to housing and education, see Martha Biondi, *To Stand and Fight: The Struggle for Civil Rights in Postwar New York City* (Harvard University Press, 2003), and Craig Steven Wilder, *A Covenant with Color: Race and Social Power in Brooklyn* (Columbia University Press, 2000).

11. "D'Agostino's Open Parkchester Unit," *Bronx Press-Review*, October 6, 1966, 8.

12. Stephen D'Agostino, interview by author, August 9, 2001.

13. Patsy D'Agostino shared Nicholas's passion for the trade, but his interests shifted in the postwar era. Patsy's involvement with trade associations and his many speaking engagements distracted him from the day-to-day operations of the stores. In the 1950s, as Patsy was drawn into the role of executive, he delegated his responsibilities as fruit buyer, with its early morning vigils at the terminal market, to Martin Tucciarone. Increasingly, Patsy assumed the role of

ambassador for the company, as he often spent business hours talking up salesmen and reporters in his office or customers out on the floor, causing some resentment from his employees and his brother.

14. All three of these organizations had their origins in the Crusades, but over time, their main function was to promote charity and the ideals of the Church. Nicholas was especially proud of his membership in the Knights of Malta, who worked with hospitals, health organizations, and children's charities throughout the world.

15. Italian Charities of America, Inc., *Italian Charities of America Bulletin*, October 1971, 1.

16. "Food Retailing: Where We Stand Today," *Progressive Grocer*, January 1965, 38.

17. "Food Retailing," 38–41. While the top ten national chains experienced a gain of over 17 percent, all other food chains had a 63 percent growth. Independent grocers enjoyed a sales increase of over 21 percent and "voluntary and cooperative independents" had a gain of nearly 35 percent, owning the largest share (50 percent) of the US retail sales.

18. In 1964, at the peak of this promotion, 81 percent of the nation's chain stores were distributing trading stamps. See "Time Capsules from 50 Years of Annual Reports," *Progressive Grocer*, April 1983, 169.

19. "Prices: Picketers and the Picketed," *Newsweek*, November 7, 1966, 78–80; "Behind the Boycotts: Why Prices Are High," *Time*, November 4, 1966, 89; and "Housewives Skewer High Food Prices," *Business Week*, October 22, 1966, 42–43. For more analysis of consumer activism and popular dissatisfaction with the food industry, see Meg Jacobs, *Pocketbook Politics: Economic Citizenship in Twentieth-Century America* (Princeton University Press, 2005), 221–61, and Lizabeth Cohen, *A Consumers' Republic: The Politics of Mass Consumption in Postwar America* (Alfred A. Knopf, 2003), 345–98.

20. Food Industry Alliance of New York State, "FIA Celebrates 100 Years," *Food Advocate/Griffin's Modern Grocer*, 2000, 38. Unit pricing refers to the system in which the price per pound of packaged items must be listed on supermarket shelves. The application of comprehensive nutritional labeling for food came in 1973. See "F.D.A. Proposes Sweeping Change in Food Labeling," *New York Times*, January 18, 1973, 1.

21. *Progressive Grocer* reported that the developments of 1973, including the sunsetting of Nixon's price ceilings, ended the "Era of Cheap Food," as grocery store sales topped the $100 billion mark for the first time. Of course, stores' collective after-tax net profit continued a steady decline that had begun in the mid-1960s—a worrying trend that was particularly painful for chains. See "The Crisis at the Check-Out Counter," *Newsweek*, April 10, 1972, 15–16; "War in the Aisles," *Newsweek*, October 9, 1972, 82; "Critics Rail, but Supermarkets Ask: Why Us?," *Business Week*, April 22, 1972, 97–98; "Irked Consumers Cutting Corners," *New York Times*, April 9, 1972, 19; "The High Cost of Eating," *Newsweek*, March 5, 1973, 52–59; "The High Price of Food Prices," *Fortune*, September 1973, 25–26; and "Time Capsules from 50 Years," 169.

22. "Food Calms Down," *Time*, April 19, 1976, 71. In New York, the city's Department of Consumer Affairs found that the price of feeding a family of four (a "market basket") rose over 45 percent between 1973 and 1978. See Lawrence Van Gelder, "Market Basket Cost Up 45% in 5 Years," *New York Times*, May 17, 1978, C4.

23. Food Industry Alliance of New York, "FIA Celebrates 100 Years," 56. See also Allan J. Mayer, "Supermarkets in a Crunch," *New York Times Magazine*, February 8, 1976, 10–12+; "Shopping for Food: How It's Changing," *U.S. News & World Report*, May 30, 1966, 12; "The Great Check-Out," *Newsweek*, November 27, 1978, 89; Ralph Blumenthal, "Supermarkets' Super Woes: High Costs and Slim Profits," *New York Times*, May 4, 1980, sec. 3, 1; and "The Unsuper Markets," *Newsweek*, January 16, 1978, 65.

24. "Today the Shopping Center, Tomorrow the Superstore," *Harvard Business Review* 52, no. 1 (January 1974): 89–98.

25. "Prices Up, Profits Down," *Forbes*, June 15, 1973, 34–35, and John T. McGrath, "Is the Supermarket Obsolete?," *Newsweek*, February 10, 1975, 9.

26. The barcode would be particularly revolutionary when used in conjunction with computers, as it would save millions of dollars each year on inventory control and checkout costs while lessening the need for skilled cashiers. Computer scanning at the checkout would not be fully implemented until the 1980s.

27. James M. Mayo, *The American Grocery Store: The Business Evolution of an Architectural Space* (Greenwood, 1993), 215.

28. "No-Frills Food," *Business Week*, March 23, 1981, 70–80, and Walter Heller, "Economy-Store Census: Warehouse Stores and Limited Assortment Stores Approach 2,000 Mark and $10 Billion in Sales," *Progressive Grocer*, May 1981, 89–91+. This type of operation had been developing since the late 1950s, as three distinct models—the discount warehouse, the supermarket, and the department store—began to fuse. Over the next two decades, by necessity, discount warehouses became more service-conscious while supermarkets became more price-conscious, even expanding their nonfood lines to include everything from appliances to drugs. See "Retailer Fusion: Who Will Win?," *Printer's Ink*, August 18, 1961, 21–24.

29. "Today the Shopping Center, Tomorrow the Superstore," 89–98, and Blumenthal, "Supermarkets' Super Woes," sec. 3, 1.

30. According to *Progressive Grocer*, between 1970 and 1980, 1,691 food stores in the New York area failed; 131 of these qualified as supermarkets (stores that did more than a million dollars' worth of business). In postwar New York, merchants had struggled to establish the supermarket model within the city's limited geography, even converting old movie houses into deluxe groceries. At the end of the 1970s, the struggles of the urban supermarket were illustrated by the conversion of a 6,400-square-foot Food City store into warehouse stores for Pottery Barn and The Gap. (See George Goodman, "Food Chains Find Leases No Bargain," *New York Times*, July 13, 1980, sec. 8, 1.)

31. "Grocers See New Hope in Limited-Line Stores," *Business Week*, December 4, 1978, 29–30, and Blumenthal, "Supermarkets' Super Woes," sec. 3, 1.

32. Blumenthal, "Supermarkets' Super Woes," sec. 3, 15. In the early 1980s, Sloan's was one of D'Agostino's primary competitors, with its ability to adapt to the evolving needs of its neighborhood customers and its pursuit of a similar demographic. In the 1990s, the chain would be bought by John Catsimatidis of the Red Apple Chain and Gristede's, who would later target D'Agostino's for acquisition. See Gerri Hirshey, "The Supermarket That's Eating Manhattan," *New York*, March 17, 1980, 48–52.

33. Leonard Daykin, "Is Inner City Food Retailing Dying?," *Progressive Grocer*, June 1969, 71–79.

34. "'Mom and Pop' Groceries Dying Under Competition," *New York Times*, December 4, 1976, 31. There was a vacuum created by the disappearance of the "mom and pop" grocery. While a new generation of ethnic bodegas would emerge to serve the needs of many urban communities, in suburbs across the US convenience store franchises such as Circle K and 7-Eleven would proliferate, becoming a multibillion-dollar industry in the 1970s. See "Convenience Stores: A $7.4 Billion Mushroom," *Business Week*, March 21, 1977, 61–64, and Mayo, *American Grocery Store*, 204–7.

35. William K. West, "Inner City Supers: Is There a Future?," *Progressive Grocer*, June 1978, 75.

36. For more on the successes of Dominican and Puerto Rican retailers, see Francis X. Clines, "The New Bodegueros," *New York Times*, March 25, 1978, 17; "Bodega," *New Yorker*, September 23, 1972, 27–30; Nancy Foner, *From Ellis Island to JFK: New York's Two Great Waves of Immigration* (Yale University Press, 2000), 97; and Frederick M. Binder and David M. Reimers, *All the Nations Under Heaven: An Ethnic and Racial History of New York City* (Columbia University Press, 1995), 227.

37. "A New Revolution in the Kitchen," *U.S. News & World Report*, February 19, 1969, 70. The article noted that some 15 million women worked outside the home by 1968, twice the total of the mid-1940s. It also attributed the shift in eating habits to America's continued move from rural to urban areas, and to teenagers snacking on their own throughout the day, rather than having a meal with their families.

38. "Better Days for Housewives as Food Industry Changes," *U.S. News & World Report*, March 22, 1965, 118–20.

39. "New Revolution in the Kitchen," 68–71.

40. Glenn Snyder, "Why Your Produce Department Will Make a Comeback in the 60's," *Progressive Grocer*, February 1960, 48–49. The secretary of United Fruit, Bernard Imming, argued that produce was declining as an aspect of the supermarket business because of the lack of produce men in management positions—making fruit and vegetable operations a mystery to the executives who were ruling the grocery business.

41. "Up-Turn in Pre-Packaging," *Modern Packaging*, July 1960, 89–90. The survey cited by *Modern Packaging* was conducted by *Food Merchandising* magazine. This figure represented a 27 percent increase over the previous two decades.

42. "The Supermarkets Fight Back," *Dun's Review*, October 1977, 109.

43. "New Revolution in the Kitchen," 70.

44. "Study Finds Rise in Materialism Amid Economic Gloom," *New York Times*, May 9, 1979, C8.

45. "Better Days for Housewives," 118.

46. Jo-Ann Zbytniewski, "Working Women: Less Time, More Money," *Progressive Grocer*, June 1979, 56–58+.

47. "Supermarkets Fight Back," 108–10.

48. Lee Flaherty, "Change in Woman's Status Spurs Battle of Supermarkets vs. Fast-Food Chains," *Advertising Age*, May 23, 1977, 58+.

49. "Big Appetite for Gourmet Foods," *Business Week*, August 23, 1958, 55–56, and "U.S. Grows an Educated Palate," *Business Week*, January 31, 1959, 28–30.

50. For more on the nascent gourmet food movement, see Ruth Reichl, *Comfort Me with Apples: More Adventures at the Table* (Random House, 2001); Patrick Kuh, *The Last Days of Haute Cuisine* (Viking, 2001); and Noel Fitch, *Appetite for Life: The Biography of Julia Child* (Doubleday, 1997).

51. "The Kitchen: America's Playroom," *Forbes*, March 15, 1976, 24–25.

52. Walter Kiechel III, "The Food Giants Struggle to Stay in Step with Consumers," *Fortune*, September 11, 1978, 50.

53. "Kitchen: America's Playroom," 24–28. The critic in question is William Rice of *The Washington Post*.

54. "Kitchen: America's Playroom," 24–28.

55. Here, one must also note that immigration in the 1960s and '70s also served to diversify the tastes and consumer habits of Americans, particularly with the growing popularity of Asian and Mexican cuisine. For more on this evolution, see Donna Gabaccia, *We Are What We Eat:*

Ethnic Food and the Making of Americans (Harvard University Press, 1998), 202–24, and Richard Pillsbury, *No Foreign Food: The American Diet in Time and Place* (Westview, 1998).

56. "Kitchen: America's Playroom," 24–28. The rise of the young female gourmet reversed a curious trend from the 1950s—according to a former editor at *Gourmet* magazine, its older disciples were often men. Before its boom in the 1960s, the magazine survived on the patronage of a small male readership, while female cooks often looked to *Good Housekeeping* for their inspiration.

57. Robert A. Wright, "Health Foods—Only a Fad?," *New York Times*, October 15, 1972, F1.

58. For insight into how the politics of the sixties reshaped American food, see Warren J. Belasco's *Appetite for Change: How the Counterculture Took On the Food Industry, 1966–1988* (Cornell University Press, 1993). Belasco explains not only how the cultural values of radicals evolved into an ethos of consumption, but also how their attitudes toward food gained broader acceptance in the American mainstream.

59. Anne Colamosca, "Health Foods Prosper Despite High Prices," *New York Times*, November 17, 1974, F3. Colamosca noted that many supermarkets, including A&P and Grand Union, that had added health food lines in the early 1970s were actually seeing their sales suffer. Apparently, the marriage of mainstream grocers and health foods would have to wait until the 1980s and '90s to find success.

60. Jane E. Brody, "America Leans to a Healthier Diet," *New York Times Magazine*, October 13, 1985, 34.

61. Nancy Jenkins, "Health Food and the Change in Eating Habits," *New York Times*, April 4, 1984, C6. The industry had already ascended from its nadir in the early 1960s, as dollar sales of fresh produce grew from $4 billion to $6 billion between 1959 and 1969 ("The Super Market of the 70's, Part II: More Sales, Profits, Prestige Ahead for Produce," *Progressive Grocer*, November 1969, 186).

62. Brody, "America Leans to a Healthier Diet," 34. The national shift from the meat-heavy diet of the 1950s and 1960s was also due to the rising price of food in the 1970s, as Americans ate more vegetables and homemade soups, less red meat, smaller portions, and more leftovers.

63. Judy Klemsrud, "Vegetarianism: Growing Way of Life, Especially Among the Young," *New York Times*, March 21, 1975, 43.

64. Kiechel, "Food Giants Struggle," 50–56.

65. Robert O'Neill, "Produce Manager: Guiding the Renaissance of Fresh," *Progressive Grocer*, February 1980, 41–61. How was the "renaissance" of produce affecting store design? The necessity of having speedy checkout lines before the era of scanning and electronic scales had once encouraged retailers to limit the varieties of fruits they sold or to opt for prepackaged produce—as clerks at the checkout would otherwise have to price and weigh each piece of fruit. Now that consumers wanted a larger quantity and variety of fresh fruits and vegetables, many merchants were opting for the bulk displays and open crates of old-fashioned produce markets.

66. "A New Twist: Supermarkets with All the Frills," *Business Week*, August 17, 1981, 122.

67. Salad bars were an especially profitable venture for grocers because they played into consumers' new fixation on freshness and health, while serving their continuing desire for convenience. With salad bars, and later additions such as delis that sold cooked rotisserie-style chickens, merchants could charge a premium for unsold produce and meat that was beginning to show its age and was destined for the garbage.

68. In 1969, *Progressive Grocer* examined the lack of qualified produce workers, particularly as the older generation of fruit and vegetable men aged and retired. According to the article, supermarkets often sent junior employees to work in produce without sufficient training,

leaving one veteran to warn, "This is a mistake. Produce is a living, breathing thing, sensitive to its surroundings, easily made worthless through mishandling. On the other hand, with care and ingenuity nothing repays a store so handsomely." Of course, this trend not only reflected management's lack of respect for produce as a source of revenue, but also the transitory nature of employment in the modern supermarket. See "The Super Market of the 70's: Where Will Tomorrow's Produce Men Come From?," *Progressive Grocer*, November 1969, 189.

69. "New Twist," 122.

70. According to *Business Week*, "prestige stores" used an effective strategy of having a sufficient stock of affordable goods to attract more middling customers while trying to entice them to "trade up" for higher quality. These stores carried a profit margin that was 50 percent higher than the industry average ("New Twist," 122).

71. For more on the consumer habits of Young Urban Professionals, including their relationship to food culture, see "The Year of the Yuppie," *Newsweek*, December 31, 1984, 14–31.

72. "A Fancy Future for Pricey Foods," *Business Week*, November 10, 1980, 83.

73. Mary Ann Linsen, "Gourmet: The Democraticization of Fine Foods," *Progressive Grocer*, February 1983, 34–36 and 44. *Progressive Grocer* also studied how D'Agostino's and competitors such as Food Emporium were using store design in new locations to create the gourmet image. In their new units, such as their store in Chelsea, D'Agostino's chose a "contemporary 'high tech' look" to create a trendy, upscale feel.

74. Stephen D'Agostino, interview by author, August 9, 2001.

75. Stephen D'Agostino, interview.

76. Stephen D'Agostino, interview.

77. Stephen D'Agostino, interview.

78. Selling packaged meat from a central processing plant had become a widespread practice among grocers by the 1960s. The company had already started this transition in the early 1950s with the installation of self-service meat counters.

79. Stephen D'Agostino, interview by author, August 9, 2001.

80. Stephen D'Agostino, interview. Years later, Stephen himself would become a member of the Union League.

81. "Shift D'Agostino Execs," *Food Merchants Advocate*, February 1979, 2. Under the new leadership structure, Nicholas D'Agostino became the company's chairman emeritus but was given the formal title of chairman of the executive committee. In addition to serving as president, Nick D'Agostino Jr. also became the chief operating officer of the business, a position he would hold until 1982.

82. Expanding the labor pool became necessary for two reasons. The city's population was changing and as D'Agostino's continued to grow, the number of Italians looking to work in the grocery business was declining. Meanwhile, the crew of potential clerks, checkers, and stockboys became more diverse, in terms of both ethnicity and age (as more teenagers sought part-time or temporary jobs).

83. According to Stephen, it was his younger brother Nick who brought many modern human resource techniques into the company early in his career.

84. Stephen recalled that the Supermarket Institute was dedicated to educating its membership by serving as an informal "graduate program for grocers." The National Association of Food Chains was founded to lobby the federal government on behalf of chain supermarkets. Stephen was certain that his decision to join the National Association of Food Chains would have upset his uncle—who saw its membership as the enemy. Stephen recalls one of the grocery

journals declaring, "Poor Patsy would be turning over in his grave" (S. D'Agostino, interview by author, August 9, 2001). In 1977, Stephen would also help found the Food Marketing Institute, which was dedicated to lobbying Congress and the presidency on behalf of food retailers. He soon became national president of the 1,200-member organization, despite the modest size of his own company.

85. Stephen D'Agostino, interview by author, August 9, 2001.

86. Stephen D'Agostino, interview.

87. Stephen D'Agostino, interview.

88. Isadore Barmash, "D'Agostino's Aims for Top Recognition: Small Chain in Manhattan Seeks Key Role," *New York Times*, June 23, 1981, D6.

89. Barmash, "D'Agostino's Aims for Top Recognition," D6.

90. Patsy D'Agostino, "I Found $5,000,000 in a Pushcart," *American Magazine*, September 1952, 108. Given their personalities, one might expect that Patsy would preach expansion and Nicholas would argue that the business should be prudent about growth. Yet, up until his death, Patsy D'Agostino was concerned about overexpansion. His caution was another source of conflict between him and his brother, who believed that the company should continue to reinvest its profits to avoid excessive taxation.

91. Barmash, "D'Agostino's Aims for Top Recognition," D6.

92. Stephen and his brother Nick also took the opportunity to install high-end bakeries and delis in their stores, which allowed them to compete with "gourmet groceries" like Zabar's. By contrast, in 1966, when Nicholas Sr. made a grand defense of his methods, he cited D'Agostino's refusal to install delicatessens as proof of its commitment to quality.

93. In a 1951 issue of *Business Week*, Patsy D'Agostino observed, "Why do you spend all your money on men to tell everybody your company is something it isn't? Pay your employees well instead, and they will tell the world how wonderful you are" ("A Gospel for Independent Grocers," *Business Week*, October 27, 1951, 79).

94. In the 1950s and early 1960s, D'Agostino's did limited advertising in local newspapers and in smaller weeklies such as *The Town and Village* (the paper of Stuyvesant Town and Peter Cooper Village). Most of these ads were focused on price, the week's specials, or the features of the store itself—though some contained holiday themes, simple graphics, or brief features on the company's personnel. One ad even described the brothers' origins on the pushcart, as discussed in the previous chapter. In these efforts, one can see the beginnings of the company's image-oriented strategy.

95. "Supermarket Ads: Creative at Last," *Printer's Ink*, May 10, 1963, 40. Observers attributed the industry's inattention to the nuances of advertising to customers' enthusiasm for the novelty of early supermarkets, as they believed that a supermarket "had only to open its doors and all the business it needed to make a handsome profit came spilling in." By the early 1960s, many grocers had also tried to incorporate contests, promotions, and coupons into their ads to bring in business. One frustrated industry analyst complained that grocers had produced "a stream of tasteless 'laundry lists,' featuring not food, but foolishness. The measure of grocery advertising today is not beauty or inherent quality. It is, instead, the number of items that can be squeezed between the gimmicks and giveaways." He concluded that coupon-driven advertising was also "sterile as a blank sheet." In a speech to a grocers' association, another ad executive declared that supermarkets practiced "stiff and stifled advertising," which reflected a "cubbyhole approach" that violated consumers' inherent "right not to be bored." See "Good Grocery Ads: Where Did They Go?," *Printer's Ink*, January 18, 1963, 68, and "'Supermart Ads Are Stiff,

Stifled,' Hurvis Charges," *Advertising Age*, November 20, 1967, 24. The executive in question is Thomas Hurvis, speaking to the National American Wholesale Grocers Association.

96. For example, if a grocer entered into an agreement with the Del Monte Company, he had to feature Del Monte brands prominently in his ads. These national food brands preferred the "price-item" style of advertising because it promoted their products and because it was cheaper. At the same time, the grocer usually had agreements with different companies, thus requiring him to feature all of them in a single, chaotic ad.

97. "Supermarket Ads: Creative at Last," 40.

98. Stephen D'Agostino, interview by author, August 9, 2001, and Nicholas D'Agostino Jr., interview by author, May 15, 2001.

99. Stephen D'Agostino, interview by author, August 9, 2001.

100. Jo Foxworth, *Boss Lady: An Executive Woman Talks About Making It* (Warner Books, 1978), 15–42.

101. Considering her decision to become her own boss, Foxworth mused, "I love writing advertising, but I don't like working for dummies" (Phillip H. Dougherty, "Messages with a Bit of Humor," *New York Times*, July 7, 1981, D20). In trying to describe Stephen D'Agostino, Foxworth recalled that he once said, "Conventional wisdom means general agreement, and when just about everybody thinks something, it isn't likely to be wise" (Foxworth, *Boss Lady*, 233).

102. Foxworth, *Boss Lady*, 233.

103. As previously noted, the campaign was based on an actual episode during the 1950s. A female customer was so overjoyed with receiving a particularly fine cut of meat that she planted a big kiss on the cheek of Nicholas D'Agostino, to the dismay of his wife, Josephine.

104. Foxworth, *Boss Lady*, 233.

105. Jo Foxworth and her staff recognized that the "D'Ag Bag" made a useful rhyme and a clever logo. But according to Stephen D'Agostino, "D'Ag's" was also a nickname that New York customers gave to the stores themselves because it was easier to say than "D'Agostino" and, thus, might be read as an Anglicization of the family name.

106. Barmash, "D'Agostino's Aims for Top Recognition," D6.

107. "D'Agostino: Innovation, Sensitivity: Success," *Food Merchants Advocate*, December 1982, 20A. The company would take an active part in making its "D'Ag Bags" symbols of status over the next decade by supplying television programs, magazines, and fashion photographers that wanted to brand their subjects as "New York" with company paraphernalia free of charge.

108. Dougherty, "Messages with a Bit of Humor," D20.

109. Dougherty, "Messages with a Bit of Humor," D20.

110. Mona Doyle, "Food Ads Need to Get with It," *Progressive Grocer*, October 1983, 26. Doyle wrote that ads "appear to consumers to be geared to homemakers and large families—in spite of the fact that one- and two-person households with two wage earners have been growing at a vastly higher rate than the population as a whole. People in these spending growth segments feel the ads are seldom addressed to them or their information needs."

111. Judy Greenwald, "D'Agostino Has Fresh Ad Approach," *Supermarket News*, May 5, 1980, 10.

112. The ads usually appeared in the paper's Wednesday "Living" section.

113. For more on the concept of *The New Yorker* "village," see Mary F. Corey, *The World Through a Monocle: "The New Yorker" at Midcentury* (Harvard University Press, 1999), 1–18.

114. Corey, *World Through a Monocle*, 105–6.

115. Due to the prohibitive cost of advertising on television, D'Agostino's devoted most of its ad budget to print media and radio. However, the signature elements of the company's advertising would find their expression in a series of memorable TV commercials that aired in New York in the 1980s. Each featured Marvin Glass's animated figures cooking, shopping, and eating, along with musical versions of D'Agostino slogans, including "Please Mr. D'Agostino, move closer to me" and "Love that D'Agostino." Despite their success, the ads were eventually discontinued for financial reasons.

116. Stephen acknowledged that his cozy relationship with the paper—based on years of company advertising and interactions with the editorial staff—also aided D'Agostino's *New York Times* campaign.

117. Blake Fleetwood, "The New Elite and an Urban Renaissance," *New York Times Magazine*, January 14, 1979, 20. This erosion would continue in ensuing decades, as between 1950 and 1989, the city lost 65 percent of its manufacturing jobs. See Jonathan Soffer, *Ed Koch and the Rebuilding of New York City* (Columbia University Press, 2010), 2.

118. Leonard Wallock, "New York City: Capital of the Twentieth Century," in *New York: Culture Capital of the World, 1940–65*, ed. Leonard Wallock (Rizzoli International, 1988), 30–31; Freeman, *Working-Class New York*, 26–28; and Foner, *From Ellis Island to JFK*, 11–13. These figures were due to both immigration and natural increase. While both of these groups came to New York because of the lack of economic opportunity in their native regions, Puerto Ricans also suffered from the effects of overpopulation on their home island. As US citizens, they faced none of the legal quotas that were impeding newcomers from other countries—which helps explain the scale of their relocation.

119. Lankevich, *American Metropolis*, 211 and 226. It is estimated that 1.6 million white residents left New York between 1950 and 1970. In addition, between 1970 and 1976, nearly a half million African American and Latino New Yorkers also left the city, no longer seeing it as a place of opportunity. Even with this out-migration, the 1980 census revealed that there were still 1.7 million African Americans and 1.4 million Latinos living in New York.

120. Lankevich, *American Metropolis*, 206.

121. "New York City: Disaster Area?," *U.S. News & World Report*, November 4, 1968, 49–51; "New York: Crucible of the Urban Crisis," *Business Week*, November 16, 1968, 73; and Edward Logue, "New York: Are Cities a Bust?," *Look*, April 1, 1969, 70–73.

122. See "Why the Growing Flight of Business from New York City," *U.S. News & World Report*, March 6, 1967, 45; "Who Can Afford Manhattan?," *Time*, December 26, 1969, 49; and "Exodus from New York City: What Makes Businesses Leave," *U.S. News & World Report*, December 7, 1970, 50–53.

123. "New York's Last Gasp," *Newsweek*, August 4, 1975, 18–20+. For other examples of the national commentary on New York's fiscal woes, see "Brother, Can You Spare a Billion?," *Newsweek*, May 26, 1975, 28+; Wyndham Robertson, "Going Broke the New York Way," *Fortune*, August 1975, 144–49+; Robert J. Samuelson, "No Funds for Fun City," *New Republic*, May 10, 1975, 17–19; and "How New York City Lurched to the Brink," *Time*, June 16, 1975, 16+.

124. In assessing the causes of New York's fiscal crisis, it is important to note that the city's annual expenditures increased from $2.5 billion to over $10 billion over the course of the 1960s and early '70s, mainly to maintain its system of welfare, health care, and education (Phillips-Fein, *Fear City*, 23). Meanwhile, from 1946 to 1975, the number of city employees had increased from around 100,000 to around 295,000 (Binder and Reimers, *All the Nations Under Heaven*). As New York struggled with declining tax revenue and federal support in a period of

economic recession, mayors John Lindsay and Abe Beame used budgetary gymnastics to keep the city solvent, which became increasingly problematic. See Auletta, *The Streets Were Paved with Gold*, 29–92 and 145–190; Freeman, *Working-Class New York*, 256–87; and Phillips-Fein, *Fear City*, 28–202.

125. For more on the blighting of New York's neighborhoods in this period, see Freeman, *Working-Class New York*, 272–83, and Schneider, *Vampires, Dragons, and Egyptian Kings*, 217–45.

126. See James Goodman's *Blackout* (North Point Press, 2003) for a captivating portrait of how the Blackout of 1977 symbolized the decade's tensions, anxieties, and conflicts.

127. A D'Agostino store even provided the setting for several scenes in Bronson's film.

128. For an engaging history of this marketing campaign, including how the branding of New York helped direct the city's priorities and serve the interests of the private sector, see Miriam Greenberg, *Branding New York: How a City in Crisis Was Sold to the World* (Routledge, 2008). Greenberg's analysis is especially helpful for understanding how the image of the city as a hub for tourism and commerce, as well as its transformation in the 1970s and '80s, marginalized New York's ethnically diverse, working-class culture.

129. Christopher Pellnat, "D'AG's Is New York: Nicholas D'Agostino, Jr. Sees a Promising Future for D'Agostino Supermarkets," *Food Merchants Advocate*, September 1993, 16.

130. Fleetwood, "New Elite," 16–7.

131. Fleetwood, "New Elite," 22 and 34. In the 1950s, the average age of residents in suburbs such as Rye was thirty-six; in the late 1970s it was forty-seven. Meanwhile, New York neighborhoods such as the Upper West Side, Greenwich Village, Chelsea, and Yorkville saw the average age of their residents drop dramatically with the arrival of young professionals. For more on the politics of the "Brownstone Revolution" as it was occurring in Brooklyn, see Suleiman Osman, "The Decade of the Neighborhood," in *Rightward Bound: Making American Conservative in the 1970s*, ed. Bruce J. Schulman and Julian E. Zelizer (Harvard University Press, 2008), 106–27.

132. Fleetwood, "New Elite," 20. Despite its declining reputation, in the early 1970s New York still earned 10 percent of all the money made in America, hosted ninety-six of the companies in the vaunted Fortune 500, and was home to six of the nation's ten biggest banks, four of its largest insurance companies, and 90 percent of its top advertising firms.

133. James B. Lindheim, "The New Class," *Harper's*, August 1975, 6. The article's labeling of young baby boomers as "hippoisie" conveyed the sensibility of Parisian coffeehouses and the fading counterculture. With the rise of the yuppie in the next decade, however, urban sophisticates would affect a more privileged identity.

134. "D'Agostino at GMR, Asks Suppliers for Involvement," *Food Merchants Advocate*, March 1973, 1.

135. Cynthia Rigg, "D'Agostino's Fresh Approach," *Crain's New York Business*, January 2, 1989, 28.

136. William Foote Whyte, *Street Corner Society: The Social Structure of an Italian Slum* (1943; University of Chicago Press, 1955), and Herbert Gans, *The Urban Villagers: Group and Class in the Life of Italian-Americans* (Free Press, 1962). Other notable works that analyzed the social condition of Italians in this period include Nathan Glazer and Daniel P. Moynihan, *Beyond the Melting Pot: The Negroes, Puerto Ricans, Jews, Italians, and Irish of New York City* (MIT Press, 1963); Edward Banfield, *The Moral Basis of a Backwards Society* (Free Press, 1958); and Leonard Covello, *The Heart Is the Teacher* (McGraw-Hill, 1958) and *The Social Background of the Italo-American School Child* (Brill, 1967).

137. In this regard, New York's Italian community benefited from the tremendous expansion of the municipal payroll after World War II. From 1946 to 1975, the number of city employees increased from around 100,000 to around 295,000 (Binder and Reimers, *All the Nations Under Heaven*, 202–3).

138. In the 1940s and '50s, Italian Americans in New York also enjoyed some of their greatest victories as a community in the realm of politics—electing two mayors and several city representatives.

139. On a local level, by 1972, 34,000 of the nearly 170,000 students in the City University of New York system were Italian (Binder and Reimers, *All the Nations Under Heaven*, 200).

140. Richard Alba, "Italian Americans and Assimilation," in *The Routledge History of Italian Americans*, ed. William J. Connell and Stanislao G. Pugliese (Routledge, 2018), 496–97.

141. For compelling analysis of the battle between Italians and African Americans over urban space amid the charged atmosphere of the 1960s and '70s, see Jonathan Rieder, *Canarsie: The Jews and Italians of Brooklyn Against Liberalism* (Harvard University Press, 1985).

142. Because of their representation in the construction and manufacturing sectors, New York's Italian community was especially affected by the shrinking of the city's industrial economy.

143. Protests from the Anti-Defamation League of B'nai B'rith subsequently caused the group to change its name to Americans of Italian Descent, Inc. For a sampling of articles debating the reality of anti-Italian discrimination in this period, see Mario Puzo, "The Italians, American Style," *New York Times Magazine*, August 6, 1967, 7+; Nicholas Pileggi, "How We Italians Discovered America and Kept It Clean and Pure While Giving It Lots of Singers, Judges, and Other Swell People," *Esquire*, June 1968, 80–82+; and Richard Gambino, "Twenty Million Italian-Americans Can't Be Wrong," *New York Times Magazine*, April 30, 1972, 20–22+. Puzo and Pileggi were critical of these organizations for their sensitivity toward ethnic caricatures, while Gambino (a historian and memoirist of Italian life in America) focused on the continued struggles of Italian Americans.

144. "Protest: 'Bless You, Joe,'" *Newsweek*, July 13, 1970, 34, and "Protest: Italian Power," *Newsweek*, June 22, 1970, 22.

145. The American public had always maintained a fascination with gangster films, but the popular reception of Coppola's film caused critics to debate how its success reflected social attitudes. Academic theorists such as Fredric Jameson even mused that the popularity of *The Godfather* stemmed from its implicit critique of the trappings of corporate America and its glorification of the concepts of honor, loyalty, and family at the center of Old World immigrant culture. For more on the social significance of the film, see Thomas Ferraro's "Blood in the Marketplace: The Business of Family in the *Godfather* Narratives," in *The Invention of Ethnicity*, ed. Werner Sollors (Oxford University Press, 1989), and Bruce J. Schulman's *The Seventies: The Great Shift in American Culture, Society, and Politics* (Da Capo, 2001).

146. Matthew Frye Jacobson, *Roots, Too: White Ethnic Revival in Post–Civil Rights America* (Harvard University Press, 2006).

147. *Italian Charities of America Bulletin*, 1971, 4.

148. When asked about the connection between the company's business practices and its ethnic identity, Stephen would later muse, "I don't identify myself as being Italian. I like Italian food, I like to go to Italy . . . but if my success depends on me being Italian, I probably wouldn't be very successful" (Stephen D'Agostino, interview by author, August 9, 2001).

149. Isadore Barmash, "D'Agostino Chain Chief Leaving to Join Bottler," *New York Times*, September 13, 1982, D1.

150. Stephen D'Agostino, interview by author, August 9, 2001.

151. Stephen D'Agostino, interview.

152. Stephen D'Agostino, interview.

153. Evidence of the company's growth under Stephen D'Agostino's leadership can be seen in both its sales and the number of stores. Between 1952 and 1981, company sales grew from $5 million to $100 million. From 1943 to 1960, the number of D'Agostino stores had expanded from three to seven, with most of these based in Manhattan's Upper East Side. Between 1960 and 1982, however, the number of D'Agostino's stores expanded from seven to eighteen, with the company venturing into the Bronx, Westchester County, and Brooklyn while continuing its investment in newly gentrified neighborhoods like Chelsea and the Upper West Side.

154. Barmash, "D'Agostino Chain Chief Leaving," D4. In a few short years, Stephen would leave JTL and return with his family to the New York area. Still, years later, Stephen believed that his resolution to leave D'Agostino's for the corporate world was "the best decision he ever made" and his years as a CEO at JTL were "the proudest moments of my life" (Stephen D'Agostino, interview by author, August 9, 2001).

155. Barmash, "D'Agostino Chain Chief Leaving," D4.

156. The issue of whether the next generation of D'Agostinos would succeed Stephen and Nick D'Agostino Jr. was also reminiscent of some of the disagreements between Patsy and Nicholas. According to Stephen, he did not want his children to work for the company, while Nick hoped his sons would continue the family dynasty. Stephen later quipped, "His kids are very happy they're in the business. My kids are probably not happy they're not in the business." Stephen's distaste for the family business as an entity and as a controlling factor in the interior lives of its members continued long after his retirement. He would argue that family businesses inevitably led to fathers lording their power over their sons, and to older children dominating their younger siblings while younger siblings resented having their talents and smarts being undervalued. When asked if he thought family businesses naturally regenerated such rivalries over time, he replied, "Excuse me, you're an educated person, right? You've read enough Shakespeare. Nothing's changed. It happens.... It's the nature of the world" (Stephen D'Agostino, interview by author, August 9, 2001).

157. D'Agostino's advertising consultant Jo Foxworth actually discovered the award's existence in a conversation with one of her associates, and she helped Nicholas apply for it.

158. Horatio Alger Association of Distinguished Americans, *Only in America: Opportunity Still Knocks, Volume II* (Horatio Alger Association, 1982).

159. Ralph Kinney Bennett, "Review of 'Free to Choose,' by Milton Friedman," *Reader's Digest*, January 1980, 165.

160. Ronald Reagan himself was a Horatio Alger alumnus, having been honored while he was governor of California.

161. Jo Foxworth, interview with the author, August 8, 2001, and Loretta D'Agostino Schmitz, unpublished personal journal, collection of the author, 2002.

5. New York's Family Grocer (1982–2025)

1. Jonathan Soffer, *Ed Koch and the Rebuilding of New York City* (Columbia University Press, 2010), 1–11, 145–60, and 255–75.

2. George J. Lankevich, *American Metropolis: A History of New York City* (New York University Press, 1998), 230 and 239.

3. For more on Wall Street's influence on the culture of New York in the 1980s, see Steve Fraser, *Every Man a Speculator: A History of Wall Street in American Life* (HarperCollins, 2005), 525–72.

4. Beneath this heady atmosphere of prosperity lurked a host of corrosive social problems. In the 1980s, the chasm between classes of New Yorkers seemed as wide as ever. While cocaine continued to be a recreational dalliance for Uptown socialites and stockbrokers, "crack" ravaged the city's Black and Latino neighborhoods, fueling violence, gang activity, and mass incarceration. The AIDS virus also exacted thousands of casualties, as throughout the 1980s, New York accounted for more than a quarter of all AIDS cases in the US. As some New Yorkers reveled in the new wealth of Wall Street, the city saw its poverty rate rise to 25 percent by the middle of the decade while the unhoused became ubiquitous. The decade's tense racial atmosphere added to the sense that New York was a city divided. When David Dinkins was elected mayor in 1990, he received only 27 percent of the white vote. Notorious incidents in the communities of Howard Beach, Bensonhurst, and Crown Heights embodied the seething racial tensions in the city's neighborhoods. Meanwhile, in 1989, white New Yorkers' anxieties about the inherent danger of their city seemed borne out by the notorious rape and beating of a female stockbroker who was jogging in Central Park—which led to the unjust prosecution and conviction of five young men of color. For more on the city's social problems in the 1980s, see Lankevich, *American Metropolis*, 235–54, and Robert Fitch, *The Assassination of New York* (Verso, 1993), 3–30.

5. John Marks, "New York, New York," *U.S. News & World Report*, September 29, 1997, 47. The quoted analyst is the urban historian Fred Siegel.

6. Marks, "New York, New York," 48–49. In this period, the city's murder rate declined by nearly 60 percent, while the rates of burglary, robbery, and auto theft were halved. Critics have noted that Giuliani has often been given undue credit for the city's revival. During his administration, Ed Koch committed billions of dollars for housing, while in the late 1980s and early 1990s city and state administrations granted hundreds of millions of dollars to blighted zones in the Bronx and Manhattan for their rebuilding efforts. David Dinkins put more than two thousand new police officers on the street and began the process of reforming the police department. And several community activists deserved credit for aiding residents in their efforts to keep decaying neighborhoods alive. Other observers have focused on the role of corporations in revitalizing the city's landscape, with some wags labeling the renewal of spaces like Times Square as the "Disney-fication" of New York (as the Walt Disney Co. invested heavily in the theater district to make it safe for family audiences).

7. Lankevich, *American Metropolis*, 252. According to the Office of the Comptroller of the State of New York, the city received 66 million visitors in 2019.

8. For more on how gentrification transformed the neighborhoods of New York, see DW Gibson, *The Edge Becomes the Center: An Oral History of Gentrification in the 21st Century* (Overlook, 2015), and Jeremiah Moss, *Vanishing New York: How a Great City Lost Its Soul* (Dey Street/HarperCollins, 2017).

9. Christopher Pellnat, "D'AG's Is New York: Nicholas D'Agostino, Jr. Sees a Promising Future for D'Agostino Supermarkets," *Food Merchants Advocate*, September 1993, 16.

10. Cynthia Rigg, "Against the Odds, Minding the Store: The Crain's All-Stars," *Crain's New York Business*, April 23, 1990, 48.

11. Rigg, "Crain's All-Stars," 47–49.

12. While not as prominent as his brother, Nick D'Agostino Jr. did take an active role in trade associations. He was involved in the National Grocers Association and served on the

board of the Food Marketing Institute. In 1982, months after he had assumed his brother's position as president of D'Agostino Supermarkets, Nick became the chairman of the New York State Food Merchants Association. In 1989, the NYSFMA honored him with its Distinguished Public Affairs Award for his work with legislators in Albany and in Washington, DC. See "Nick D'Agostino, Jr. NYSFMA Chairman; 7 New Directors Elected," *Food Merchants Advocate*, October 1982, 1, and "NYSFMA Public Affairs Award for D'Agostino," *Food Merchants Advocate*, November 1989, 1.

13. Rigg, "Crain's All-Stars," 48.
14. Bob Gatty, "Profiles in Leadership: Nicholas D'Agostino," *Grocery Marketing*, February 1989, 4.
15. Nicholas D'Agostino Jr., interview by author, May 15, 2001.
16. Nicholas D'Agostino Jr., interview.
17. "Nick D'Agostino, Jr.: Dedicated to Improving the Quality of Life for All New York," *Food Merchants Advocate*, December 1982, 36.
18. Gatty, "Profiles in Leadership: Nicholas D'Agostino," 4.
19. Pellnat, "D'AG's Is New York," 16.
20. Nicholas D'Agostino Jr., interview.
21. Rigg, "Crain's All-Stars," 47.
22. "Community Service: NYO and UHF Honor D'Agostino," *KPMG Peat Marwick*, September–October 1989, 3.
23. "Small Change at the Checkout," *New York Times*, February 9, 1989, A26.
24. "Schools Get Market's Computers," *Crain's New York Business*, June 10, 1991, 17.
25. Pellnat, "D'AG's Is New York," 16.
26. "D'Ag's Loves the Big Apple," *Twin County Grocers Association Newsletter*, 1982, 11.
27. "Nick D'Agostino, Jr.: Dedicated," 16.
28. "D'Agostino: Innovation, Sensitivity: Success," *Food Merchants Advocate*, December 1982, 20A.
29. Pellnat, "D'AG's Is New York," 16.
30. Nicholas D'Agostino Jr., interview by author, May 15, 2001.
31. Nicholas D'Agostino Jr., interview.
32. Stephen D'Agostino, interview by author, August 9, 2001.
33. Stephen D'Agostino, interview.
34. "The American Dream: A Second Generation," *Chain Store Age/Supermarkets*, December 1982, 17. The article noted that D'Agostino's had over 1,000 employees at the time of publication.
35. "D'Agostino: Innovation, Sensitivity: Success," 20.
36. Judy Greenwald, "D'Agostino Has Fresh Ad Approach," *Supermarket News*, May 5, 1980, 28.
37. Nicholas D'Agostino Jr., interview by author, May 15, 2001.
38. Pellnat, "D'AG's Is New York," 16.
39. Steve Weinstein, "Motivating Forces," *Progressive Grocer*, September 1996, 34+. See also Steve Weinstein, "How to Hire the Best," *Progressive Grocer*, July 1993, 119.
40. Pellnat, "D'AG's Is New York," 16.
41. Pellnat, "D'AG's Is New York," 16.
42. "Nick D'Agostino, Jr.: Dedicated," 16.
43. Nicholas D'Agostino Jr., interview by author, May 15, 2001.
44. Pellnat, "D'AG's Is New York," 16.

45. Steve Weinstein, "Tyranny Is Out, Teamwork Is In," *Progressive Grocer*, December 1987, 151 and 156.

46. Weinstein, "Tyranny Is Out, Teamwork Is In," 152.

47. "D'Ag's Loves the Big Apple," 11.

48. Rigg, "Crain's All-Stars," 48. Late in his career, Nick admitted that his management style had evolved with the company's scale, as well as with the times. In his early days as a vice president, "ownership was on premises in every store, every day. . . . If a manager would get sick, I'd go manage the store. . . . When I was first in the business and I would sign payroll by hand, we had eight or ten stores, I not only knew every employee that I was signing the payroll for, I knew how many hours they worked. . . . As the company doubled and tripled in size, you couldn't do that anymore." Over time, Nick and Stephen "became more concerned about the culture of our company, as opposed to the day-to-day running of our business" (Nicholas D'Agostino Jr., interview by author, May 15, 2001).

49. *D'Agostino Supermarkets, Inc. Estate Tax Pamphlet*, Prepared for The Food Marketing Institute by Bernish Communication Associates and On the Mark, LLC, 2001–02.

50. Nicholas D'Agostino Jr., interview by author, May 15, 2001.

51. Nicholas D'Agostino Jr., interview.

52. Pellnat, "D'AG's Is New York," 20.

53. "D'Ag's Loves the Big Apple," 10.

54. "D'Ag's Loves the Big Apple," 10.

55. "D'Ag's Loves the Big Apple," 10.

56. "Advertise Your Store's People, Not Just Your Prices," *Progressive Grocer*, August 1981, 16. Zal Venet of New York's Venet Advertising firm is the quoted speaker.

57. "D'Ag's Loves the Big Apple," 10.

58. Pellnat, "D'AG's Is New York," 20.

59. Pellnat, "D'AG's Is New York," 20.

60. The company also used "New York's Original Grocer" to promote its lineage.

61. Jo Foxworth, interview by author, August 8, 2001.

62. This invocation of the family's ethnic heritage was largely cosmetic. By the late 1980s, D'Agostino's iconography, from stationery to awnings, featured the Italian tricolor along with the image of a tomato—which called to mind the company's roots on the pushcart. The company had the encouragement and input of its chief advertising resource, Jo Foxworth, in this design decision. For many years, Foxworth had wanted the company to promote its Italian heritage.

63. The Estate Tax is a federal tax assessed on the deceased's property before it is passed to his or her heirs. Though the tax has a high threshold (i.e., only applying to the very wealthy) and has produced significant revenue for the government, it has drawn public animus because it can be assessed on businesses and properties that are passed to the next generation of a family. Over the last two decades, abolition of the so-called death tax has enjoyed fervent support from entrepreneurs, farmers, and political conservatives.

64. *D'Agostino Supermarkets, Inc. Estate Tax Pamphlet*.

65. *D'Agostino Supermarkets, Inc. Estate Tax Pamphlet*.

66. *D'Agostino Supermarkets, Inc. Estate Tax Pamphlet*.

67. "The American Dream: A Second Generation," *Chain Store Age/Supermarkets*, December 12, 1982, 17.

68. "American Dream: A Second Generation," 17.

69. "American Dream: A Second Generation," 17.

70. "American Dream: A Second Generation," 17.

71. Bruce Fox, "At D'Agostino Computer Handles Phoned-In Orders," *Supermarket News*, January 5, 1987, 13.

72. Jo Foxworth called Tele-Dag an "expensive experiment," especially the cost of building, stocking, and maintaining the warehouse in the Bronx, and explained that the service "was losing a million dollars a year.... We never got enough orders to justify it. We could not deliver on time" (Jo Foxworth, interview by author, August 8, 2001).

73. "American Dream: A Second Generation," 17.

74. Fox, "Computer Handles Phoned-In Orders," 13.

75. "America's Supermarket Miracle," *Business Week*, May 4, 1987, 127–30+.

76. Thomas McCarroll, "Grocery-Cart Wars," *Time*, March 30, 1992, 49. "How New York City Lurched to the Brink," *Time*, June 16, 1975, 16+.

77. Over the course of the 1980s, six of the top twelve supermarket chains (including Safeway, Jewel, and Lucky's) were "bought out" by various corporations and competitors (McCarroll, "Grocery-Cart Wars," 49).

78. Michael Ruhlman, *Grocery: The Buying and Selling of Food in America* (Abrams, 2017), 16.

79. McCarroll, "Grocery-Cart Wars," 49.

80. Michael Quint, "D'Agostino to Accept Debit Cards for Purchases," *New York Times*, May 19, 1990, 43, and Jeanne Iida, "Grocery Chain Does Well in Accepting Debit Cards," *American Banker*, March 22, 1991, 3. It is important to note that D'Agostino's innovation was not ahead of the national curve; New York grocery stores had been slow to adopt this new technology.

81. McCarroll, "Grocery-Cart Wars," 49, and "D'Agostino Steps Up Its Rewards," *Chain Store Age*, January 2005, 118.

82. See Victor J. Orler and David H. Friedman, "Consumer-Direct: Here to Stay," *Progressive Grocer*, January 1988, 51–52; Michael Garry, "Home Shopping Comes of Age," *Progressive Grocer*, September 1995, 81–83; "A Woman's Place Is on the Net," *Chain Store Age*, June 1997, 16–18; "Checking Out the Corner Cyberstore," *Business Week*, May 10, 1999, 130; and Karen Springen and Karen Kushner, "From Soup to Nuts," *Newsweek*, March 16, 1998, 77–78.

83. Warren Thayer, "Electronic Mom and Pop," *Progressive Grocer*, May 1989, 94–96, and Tim Dorgan, "Belief in the Future," *Progressive Grocer*, February 1997, 67–68.

84. See "Videotex Service in D'Agostino?," *Crain's New York Business*, February 13, 1989, 1, and McCarroll, "Grocery-Cart Wars," 49.

85. "New Internet Business to Enable Consumers to Name and Get Private Prices Before They Shop," *Business Wire*, September 21, 1999; "Grocer Shoppers Always Get Lowest Prices Through Priceline.com's WebHouse Club," *Business Wire*, November 3, 1999; and "Food Fight," *Chain Store Age*, November 1999, 168–71. Other name retailers who joined the WebHouse Club Network included ShopRite, A&P, King Kullen, Waldbaum's, Gristedes, Sloan's, and the Food Emporium.

86. "Online Grocery Shopping Comes to New York City," *Business Wire*, February 15, 2001.

87. Terry Pristin, "Ordering Groceries in Aisle 'www,'" *New York Times*, May 4, 2002, B3. MyWebGrocer was also responsible for designing and maintaining the company website. D'Agostino charged $10 for deliveries under $75, and $8 for over that amount. Despite the company's hyping of its online service, internet shopping accounted for only 1 to 3 percent of sales even as it expanded to all 23 of its stores.

88. Pristin, "Ordering Groceries in Aisle 'www,'" B3.

89. FreshDirect introduced a couple of key innovations to online food shopping to make the service more appealing to Manhattan professionals. First, the company targeted upscale neighborhoods with a product mix that consisted of 70 percent produce, perishables, and prepared meals, and only 30 percent dry goods—the opposite of traditional supermarkets. Second, FreshDirect looked to compete with other upscale retailers by offering quality produce, freshly roasted coffee, prepared foods, and freshly baked breads at lower prices. FreshDirect was founded by Joe Fedele (formerly of the Fairway market) and Jason Ackerman, with the help of $100 million from Wall Street investors. See Chris Smith, "Splat," *New York*, May 24, 2004, 36–41. The company claimed they could charge less than the competition because they made direct deals with manufacturers and farmers' markets, and kept a staff of a thousand bakers, butchers, and chefs at their 30,000-square-foot warehouse in Long Island City. See Lisa Fickenscher, "Grocer Finds Online Strategy That Delivers," *Crain's New York Business*, April 7–13, 2003, 48; Lisa Fickenscher, "Online Grocer Clicks," *Crain's New York Business*, February 21–27, 2005, 3 and 34; and Julia Moskin, "Online Shopping Makes New York a Cardboard Jungle," *New York Times*, April 6, 2005, F1.

90. Moskin, "Online Shopping," F1.

91. Constance Gustke, "Prices and Possibilities," *Progressive Grocer*, January 1, 2002, 66–68. In 2003, DemandTec boosted company revenue by almost 10 percent, unit volume by over 6 percent, and net profits by almost 2 percent—amounts promising enough to justify the millions of dollars the software cost. See John Karolefski, "D'Agostino Supermarket Pricing Strategy Boosts Sales," *Food Logistics*, November/December 2003, 20. Of course, the software meant D'Agostino's would cut prices on staples and raise prices on high-end items. For its successful implementation of the demand-based management system, the company was honored by the computer industry ("Best in Corporate Systems" at Retail Systems 2002 Achievement Awards). See "CVS SVP/CIO Receives Career Achievement Award at Retail Systems 2002/VICS Collaborative Commerce," *Business Wire*, June 25, 2002.

92. Cynthia Rigg, "Area Food Brokers Seek Shelf Esteem," *Crain's New York Business*, January 7, 1991, 3.

93. What were the factors that created this new wave of immigrants? Earlier legislation, including the 1882 Chinese Exclusion Act, the Immigration Act of 1924 (which affirmed the national origins quota system), and the accompanying Asian Exclusion Act, had limited immigration from Europe while prohibiting new arrivals from Asia. Then, under the auspices of Lyndon Johnson's "Great Society" program, Congress enacted the Immigration and Nationality Act of 1965, which ended preferential quotas for Northern Europeans and restrictions against Asian immigration. In the two decades that followed, the US welcomed millions of newcomers from China, Korea, Southeast Asia, and India. Meanwhile, Cold War–inspired conflicts and political unrest spurred immigration from El Salvador, Nicaragua, Guatemala, Colombia, and the Caribbean. The Immigration Act of 1990 then included provisions to attract skilled workers (the H-1B visa) and a diversity lottery system that increased populations from Asia and Africa. For more on this recent immigration, see Nancy Foner, *From Ellis to JFK: New York's Two Great Waves of Immigration* (Yale University Press, 2000) and Nancy Foner, ed., *One Out of Three: Immigrant New York in the Twenty-First Century* (Columbia University Press, 2013); Frederick M. Binder and David M. Reimers, *All the Nations Under Heaven: An Ethnic and Racial History of New York City* (Columbia University Press, 1995); David M. Reimers, *Still the Golden Door: The Third World Comes to America* (1985; Columbia University Press, 1992); Tyler Anbinder, *City of Dreams: The 400-Year Epic History of Immigrant New York* (Houghton Mifflin Harcourt, 2016); Lawrence H. Fuchs, *The American Kaleidoscope: Race, Ethnicity, and*

the Civic Culture (Wesleyan University Press, 1990); Reed Ueda, *Postwar Immigrant America: A Social History* (Bedford/St. Martin's, 1994); and Roger Daniels, *Coming to America: A History of Immigration and Ethnicity in American Life* (HarperCollins, 1990).

94. Lankevich, *American Metropolis*, 240.

95. Nancy Foner, "Introduction: Immigrants in New York City in the New Millennium," in *One Out of Three*, ed. Foner, 1. See also "The Global Apple," *Economist*, March 16, 1996, 28.

96. Binder and Reimers, *All the Nations Under Heaven*, 226–27. The city's largest cohort of immigrants after 1970 hailed from the Caribbean. Including their American-born children, there were about 300,000 Dominicans in New York in 1990.

97. Foner, *One Out of Three*, 17.

98. Foner, *One Out of Three*, 12.

99. Foner, *One Out of Three*, 21.

100. "Global Apple," 28.

101. Clines, "New Bodegueros," 17.

102. For more on the intricacies of the city's Korean community, see Pyong Gap Min, "Koreans: Changes in New York in the Twenty-First Century," in *One Out of Three*, ed. Foner, 148–75.

103. Why were so many Korean immigrants drawn to the food trade? In the early 1970s, a generation of aging Italian, Greek, and Jewish merchants were retiring without any heirs who were willing to continue running their shops. Many of these merchants were convinced that the neighborhood grocery was doomed by urban blight and the growth of supermarkets, so they were anxious to sell their stores at any price. While Korean immigrants were often well educated, issues of language, credentials, and discrimination barred them from the professions. Owning a business could mean financial success, respectability, and self-determination. Korean immigrants also saw that produce markets required only a small capital investment and did not require much formal training or knowledge of English.

104. Marlys Harris, "Making It: How the Koreans Won the Green-Grocer Wars," *Money*, March 1983, 192.

105. Harris, "Making It," 196.

106. Elizabeth Hawes, "New Greengrocers," *New Yorker*, July 4, 1977, 21.

107. Hawes, "New Greengrocers," 20 and 23.

108. "Breathing New Life into Small Business," *Forbes*, September 17, 1979, 197.

109. "Breathing New Life into Small Business," 197.

110. Harris, "Making It," 192 and 194.

111. Harris, "Making It," 192. One can again observe a parallel with the case of Italian merchants, seen in Mark Murphy's descriptions in *The New Yorker*, of the frontier atmosphere at the Bronx Terminal Market where Patsy D'Agostino went to procure the inventory for his stores. See Mark Murphy, "If Trouble Can Be Avoid," *New Yorker*, May 15, 1943, 25–35.

112. The Korean grocers who served predominantly African American communities in Brooklyn and Harlem became figures of controversy throughout this period. Some residents viewed the Korean retailers as interlopers who had little respect for their customers, or as symbols of the need for more Black-owned businesses. Korean grocers, on the other hand, often struggled to cope with communities that were hostile to their presence. This situation resulted in several well-publicized conflicts in the 1980s and '90s.

113. Harris, "Making It," 193.

114. Harris, "Making It," 192.

115. Harris, "Making It," 192.

116. Hawes, "New Greengrocers," 20.
117. Murphy, "If Trouble Can Be Avoid," 25–26.
118. Hawes, "New Greengrocers," 22.
119. Harris, "Making It," 198.
120. Among New York retailers, D'Agostino Supermarkets became a pioneer for establishing private-label goods as prestige items. See Cynthia Rigg, "Stores Put Stock in Private Labels," *Crain's New York Business*, November 28, 1993, 1; Richard Turcsik, "A Run for the Money," *Progressive Grocer*, November/December 2001, 85–90; Jennifer Lawrence, "Grocers Pitch Private-Label Brands," *Advertising Age*, January 24, 1994, 15; and Priscilla Donegan, "Private Label is Alive and Well," *Progressive Grocer*, February 1989, 61–65+.
121. Cynthia Rigg, "D'Agostino's Fresh Approach," *Crain's New York Business*, January 2, 1989, 28.
122. Rigg, "D'Agostino's Fresh Approach," 28.
123. "Downsized D'AG's Offsets Rent," *Chain Store Age Executive*, February 1989, 20–21.
124. "Downsized D'AG's Offsets Rent," 20–21.
125. Rigg, "D'Agostino's Fresh Approach," 28.
126. "Downsized D'AG's Offsets Rent," 20–21.
127. Rigg, "D'Agostino's Fresh Approach," 28.
128. "D'Ag's Loves the Big Apple," 10.
129. For a comprehensive study of the origins of the ethnic revival, particularly its relationship to identity, popular culture, and Americans' newfound obsession with heritage, see Matthew Frye Jacobson, *Roots, Too: White Ethnic Revival in Post–Civil Rights America* (Harvard University Press, 2006). Jacobson argues that over the course of the 1970s and '80s, the so-called Ellis Island immigrant was reimagined as the embodiment of American values. For more on the connection between heritage and commerce, see Marilyn Halter, *Shopping for Identity: The Marketing of Ethnicity* (Schocken Books, 2000).
130. One of the chief critics of this revival was sociologist Herbert Gans, who argued that "symbolic ethnicity" was mainly illusory. See "Symbolic Ethnicity: The Future of Ethnic Groups and Cultures in America," *Ethnic and Racial Studies* 2, no. 1 (January 1979): 1–20. Werner Sollors, ed., *The Invention of Ethnicity* (Oxford University Press, 1989) and David A. Hollinger, *Post-Ethnic America* (Basic Books, 1995) also examined this phenomenon, though Sollors affirmed the integrity of symbolic ethnicity.
131. Stephen S. Hall, "Italian-Americans: Coming into Their Own," *New York Times Magazine*, May 15, 1983, sec. 6, 28–58. Amid these advances, New York's blue-collar Italians still struggled with the stability and identity of their communities in the 1980s. In a decade marked by racial tension, the battle over school desegregation and housing in Brooklyn's Canarsie neighborhood continued. In 1986 in Howard Beach, another Italian enclave, three Black men were killed after being chased onto an expressway by a gang of white locals. Then, in 1990, an African American teenager was shot in the Bensonhurst section of Brooklyn, and residents who witnessed the crime refused to testify. Italian neighborhoods also grappled with the loss of thousands of longtime residents who had died or moved to the suburbs. By the late 1980s, for example, only 1,000 Italians lived in an area of East Harlem that had housed as many as 85,000 of them in the 1920s. In the wake of this demographic shift, residents often used traditional community and commercial institutions to maintain a symbolic Italian character for their neighborhoods. On Saturdays, Italians often returned to venerable specialty shops in the Bronx or Lower Manhattan, where they mixed with Asian and Latino residents or the "old-timers" who remained in the neighborhood. Cafes and restaurants also served as ethnic standard-bearers,

providing cultural stability amid demographic change. (See Jane Gross, "Savory Shops Give an Ethnic Flavor to a Bronx Avenue," *New York Times*, March 25, 1985, B1, and "Businesses That Ride a Rebirth of Ethnic Pride," *Business Week*, October 22, 1979, 149+.)

132. Binder and Reimers, *All the Nations Under Heaven*, 244.

133. For more on the origins of this modern renaissance of Italian culture, see Donna Gabaccia, *Italy's Many Diasporas* (University of Washington Press, 2000), 165.

134. "Quinta Strada," *Time*, May 31, 1976, 57–59.

135. For more on the rise of the Italian suit and the government's "Made in Italy" label campaign to bolster high-end exports, see Courtney Ritter, "The Double Life of the Italian Suit: Italian Americans and the 'Made in Italy' Label," in *Making Italian America: Consumer Culture and the Production of Ethnic Identities*, ed. Simone Cinotto (Fordham University Press, 2014), 196–206.

136. Gabaccia, *Italy's Many Diasporas*, 187–88.

137. Trish Hall, "Italian Allure, Armani to Zabaglione," *New York Times*, August 10, 1988, C1 and 6.

138. Hall, "Italian Allure," C1. The trade representative was Lucio Caputo, the president of the Italian Wine and Food Institute.

139. Hall, "Italian Allure," C1.

140. Hall, "Italian Allure," C1, and Bryan Miller, "In Manhattan, Trattorias Bloom," *New York Times*, August 17, 1988, C1. The claim about the popularity of Italian food was made by the National Restaurant Association.

141. Miller, "In Manhattan, Trattorias Bloom," C1.

142. Jo Foxworth, interview by author, August 8, 2001.

143. Stephen D'Agostino, interview by author, August 9, 2001.

144. Nicholas D'Agostino Jr., interview by author, May 15, 2001.

145. Foner, *From Ellis Island to JFK*, 231–35, and Richard Alba, "Italian Americans: A Century of Ethnic Change," in *Origins and Destinies: Immigration, Race and Ethnicity in America*, ed. Silvia Pedraza and Ruben Rumbaut (Wadsworth, 1996), 172–81.

146. Alba, "Italian Americans," 179.

147. See Richard Alba, *Ethnic Identity: The Transformation of White America* (Yale University Press, 1990), and "The Twilight of Ethnicity Among Americans of European Ancestry: The Case of Italians," *Ethnic and Racial Studies* 8, no. 1 (January 1985): 134–58; Mary Waters, *Ethnic Options: Choosing Identities in America* (University of California Press, 1990); Micaela di Leonardo, *The Varieties of Ethnic Experience: Kinship, Class, and Gender Among California Italian-Americans* (Cornell University Press, 1984); and Peter Kivisto, ed., *The Ethnic Enigma: The Salience of Ethnicity for European-Origin Groups* (Associated University Presses, 1989). Waters's assertion that "symbolic ethnicity" persists because of Americans' desire for community without individual cost also informs an understanding of how the marketing of ethnic and family roots has appeal in the marketplace, especially in New York. Di Leonardo represented Italian American culture as encompassing multiple classes, levels of education, and regions, and profoundly influenced by its female members. Donald Tricarico's essay "In a New Light: Italian-American Ethnicity in the Mainstream" in Kivisto, *Ethnic Enigma*, 24–46, emphasizes that not only is an ethnic sensibility integral to the daily lives of white-collar Italian Americans, but that the third generation preserves and transforms ethnic identity as they assimilate.

148. Steve Weinstein, "The Battle of Broadway," *Progressive Grocer*, April 1999, 60–66. Weinstein's article focuses on the intense competition on the Upper West Side between Food Emporium, D'Agostino's, Citarella, Zabar's, and Gristedes. In Midtown, Dean & DeLuca

was joined by groceries like Ninth Avenue International Foods and Ernest Klein & Company International Supermarket, a 7,000-square-foot store which boasted a clientele of Donald Trump, Calvin Klein, and Tony Bennett. See Bob Ingram, "Store of the Stars," *Supermarket Business*, November 1998, 104.

149. Barbara Costikyan, "The Joy of Shops," *New York*, December 23–30, 1991, 85–91.

150. Len Lewis, "Papaya, Pagliacci and Pork Chops," *Progressive Grocer*, June 1998, 26–32.

151. Bruce Fox, "At Fairway, the Buyers Taste the Food," *Chain Store Age*, May 1996, 37–38.

152. As quoted in Fox, "At Fairway," 37.

153. Fox, "At Fairway," 38.

154. Fox, "At Fairway," 37.

155. Costikyan, "Joy of Shops," 88.

156. Barbara Stewart, "How to Keep the Greenmarket in the Pink," *New York Times*, August 3, 1997, sec. 13, 4.

157. Dana Canedy, "'Big Guys' Have No Love for Big Apple," *New York Times*, November 13, 1998, C5.

158. Sarah Ferguson, "The Invasion of the Superstores," *New York*, March 13, 1995, 56–59.

159. Ferguson, "Invasion of the Superstores," 58. The mayor's proposal included provisions that would allow stores of up to 200,000 square feet to move into areas formerly designated for manufacturers, but it was blocked by the New York City Council and the City Planning Commission. Its defenders argued that retailers like Woolworth's had served as superstores for a previous generation of New Yorkers. However, in the 1990s, other forces—including rising commercial rents, preferred treatment from landlords and lenders, and consumers' "suburban tastes"—promoted big-box and chain stores at the expense of local businesses. See Sarah Kershaw, "Supermarkets Are Few, Stores Many," *New York Times*, February 19, 1997, B4, and Moss, *Vanishing New York*, 279–89.

160. Smith, "Splat," 36.

161. Lisa Chamberlain, "A Destination for Serious Eating," *New York Times*, April 24, 2005, sec. 11, 10.

162. Chamberlain, "Destination for Serious Eating," 10.

163. John Holusha, "Food Stores: A Broader Menu," *New York Times*, May 9, 2004, sec. 11, 1.

164. Holusha, "Food Stores: A Broader Menu," 1.

165. Holusha, "Food Stores: A Broader Menu," 1. The quoted speaker is Faith Consolo, of the retail brokerage firm Garrick-Aug.

166. Denise Frenner, "From Piano to Sushi Bars, Grocers Jazz Up Service," *Advertising Age*, May 4, 1987, S1.

167. Cynthia Valentino, "In a Fragmented Market, Grocers Cover the Niches," *Advertising Age*, May 4, 1987, S8. See also Steve Weinstein, "Competition: Intense and Non-Traditional," *Progressive Grocer*, July 1989, 20–22+.

168. Ryan Mathews, "Lessons of War," *Progressive Grocer*, November 1995, 29.

169. Ryan Mathews, "Welcome to the Logistics Museum," *Progressive Grocer*, December 1997, 6–7.

170. Nicholas D'Agostino Jr., interview by author, May 15, 2001.

171. Michael Ruhlman, *Grocery: The Buying and Selling of Food in America* (Abrams, 2017), 29.

172. Greg Burns, "All Together Now: 'Make That to Go,'" *Business Week*, January 8, 1996, 105.

173. Stacy Perman, "The Joy of Not Cooking," *Time*, June 1, 1998, 66–68.

174. Mimi Sheraton, "Taking Out, Eating In," *Time*, April 11, 1988, 75–76.

175. For a sampling of the generational issues that food retailers faced in the 1990s, see Carol Radice, "Targeting Tomorrow's Consumers," *Progressive Grocer*, July 1998, 55–56; Steve Weinstein, "The Graying of American Shoppers," *Progressive Grocer*, May 1996, 55–60; Priscilla Donegan, "Older Shoppers: A Super Market," *Progressive Grocer*, August 1986, 91–98; and Michael Sansolo, "Riding the Age Wave," *Progressive Grocer*, June 1993, 83–84. For more on grocers' relationship with the growing demographic of Latino consumers, see Steve Weinstein, "The Challenge of the '90s: Pinning Down the Hispanic Market," *Progressive Grocer*, June 1990, 69–74; Len Lewis, "Culture Shock," *Progressive Grocer*, April 1998, 23–28; Michael Friedman, "Executive Report—Hispanic Marketing: Culture Shock," *Progressive Grocer*, October 2000, 109–13; and Terry Hennessy, "Traditional Wisdom," *Progressive Grocer*, February 1999, 87–94.

176. Corby Kummer, "Designs for Shopping," *Atlantic Monthly*, May 1987, 84–85. For more on this two-tiered differentiation see Steve Weinstein, "Back and Forward to Basics," *Progressive Grocer*, March 1987, 93–106, and Valentino, "In a Fragmented Market," S8–15.

177. For examples of the food industry's anxious reaction to Walmart and the development of the supercenter format, see Wendy Zellner, "Look Out, Supermarkets—Wal-Mart Is Hungry," *Business Week*, September 14, 1998, 98–99; Wendy Zellner, "Wal-Mart: Retailer of the Century," *Chain Store Age*, special issue, December 1999, 12–24; Michael Sansolo, "It's Not Over . . . Yet," *Progressive Grocer*, July 1993, 4; Michael Sansolo, "It's the Stores . . . ," *Progressive Grocer*, May 1993, 6; Ryan Mathews, "Under Siege," *Progressive Grocer*, May 1995, 34–42; Lawrence J. Ring, "Supermarkets at Risk," *Chain Store Age*, July 1999, 56–62; Steve Weinstein, "Supercenters: The Ultimate Weapon?," *Progressive Grocer*, September 1999, 25–34; and Jacqueline Pollok, "Supermarkets: Caught in the Crossfire," *Chain Store Age*, August 1995, 17A–21A.

178. See Frenner, "From Piano to Sushi Bars," S1–2; Alice Bredin, "Supermarkets: Upscale Is on the Upswing," *Chain Store Age Executive*, November 1987, 132–36; Mary Ann Linsen, "Too Much of a Good Thing?," *Progressive Grocer*, February 1988, 91–92+; and Larry Schaeffer, "A Guide to Going Upscale," *Progressive Grocer*, May 1985, 35–42.

179. Weinstein, "Back and Forward to Basics," 96.

180. Kershaw, "Supermarkets Are Few, Stores Many," B4. For more on supermarkets in underserved communities at the end of the twentieth century, and the possibilities for new investment, see Barry Janoff, "Urban Renewal," *Progressive Grocer*, October 1999, 22–30; Murray Raphel and Neil Raphel, "Myths of the Inner City," *Progressive Grocer*, May 1993, 13–14; Michael Garry, "Back to the Cities," *Progressive Grocer*, September 1995, 73–78; Bob Ingram, "Urban Urgency," *Supermarket Business*, July 1999, 13; Steve Weinstein, "Too Little, Too Late?," *Progressive Grocer*, May 2000, 113–22; Bill Turque et al., "Where the Food Isn't," *Newsweek*, February 24, 1992, 36–37; "Are N.Y.C. Stores Milking the Poor?," *Progressive Grocer*, May 1991, 9; Michael Sansolo, "Hit 'Em Where They Are," *Progressive Grocer*, November 1991, 4; Stephen Bennett, "Is There Profit in the Inner City?," *Progressive Grocer*, December 1988, 47–49+; Ronald Tanner, "New Life for City Supers," *Progressive Grocer*, February 1985, 21; Cara Trager, "Bodegas' Facelifts Offer Them a New Lease on Life," *Advertising Age*, February 9, 1987, S21; Isadore Barmash, "Pathmark and Its Superstores,"

New York Times, April 17, 1983, sec. 3, 4; Richard Turcsik, "Taking Root: A Suburban-Style Pathmark Blossoms in New York's Harlem," *Progressive Grocer*, July 1999, 64–69; Karen Springen, "Supermarket Solutions," *Newsweek*, August 11, 1997, 45; and Monique Brown, "Supermarket Blackout," *Black Enterprise*, July 1999, 81–82+.

181. Nicholas D'Agostino Jr., interview by author, May 15, 2001.
182. Nicholas D'Agostino Jr., interview.
183. Weinstein, "Back and Forward to Basics," 93–106.
184. Kummer, "Designs for Shopping," 85.
185. Holusha, "Food Stores: A Broader Menu," 1.
186. Nicholas D'Agostino Jr., interview.
187. Nicholas D'Agostino Jr., interview.
188. Stephen Bennett, "A Healthy Prognosis for Produce," *Progressive Grocer*, January 1994, 81–83, and Mary Ann Linsen, "And the Produce Beat Goes On," *Progressive Grocer*, June 1988, 131–37.
189. Stephen Bennett, "How to Handle Produce," *Progressive Grocer*, February 1995, 99–102.
190. Mary Ann Linsen, "The Decade of the Fresh & Fast," *Progressive Grocer*, October 1989, 31–34+. The quoted executive is Jules Rose of Sloan's.
191. Stephen Bennett, "The Power of Produce," *Progressive Grocer*, December 1994, 97–104, and "How to Handle Produce," 99–102. By the end of the decade, many retailers carried well over four hundred produce items.
192. Steve Weinstein, "Sophisticated Shoppers—Sticky Issues," *Progressive Grocer*, September 1989, 175–76+. The quoted speaker is Mary Moore, the company's director of communications.
193. Nicholas D'Agostino Jr., interview by author, May 15, 2001.
194. Seth Lubove, "Food Porn," *Forbes*, February 14, 2005, 102. In this campaign, Whole Foods was aided by $4.5 million in venture capital and another $23 million from a 1992 IPO.
195. Lubove, "Food Porn," 102. In addition, in the mid-2000s, Whole Foods' stock was valued at $6 billion, and its annual sales-per-square-foot was $800.
196. Lubove, "Food Porn," 102.
197. Lubove, "Food Porn," 102.
198. Adam Gopnik, "Just Looking: A New Mall," *New Yorker*, March 1, 2004, 36.
199. Gopnik, "Just Looking," 36. Whole Foods was not without its detractors, who railed at the company's prices and pretensions. Critics labeled Whole Foods' "food as theater" marketing "food porn" and charged that the company embodied the egoism, vanity, and self-indulgence of the "Baby Boom" generation. Another journalist labeled Whole Foods "a wolf in vegetarian's clothing" for its ruthless acquisition strategies and for co-opting the oppositional politics of the counterculture. See Lubove, "Food Porn," 102, and Andrew Ferguson, "Supermarket of the Vanities," *Fortune*, June 10, 1996, 10+.
200. Lubove, "Food Porn," 102.
201. Smith, "Splat," 36.
202. Lisa Fickenscher, "Shunning the Grocer," *Crain's New York Business*, April 18–24, 2005, 3.
203. Fickenscher, "Shunning the Grocer," 3. The quoted retailer is John Catsimatidis of Gristedes.
204. Kershaw, "Supermarkets Are Few, Stores Many," B4.
205. Nicholas D'Agostino Jr., interview by author, May 15, 2001.

206. Fickenscher, "Shunning the Grocer," 3.
207. Smith, "Splat," 36.
208. Nicholas D'Agostino Jr., interview by author, May 15, 2001.
209. Nicholas D'Agostino Jr., interview.
210. Kelly Beamon, "Coffeehouse Chic," *Supermarket Business*, May 15, 2000, 127.
211. "D'Agostino Tests Coffee Bar Concept," *Nation's Restaurant News*, September 9, 1996, 2. According to the National Coffee Association, the number of "gourmet coffeehouses" in the US grew from 450 to 7,500 between 1991 and 2000.
212. Nicholas D'Agostino Jr., interview by author, May 15, 2001.
213. Nicholas D'Agostino Jr., interview.
214. "Grocer Bags Ad Prizes with Creative Approach," *Advertising Age*, May 20, 1985, 51.
215. Belinda Hulin-Salkin, "Shops Eager to Rescue Stores from Price-Ad Rut," *Advertising Age*, October 3, 1988, S18.
216. Belinda Hulin-Salkin, "Food Stores Turn Shopping into a Carefully Catered Affair," *Advertising Age*, October 3, 1988, S1.
217. Jo Foxworth, interview by author, August 8, 2001.
218. Foxworth, interview.
219. Nicholas D'Agostino Jr., interview by author, May 15, 2001.
220. Emily De Nitto, "New York, New York," *Crain's New York Business*, August 26, 2002, 6.
221. "Family Album," *Spotlight Magazine*, January 1998, 20. The feature also endeavors to spread the myth that D'Agostino's was the first supermarket in America: "Did Nick and Patsy D'Agostino create the concept of the modern supermarket in Manhattan? Arguably so."
222. See Kenneth Dreyfack, "The Stage Is Set for More Megadeals," *Business Week*, January 13, 1986, 67; Ryan Mathews, "Special Report: Social Change and the Supermarket: 1976–1986, The Decade of Delusion," *Progressive Grocer*, December 1996, 79–95; and Gene Hoffman, "Merger Myopia," *Progressive Grocer*, May 1999, 160.
223. Steve Weinstein, "A Good Deal Is Hard to Find," *Progressive Grocer*, July 1987, 18–28. See also Weinstein, "Consolidations: The Urge to Merge Continues," *Progressive Grocer*, October 1989, 102–4; Eric Schine, "At the Food Chains, It's All Gulp and Swallow," *Business Week*, May 8, 1995, 85; and "Supermarket Merger Frenzy," *Chain Store Age*, August 1999, 33A–34A.
224. Steve Weinstein, "A Conversation with Nick D'Agostino," *Progressive Grocer*, September 1987, 66.
225. Weinstein, "Conversation with Nick D'Agostino," 66.
226. Weinstein, "Conversation with Nick D'Agostino," 66.
227. Gatty, "Profiles in Leadership: Nick D'Agostino," 4.
228. Pellnat, "D'AG's Is New York," 20.
229. Gatty, "Profiles in Leadership: Nick D'Agostino," 4.
230. Rigg, "Crain's All-Stars," 48.
231. Nicholas D'Agostino Jr., interview by author, May 15, 2001.
232. Gatty, "Profiles in Leadership: Nick D'Agostino," 4.
233. Steve Weinstein, "In a Family Way," *Progressive Grocer*, September 1988, 6. When Nick D'Agostino Jr. and Stanley Silverzweig founded the D'Agostino/Silverzweig Entrepreneurial Institute, their primary concern was the rash of corporate mergers that were picking off independent businesses. In 2001, the institute was still sponsoring seminars on the issues that threatened family retailers, such as the estate tax, estate planning, and generational succession. Nick testified that family entrepreneurs were notorious for their inability to plan

for the future, especially those patriarchs who refused to relinquish control. He related that the D'Agostinos had hired an outside consultant to help them manage succession. See Steve Weinstein, "All in the Family," *Progressive Grocer*, May 2001, 91, and "Breaking the Rules," *Progressive Grocer*, May 2001, 94.

234. Pellnat, "D'AG's Is New York," 20.
235. Priscilla Donegan, "Family Businesses: A Fight for Survival," *Progressive Grocer*, September 1988, 21–24.
236. Weinstein, "Conversation with Nick D'Agostino," 65–66.
237. Nicholas D'Agostino Jr., interview by author, May 15, 2001.
238. Nicholas D'Agostino Jr., interview.
239. Nicholas D'Agostino Jr., interview.
240. Stephen D'Agostino, interview by author, August 9, 2001.
241. Donegan, "Family Businesses," 21–24.
242. Nicholas D'Agostino Jr., interview.
243. Nick D'Agostino III became the company's "Vice President, Corporate Administration," Walter D'Agostino was named "Vice President, Sales and Merchandising," and David D'Agostino was promoted to "Director of Store Operations." Their father mused, "They're much more title oriented than I was when I was their age, but that's life" (Nicholas D'Agostino Jr., interview by author, May 15, 2001).
244. Nick D'Agostino Jr. would remain the company's chairman and chief executive officer through the 2000s. Nicholas D'Agostino III would eventually succeed his father as CEO.
245. Nicholas D'Agostino Jr., interview.
246. "Marks & Spencer Sells King's Super Markets," *Gourmet Retailer*, October 2002, 10.
247. Nicholas D'Agostino III had received his public introduction in an article on the "comers" in New York business (Cynthia Rigg, "40 Under 40," *Crain's New York Business*, January 30, 1989, 17). At this point, Nick III was responsible for the company's computer operations (at a company known to be "technologically ahead of most of the city's grocery chains"). For the next decade and a half, he sought to make computer technology the centerpiece of D'Agostino's retailing strategy. See "D'Agostino Names President/C.O.O. and Marketing Director," *Progressive Grocer*, June 1, 2005, 8.
248. Pellnat, "D'AG's Is New York," 20.
249. Pellnat, "D'AG's Is New York," 16. The speaker is company president, Ron Nevers.
250. "D'Agostino Names Chief," *New York Times*, September 23, 1986, D32.
251. "D'Ag Takes Bigger Bite of Market," *Crain's New York Business*, September 7, 1987, 14.
252. Theresa Agovino, "New Chairman Sends D'Agostino's Northward," *Crain's New York Business*, October 20, 1986, 26. By 2005 the company was down to twenty-two locations, only three of which were outside the Five Boroughs.
253. See Cynthia Rigg, "Three Major Rivals Bid to Buy Sloan's Chain," *Crain's New York Business*, February 5, 1990, 1; "Green Wants to Stop Deal," *Crain's New York Business*, July 16, 1990, 19; "Squashing Deal for Sloan's Won't Help Consumers," *Crain's New York Business*, July 16, 1990, 8; and Mark Green, "Consumer Abuse Must Go," *Crain's New York Business*, October 15, 1990, 10.
254. Kevin DeMarrais, "Sizing Up the Sale of King's Markets," *Bergen Record*, July 28, 2002, B1. For more on the proposed sale, see Terry Pristin, "New Yawk Grocer Ventures into the New Jersey Suburbs," *New York Times*, September 29, 2002, 44; Kevin DeMarrais, "King's Bidder Moves to Fore," *Bergen Record*, March 16, 2002, 11; Teresa McAlvey, "D'Agostino's Paying $160M for King's Chain," *Bergen Record*, July 23, 2002, L6; Lisa Marsh, "Big Changes Are in

the Bag for 70-Yr.-Old D'Agostino and King's," *New York Post*, July 28, 2002, 30; "Talks to Sell Supermarkets to D'Agostino End," *New York Times*, December 2, 2002, C4; and Juliana Ratner, "M&S King's Disposal Deal Collapses," *Financial Times*, December 2, 2002, 26.

255. Matthew Boyle, "America's Favorite Cult Grocery Tries Its Magic in New York City," *Bloomberg Businessweek*, April 10, 2019, www.bloomberg.com/news/features/2019-04-10 /america-s-favorite-cult-grocer-tries-its-magic-in-new-york-city.

256. Zachary Kussin, "Wegmans Announces Second NYC Location to Open in 2023," *New York Post*, July 29, 2021, nypost.com/2021/07/29/wegmans-announces-second-nyc -location-to-open-in-2023/.

257. Ronda Kaysen, "Where, Oh Where, Did My Supermarket Go?," *New York Times*, November 6, 2016, sec. RE, 1. See also Terry Pristin, "Square Feet: Where Have All the Supermarkets Gone?," *New York Times*, March 22, 2006, C6. Pristin notes, "Once you could find them every few blocks or so in prime neighborhoods of Manhattan, but these days the local chain supermarket seems to be heading the way of the five-and-dime."

258. In 2010, the Duane Reade chain was purchased by Walgreen but continued to operate under its own brand name. See Daniel Indiviglio, "Duane Reade Acquired by Walgreen," *The Atlantic*, February 17, 2010, www.theatlantic.com/business/archive/2010/02/duane-reade -acquired-by-walgreen/36096/.

259. Kaysen, "Where, Oh Where, Did My Supermarket Go?," 1.

260. In 2007, Sterling Investment Partners bought a majority stake in Fairway with plans to dramatically expand the retailer's East Coast footprint. But Fairway fell victim to their own bloated ambitions, as the company filed for bankruptcy in 2016 and again in 2020, leaving it with only four locations. See Ginia Bellafante, "No Longer a Market Like No Other, Fairway Fades," *New York Times*, May 7, 2016, www.nytimes.com/2016/05/08/nyregion/no-longer-a-market-like -no-other-fairway-fades.html; Rachel Abrams, "Fairway, Unable to Fend Off Rivals, Files for Bankruptcy," *New York Times*, May 3, 2016, www.nytimes.com/2016/05/04/business/dealbook /fairway-unable-to-fend-off-rivals-files-for-bankruptcy.html; Azi Payabarah et al., "Fairway Market Files for Bankruptcy," *New York Times*, January 22, 2020, www.nytimes.com/2020/01 /22/nyregion/fairway-market-bankruptcy.html; and Eileen Appelbaum and Andrew W. Park, "How Private Equity Ruined a Beloved Grocery Chain," *The Atlantic*, February 16, 2020, www .theatlantic.com/ideas/archive/2020/02/how-private-equity-ruined-fairway/606625/.

261. During COVID-19, even more Americans experimented with online shopping. Internet grocery sales jumped 103 percent in 2020, and by 2022, 28 percent of American consumers purchased the bulk of their foodstuffs online. Yet, the percentage of Americans who did most of their food shopping online declined once the pandemic receded. Analysts predicted that in the near future, many Americans would use a hybrid model in which e-commerce would supplement their usual visits to brick-and-mortar supermarkets. See Tom Ryan, "Has Online Grocery Shopping Hit Its Sales Ceiling?," *RetailWire*, June 14, 2022, retailwire.com/discussion /has-online-grocery-shopping-hit-its-sales-ceiling, and Joan Verdon, "The Pandemic Changed How We Shop for Groceries, Adobe Report Shows," *Forbes*, March 15, 2022, www.forbes.com /sites/joanverdon/2022/03/15/the-pandemic-changed-how-we-shop-for-groceries-adobe-report -shows.

262. The cited figure is Gweneth Borden, executive director of the Golden Gate Restaurant Association. See Roman Mars, host, *99% Invisible* (podcast), episode 356, "Automat," SXM Media Group, June 4, 2019, 38 min., 47 sec., 99percentinvisible.org/episode/the-automat/.

263. Alison Bechdel, *Fun Home: A Family Tragicomic* (Mariner/Houghton Mifflin, 2007), 192. Donna Tartt's acclaimed 2013 novel *The Goldfinch* also referenced D'Agostino delivery

carts as part of its Manhattan backdrop. See Tartt, *The Goldfinch* (Back Bay Books/Little, Brown, 2013), 13.

264. In 2010, D'Agostino's embarked on its first major marketing campaign in over a decade, although its aesthetics and emphasis on low prices set it apart from the earlier generation of company advertising. See Stuart Elliott, "According to D'Ag, Low Prices Are in the Bag," *New York Times*, April 19, 2010, www.nytimes.com/2010/04/19/business/media/19adnewsletter1.html.

265. The pandemic also drove many of New York's big-box retailers out of business. The vacancies left by big-box stores, combined with the construction of new residential towers in Manhattan, Brooklyn, and Queens, subsequently created opportunities for supermarkets. Whole Foods opened a 42,000-square-foot superstore on Wall Street, while Wegmans planned a third location at the former Bed Bath & Beyond on Broadway. At the same time, the continued high cost of rents in New York inspired Whole Foods to plan for smaller 7,000-to-14,000-square-foot locations—recalling a bygone era of retailing. See Lois Weiss, "Eat It: Supermarkets and Urban Grocery Concepts Are Swarming NYC," *New York Post*, April 21, 2024, nypost.com/2024/04/21/real-estate/nyc-grocery-stores-are-booming-thanks-to-big-box-extinction, and Timothy Inklebarger, "Smaller Grocers Filling Void Left by Big-Box Retailers in NYC," *Supermarket News*, April 23, 2024, www.supermarketnews.com/news/smaller-grocery-stores-filling-void-left-big-box-retailers-nyc. Perhaps the biggest victims of the changing retail landscape, post-COVID, were chain drugstores such as Duane Reade, CVS, and Rite Aid. In 2014, chain drugstores had over 650 locations throughout the Five Boroughs; by 2024, 40 percent of these had closed. This decline can be explained by the rise of online shopping, changing payment rules for pharmacies, and a glutting of the market. Because the chains were often locked into long leases, many of the locations remain vacant even as the city's real estate market has rebounded. See Stefanos Chen, "The Zombie Pharmacies That Are Holding Back New York City Retail," *New York Times*, August 6, 2024, www.nytimes.com/2024/08/06/nyregion/pharmacies-vacant-drugstores-retail.html.

266. See Nick Paumgarten, "Down in the Basement," *New Yorker*, August 8, 2011, 18–19, and Jeff Vandam, "Stuyvesant Town and Peter Cooper Village: The New Owners Get the Once-Over," *New York Times*, April 1, 2007, sec. RE, 1. Tishman Speyer defaulted on its payments in 2010 and sold the development to Blackstone and Ivanhoé Cambridge for $5.45 billion in 2015 with the stipulation that only about half of the units would continue to be rent-regulated. See Rachel A. Woldoff et al., *Priced Out: Stuyvesant Town and the Loss of Middle-Class Neighborhoods* (New York University Press, 2016).

267. Gay Talese, "Basta," *New Yorker*, May 31, 2010, 22–23.

268. Lisa Fickenscher, "'New York's Original Grocer' Struggling to Survive," *New York Post*, April 20, 2015, nypost.com/2015/04/20/new-yorks-original-grocer-struggling-to-survive/.

269. Lisa Fickenscher, "City's Last Original Grocer Quietly Shopping Manhattan Stores," *New York Post*, June 5, 2016, nypost.com/2016/06/05/citys-last-original-grocer-quietly-shopping-manhattan-stores/.

270. Teresa Novellino, "Gristedes Owner Bails Out Rival D'Agostino Supermarket Chain," *New York Business Journal*, August 26, 2016, www.bizjournals.com/newyork/news/2016/08/26/gristedes-owner-bails-out-rival-d-agostino.html. See also Jon Springer, "Gristedes-D'Agostino Merger Still On," *Supermarket News*, October 24, 2016, www.supermarketnews.com/retail-financial/gristedes-dagostino-merger-still.

271. Richard Morgan, "Red Apple Rescues Rival Supermarket Chain D'Agostino," *New York Post*, August 26, 2016, nypost.com/2016/08/26/red-apple-rescues-rival-supermarket-chain-dagostino/.

272. Jane Margolies, "A Supermarket King Expands His Inventory," *New York Times*, October 14, 2018, sec. RE, 16.

273. In an email exchange, Nicholas D'Agostino III explained that as part of their arrangement, D'Agostino Supermarkets put their operating assets into a new company called D'Agostino Markets LLC, which were then transferred to the New York Food Group. In exchange, D'Agostino's received a percentage of the New York Food Group and the NYFG assumed his company's expenses. While an agreement was put in place for the New York Food Group to eventually acquire D'Agostino Supermarkets, Inc., it was never executed. The New York Food Group is currently running D'Agostino's stores through D'Agostino Markets LLC. Meanwhile, Nicholas III continues to maintain ownership of D'Agostino Supermarkets, Inc. (Nicholas D'Agostino III, email message to author, July 13, 2023, and July 28, 2023).

274. Sabina Mollot, "Catsimatidis Giving Amazon a Supermarket Run for Its Money," *Real Estate Weekly*, September 18, 2019, rew-online.com/catsimatidis-giving-amazon-a-supermarket-run-for-its-money/.

275. Catsimatidis even speculated that he would switch the branding of certain Gristedes and D'Agostino locations depending on location and circumstance.

276. Lisa Fickenscher, "D'Agostino Executive Steps Down in Grocery Chain Shake Up," *New York Post*, June 3, 2021, nypost.com/2021/06/03/dagostinos-executive-steps-down-in-grocery-chain-shake-up/.

277. Russell Redman, "Red Apple Group Promotes Joseph Parisi to Gristedes/D'Agostino President," *Supermarket News*, June 21, 2022, www.supermarketnews.com/executive-changes/red-apple-group-promotes-joseph-parisi-gristedesd-agostino-president, and "Gristedes & D'Agostino Supermarkets Gets New President/COO," *Progressive Grocer*, June 21, 2022, https://progressivegrocer.com/search?pg%5Bquery%5D=joe%20parisi.

BIBLIOGRAPHY

Abrams, Rachel. "Fairway, Unable to Fend Off Rivals, Files for Bankruptcy." *New York Times*, May 3, 2016. www.nytimes.com/2016/05/04/business/dealbook/fairway-unable-to-fend-off-rivals-files-for-bankruptcy.html.

Adams, Charlotte. "Italian Life in New York." *Harper's Magazine*, April 1881. Reprinted in *A Documentary History of the Italian Americans*, edited by Wayne Moquin. Praeger, 1974.

Adams, Mildred. "In the Pushcart Bazaars All Things Are Sold." *New York Times*, March 30, 1930.

"Adverse Effect on Food Shops Seen in Point Rationing System." *New York Times*, March 20, 1943.

"Advertise Your Store's People, Not Just Your Prices." *Progressive Grocer*, August 1981.

Agovino, Theresa. "New Chairman Sends D'Agostino's Northward." *Crain's New York Business*, October 20, 1986.

Alba, Richard. *Ethnic Identity: The Transformation of White America*. Yale University Press, 1990.

Alba, Richard. "Italian Americans: A Century of Ethnic Change." In *Origins and Destinies: Immigration, Race, and Ethnicity in America*, edited by Silvia Pedraza and Rubén G. Rumbaut. Wadsworth, 1996.

Alba, Richard. "Italian Americans and Assimilation." In *The Routledge History of Italian Americans*, edited by William J. Connell and Stanislao G. Pugliese. Routledge, 2018.

Alba, Richard. "Social Assimilation Among American Catholic National-Origin Groups." *American Sociological Review* 41, no. 6 (December 1976): 1030–46.

Alba, Richard. "The Twilight of Ethnicity Among Americans of European Ancestry: The Case of Italians." *Ethnic and Racial Studies* 8, no. 1 (January 1985): 134–58.

"All Peddlers Barred from Midtown Area." *New York Times*, July 10, 1929.

"The American Dream: A Second Generation." *Chain Store Age/Supermarkets*, December 12, 1982.

"American Meat Institute. Advertisement." *Life*, January 3, 1955.

"America's Supermarket Miracle." *Business Week*, May 4, 1987.
Anbinder, Tyler. *City of Dreams: The 400-Year Epic History of Immigrant New York*. Houghton Mifflin Harcourt, 2016.
Appelbaum, Eileen, and Andrew W. Park. "How Private Equity Ruined a Beloved Grocery Chain." *The Atlantic*, February 16, 2020. www.theatlantic.com/ideas/archive/2020/02/how-private-equity-ruined-fairway/606625/.
"Are N.Y.C. Stores Milking the Poor?" *Progressive Grocer*, May 1991.
Ashby, Thomas. *Some Italian Scenes and Festivals*. E. P. Dutton, 1929.
Auletta, Ken. *The Streets Were Paved with Gold*. Random House, 1979.
Banfield, Edward. *The Moral Basis of a Backwards Society*. Free Press, 1958.
Barmash, Isadore. "D'Agostino Chain Chief Leaving to Join Bottler." *New York Times*, September 13, 1982.
Barmash, Isadore. "D'Agostino's Aims for Top Recognition: Small Chain in Manhattan Seeks Key Role." *New York Times*, June 23, 1981.
Barmash, Isadore. "Pathmark and Its Superstores." *New York Times*, April 17, 1983.
Barrett, James R., and David Roediger. "Inbetween Peoples: Race, Nationality and the 'New Immigrant' Working Class." *Journal of American Ethnic History* 16, no. 3 (1997): 3–44.
Battisti, Danielle. *Whom We Shall Welcome: Italian Americans and Immigration Reform, 1945–1965*. Fordham University Press, 2019.
Baughn, F. A. "We're Going to Be Closed Up Anyway: O.P.A. Driving Retailers Out of Business." *Nation's Business*, January 1943.
Beamon, Kelly. "Coffeehouse Chic." *Supermarket Business*, May 15, 2000.
Bechdel, Alison. *Fun Home: A Family Tragicomic*. Mariner/Houghton Mifflin, 2007.
"Behind the Boycotts: Why Prices Are High." *Time*, November 4, 1966.
Belasco, Warren J. *Appetite for Change: How the Counterculture Took On the Food Industry, 1966–1988*. Cornell University Press, 1993.
Bellafante, Ginia. "No Longer a Market Like No Other, Fairway Fades." *New York Times*, May 7, 2016. www.nytimes.com/2016/05/08/nyregion/no-longer-a-market-like-no-other-fairway-fades.html.
Bennett, Ralph Kinney. "Review of 'Free to Choose,' by Milton Friedman." *Reader's Digest*, January 1980.
Bennett, Stephen. "A Healthy Prognosis for Produce." *Progressive Grocer*, January 1994.
Bennett, Stephen. "How to Handle Produce." *Progressive Grocer*, February 1995.
Bennett, Stephen. "Is There Profit in the Inner City?" *Progressive Grocer*, December 1988.
Bennett, Stephen. "The Power of Produce." *Progressive Grocer*, December 1994.
"Better Days for Housewives as Food Industry Changes." *U.S. News & World Report*, March 22, 1965.
Betts, Lillian. "Italian Peasants in a New Law Tenement." *Harper's*, August 1904.
"Big Appetite for Gourmet Foods." *Business Week*, August 23, 1958.
"Biggest Appetite." *Life*, January 3, 1955.
Binder, Frederick M., and David M. Reimers. *All the Nations Under Heaven: An Ethnic and Racial History of New York City*. Columbia University Press, 1995.
Biondi, Martha. *To Stand and Fight: The Struggle for Civil Rights in Postwar New York City*. Harvard University Press, 2003.
Blumenthal, Ralph. "Supermarkets' Super Woes: High Costs and Slim Profits." *New York Times*, May 4, 1980.
"Bodega." *New Yorker*, September 23, 1972.

Boyle, Matthew. "America's Favorite Cult Grocery Tries Its Magic in New York City." *Bloomberg Businessweek*, April 10, 2019. www.bloomberg.com/news/features/2019-0410/america-s-favorite-cult-grocer-tries-its-magic-in-new-york-city.

"A Boys Town Immigrant; Italian, 15, Flies Here to Live with New Rochelle Family." *New York Times*, November 9, 1952.

Brandt, Lilian. "A Transplanted Birthright: The Development of the Second Generation of the Italians in an American Environment." *Charities*, May 7, 1904.

"Breathing New Life into Small Business." *Forbes*, September 17, 1979.

Bredin, Alice. "Supermarkets: Upscale Is on the Upswing." *Chain Store Age Executive*, November 1987.

Briggs, John W. *An Italian Passage: Immigrants to Three American Cities, 1890–1930*. Yale University Press, 1978.

Brobeck, Florence. "Outdoor Food Markets Are Moving Indoors." *New York Times*, October 11, 1936.

Brody, Jane E. "America Leans to a Healthier Diet." *New York Times Magazine*, October 13, 1985.

"Brother, Can You Spare a Billion?" *Newsweek*, May 26, 1975.

Brown, Monique. "Supermarket Blackout." *Black Enterprise*, July 1999.

Brown, Stanley H. "You're Right—Inflation Is Worse Than They're Telling You." *New York*, May 14, 1973.

Buonanno, Laura, and Michael Buonanno. *Remembering Italian America: Memory, Migration, and Identity*. Routledge, 2021.

Burck, Gilbert. "Headquarters Town." *Fortune*, February 1960.

Burns, Greg. "All Together Now: 'Make That to Go.'" *Business Week*, January 8, 1996.

"Businesses That Ride a Rebirth of Ethnic Pride." *Business Week*, October 22, 1979.

"Cake Production to Be Cut Again." *New York Times*, June 12, 1945.

"Calls for Unity in Housing Aims." *New York Times*, May 2, 1943.

Candeloro, Dominic. "World War II Changed Everything." In *The Routledge History of Italian Americans*, edited by William J. Connell and Stanislao G. Pugliese. Routledge, 2018.

Canedy, Dana. "'Big Guys' Have No Love for Big Apple." *New York Times*, November 13, 1998.

Caro, Robert. *The Power Broker: Robert Moses and the Fall of New York*. Knopf, 1974.

Carr, John Foster. "The Coming of the Italian." *Outlook*, February 24, 1906.

Chamberlain, Lisa. "A Destination for Serious Eating." *New York Times*, April 24, 2005.

"Checking Out the Corner Cyberstore." *Business Week*, May 10, 1999.

Chen, Stefanos. "The Zombie Pharmacies That Are Holding Back New York City Retail." *New York Times*, August 6, 2024. www.nytimes.com/2024/08/06/nyregion/pharmacies-vacant-drugstores-retail.html.

"Cigarettes Hoarded." *New York Times*, October 5, 1944.

Cinel, Dino. *From Italy to San Francisco: The Immigrant Experience*. Stanford University Press, 1982.

Cinotto, Simone. *The Italian American Table: Food, Family, and Community in New York City*. University of Illinois Press, 2013.

Cinotto, Simone, ed. *Making Italian America: Consumer Culture and the Production of Ethnic Identities*. Fordham University Press, 2014.

"City Fights Fraud in Weighing Foods." *New York Times*, September 28, 1934.

Clark, D. "Hard-Hitting Boss of Prices." *New York Times Magazine*, April 27, 1941.

"The Classic Years." *Progressive Grocer*, December 1988.

Clines, Francis X. "The New Bodegueros." *New York Times*, March 25, 1978.
"Closing of Pushcart Markets to Be Urged in Economy Drive." *New York Times*, January 14, 1958.
Cohen, Lizabeth. *A Consumers' Republic: The Politics of Mass Consumption in Postwar America*. Alfred A. Knopf, 2003.
Colamosca, Anne. "Health Foods Prosper Despite High Prices." *New York Times*, November 17, 1974.
"Community Service: NYO and UHF Honor D'Agostino." *KPMG Peat Marwick,* September–October 1989.
"Congressional Focus on Food Marketing." *Business Week*, October 19, 1957.
"Convenience Stores: A $7.4 Billion Mushroom." *Business Week*, March 21, 1977.
Conzen, Kathleen Neils. "The Invention of Ethnicity: A Perspective from the U.S.A." *Journal of American Ethnic History* 12, no. 1 (Fall 1992): 3–41.
"Co-Ops Spring Up." *Business Week*, November 20, 1943.
Corey, Mary F. *The World Through a Monocle: "The New Yorker" at Midcentury*. Harvard University Press, 1999.
Costikyan, Barbara. "The Joy of Shops." *New York*, December 23–30, 1991.
Covello, Leonard. *The Heart Is the Teacher*. McGraw-Hill, 1958.
Covello, Leonard. *The Social Background of the Italo-American School Child*. Brill, 1967.
"Credit Failures Remain Stable." *New York Times*, January 3, 1956.
"The Crisis at the Check-Out Counter." *Newsweek*, April 10, 1972.
"Critics Rail, but Supermarkets Ask: Why Us?" *Business Week*, April 22, 1972.
"CVS SVP/CIO Receives Career Achievement Award at Retail Systems 2002/VICS Collaborative Commerce." *Business Wire*, June 25, 2002.
"D'Ag Takes Bigger Bite of Market." *Crain's New York Business*, September 7, 1987.
D'Agostino, Nicholas. "The Four Seasons of Nicholas D'Agostino" (includes chapters "Loreta's Son," "Stephen's Son," and "Josephine's Husband"). Unpublished manuscript, 1982. Collection of the author.
D'Agostino, Patsy. *How I Made a Million*. Edited by Noah Sarlat. 1955. Reprint, Paperback Library, 1961.
D'Agostino, Patsy. "I Found $5,000,000 in a Pushcart." *American Magazine*, September 1952.
D'Agostino, Patsy. "Independents on the Band Wagon." In *Food Marketing: Twenty-Two Leaders of the Food Industry Tell How the Nation's Biggest and Most Complex Business Works—and Why*, edited by Paul Sayres. McGraw-Hill, 1950.
D'Agostino, Patsy. "Stop Treating Frozen as Stepchild, Promote Quality." *Quick Frozen Foods*, June 1958.
"D'Agostino at GMR, Asks Suppliers for Involvement." *Food Merchants Advocate*, March 1973.
"D'Agostino: Innovation, Sensitivity: Success." The Chairman's Issue, *Food Merchants Advocate*, December 1982.
"D'Agostino Names Chief." *New York Times*, September 23, 1986.
"D'Agostino Names President/C.O.O. and Marketing Director." *Progressive Grocer*, June 1, 2005.
"D'Agostino Steps Up Its Rewards." *Chain Store Age*, January 2005.
D'Agostino Supermarkets. *D'AGs Consumer Newsletter*, September/October 1982.
D'Agostino Supermarkets, Inc. Estate Tax Pamphlet. Prepared for the Food Marketing Institute by Bernish Communication Associates and On the Mark, LLC, 2001–02.
"D'Agostino Tests Coffee Bar Concept." *Nation's Restaurant News*, September 9, 1996.

"D'Agostino's Open Parkchester Unit." *Bronx Press-Review*, October 6, 1966.
"D'Ag's Loves the Big Apple." *Twin County Grocers Association Newsletter*, 1982.
Daly, Michael. "Making It: The Saga of Min Chul Shin and His Family Fruit Store." *New York*, December 20, 1982.
Daniels, Roger. *Coming to America: A History of Immigration and Ethnicity in American Life*. HarperCollins, 1990.
Davenport, William E. "The Italian Immigrant in America." *Outlook*, January 3, 1903.
Daykin, Leonard. "Is Inner City Food Retailing Dying?" *Progressive Grocer*, June 1969.
de Fiori, Vittorio, and Enrica Laglia. "The D'Agostino Brothers." *Italamerican Magazine*, October 1954.
De Nitto, Emily. "New York, New York." *Crain's New York Business*, August 26, 2002.
DeMarrais, Kevin. "King's Bidder Moves to Fore." *Bergen Record*, March 16, 2002.
DeMarrais, Kevin. "Sizing Up the Sale of King's Markets." *Bergen Record*, July 28, 2002.
"Denies Misuse of Ad Allowance." *New York Times*, June 16, 1948.
"Details Problems of Retail Grocers." *New York Times*, June 23, 1947.
Deutsch, Tracey. *Building a Housewife's Paradise: Gender, Politics, and American Grocery Stores in the Twentieth Century*. University of North Carolina Press, 2010.
di Leonardo, Micaela. *The Varieties of Ethnic Experience: Kinship, Class, and Gender Among California Italian-Americans*. Cornell University Press, 1984.
Diner, Hasia. *Hungering for America: Italian, Irish, and Jewish Foodways in the Age of Migration*. Harvard University Press, 2001.
DiPalma Castiglione, G. E. "Italian Immigration into the United States, 1901–4." *American Journal of Sociology* 11, no. 2 (1905): 183–206. Reprinted in *A Documentary History of the Italian Americans*, edited by Wayne Moquin. Praeger, 1974.
Donegan, Priscilla. "Family Businesses: A Fight for Survival." *Progressive Grocer*, September 1988.
Donegan, Priscilla. "Older Shoppers: A Super Market." *Progressive Grocer*, August 1986.
Donegan, Priscilla. "Private Label Is Alive and Well." *Progressive Grocer*, February 1989.
Dorgan, Tim. "Belief in the Future." *Progressive Grocer*, February 1997.
Dougherty, Phillip H. "Messages with a Bit of Humor." *New York Times*, July 7, 1981.
"Downsized D'AG's Offsets Rent." *Chain Store Age Executive*, February 1989.
Doyle, Mona. "Food Ads Need to Get with It." *Progressive Grocer*, October 1983.
"Draft Exemption Sought." *New York Times*, April 23, 1944.
Dreyfack, Kenneth. "Social Change and the Supermarket: 1976–1986, the Decade of Delusion." *Progressive Grocer*, December 1996.
Dreyfack, Kenneth. "The Stage Is Set for More Megadeals." *Business Week*, January 13, 1986.
"Early Shortage of Meat for Army as Result of OPA Rules Predicted." *New York Times*, May 2, 1943.
"East Side 'Suburb in City' to House 30,000 After War." *New York Times*, April 19, 1943.
Elliott, Stuart. "According to D'Ag, Low Prices Are in the Bag." *New York Times*, April 19, 2010. www.nytimes.com/2010/04/19/business/media/19adnewsletter1.html.
Ennis, Thomas. "Unused Theaters Become Markets." *New York Times*, October 21, 1956.
Ewen, Elizabeth. *Immigrant Women in the Land of Dollars: Life and Culture on the Lower East Side, 1890–1925*. Monthly Review Press, 1985.
"Exodus from New York City: What Makes Businesses Leave." *U.S. News & World Report*, December 7, 1970.
"Expanding Supers." *Business Week*, July 12, 1947.

"Family Album." *Spotlight Magazine*. New York, New Jersey, and Connecticut Edition. January 1998.
"A Fancy Future for Pricey Foods." *Business Week*, November 10, 1980.
"Farewell to Price Control." *Fortune*, August 1946.
"Farewell to the Pushcarts." *New York Times*, July 23, 1937.
"F.D.A. Proposes Sweeping Change in Food Labeling." *New York Times*, January 18, 1973.
"Fears Rise in Canned Food Use." *New York Times*, November 23, 1946.
Federal Writers' Project. *The Italians of New York*. 1938. Arno, 1969.
Ferguson, Andrew. "Supermarket of the Vanities." *Fortune*, June 10, 1996.
Ferguson, Sarah. "The Invasion of the Superstores." *New York*, March 13, 1995.
Ferraro, Thomas J. "Blood in the Marketplace: The Business of Family in the *Godfather* Narratives." In *The Invention of Ethnicity*, edited by Werner Sollors. Oxford University Press, 1989.
Fickenscher, Lisa. "City's Last Original Grocer Quietly Shopping Manhattan Stores." *New York Post*, June 5, 2016. nypost.com/2016/06/05/citys-last-original-grocer-quietly-shopping-manhattan-stores/.
Fickenscher, Lisa. "D'Agostino Executive Steps Down in Grocery Chain Shake Up." *New York Post*, June 3, 2021. nypost.com/2021/06/03/dagostinos-executive-steps-down-in-grocery-chain-shake-up/.
Fickenscher, Lisa. "Grocer Finds Online Strategy That Delivers." *Crain's New York Business*, April 7–13, 2003.
Fickenscher, Lisa. "'New York's Original Grocer' Struggling to Survive." *New York Post*, April 20, 2015. nypost.com/2015/04/20/new-yorks-original-grocer-struggling-to-survive/.
Fickenscher, Lisa. "Online Grocer Clicks." *Crain's New York Business*, February 21–27, 2005.
Fickenscher, Lisa. "Shunning the Grocer." *Crain's New York Business*, April 18–24, 2005.
Fields, Sidney. "The Immigrant Didn't Forget." *New York Daily Mirror*, May 20, 1949.
"Final Showdown on OPA." *Nation*, June 22, 1946.
Fitch, Noel. *Appetite for Life: The Biography of Julia Child*. Doubleday, 1997.
Fitch, Robert. *The Assassination of New York*. Verso, 1993.
Flaherty, Lee. "Change in Woman's Status Spurs Battle of Supermarkets vs. Fast-Food Chains." *Advertising Age*, May 23, 1977.
Fleetwood, Blake. "The New Elite and an Urban Renaissance." *New York Times Magazine*, January 14, 1979.
Foerster, Robert F. *The Italian Emigration of Our Times*. Harvard University Press, 1919.
Foner, Nancy. *From Ellis Island to JFK: New York's Two Great Waves of Immigration*. Yale University Press, 2000.
Foner, Nancy, ed. *New Immigrants in New York*. New York: Columbia University Press, 2001.
Foner, Nancy, ed. *One Out of Three: Immigrant New York in the Twenty-First Century*. Columbia University Press, 2013.
"Food Black Market Costs $1,200,000, Bowles Declares." *New York Times*, March 1, 1944.
"Food Calms Down." *Time*, April 19, 1976.
"Food Fight." *Chain Store Age*, November 1999.
"Food Independent Has Bulk of Sales." *New York Times*, June 24, 1952.
Food Industry Alliance of New York State. "FIA Celebrates 100 Years." *Food Advocate/Griffin's Modern Grocer*, 2000.
"Food Industry to Aid Boys Town in Italy." *New York Times*, May 26, 1948.
"Food Markets Discussed." *New York Times*, February 16, 1949.

"Food—Mass Luxury: A $73 Billion Market Basket." Special Issue of *Life*, January 3, 1955.
"Food Retailing: Where We Stand Today." *Progressive Grocer*, January 1965.
"Food Stores Urged to Close Full Day." *New York Times*, March 12, 1943.
"Food Trade Is Told to Put House in Order." *New York Times*, November 20, 1946.
"For Study Abroad: Retail Grocers Ask Truman to Send Experts to Europe." *New York Times*, September 23, 1947.
Fox, Bruce. "At D'Agostino Computer Handles Phoned-In Orders." *Supermarket News*, January 5, 1987.
Fox, Bruce. "At Fairway, the Buyers Taste the Food." *Chain Store Age*, May 1996.
Foxworth, Jo. *Boss Lady: An Executive Woman Talks About Making It*. Warner Books, 1978.
Franklin, Rebecca. "From Soup to Nuts to Art." *New York Times Magazine*, September 24, 1950.
Fraser, Steve. *Every Man a Speculator: A History of Wall Street in American Life*. HarperCollins, 2005.
Freeman, Joshua B. *Working-Class New York: Life and Labor Since World War II*. New Press, 2000.
Frenner, Denise. "From Piano to Sushi Bars, Grocers Jazz Up Service." *Advertising Age*, May 4, 1987.
Friedman, Michael. "Executive Report—Hispanic Marketing: Culture Shock." *Progressive Grocer*, October 2000.
"From Pushcart to Super-Market." *Town & Village*, February 23, 1950.
Fuchs, Lawrence H. *The American Kaleidoscope: Race, Ethnicity, and the Civic Culture*. Wesleyan University Press, 1990.
Gabaccia, Donna. *From Sicily to Elizabeth Street: Housing and Social Change Among Italian Immigrants, 1880–1930*. State University of New York Press, 1984.
Gabaccia, Donna. *From the Other Side: Women, Gender, and Immigrant Life in the U.S., 1820–1990*. Indiana University Press, 1994.
Gabaccia, Donna. *Italy's Many Diasporas*. University of Washington Press, 2000.
Gabaccia, Donna. *We Are What We Eat: Ethnic Food and the Making of Americans*. Harvard University Press, 1998.
Gambino, Richard. "Twenty Million Italian-Americans Can't Be Wrong." *New York Times Magazine*, April 30, 1972.
Gans, Herbert. "Symbolic Ethnicity: The Future of Ethnic Groups and Cultures in America." *Ethnic and Racial Studies* 2, no. 1 (January 1979): 1–20.
Gans, Herbert. *The Urban Villagers: Group and Class in the Life of Italian-Americans*. Free Press, 1962.
"Gardens to Bloom on 'Gas House' Site." *New York Times*, January 4, 1945.
Garry, Michael. "Back to the Cities." *Progressive Grocer*, September 1995.
Garry, Michael. "Home Shopping Comes of Age." *Progressive Grocer*, September 1995.
Gatty, Bob. "Profiles in Leadership: Nicholas D'Agostino." *Grocery Marketing*, February 1989.
Gibson, DW. *The Edge Becomes the Center: An Oral History of Gentrification in the 21st Century*. Overlook, 2015.
Giordano, Paolo A., and Anthony Julian Tamburri, eds. *Beyond the Margin: Readings in Italian Americana*. Fairleigh Dickinson University Press, 1998.
Glazer, Nathan, and Daniel P. Moynihan. *Beyond the Melting Pot: The Negroes, Puerto Ricans, Jews, Italians, and Irish of New York City*. MIT Press, 1963.
"The Global Apple." *Economist*, March 16, 1996.

"Good Grocery Ads: Where Did They Go?" *Printer's Ink*, January 18, 1963.
Goodman, George. "Food Chains Find Leases No Bargain." *New York Times*, July 13, 1980.
Goodman, James. *Blackout*. North Point Press, 2003.
Gopnik, Adam. "Just Looking: A New Mall." *New Yorker*, March 1, 2004.
"A Gospel for Independent Grocers." *Business Week*, October 27, 1951.
"The Great Check-Out." *Newsweek*, November 27, 1978.
Green, Mark. "Consumer Abuse Must Go." Editorial. *Crain's New York Business*, October 15, 1990.
"Green Stamps Stick Around." *Marketing News*, December 15, 2004.
"Green Wants to Stop Deal." *Crain's New York Business*, July 16, 1990.
Greenberg, Miriam. *Branding New York: How a City in Crisis Was Sold to the World*. Routledge, 2008.
Greenhouse, Steven. "Nicholas D'Agostino Sr., 86, Founder of Grocery Chain." Obituary. *New York Times*, June 25, 1996.
Greenwald, Judy. "D'Agostino Has Fresh Ad Approach." *Supermarket News*, May 5, 1980.
"Gristedes & D'Agostino Supermarkets Gets New President/COO." *Progressive Grocer*, June 21, 2022. https://progressivegrocer.com/search?pg%5Bquery%5D=joe%20parisi.
"Grocer Bags Ad Prizes with Creative Approach." *Advertising Age*, May 20, 1985.
"Grocer Horns In on Druggist." *Business Week*, February 16, 1952.
"Grocer Shoppers Always Get Lowest Prices Through Priceline.com's WebHouse Club." *Business Wire*, November 3, 1999.
"Grocers Demand Fair Opportunity." *New York Times*, June 21, 1948.
"Grocers' Group Head Urges Lower Prices." *New York Times*, April 28, 1947.
"Grocers Say Cost Cuts Their Profit." *New York Times*, November 3, 1947.
"Grocers See New Hope in Limited-Line Stores." *Business Week*, December 4, 1978.
"Grocers, Tired of Abuse, Drop Cigarette Sales." *New York Times*, February 2, 1945.
Gross, Jane. "Savory Shops Give an Ethnic Flavor to a Bronx Avenue." *New York Times*, March 25, 1985.
Grutzner, Charles. "City's Food Buying Normal; Consumers' 'Sense' Praised." *New York Times*, May 11, 1948.
Guglielmo, Jennifer, and Salvatore Salerno. *Are Italians White? How Race Is Made in America*. Routledge, 2003.
Guglielmo, Thomas A. *White on Arrival: Italians, Race, Color, and Power in Chicago, 1890–1945*. Oxford University Press, 2003.
Gustke, Constance. "Prices and Possibilities." *Progressive Grocer*, January 1, 2002.
Hall, Stephen S. "Italian-Americans: Coming into Their Own." *New York Times Magazine*, May 15, 1983.
Hall, Trish. "Italian Allure, Armani to Zabaglione." *New York Times*, August 10, 1988.
Hallberg, Garth Risk. *City on Fire*. Vintage Books, 2016.
Halter, Marilyn. *Shopping for Identity: The Marketing of Ethnicity*. Schocken Books, 2000.
Hamill, Katherine. "Caviar in the Supermarket." *Fortune*, January 1959.
Harris, Marlys. "Making It: How the Koreans Won the Green-Grocer Wars." *Money*, March 1983.
Hartt, Rollin Lynde. "Made in Italy." *The Independent*, July 23, 1921.
Hawes, Elizabeth. "New Greengrocers." *New Yorker*, July 4, 1977.
Heller, Walter. "Economy-Store Census: Warehouse Stores and Limited Assortment Stores Approach 2,000 Mark and $10 Billion in Sales." *Progressive Grocer*, May 1981.
Hennessy, Terry. "Fresh Ideas." *Progressive Grocer*, March 2000.

Hennessy, Terry. "Traditional Wisdom." *Progressive Grocer*, February 1999.
"The High Cost of Eating." *Newsweek*, March 5, 1973.
"The High Price of Food Prices." *Fortune*, September 1973.
Hirshey, Gerri. "The Supermarket That's Eating Manhattan." *New York*, March 17, 1980.
Hoffman, Gene. "Merger Myopia." *Progressive Grocer*, May 1999.
"Holiday Prospects for Turkey Vanish." *New York Times*, October 28, 1944.
Hollinger, David A. *Post-Ethnic America*. Basic Books, 1995.
Holt, Jane. "The Post-War Store." *New York Times Magazine*, April 1, 1945.
Holusha, John. "Food Stores: A Broader Menu." *New York Times*, May 9, 2004.
Horatio Alger Association of Distinguished Americans. *Only in America: Opportunity Still Knocks, Volume II*. Horatio Alger Association, 1982.
"Housewives Skewer High Food Prices." *Business Week*, October 22, 1966.
"Housing Plan Disapproved." *New York Times*, June 1, 1943.
"Housing Plan Seen as a 'Walled City.'" *New York Times*, May 20, 1943.
"Housing 'Slicks Up' East Side's Stores." *New York Times*, January 24, 1950.
"How New York City Lurched to the Brink." *Time*, June 16, 1975.
"How They Killed O.P.A." *New Republic*, September 23, 1946.
"How to Succeed: Four Textbook Examples." *Crain's New York Business*, April 23, 1990.
Howard, Vicki. *From Main Street to Mall: The Rise and Fall of the American Department Store*. University of Pennsylvania Press, 2015.
Hughes, Lawrence M. "Patsy D'Agostino: Neighborly Grocer." *Catholic Digest*, May 1956.
Hulin-Salkin, Belinda. "Food Stores Turn Shopping into a Carefully Catered Affair." *Advertising Age*, October 3, 1988.
Hulin-Salkin, Belinda. "Shops Eager to Rescue Stores from Price-Ad Rut." *Advertising Age*, October 3, 1988.
Huston, L. "GHQ for Our Daily Life: Leon Henderson's OPA Headquarters." *New York Times Magazine*, May 10, 1942.
Iida, Jeanne. "Grocery Chain Does Well in Accepting Debit Cards." *American Banker*, March 22, 1991.
Indiviglio, Daniel. "Duane Reade Acquired by Walgreen." *The Atlantic*, February 17, 2010. www.theatlantic.com/business/archive/2010/02/duane-reade-acquired-by-walgreen/36096/.
Ingram, Bob. "Store of the Stars." *Supermarket Business*, November 1998.
Ingram, Bob. "Urban Urgency." *Supermarket Business*, July 1999.
Inklebarger, Timothy. "Smaller Grocers Filling Void Left by Big-Box Retailers in NYC." *Supermarket News*, April 23, 2024. www.supermarketnews.com/news/smaller-grocery-stores-filling-void-left-big-box-retailers-nyc.
"Irked Consumers Cutting Corners." *New York Times*, April 9, 1972.
Italian Charities of America, Inc. *Italian Charities of America Bulletin*, October 1971.
Jacobs, Meg. *Pocketbook Politics: Economic Citizenship in Twentieth-Century America*. Princeton University Press, 2005.
Jacobson, Matthew Frye. *Roots, Too: White Ethnic Revival in Post–Civil Rights America*. Harvard University Press, 2006.
Jacobson, Matthew Frye. *Whiteness of a Different Color: European Immigrants and the Alchemy of Race*. Harvard University Press, 1998.
Janoff, Barry. "Urban Renewal." *Progressive Grocer*, October 1999.
Jenkins, Nancy. "Health Food and the Change in Eating Habits." *New York Times*, April 4, 1984.

Karolefski, John. "D'Agostino Supermarket Pricing Strategy Boosts Sales." *Food Logistics*, November/December 2003.

Kaysen, Ronda. "Where, Oh Where, Did My Supermarket Go?" *New York Times*, November 6, 2016.

Kershaw, Sarah. "Supermarkets Are Few, Stores Many." *New York Times*, February 19, 1997.

Kessner, Thomas. *The Golden Door: Italian and Jewish Immigrant Mobility in New York City, 1880–1915*. Oxford University Press, 1977.

Kiechel, Walter, III. "The Food Giants Struggle to Stay in Step with Consumers." *Fortune*, September 11, 1978.

"The Kitchen: America's Playroom." *Forbes*, March 15, 1976.

Kivisto, Peter, ed. *The Ethnic Enigma: The Salience of Ethnicity for European-Origin Groups*. Associated University Presses, 1989.

Klemsrud, Judy. "Vegetarianism: Growing Way of Life, Especially Among the Young." *New York Times*, March 21, 1975.

Krinsky, Carol Herselle. "Architecture in New York City." In *New York: Culture Capital of the World, 1940–65*, edited by Leonard Wallock. Rizzoli, 1988.

Kuh, Patrick. *The Last Days of Haute Cuisine*. Viking, 2001.

Kummer, Corby. "Designs for Shopping." *Atlantic Monthly*, May 1987.

Kussin, Zachary. "Wegmans Announces Second NYC Location to Open in 2023." *New York Post*, July 29, 2021. nypost.com/2021/07/29/wegmans-announces-second-nyc-location-to-open-in-2023.

Lang, D. "Menus, Nylons, Wiping Cloths and Abdullahs." *New Yorker*, July 14, 1945.

Lankevich, George J. *American Metropolis: A History of New York City*. New York University Press, 1998.

Lawrence, Jennifer. "Grocers Pitch Private-Label Brands." *Advertising Age*, January 24, 1994.

Levenstein, Harvey. *Paradox of Plenty: A Social History of Eating in Modern America*. Oxford University Press, 1993.

Levenstein, Harvey. *Revolution at the Table: The Transformation of the American Diet*. Oxford University Press, 1988.

Levi, Carlo. *Christ Stopped at Eboli: The Story of a Year*. 1947. Translated by Frances Frenaye. Reprint, Farrar, Straus, and Giroux, 1980.

Levinson, Marc. *The Great A&P and the Struggle for Small Business in America*. Hill and Wang, 2011.

Lewis, Len. "Culture Shock." *Progressive Grocer*, April 1998.

Lewis, Len. "Papaya, Pagliacci and Pork Chops." *Progressive Grocer*, June 1998.

Lieberson, Stanley. "Unhyphenated Whites in the United States." *Ethnic and Racial Studies* 8, no. 1 (January 1985): 159–80.

Lindheim, James B. "The New Class." *Harper's*, August 1975.

Lingeman, Richard R. "Remembrance of Rationing Past." *New York Times Magazine*, September 9, 1973.

Linsen, Mary Ann. "And the Produce Beat Goes On." *Progressive Grocer*, June 1988.

Linsen, Mary Ann. "The Decade of the Fresh & Fast." *Progressive Grocer*, October 1989.

Linsen, Mary Ann. "Gourmet: The Democratization of Fine Foods." *Progressive Grocer*, February 1983.

Linsen, Mary Ann. "Too Much of a Good Thing?" *Progressive Grocer*, February 1988.

"Little Meat Here Again This Week." *New York Times*, May 26, 1945.

"Local Supermarkets' Business Is Growing." *Business Week*, July 17, 1948.

Logue, Edward. "New York: Are Cities a Bust?" *Look*, April 1, 1969.
Lombardo, Anthony. *The Italians in America*. Claretian, 1973.
Lowe, Jeanne R. *Cities in a Race with Time: Progress and Poverty in America's Renewing Cities*. Random House, 1967.
Lubove, Seth. "Food Porn." *Forbes*, February 14, 2005.
Luconi, Stefano. *From Paesani to White Ethnics: The Italian Experience in Philadelphia*. State University of New York Press, 2001.
MacFadyen, J. Tevere. "The Rise of the Supermarket." *American Heritage*, October/November 1985.
Mangano, Antonio. "The Associated Life of the Italians in New York City." *Charities*, May 7, 1904.
Margolies, Jane. "A Supermarket King Expands His Inventory." *New York Times*, October 14, 2018.
Margolius, Sidney. "Super Business of Supermarkets." *New York Times Magazine*, March 29, 1959.
Marinari, Maddalena. "'In the Name of God . . . and in the Interest of Our Country': The Cold War, Foreign Policy, and Italian Americans' Mobilization Against Immigration Restriction." In *New Italian Migrations to the United States*, edited by Laura E. Ruberto and Joseph Sciorra. University of Illinois Press, 2017.
"Markets Here Not Super?" *New York Times*, December 2, 1954.
Marks, John. "New York, New York." *U.S. News & World Report*, September 29, 1997.
"Marks & Spencer Sells King's Super Markets." *Gourmet Retailer*, October 2002.
Mars, Roman, host. *99% Invisible*. Podcast, episode 356, "Automat." SXM Media Group, June 4, 2019. 38 min., 47 sec. 99percentinvisible.org/episode/the-automat/.
Marsh, Lisa. "Big Changes Are in the Bag for 70-Yr.-Old D'Agostino and King's." *New York Post*, July 28, 2002.
Martin, Douglas. "For 100 Years, Providing a Tie to Italian Culture." *New York Times*, December 21, 1988.
Martino, Marcel. "The Family Grocer." *New York Times*, May 23, 1951.
Mathews, Ryan. "Lessons of War." *Progressive Grocer*, November 1995.
Mathews, Ryan. "Marketing to a New World of Taste." *Progressive Grocer*, July 1995.
Mathews, Ryan. "Special Report: Social Change and the Supermarket: 1976–1986, The Decade of Delusion." *Progressive Grocer*, December 1996.
Mathews, Ryan. "Under Siege." *Progressive Grocer*, May 1995.
Mathews, Ryan. "Welcome to the Logistics Museum." *Progressive Grocer*, December 1997.
Mayer, Allan J. "Supermarkets in a Crunch." *New York Times Magazine*, February 8, 1976.
Mayo, James M. *The American Grocery Store: The Business Evolution of an Architectural Space*. Greenwood, 1993.
"Mayor Forecasts 'Four More Years.'" *New York Times*, July 22, 1937.
"Mayor Orders Curb on Pushcarts Permits." *New York Times*, November 13, 1934.
McAlvey, Teresa. "D'Agostino's Paying $160M for King's Chain." *Bergen Record*, July 23, 2002.
McCarroll, Thomas. "Grocery-Cart Wars." *Time*, March 30, 1992.
McDonald, John. "The $2-Billion Building Boom." *Fortune*, February 1960.
McGrath, John T. "Is the Supermarket Obsolete?" *Newsweek*, February 10, 1975.
McGreevy, John T. *Parish Boundaries: The Catholic Encounter with Race in the Twentieth-Century Urban North*. University of Chicago Press, 1996.
"Meat, Butter, Eggs Take Another Dip." *New York Times*, September 23, 1947.

"Meat Prices Seen Remaining at Peak." *New York Times*, August 8, 1951.
"Meat Situation." *Life*, January 3, 1955.
Miller, Bryan. "In Manhattan, Trattorias Bloom." *New York Times*, August 17, 1988.
Min, Pyong Gap. "Koreans: Changes in New York in the Twenty-First Century." In *One Out of Three: Immigrant New York in the Twenty-First Century*, edited by Nancy Foner. Columbia University Press, 2013.
Mitgang, Herbert. "Thrilling Adventure: Man and Supermarket." *New York Times Magazine*, November 24, 1957.
"The Modern Grocer: All-American Success Story." *Progressive Grocer*, June 1958.
Mollot, Sabina. "Catsimatidis Giving Amazon a Supermarket Run for Its Money." *Real Estate Weekly*, September 18, 2019. rew-online.com/catsimatidis-giving-amazon-a-supermarket-run-for-its-money/.
"'Mom and Pop' Groceries Dying Under Competition." *New York Times*, December 4, 1976.
Moquin, Wayne, ed. *A Documentary History of the Italian Americans*. Praeger, 1974.
"More Pushcarts to Vanish." *New York Times*, September 20, 1936.
Morgan, Richard. "Red Apple Rescues Rival Supermarket Chain D'Agostino." *New York Post*, August 26, 2016. nypost.com/2016/08/26/red-apple-rescues-rival-supermarket-chain-dagostino/.
Morris, Charles. *American Catholic: The Saints and Sinners Who Built America's Most Powerful Church*. Vintage Books, 1997.
Moskin, Julia. "Online Shopping Makes New York a Cardboard Jungle." *New York Times*, April 6, 2005.
Moss, Jeremiah. *Vanishing New York: How a Great City Lost Its Soul*. Dey Street/HarperCollins, 2017.
Murphy, Mark. "If Trouble Can Be Avoid." *New Yorker*, May 15, 1943.
Nagle, James. "Small Grocers Keep a Foothold." *New York Times*, March 16, 1958.
Nelli, Humbert S. *From Immigrants to Ethnics: The Italian Americans*. Oxford University Press, 1983.
Nelli, Humbert S. "Italians in Urban America." In *The Italian Experience in the United States*, edited by Silvano M. Tomasi and Madeline H. Engel. Center for Migration Studies, 1970.
"Never Say Die." *New York Times*, March 3, 1955.
"New Ceilings Set for 7 Vegetables to Restore Supply." *New York Times*, March 14, 1943.
"The New City." *Fortune*, February 1960.
"New Internet Business to Enable Consumers to Name and Get Private Prices Before They Shop." *Business Wire*, September 21, 1999.
"A New Revolution in the Kitchen." *U.S. News & World Report*, February 19, 1969.
"A New Twist: Supermarkets with All the Frills." *Business Week*, August 17, 1981.
New York, Supreme Court, Appellate Division, First Department. *Foley, John, et al., as executors of Patsy D'Agostino, Deceased v. Nicholas D'Agostino et al., Defendants* 21 A.D. 2d 60; 248 N.Y.S. 2d 121, 1964. New York State Law Reporting Bureau.
"New York City: Disaster Area?" *U.S. News & World Report*, November 4, 1968.
"New York: Crucible of the Urban Crisis." *Business Week*, November 16, 1968.
"New York Pushcarts Do $35,000,000 Trade." *New York Times*, May 25, 1925.
"New York's Last Gasp." *Newsweek*, August 4, 1975.
"New York's Many Miles of Pushcarts." *New York Times*, November 30, 1924.
Newton, Marshall. "Fear Meat Costs Will Soar Dims Relief of Housewives." *New York Times*, October 15, 1946.

"Nick D'Agostino, Jr.: Dedicated to Improving the Quality of Life for All New York." The Chairman's Issue. *Food Merchants Advocate*, December 1982.

"Nick D'Agostino, Jr. NYSFMA Chairman; 7 New Directors Elected." *Food Merchants Advocate*, October 1982.

"No-Frills Food." *Business Week*, March 23, 1981.

Novak, Michael. *The Rise of the Unmeltable Ethnics*. Macmillan, 1972.

Novellino, Teresa. "Gristedes Owner Bails Out Rival D'Agostino Supermarket Chain." *New York Business Journal*, August 26, 2016. www.bizjournals.com/newyork/news/2016/08/26/gristedes-owner-bails-out-rival-d-agostino.html.

"NYSFMA Public Affairs Award for D'Agostino." *Food Merchants Advocate*, November 1989.

"'Oleo' Now Harder to Get Than Butter, Stores Find." *New York Times*, November 30, 1944.

O'Neill, Robert. "Produce Manager: Guiding the Renaissance of Fresh." *Progressive Grocer*, February 1980.

"Online Grocery Shopping Comes to New York City." *Business Wire*, February 15, 2001.

"OPA's Police Job." *Business Week*, March 28, 1942.

"Opening Anti-Pushcart Drive." *New York Times*, February 28, 1935.

"Orange Prices Rise on Black Market." *New York Times*, June 17, 1945.

Orler, Victor J., and David H. Friedman. "Consumer-Direct: Here to Stay." *Progressive Grocer*, January 1988.

Orsi, Robert A. *The Madonna of 115th Street: Faith and Community in Italian Harlem, 1880–1950*. Yale University Press, 1985.

Osman, Suleiman. "The Decade of the Neighborhood." In *Rightward Bound: Making America Conservative in the 1970s*, edited by Bruce J. Schulman and Julian E. Zelizer. Harvard University Press, 2008.

Packard, Vance. *The Status Seekers*. 1959. Reprinted in *American Social Classes in the 1950s: Selections from Vance Packard's "The Status Seekers,"* edited by Daniel Horowitz. Bedford/St. Martin's, 1995.

"Pasquale D'Agostino, 55, Dies; Supermarket-Chain President." *New York Times*, July 27, 1960.

Paumgarten, Nick. "Down in the Basement." *New Yorker*, August 8, 2011.

Payabarah, Azi, Andrea Salcedo, Matthew Haag, and Amie Tsang. "Fairway Market Files for Bankruptcy." *New York Times*, January 22, 2020. www.nytimes.com/2020/01/22/nyregion/fairway-market-bankruptcy.html.

Pellnat, Christopher. "D'AG's Is New York: Nicholas D'Agostino, Jr. Sees a Promising Future for D'Agostino Supermarkets." *Food Merchants Advocate*, September 1993.

Perman, Stacy. "The Joy of Not Cooking." *Time*, June 1, 1998.

Phillips-Fein, Kim. *Fear City: New York's Fiscal Crisis and the Rise of Austerity Politics*. Metropolitan Books, 2017.

Pileggi, Nicholas. "How We Italians Discovered America and Kept It Clean and Pure While Giving It Lots of Singers, Judges, and Other Swell People." *Esquire*, June 1968.

Pillsbury, Richard. *No Foreign Food: The American Diet in Time and Place*. Westview, 1998.

Plunz, Richard. *A History of Housing in New York City: Dwelling Type and Social Change in the American Metropolis*. Columbia University Press, 1990.

"Point-Cutting War on Rationed Food in the City Is Begun." *New York Times*, April 4, 1943.

"Poll Shows D'ag's Bag Is Best Buy." *New York Daily News*, May 11, 1978.

Pollok, Jacqueline. "Supermarkets: Caught in the Crossfire." *Chain Store Age*, August 1995.

Pope, Paul David. *The Deeds of My Fathers: How My Grandfather and Father Built New York and Created the Tabloid World of Today*. Rowan & Littlefield, 2010.

"Poultry Shortage Feared by Dealers." *New York Times*, March 6, 1943.
Pozzetta, George E., and Gary R. Mormino. *The Immigrant World of Ybor City: Italians and Their Latin American Neighbors in Tampa, 1885–1985*. University of Illinois Press, 1990.
"Price Education: OPA Trying to Educate the Retailer." *Business Week*, May 23, 1942.
"Prices: Picketers and the Picketed." *Newsweek*, November 7, 1966.
"Prices Up, Profits Down." *Forbes*, June 15, 1973.
Pristin, Terry. "New Yawk Grocer Ventures into the New Jersey Suburbs." *New York Times*, September 29, 2002.
Pristin, Terry. "Ordering Groceries in Aisle 'www.'" *New York Times*, May 4, 2002.
Pristin, Terry. "Square Feet: Where Have All the Supermarkets Gone?" *New York Times*, March 22, 2006.
"Protest: 'Bless You, Joe.'" *Newsweek*, July 13, 1970.
"Protest: Italian Power." *Newsweek*, June 22, 1970.
Pugliese, Stanislao. "Fascism and Anti-Fascism in Italian America." In *The Routledge History of Italian Americans*, edited by William J. Connell and Stanislao G. Pugliese. Routledge, 2018.
"Pushcart Market Planned." *New York Times*, June 16, 1912.
"Pushcart Markets." *New York Times*, November 21, 1912.
"The Pushcart Markets." *New York Times*, April 1, 1913.
"Pushcart Markets Found Insanitary." *New York Times*, February 27, 1930.
"Pushcart Markets Now." *New York Times*, December 10, 1912.
"Pushcart Men's Problems." *New York Times*, June 18, 1912.
"Pushcarts Losing Ground." *New York Times*, August 25, 1935.
Puzo, Mario. "The Italians, American Style." *New York Times Magazine*, August 6, 1967.
Quint, Michael. "D'Agostino to Accept Debit Cards for Purchases." *New York Times*, May 19, 1990.
"Quinta Strada." *Time*, May 31, 1976.
Radice, Carol. "Targeting Tomorrow's Consumers." *Progressive Grocer*, July 1998.
"Raid Pushcart Peddlers." *New York Times*, December 24, 1910.
Raphel, Murray, and Neil Raphel. "Myths of the Inner City." *Progressive Grocer*, May 1993.
Ratner, Juliana. "M&S King's Disposal Deal Collapses." *Financial Times*, December 2, 2002.
Redman, Russell. "Red Apple Group Promotes Joseph Parisi to Gristedes/D'Agostino President." *Supermarket News*, June 21, 2022. www.supermarketnews.com/executive-changes/red-apple-group-promotes-joseph-parisi-gristedesd-agostino-president.
Reichl, Ruth. *Comfort Me with Apples: More Adventures at the Table*. Random House, 2001.
Reimers, David M. *Still the Golden Door: The Third World Comes to America*. 1985. Reprint, Columbia University Press, 1992.
"Retail Self-Service Urged." *New York Times*, October 8, 1948.
"Retailer Fusion: Who Will Win?" *Printer's Ink*, August 18, 1961.
"Retailers Moving to Diversify Lines." *New York Times*, October 9, 1949.
Richards, David A. J. *Italian American: The Racializing of an Ethnic Identity*. New York University Press, 1999.
Rieder, Jonathan. *Canarsie: Jews and Italians of Brooklyn Against Liberalism*. Harvard University Press, 1985.
Rigg, Cynthia. "Against the Odds, Minding the Store: The Crain's All-Stars." *Crain's New York Business*, April 23, 1990.
Rigg, Cynthia. "Area Food Brokers Seek Shelf Esteem." *Crain's New York Business*, January 7, 1991.

Rigg, Cynthia. "D'Agostino's Fresh Approach." *Crain's New York Business*, January 2, 1989.
Rigg, Cynthia. "40 Under 40." *Crain's New York Business*, January 30, 1989.
Rigg, Cynthia. "Stores Put Stock in Private Labels." *Crain's New York Business*, November 28, 1993.
Rigg, Cynthia. "Three Major Rivals Bid to Buy Sloan's Chain." *Crain's New York Business*, February 5, 1990.
Ring, Lawrence J. "Supermarkets at Risk." *Chain Store Age*, July 1999.
Ritter, Courtney. "The Double Life of the Italian Suit: Italian Americans and the 'Made in Italy' Label." In *Making Italian America: Consumer Culture and the Production of Ethnic Identities*, edited by Simone Cinotto. Fordham University Press, 2014.
Robertson, Wyndham. "Going Broke the New York Way." *Fortune*, August 1975.
Robey, R. "OPACS: The New Price Control Organization." *Newsweek*, April 21, 1941.
Roediger, David R. *Working Toward Whiteness: How America's Immigrants Became White*. Basic Books, 2005.
Rose, Philip M. *The Italians in America*. George H. Doran, 1922.
Ruhlman, Michael. *Grocery: The Buying and Selling of Food in America*. Abrams, 2017.
Ryan, Tom. "Has Online Grocery Shopping Hit Its Sales Ceiling?" *RetailWire*, June 14, 2022. retailwire.com/discussion/has-online-grocery-shopping-hit-its-sales-ceiling.
"Sales of Meat Drop Little on 1st 'Meatless' Tuesday." *New York Times*, October 8, 1947.
Samuelson, Robert J. "How New York City Lurched to the Brink." *Time*, June 16, 1975.
Samuelson, Robert J. "No Funds for Fun City." *New Republic*, May 10, 1975.
Sansolo, Michael. "Hit 'Em Where They Are." *Progressive Grocer*, November 1991.
Sansolo, Michael. "It's Not Over . . . Yet." *Progressive Grocer*, July 1993.
Sansolo, Michael. "It's the Stores . . ." *Progressive Grocer*, May 1993.
Sansolo, Michael. "Riding the Age Wave." *Progressive Grocer*, June 1993.
"Sausages Spoiling, Retailers Assert." *New York Times*, April 20, 1943.
Sayres, Paul. "The World's Biggest Business." In *Food Marketing: Twenty-Two Leaders of the Food Industry Tell How the Nation's Biggest and Most Complex Business Works—and Why*, edited by Paul Sayres. McGraw-Hill, 1950.
Schaeffer, Larry. "A Guide to Going Upscale." *Progressive Grocer*, May 1985.
Schine, Eric. "At the Food Chains, It's All Gulp and Swallow." *Business Week*, May 8, 1995.
Schine, Eric. "Supermarket Merger Frenzy." *Chain Store Age*, August 1999.
Schneider, Eric C. *Vampires, Dragons, and Egyptian Kings: Youth Gangs in Postwar New York*. Princeton University Press, 1999.
"Schools Get Market's Computers." *Crain's New York Business*, June 10, 1991.
Schulman, Bruce J. *The Seventies: The Great Shift in American Culture, Society, and Politics*. Da Capo, 2001.
Schumach, Murray. "The East River Shore Regains Its Glory." *New York Times Magazine*, January 19, 1947.
Schwartz, Joel. *The New York Approach: Robert Moses, Urban Liberals, and Redevelopment of the Inner City*. Ohio State University Press, 1993.
"Seeks to Curb Peddlers." *New York Times*, February 10, 1935.
"Sees Food Pipeline No Longer Clogged." *New York Times*, February 4, 1947.
Sheraton, Mimi. "Taking Out, Eating In." *Time*, April 11, 1988.
"Shift D'Agostino Execs." *Food Merchants Advocate*, February 1979.
"Shopper's Delight." *Life*, January 3, 1955.
"Shopping for Food: How It's Changing." *U.S. News & World Report*, May 30, 1966.

Silberman, Charles E. "The Home of the Middle Class." *Fortune*, February 1960.
Simon, Arthur. *Stuyvesant Town, U.S.A.: Pattern for Two Americas*. New York University Press, 1970.
Singer, Caroline. "An Italian Saturday." *The Century*, March 1921.
"Size Means Sales." *Business Week*, June 18, 1949.
"Small Change at the Checkout." *New York Times*, February 9, 1989.
"Small Grocers Fight Back." *Business Week*, April 12, 1947.
"The Smaller Food Chains Come Up Fast." *Business Week*, May 20, 1950.
Smith, Chris. "Splat." *New York*, May 24, 2004.
Smith, Patti. *Just Kids: An Autobiography*. Ecco, 2010.
Snyder, Glenn. "Why Your Produce Department Will Make a Comeback in the 60's." *Progressive Grocer*, February 1960.
Soffer, Jonathan. *Ed Koch and the Rebuilding of New York City*. Columbia University Press, 2010.
Sollors, Werner, ed. *The Invention of Ethnicity*. Oxford University Press, 1989.
Sparkes, Boyden. "Can the Cities Come Back?" *Saturday Evening Post*, November 4, 1944.
Springen, Karen. "Supermarket Solutions." *Newsweek*, August 11, 1997.
Springen, Karen, and Karen Kushner. "From Soup to Nuts." *Newsweek*, March 16, 1998.
Springer, Jon. "Gristedes-D'Agostino Merger Still On." *Supermarket News*, October 24, 2016. www.supermarketnews.com/retail-financial/gristedes-dagostino-merger-still.
"Squashing Deal for Sloan's Won't Help Consumers." Editorial. *Crain's New York Business*, July 16, 1990.
Stewart, Barbara. "How to Keep the Greenmarket in the Pink." *New York Times*, August 3, 1997.
Straight, M. "Why Henderson Goes." *New Republic*, December 28, 1942.
Stuart, John. "'Old Time' Store Passing Swiftly." *New York Times*, February 17, 1952.
"Study Finds Rise in Materialism Amid Economic Gloom." *New York Times*, May 9, 1979.
"Stuyvesant Town Approved by Board." *New York Times*, June 4, 1943.
"Stuyvesant Town Defended." *New York Times*, June 3, 1943.
"The Super Market of the 70's: Where Will Tomorrow's Produce Men Come From?" *Progressive Grocer*, November 1969.
"The Super Market of the 70's Part II: More Sales, Profits, Prestige Ahead for Produce." *Progressive Grocer*, November 1969.
"Super Markets Planning Outlay of $375,000,000." *New York Times*, May 18, 1951.
"'Superette' Held Answer to Chains." *New York Times*, March 13, 1950.
"Supermarket Ads: Creative at Last." *Printer's Ink*, May 10, 1963.
"Supermarket Study." *New York Times*, January 13, 1953.
"The Supermarket: The Revolution in Retailing." *Business Week*, June 28, 1952.
"The Supermarkets Fight Back." *Dun's Review*, October 1977.
"Supermarkets Plus." *Business Week*, October 12, 1946.
"'Supermart Ads Are Stiff, Stifled,' Hurvis Charges." *Advertising Age*, November 20, 1967.
Talese, Gay. "Basta." *New Yorker*, May 31, 2010.
"Talks to Sell Supermarkets to D'Agostino End." *New York Times*, December 2, 2002.
Tanner, Ronald. "New Life for City Supers." *Progressive Grocer*, February 1985.
Tartt, Donna. *The Goldfinch*. Back Bay Books/Little, Brown, 2013.
Tedlow, Richard S. *New and Improved: The Story of Mass Marketing in America*. Basic Books, 1990.

Thayer, Warren. "Electronic Mom and Pop." *Progressive Grocer*, May 1989.
"A Thriving Business." *New York Times*, August 3, 1930.
"Time Capsules from 50 Years of Annual Reports." *Progressive Grocer*, April 1983.
Tirabassi, Maddalena. "Why Italians Left Italy: The Physics and Politics of Migration." In *The Routledge History of Italian Americans*, edited by William J. Connell and Stanislao G. Pugliese. Routledge, 2018.
"To Regulate Peddlers." *New York Times*, April 16, 1910.
"Today the Shopping Center, Tomorrow the Superstore." *Harvard Business Review* 52, no. 1 (January 1974): 89–98.
"Today's Food Stores Cost 12 Times 1940's." *New York Times*, April 26, 1953.
Tomasi, Silvano M. "The Ethnic Church and the Integration of Italian Immigrants in the United States." In *The Italian Experience in the United States*, ed. Silvano M. Tomasi and Madeline H. Engel. Center for Migration Studies, 1970.
Trager, Cara. "Bodegas' Facelifts Offer Them a New Lease on Life." *Advertising Age*, February 9, 1987.
Trends in the United States: Consumer Attitudes and the Supermarket. Food Marketing Institute Research Department, 1996.
Tricarico, Donald. "In a New Light: Italian-American Ethnicity in the Mainstream." In *The Ethnic Enigma: The Salience of Ethnicity for European-Origin Groups*, edited by Peter Kivisto. Associated University Presses, 1989.
Trillin, Calvin. "The Italian Thing." *New Yorker*, November 19, 1990.
"A Triumph and an Obligation." *Life*, January 3, 1955.
Turcsik, Richard. "A Run for the Money." *Progressive Grocer*, November/December 2001.
Turcsik, Richard. "Taking Root: A Suburban-Style Pathmark Blossoms in New York's Harlem." *Progressive Grocer*, July 1999.
Turque, Bill. "Where the Food Isn't." *Newsweek*, February 24, 1992.
Ueda, Reed. *Postwar Immigrant America: A Social History*. Bedford/St. Martin's, 1994.
"The Unsuper Markets." *Newsweek*, January 16, 1978.
"Up-Turn in Pre-Packaging." *Modern Packaging*, July 1960.
U.S. Congress. House. Committee on Education and Labor, Special Subcommittee of the Committee on Education and Labor. *Hearings on Labor Practices in the Food Industry*. 80th Congress, 1st Session, July 11, 1947.
U.S. Congress. House. Select Committee to Conduct a Study and Investigation of the National Defense Program in Its Relation to Small Business in the United States. *Hearings on Small Business*. 78th Congress, 1st Session, June 7, 1943.
"U.S. Grows an Educated Palate." *Business Week*, January 31, 1959.
Valentino, Cynthia. "In a Fragmented Market, Grocers Cover the Niches." *Advertising Age*, May 4, 1987.
Van Gelder, Lawrence. "Market Basket Cost Up 45% in 5 Years." *New York Times*, May 17, 1978.
Van Marter Beede, Vincent. "The Italians in America." *The Chautauquan*, January 1902.
Vandam, Jeff. "Stuyvesant Town and Peter Cooper Village: The New Owners Get the Once-Over." *New York Times*, April 1, 2007.
Verdon, Joan. "The Pandemic Changed How We Shop for Groceries, Adobe Report Shows." *Forbes*, March 15, 2022. www.forbes.com/sites/joanverdon/2022/03/15/the-pandemic-changed-how-we-shop-for-groceries-adobe-report-shows.
"Videotex Service in D'Agostino?" *Crain's New York Business*, February 13, 1989.

Wallock, Leonard. "New York City: Capital of the Twentieth Century." In *New York: Culture Capital of the World, 1940–1965*, edited by Leonard Wallock. Rizzoli International, 1988.
Walsh, John P. *Supermarkets Transformed: Understanding Organizational and Technological Innovations*. Rutgers University Press, 1993.
"Want the Pushcarts Back." *New York Times*, June 14, 1912.
"War in the Aisles." *Newsweek*, October 9, 1972.
Ward, Barbara McLean, ed. *Produce and Conserve, Share and Play Square: The Grocer and the Consumer on the Home-Front Battlefield During World War II*. Strawberry Banke, 1994.
Waters, Mary. *Ethnic Options: Choosing Identities in America*. University of California Press, 1990.
Weinstein, Michael. "The Crowded World of Urban Supermarkets." *New York Times*, December 18, 1977.
Weinstein, Steve. "All in the Family." *Progressive Grocer*, May 2001.
Weinstein, Steve. "Back and Forward to Basics." *Progressive Grocer*, March 1987.
Weinstein, Steve. "The Battle of Broadway." *Progressive Grocer*, April 1999.
Weinstein, Steve. "Breaking the Rules." *Progressive Grocer*, May 2001.
Weinstein, Steve. "The Challenge of the '90s: Pinning Down the Hispanic Market." *Progressive Grocer*, June 1990.
Weinstein, Steve. "Competition: Intense and Non-Traditional." *Progressive Grocer*, July 1989.
Weinstein, Steve. "Consolidations: The Urge to Merge Continues." *Progressive Grocer*, October 1989.
Weinstein, Steve. "A Conversation with Nick D'Agostino." *Progressive Grocer*, September 1987.
Weinstein, Steve. "A Good Deal Is Hard to Find." *Progressive Grocer*, July 1987.
Weinstein, Steve. "The Graying of American Shoppers." *Progressive Grocer*, May 1996.
Weinstein, Steve. "How to Hire the Best." *Progressive Grocer*, July 1993.
Weinstein, Steve. "In a Family Way." *Progressive Grocer*, September 1988.
Weinstein, Steve. "Motivating Forces." *Progressive Grocer*, September 1996.
Weinstein, Steve. "Sophisticated Shoppers—Sticky Issues." *Progressive Grocer*, September 1989.
Weinstein, Steve. "Supercenters: The Ultimate Weapon?" *Progressive Grocer*, September 1999.
Weinstein, Steve. "Too Little, Too Late?" *Progressive Grocer*, May 2000.
Weinstein, Steve. "Tyranny Is Out, Teamwork Is In." *Progressive Grocer*, December 1987.
Weiss, Lois. "Eat It: Supermarkets and Urban Grocery Concepts Are Swarming NYC." *New York Post*, April 21, 2024. nypost.com/2024/04/21/real-estate/nyc-grocery-stores-are-booming-thanks-to-big-box-extinction.
West, William K. "Inner City Supers: Is There a Future?" *Progressive Grocer*, June 1978.
"What Is to Be Done?" *New Yorker*, November 15, 1993.
White, Frank Marshall. "Black Hand Holds Sway in Italian New York." *Literary Digest*, August 30, 1913.
White, Frank Marshall. "The Black Hand in Control in Italian New York." *Outlook*, August 16, 1913.
White, Frank Marshall. "To Rid This Country of Foreign Criminals." *Harper's Weekly*, June 27, 1908.
"Who Can Afford Manhattan?" *Time*, December 26, 1969.
"Why the Growing Flight of Business from New York City." *U.S. News & World Report*, March 6, 1967.

"Why Your Produce Department Will Make a Comeback in the 60's." *Progressive Grocer*, February 1960.

Whyte, William Foote. *Street Corner Society: The Social Structure of an Italian Slum.* 1943. Reprint, University of Chicago Press, 1955.

Whyte, William H., Jr. *The Organization Man.* Simon and Schuster, 1956.

Wilcox, C. "In Defense of Price Control." *New York Times Magazine*, October 10, 1943.

Wilder, Craig Steven. *A Covenant with Color: Race and Social Power in Brooklyn.* Columbia University Press, 2000.

Williams, Jim. "We Gain New $200 Stop." *Arnold Bakers' Breadwinner*, March 1950.

Woldoff, Rachael A., Lisa M. Morrison, and Michael R. Glass. *Priced Out: Stuyvesant Town and the Loss of Middle-Class Neighborhoods.* New York University Press, 2016.

"A Woman's Place Is on the Net." *Chain Store Age*, June 1997.

Wright, Robert A. "Health Foods—Only a Fad?" *New York Times*, October 15, 1972.

Yans-McLaughlin, Virginia. *Family and Community: Italian Immigrants in Buffalo, 1880–1930.* Cornell University Press, 1977.

"The Year of the Yuppie." *Newsweek*, December 31, 1984.

Young, Nancy Beck. *Wright Patman: Populism, Liberalism, and the American Dream.* Southern Methodist University Press, 2000.

Zbytniewski, Jo-Ann. "Working Women: Less Time, More Money." *Progressive Grocer*, June 1979.

Zellner, Wendy. "Look Out, Supermarkets—Wal-Mart Is Hungry." *Business Week*, September 14, 1998.

Zellner, Wendy. "Wal-Mart: Retailer of the Century." Special issue, *Chain Store Age*, December 1999.

Zwiebach, Elliot. "New Breed of Industry Leader Urged by D'Agostino." *Supermarket News*, April 6, 1981.

INDEX

All family relationships indicated in parentheses use Patsy and Nicholas D'Agostino Sr. as the focal points. Page numbers in *italics* refer to images.

Abruzzi, Italy, 35–38, 40–41, 104, 118–19
Ackerman, Jason, 288n89
advertising: Antiquary Scotch, *127*, 161; *Chain Store Age*, 162; Chase Manhattan Bank, 189; community and service, 188–89; customer targeting, 142, 198, 279n110; *Food Merchants Advocate*, 162; "I Love New York" campaign, 165, 281n128; Lord Calvert whiskey, *127*, 161, 189, 265n86; mass marketing, 10, 98, 200, 217; "Men of Distinction" campaign, 265n86; in *New Yorker*, 160; *New York Times*, *128*, 161; *Only in America*, 172–73; OPA giving large retailers free advertising, 63; supermarkets, 156, 158, 226–27, 278–79nn95–96
advertising, D'Agostino, *125*; "15 Minutes of Fame…" campaign, *175*, 191; author's overview, 10–11; *Avenue*, 189–90; commodification of private lives for, 11, 86–87, 189–94, 213; company origins central theme, 189–92, 193–94; connection to NYC, 4, 160–61, 192, 227; cost of, 227; customer base targeted, 142, 156, 158–59, 160, 190–91; "D'Ag Bag" campaign, *124*, 157–58, 160, 227, 240, 279n105, 279n107; "D'AG/NYC" crest, 188; early print advertising, 278n94; employing African American model, *124*, 158–59; ethnic roots of company, 191–92; falling into disuse, 226–27; "familiar face of the company chairman," 189; family angle, 227, 239–40; featuring Nicholas Sr., *x*, 1-2, 192; in film and television, 188, 240, 280n115; Fresh Markets, 212; "Hello, Young Lovers!" campaign, *175*, 190–91; humanizing the company, 189; "Hurry in to the big D'Agostino Love-In" campaign, *125*, 160; iconography over information, 159, 278n94; "If there's no D'Agostino near you…move!" campaign, *124*, *125*, 158, 160, 226; immigrant family as institution and product, 2, 4; introducing merchant to customer, 155; "Keep New York Delicious…" campaign, *124*, 159; key part of brand, 155, 159; "markets of distinction," 91, 265n86; *New Yorker*-style

advertising, D'Agostino (*continued*)
cartoons, 11, *125*, 160; *New York Times* spots, 159, 189, 280n116; "One of the nice things about New York" campaign, *126*, 165; "Only in New York" campaign, 1–2, 192; Patsy's resistance to, 97–98, 278n93; "Please Don't Kiss the Butcher" campaign, 156–57; reduction in, 240; seen as extravagant, 10; self-deprecating wit, 158, 160–61; visual style, 159; "What's Hot…What's New York!" campaign, *127*, 161; "Would I kid you about a cookie?" campaign, *128*. See also branding

Agnew, Spiro, 135
AIDS, 182, 284n4
Alba, Richard, 213, 249n23, 249n24
Alger, Horatio, 11
Amazon, 238
American Committee on Italian Migration, 269–70n151
American dream: at D'Agostino's, 194; fragility for first generation immigrants, 42; Great Depression and, 45; individualism and entrepreneurship, 65, 101; jeopardized by OPA regulations, 61, 64; Korean greengrocers, 202–7; return to Italy affirming, 119; as tale of feminine disappointment, 39, 45–46; as tale of masculine triumph, 39; through food retailing, 202. See also media profiles
American Italian Anti-Defamation League, 168, 282n143
Americans of Italian Descent, Inc., 282n143
Anderson, George, 101
Andronico's, 221
Anti-Defamation League of B'nai B'rith, 282n143
A&P: antitrust case, 259n8; competition with D'Agostino's, 214, 218, 237–38; decline, 138, 259–60n10; OPA advertising for, 63; revenue and profits, 77, 276n59; store closures, 25, 138; supermarket pivot, 25, 79
Archdiocese of New York, 181
Armani, 211, 212

Arnold Bakers, 86
As Good as It Gets, 188
Asian Exclusion Act, 288–89n93
Austin & Clements, 99–100, 105
Avventuriero, Gaetano, 116

Balducci's, 214
Barnes & Noble, 215, 216
Barney Miller, 164–65
Barrett, James, 17
Beame, Abe, 280–81n124
Bechdel, Alison, 240
Bed, Bath & Beyond, 215, 292n159
Benetton, 211, 212
Bennett, Ralph Kinney, 173
BlackRock Realty, 241
Blackstone, 298n266
blind shopping, 196–97
Bohack, 138, 214
Borders, 216
Boys' Town of Italy, 71, 106, 107, 115, 118, 269–70n151, 270n156
branding: advertising key part of, 155, 159; after acquisition by Catsimatidis, 299n275; contemporary version of traditional family business, 179; corporate personality projection of president, 155–56, 161–62, 178–79, 236–37; family business, 2, 183, 189–90; "family owned and family operated," 2, 13, 189; iconography, 286n62; "New York's Grocer," 187, 193, 239; "New York's Original Grocer," 286n60; store name, 86, 156, 256n68, 263n60; "Supermarkets of Distinction," 108. See also advertising, D'Agostino
Brandt, Lilian, 21
Bread & Circus, 221
Bronson, Charles, 164, 281n127
Bronx Terminal Market Merchants Association, 77
Bronx Zoo, 135
Brooklyn Bridge, *125*, 160
Buford, Bill, 224
Bugnara, Abruzzi, Italy, 35–38, 40–41, 118–19
Burns, Joseph, 159

Butterfield Market, 29, 50–52
Buy-Low Grocery Company, 79, 148

Caldwell, Harry, 101
Carcone, Gerard (cousin's brother-in-law), 29, 50–52
Cardinal Cooke's Commission for the Laity, 118, 134
Carroll-Abbing, John, 71, 108, 115, 269–70n151
Carter, Jimmy, 162
Caruso, Enrico, 116
Catholic Charities of Greater New York, 107, 118, 134
Catholicism: 1950s as "brick and mortar" period, 107; Catholic education, 270n160; of D'Agostino family, 71, 73, 107–8, 117–18, 134, 181; identity of D'Agostino Supermarkets, 108, 118; Italian immigrants' relationship with, 117, 249–50n25, 270n159
Catsimatidis, John, 7, 242–43, 274n32, 299n275
Central Park Zoo, 125, 160
Child, Julia, 142, 145
Chinese Exclusion Act (1882), 288–89n93
Cinotto, Simone, 49, 66, 251n48
Circiello, Gino, 116, 241
Citarella, 214, 223
City College of New York (CCNY), 101, 104
Citymeals-on-Wheels, 182
Clausen, Charlie, 101
Clemente, Domenick (Dick Clements), 99–100, 105
Colamosca, Anne, 276n59
Cold War, 129, 271n2
Columbus Hospital, 114
computer shopping, 194–95. *See also* online shopping
Contract Labor Law (1885), 248n9
Cooke, Terence, 73
Cooley, Harold, 95
Coppola, Francis Ford, 169, 282n145
Corey, Mary, 31, 90, 160, 253n4, 265n86
Corsi, Edward, 270n158
Costco, 195, 215, 238
COVID-19, 297n260, 298n265

Crain's New York Business, 183
Cullen, Michael, 24–25
Cuomo, Mario, 210
Curley, James Michael, 61
customers: advertising targeting, 142, 156, 158–59, 160, 190–91, 198, 279n110; cost-conscious, 137; "culture of consensus," 9, 90, 138; decline of supermarkets, 223–24, 239; desire for produce, 220; dynamic between grocers and, 137, 138–39, 235, 257n85; expectations of, 145, 219–20, 223, 225; foodies and gourmets, 142–45, 146, 205, 240, 276n56; healthy eating, 220, 224; marketplace segmentation and diversity, 218, 219; "Mrs. Consumer," 217; nature of changing, 93–94, 139, 142, 143, 166–67, 223; tactics for attracting, 142; women's changing role, 142, 217; younger customers avoiding supermarkets, 239. *See also* advertising
customers, D'Agostino: adjusting to customers' changing tastes, 265n89; affinity with customers, 189; changing customer base, 90–91; discerning consumers targeted, 87–89; driving expansion, 253n4; expectations of, 212, 219; gentrification and, 147, 167, 219, 224–25; loss of, 214, 223, 239; new middle-class base, 87, 90–92; Nicholas Sr.'s assumptions, 132–33; older and more modest means, 240; Patsy and female customers under OPA, 257n85; price-conscious customers sought, 226; retention of, 132, 181, 207–8, 217; surveying customer base, 147; treatment of, 74–75; trust and loyalty of, 74–75, 94, 95–96, 132–34, 160, 187–88, 193; wealth and status of, 2–3, 4, 58, 82, 146, 159–61, 185; working professionals, 139, 142, 156; young customers sought, 190–91
CVS, 298n265

D'Agostino, Baron (no relation), 41, 270–71n161
D'Agostino, David (Nicholas's grandson), 176, 199, 296n243

D'Agostino, Ignazio "Ignatius" Stephen (father): anti-Italian prejudice, 43, 98-99; bringing Patsy to US, 33, 40; courting and marrying Loreta, 38-39, 253n13; early years in US, 42-43; impact of emigration on family, 37-38; issues with alcohol, 43, 48; Josephine's godfather, 54; limits of success, 57, 65-66, 99, 103, 150; pushcart peddling, 33-34, 43, 49; relationship with Frank Tucciarone, 44; shaping Patsy's expectations of US, 98. *See also* family and personality conflicts

D'Agostino, Irene (Patsy's wife), 29, 34, 53, 72, 110-11

D'Agostino, Josephine (Nicholas's wife), 28, 29, 72; childhood, 46; courtship and marriage to Nicholas, 47, 53-55, 56, 189-90, 256n59; housing situation, 109, 110-13; Ignatius's goddaughter, 54; reaction to Stephen's resignation, 172; representing "new woman" of 1920s, 46; role in founding D'Agostino's, 47, 55, 267n121; role in Tucciarone business, 45-47; social habits, 47; suburban life, 112-13

D'Agostino, Loreta (mother), 27, 38-40, 41, 118-19, 253n13, 270-71n161

D'Agostino, Nicholas, Jr. (Nicholas's son), 29, 72, 176; advertising embraced by, 10-11, 157; apprenticeship in family business, 180; awards and recognitions, 182, 183, 284-85n12; burden of carrying company name, 232; Catholicism of, 181; on the competition, 218-19, 223, 224-25; computer innovations adopted, 194-97; D'Agostino/Silverzweig Entrepreneurial Institute, 231, 295-96n233; ethos of family business, 181, 185-86; expansion under, 178, 230; family as organizing principle, 4, 181, 183, 189-93, 212-13, 228, 229-33, 234; fostering sense of community, 187-88; gourmet trend response, 147; industry leadership, 180, 182-83, 284-85n12; Italian identity, 212-13; joining family business, 120-21, 123, 171; leadership and management style, 179-83, 186-87, 286n48; on organic produce, 220-21; philanthropy, 179, 181-83; political activities, 192-93; on product selection, 217; public face of company, 180, 186, 189; relationships with film and television companies, 188; relationship with employees, 183, 185-86, 187, 229, 231, 286n48; role in company, 4, 151, 170, 180-81, 277n81; spokesperson for other companies, 189; stewardship and fairness principles, 229, 231; store as New York institution, 165; store location selection, 167; succession planning, 229-33, 283n156, 295-96n233. *See also* customers, D'Agostino; media profiles, Nicholas Jr.

D'Agostino, Nicholas III (Nicholas's grandson), 176; D'Agostino's acquisition negotiated, 242-43, 299n273; expansion under, 233-34; industry leadership, 192-93; role in company, 7, 231, 233, 242-43, 296n243; technological innovations embraced, 199, 296n247

D'Agostino, Nicola "Nicholas" Sr., 29, 67, 68, 71, 176; American dream, 119; audience with Pope Pius XII, 107, 118; awards and recognitions, 135, 172-74; business acumen and vision, 121, 132-33; butcher's training, 51, 53, 57, 89, 91, 267n122; Butterfield Market, 51-52; buying out Frank Tucciarone, 34, 45, 55-56, 267n121; Catholicism of, 71, 73, 117-18, 134; character profile, 4-5, 47, 52-53, 134; childhood, 37-38, 40-41; courting and marrying Josephine, 47, 53-55, 56, 189-90, 256n59; D'Agostino's as extension of identity, 133, 171, 192; declaration of masculinity, 41-42; desire for success and recognition, 38, 40, 47, 57, 135-36; early years in food business, 49-51; emigration to US, 41-42, 48-49; expansion under, 133-34; face of business, 135; Grand Royal market, 55; housing situation, 109, 110-13; impact of Ignatius's drinking, 48; industry leadership, 114; Italian community activism, 169; limits of success, 150, 153; micromanaging tendencies,

133, 171; moral responsibility, 132; narrative of business success, 121, 122; outward migration and upward mobility, 110–13; on Patsy as industry spokesperson, 135; philanthropy, 106–7, 114, 115–16, 117, 134–36; power of quality, 132–34; public and political influence, 116, 135; pushcart peddling, 26, 49, 133, 267n122; reaction to Stephen's resignation, 172; resistance to modernization efforts, 153; retirement, 174; return visits to Abruzzi, 72, 75–76, 118–19, 134; role in company, 3, 131, 151, 277n81; sidelined in media profiles, 34, 100, 121; social habits and clubs, 53, 113, 116, 134; working at young age, 37–38, 40. *See also* D'Agostino brothers; family and personality conflicts; media profiles, Nicholas Sr.

D'Agostino, Pasquale "Patsy," 27, 29, 67, 68, 70, 71, 72; on advertising, 97–98, 155, 278n93; anxieties about loss of individuality, 102; appearance before Congress, 61–65, 258n89; audience with Pope Pius XII, 107, 118; cancer diagnosis and death, 120–21; Catholicism of, 71, 107–8, 117–18; childhood, 40; criticisms of organized labor, 62, 258n89; desire for success and recognition, 40; dislike of OPA regulations, 60–64, 257n85; ditch digging, 102; emigration to US, 33, 39, 40, 98; First National, 102, 154–55; on frozen foods, 88–89; gift of charm, 57, 66, 67, 97; housing, 110–11, 268n143; *How I Made a Million*, 103–4; immigrant narrative and mythos, 21, 32–35, 62–64, 65, 121–22; industry leadership, 3, 60, 77, 96, 106, 114, 116, 265n95, 272–73n13; language and assimilation, 104, 266n108; lecturing on economics, 101, 104; limiting Josephine's role, 47; marriage to Irene, 53; outward migration and upward mobility, 110–11, 114; partnership with Frank Tucciarone, 34, 45, 102–3; "Pat Austin," 99–100, 105; philanthropy, 106–7, 114, 115–16, 117; public face of company, 121, 272–73n13; public identity, 60, 62–63, 65; pushcart peddling, 22, 26, 33–34, 43, 65–66, 100, 253n7; relationship with employees, 102; relationship with nephew Stephen, 123, 151, 170–71; return visits to Abruzzi, 75–76, 118; role in company, 3; on running a business, 77, 78, 79, 80–81, 102, 103, 121–22, 154–55, 278n90; social clubs, 116; spokesperson for Lord Calvert whiskey, 127, 161, 265n86; succession planning, 34–35, 81–82; symbol for virtues of immigrant class, 32; temper and contrarianism, 52–53; value of self-education, 104; well-suited for life of a merchant, 66. *See also* customers, D'Agostino; D'Agostino brothers; family and personality conflicts; media profiles, Patsy

D'Agostino, Stephen (Nicholas's son), 29, 72, 176; business acumen, 149–50, 152–55; on the competition, 146; distance from family business, 283n156; on employees, 184; ethnicity in business, 212; expansion under, 151–52, 155; industry leadership, 151, 161–62, 277–78n84; Italian identity, 282n148; joining family business, 120–21, 123, 147–49, 151; JTL Corporation, 170, 172; marketing and advertising, 156; meeting with President Carter, 162; public profile, 153–55, 161; pushing company away from ethnic roots, 191; relationship with Patsy, 123, 151, 170–71; resenting family divisions, 151, 271n171; resignation, 170, 171–72; responding to gourmet trend, 147; role in company, 3–4, 151, 179; spokesperson for other companies, 127, 128, 161, 189; succession planning, 283n156; vision of NYC, 170. *See also* customers, D'Agostino; family and personality conflicts

D'Agostino, Stephen (Patsy's son), 29, 120–21, 154, 176, 271n168

D'Agostino, Walter (Nicholas's grandson), 176, 231, 233, 296n243

D'Agostino brothers: business acumen and knowledge, 55–56, 57, 66, 67, 91;

D'Agostino brothers (*continued*)
business arrangement between, 55–56; Buy-Low Grocery Company, 79; complicated relationship, 3, 106, 109, 110–11, 135; family history, business history, and identity, 3, 9, 42, 75, 86–87, 96, 98–99, 121; indebted to Tucciarone brothers, 43, 45; Joint Merchants Produce Co-Op, 79; litigation, 121-22; loyalty to family, 59; Metropolitan Life contract, 85–86, 87; obstacles to success, 35; pros and cons of postwar success, 75–76; prototypical story of Americanization, 65; quest for literacy, 66; supermarket model, 2, 93; transnational identity, 59, 60; wholesale cooperatives formed, 75, 78–79; WWII period of struggle for, 58–64. *See also* customers, D'Agostino; D'Agostino, Nicola "Nicholas" Sr.; D'Agostino, Pasquale "Patsy"; family and personality conflicts; media profiles, Nicholas Sr.; media profiles, Patsy

D'Agostino Brothers (company). *See* D'Agostino Supermarkets

D'Agostino Markets LLC, 299n273

D'Agostino/Silverzweig Entrepreneurial Institute, 231, 295–96n233

D'Agostino Supermarkets, 69; as all-in-one store, 56, 57; association with Manhattan chic, 157–58, 161, 169–70; bakery and deli, 278n92; business model, 55–57, 59, 81, 132–33, 146–47, 151; business overview, 2–4, 7, 235–37; Buy-Low Grocery Company, 79, 148; "Career in Focus" initiative, 185–86; Catholic culture in identity of, 108, 118; as chain retailer, 261n32; city and market challenges, 218–19; Coffee Works, 226; commitment to community, 179; competition, standing out from, 183, 214, 218–19; competition from chain supermarkets, 146; competition from ethnic groceries, 179, 207, 208–9, 217; competition from gourmet groceries, 179, 207, 214–15, 217, 226, 237; competition from megastores and elite supermarkets, 207, 217–20, 223, 237; contraction, 237–43; corporate personality as projection of president, 155–56, 161–62, 178–79, 236–37; as cultural barometer, 161; "D'Ag Bagazette," 186; dairy selection, 91; employees, 94, 152, 183–86, 187, 229, 231, 277n82, 286n48; evolution of, 75, 81, 87, 90–92, 208–9; expansion under Nicholas Jr., 178, 230, 234; expansion under Nicholas Sr., 133–34; expansion under Stephen, 151–52, 155, 179–80, 283n153; in film and television, 188, 281n127; financial and organizational challenges, 241–43; founding, 42, 47, 55, 267n121; Fresh Markets, 208–9, 212; frozen foods, 88–89, 264n72; gourmet culture embraced, 92, 145–47; identity as multigenerational family business, 122; identity crisis, 224–25, 235, 239; innovations and new technologies, 75, 154, 179, 194–97, 198, 199, 200, 226, 288n91; interior design, presentation, and display, 89, 133, 277n73; Josephine's pivotal role, 47, 55, 267n121; landmark status and heritage, 1–2, 4; "Lunch with the President" days, 186; market dominance, 153; Marketta, 227–28; merchandising revolution, 87–88; mergers and acquisitions, 7, 234–35, 242–43; muting of ethnicity, 169–70, 212, 213, 286n62; name changes, 86, 156, 256n68, 263n60; narratives surrounding, 12, 42, 121–22, 192–93; NYC partner in success of, 9, 157–58, 161, 212; NYC's renaissance and gentrification, 167, 177–79, 241; NYC urban renewal benefitting, 75, 85–87, 91–92; online retailing, 199–200, 226, 287n87; organizational structure, 146–47, 151; philanthropy and corporate culture, 186; postwar success, 81, 91; private-label goods as prestige items, 207, 290n120; product expansion to drugstore items, 89; red meat bolstering, 59, 91; reputation's decline, 179, 225–26; "a responsible company," 132; revenue and profits, 97–98, 108,

INDEX · 327

133, 154, 155, 179, 180, 208–9, 234, 263n62, 283n153; self-service model, 78, 81, 88; store opening celebrations, 68, 71, 73, 86, 108, 118; superette model, 78; supermarket not specialty store, 219–20; TeleDag, 196–97, 239; Tucciarone family's involvement, 43, 45, 55, 267n121; Yorkville Food Shoppe, 56, 86, 89, 256n68. *See also* advertising, D'Agostino; branding; customers, D'Agostino; media profiles, D'Agostino; *individual family members*

D'Agostino Supermarkets, locations: 20th St., 68, 75, 85–87, 90; 56th St., 116; 72nd St., 116; 77th St. and Third Ave., 58; 80th St., 116; 83rd St. and Lexington Ave., 34, 58, 103, 157, 193; 85th St., 58, 81; the Bronx, 133, 152, 234, 283n153; Brooklyn, 133, 152, 234, 283n153; Chelsea, 147, 277n73, 283n153; Greenwich Village, 147; Mount Vernon, 3, 58, 82, 261n39, 263n60; Rye Brook, 227–28; Upper East Side, 3; Upper West Side, 147, 151, 235, 283n153, 291n148; Westchester County, 154, 234, 283n153

Dean & DeLuca, 145, 214
Death Wish (Bronson), 164
DemandTec, 288n91
Democratic Club, 114
department stores, 264n76
DeSapio, Carmine, 270n158
D'Espinosa, Bill (cousin), 100, 105
D'Espinosa, Loreta. *See* D'Agostino, Loreta (mother)
D'Espinosa, Tony (uncle), 38, 49, 54–55
Deutsch, Tracey, 25, 257n85
Di Leonardo, Micaela, 213, 291n147
Diner, Hasia, 251n48
Dinkins, David, 284n4, 284n6
Doyle, Mona, 279n110
drugstores, 238–39, 298n265
Duane Reade, 238, 297n258, 298n265

Ecker, Frederick, 84, 262–63n51
Emergency Price Control Act, 61–64
Estate Tax, 192–93, 286n63

ethnic entrepreneurship: assimilation and social mobility, 20–21, 114–15, 207; demise of neighborhood grocer and, 140; ethnic grocer as pastoral other, 31, 65–66; food deserts and, 140; generational success and failure, 35, 42–45, 52, 56–57, 150, 153; H-1B visas, 201–2; Italian immigrants' engagement in, 20–21; Korean greengrocers, 202–7, 208; NYC renaissance and, 202; opportunities and hazards facing, 50; personal history as public representation, 11; political symbolism of small businessmen, 61; pushcart peddling, 20, 22–24, 26, 100, 144; transforming immigrant identities, 8–9
ethnicity, symbolic, 290n130, 291n147
ethnic revival, 8, 167–69, 209, 290nn129–30

Fairway, 214–15, 223, 237, 239, 297n260
Falkenberg, Jinx, 263n59
family and personality conflicts: generated by family-run businesses, 76, 232–33, 237; generational divisions, 42, 52, 53–55; media profiles causing tension, 34; Nicholas Sr. and Irene, 53; Nicholas Sr. and Stephen, 170–71, 172; Nicholas Sr. at Butterfield Market, 52; Nicholas Sr.'s courtship of Josephine, 54–55; Patsy and Ignatius, 41, 99; Patsy and Nicholas Sr., 47, 49, 278n90; Patsy's death and succession, 76, 120–23, 151, 229, 231, 271n171; Stephen and Nicholas Jr., 170–71, 172, 283n156; T. Mazzucco and G. Carcone, 52; Walter's departure from business, 233
family businesses, generally: author's overview, 2, 10; blurred lines between family and commerce, 11, 12; competing narratives, 47; decline of, 231–32; family laying groundwork for success, 42; primogeniture, 36, 171, 230; tensions between business and family, 76, 232–33, 237
farmers' markets, 215, 225, 239
fast-food franchises, 141–42, 145

Fedele, Joe, 215, 288n89
Federal-Aid Highway Act (1956), 268n145
Federal Housing Administration, 268n140
Fellini, Federico, 210
Ferraro, Geraldine, 210
Fiddler on the Roof, 169
Finchley's, 134
Fiori, Vittorio de, 104–7
First National, 34, 102, 154–55
Foerster, Robert, 18, 36, 65
Foner, Nancy, 201, 213, 249n24, 255n44
Food Emporium, 145, 147, 183, 214, 277n73
Food Fair, 138
food industry and culture: American symbolism, 93, 136; anonymity of shopping and, 94; artificial flavors and food dyes, 143; canned foods, 44, 264n69; convenience foods, 140, 143, 145; dining out, 143; ethnic revival and, 169, 205, 211–12, 213; fast food, 141–42, 145; food as status symbol, 178; "foodie" ethos, 224; frozen foods, 88–89, 140, 145, 264n72; gourmet foods, 92, 142–45, 146, 221, 265n91; health food, 144, 276n59; healthful eating, 205; home cooking's popularity, 142–43; merchandising revolution, 87–88, 93, 141; microwave ovens, 140; natural foods, 142, 144, 224; organic food movement, 220–21, 224; prepared meals, 222; price controls, 137; produce consumption, 93, 140–41, 144, 275n40, 276n61; red meat consumption, 91, 137, 144, 263n64, 276n62; rising prices, 137; vegetarianism, 144, 145. *See also* food retailers
Food Marketing Institute, 162, 192–93, 277–78n84, 284–85n12
food rationing, 59, 60–61, 253n2, 256n71, 257n85
food retailers: bodegas, 202, 239, 274n34; chain growth, 137–38, 273n17; challenges in the 1960s and '70s, 137–40; cheese shops, 143; competition from restaurants, 239; computerized shopping, 193–97; corner stores, 22, 205; decline of family-run firms, 231–32; displays and store design, 89, 276n65; drugstores and, 89–90, 94, 238–39, 264–65n80; employees, 94, 184–85, 220, 271nn3–4; ethnic grocery stores, overview, 9–10; farmers' markets, 215, 225, 239; food deserts, 140; fruit stands, 20–21, 251n51; gourmet groceries, 145–46, 214–15, 217, 218, 226, 237, 277n70; hierarchy and network of urban merchants, 2; independents *vs.* chain stores, 76–79, 80–81, 94–95, 260–61n28, 265n95; Korean greengrocers, 202–9, 289n103, 289n112; local groceries closing, 238–39; "malaise days," 137–39; market segmentation, 138, 145, 146–47, 198; megastores, 216; merchandising revolution, 87–88, 93; mergers and takeovers, 197–98, 229; mom and pop groceries, 75, 95, 139–40, 144, 202, 216, 228, 274n34; online shopping, 198–200, 297n261; opportunities for immigrants, 20–21; produce stands, 20–21, 143, 202–9, 251n51; profit margins and revenue, 136, 221–22; promotional strategies, 137; retail arms race, 78; return to pre-supermarket past, 219; rising importance of produce selection, 220; rising prices, 137; salad bars and delis, 276n67; self-service model, 80–81; social advancement, 129–30; specialty stores assuming role of supermarkets, 219; technological innovations, 138, 198–99; threats to, 136–37; types of postwar, 77, 259n6, 260n11, 260n22, 260n23; volume dealers, 218; wholesalers and wholesale cooperatives, 75, 78–79, 139, 260n23. *See also* advertising; customers; ethnic entrepreneurship; pushcart peddling; supermarkets; *individual retailers and stores*
Foxworth, Jo: advertising themes and strategies, 188, 189, 190–91, 213, 279n105, 286n62; on being her own boss, 279n101; conflict with Ron Nevers, 227; creating D'Agostino advertising,

156–57, 159–60; Horatio Alger award for Nicholas Jr., 283n157; uniqueness of D'Agostino advertising, 158
Francis, Arlene, 263n59
Frank Tucciarone and Company, 2, 45
Freeman, Joshua, 162
FreshDirect, 199, 239, 288n89
Fresh Fields, 221
Friedman, Milton, 173
Friends, 188

Gabaccia, Donna, 17, 113–14, 210, 248n12, 254n28
Gans, Herbert J., 167, 290n130
General Foods, 229
Gentile, Gennaro, 34, 102
Gerosa, Lawrence, 270n158
GI Bill (1944). *See* Servicemen's Readjustment Act (1944)
Gimbel family, 58
Gino's Restaurant, 151, 241, 270n155
Giuliani, Rudolph, 178, 210, 216, 238, 284n6
Glaser, Milton, 165
Glass, Marvin, 125, 159–61, 227, 280n115
Godfather films (Coppola), 169, 282n145
Goodman, Sylvan, 25
Gopnik, Adam, 222
Grand Royal market, 55
Grand Union, 77, 264n74, 276n59
Great Atlantic & Pacific Tea Company (A&P). *See* A&P
Great Depression, 24, 45, 255n54
Great Society, 163, 288–89n93
Greenberg, Miriam, 281n128
Gristedes, 154, 183, 214, 218, 223, 242, 274n32
grocery stores. *See* food retailers; supermarkets; *individual retailers and stores*
Guglielmo, Thomas, 17, 268n140

Hallberg, Garth Risk, 241
Harding, Warren G., 33
Harry, Debbie, 157
Hart-Cellar Act. *See* Immigration and Nationality Act (1965)
Hartley, Fred A., 258n89

Hitler, Adolph, 64
HIV/AIDS, 182, 284n4
Hoffman, Jane, 124, 158–59
Home Depot, 215
HomeRuns, 198
Hope, Bob, 173
Horatio Alger Association of Distinguished Americans, 172–74
Hughes, Lawrence, 107–8

Iacocca, Lee, 210
Il Progresso Italo-Americano, 59, 115
immigrant identity: ambiguity of Italian identity, 15, 17, 99–100; assimilation, 14, 15, 16–17; growing cohesiveness among Italian Americans, 248n14; hyphenated identity cutting both ways, 64; Italian identity in business marketing, 266n113; outward migration and, 110; parochialism, 15, 16–17; rebranding Italian identity, 210–12, 213; store names and, 56; transnational existence complicating, 15, 248n12; WWII challenging, 59–60, 62–64
immigrants and immigration: American dream, 202; assimilation, 66, 75–76, 105; H-1B visa, 201–2, 288–89n93; isolation of women, 39; Korean immigrants to NYC, 201–7, 208–209, 289n103, 289n112; part of NYC renaissance, 201–2. *See also* American dream; ethnic entrepreneurship; immigrant identity; Italian immigrants and immigration
Immigration Act (1924), 17, 250n30, 288–89n93
Immigration Act (1990), 288–89n93
Immigration and Nationality Act (1965), 178, 201, 269–70n151, 288–89n93
Imming, Bernard, 275n40
Impelliteri, Vincent, 270n158
independent, notion of, 101–3, 261n32
Independent Grocers' Alliance, 264n79
Instacart, 239
Italian American Grocers Association, 59–60
Italian Benevolent Institute, 114
Italian Charities of America, 106, 115, 135

Italian Executives of America, 135
Italian immigrants and immigration: assimilation, 8–9, 14, 168, 213, 249n24, 251n44; author's overview, 14–19, 247n5; Catholicism and, 16–17, 117, 249–50n25, 270n159; effects on Italy, 36–38; ethnic revival, 167–69; forming flexible and contingent households, 49; generational divide, 21, 52; housing, 15, 16, 109–10; impact on US Italian community, 247n5; impetus for, 36–37; Italian American culture, 291n147; Italian culture and labor, 15–16, 39; literacy and education, 14, 17, 18, 249n24; myth of the pastoral Italian, 9; "natural affinity" for produce, 20–21; new class of, 211; opportunities from labor, 19, 39; outward migration and upward mobility, 19, 109–13; padrone system, 248n9; philanthropy, 269–70n151; political apathy, 16–17, 249n25; purpose and intended duration, 8, 14–15; pushcart peddling, 22, 26; reliance on community, 50, 255n52; role of food, 251n48; sentimentalization, 251n44; social mobility, 19–20, 22, 209–12, 213, 282nn137–39; status of laborers, 248n8; stereotypes and prejudices against, 17–18, 20, 43, 102, 167–69, 251n44, 282n145; tensions with Black and Puerto Rican communities, 268n140; unstable business climate, 50, 52; whiteness, 17, 268n140; wives' difficulty acclimating, 39. *See also* ethnic entrepreneurship; immigrant identity
Italian Immigration Commission, 15
Italian Trade Commission, 211
Italy, 35–38, 40–41, 104, 115, 118–19, 135
Ivanhoé Cambridge, 298n266

Jacobson, Matthew, 17, 169
Jae Ok Kim, 203–4
Jameson, Fredric, 282n145
Johnson, Lyndon, 163, 288–89n93
Joint Merchants Produce Co-Op, 79
JTL Corporation, 170, 172

Kefauver, Estes, 61, 64
Kennedy, John F., 258n89
Kentucky Fried Chicken, 141
Key Food Stores Co-operative, 242
Khrushchev, Nikita, 129, 271n2
King, John Reed, 263n59
King Kullen Market, 24–25, 89
King's, 234–35
Kivisto, Peter, 213
Knights of Malta, 118, 134, 273n14
Knights of St. John Lateran, 118, 134
Knights of the Holy Sepulchre, 134
Koch, Ed, 164, 177–78, 284n6
Korean immigrants, 201–7, 208, 289n103, 289n112
Kozmo, 198
Kroger, 25, 77, 79

La Follette, Robert, Jr., 61
Laglia, Enrica, 104–7
La Guardia, Fiorello, 24, 26, 116
Landry, Tom, 173
language, 66, 104, 266n108
Lannon, Dave, 223
Lei, 158
Levenstein, Harvey, 264n73
Levi, Carlo, 14
Levinson, Marc, 25
Lincoln Center, 135
Lindsay, John, 280–81n124
Luconi, Stefano, 17, 268n140

Mackey, John, 221
Mad About You, 188
Madison Square Boys and Girls Club, 181
Mafia, 17, 116, 168–69, 282n145
Manhattan Grocers Cooperative, 114
Marchisio, Juvenal, 115, 269–70n151
Marks and Spencer, 234
Martino, Marcel, 77, 78
Masciarelli, Anthony, 95
masculinity, 39, 41–42, 49, 55
Mathews, Ryan, 217
Mayo, James, 256n71
Mazzucco, Celeste, 44
Mazzucco, Philip (uncle), 49, 50
Mazzucco, Tommy (cousin), 29, 50–52

McCarran-Walter Act (1952), 269–70n151
McCray, Tex, 263n59
McDonald's, 141
McKinnon, George, 258n89
media profiles, D'Agostino: D'Ag Bags, 157; interior design, 89; New York's grocer, 188; philanthropy and corporate culture, 182–83; store defining NYC's character, 179; store opening celebrations, 86; "Biggest Appetite" (*Life*), 74; "D'Agostino Has Fresh Ad Approach" (*Supermarket News*), 159; "D'Agostino: Innovation, Sensitivity; Success" (*Food Merchants Advocate*), 183; "D'AG's Is New York" (*Food Merchants Advocate*), 188; *New York Times*, 157
media profiles, Nicholas Jr.: American dream, 194; management style, 187; New York's grocer, 187–88; paradigm of family businessman, 181, 230; philanthropy and corporate culture, 182–83; reflects D'Agostino image, 189; "D'AG's Is New York" (*Food Merchants Advocate*), 188; "Nick D'Agostino, Jr." (*Food Merchants Advocate*), 182–83; "The American Dream" (*Chain Store Age*), 194
media profiles, Nicholas Sr.: archetypal, self-made man, 12, 75; assimilation of immigrants and Catholics, 106–8; form of store promotion, 155; life story as morality play, 106; philanthropic leadership, 106–7; trinity of business, national pride, and family, 104, 106–7; "The D'Agostino Brothers" (*Italamerican*), 104, 106–7
media profiles, Patsy: American dream, 98–103; archetypal, self-made man, 11–12; business ethos, 61, 79–82, 96, 97–103, 106; favorite of local reporters, 60; form of store promotion, 155; Italian identity, 30, 32–33, 34–35, 67, 75, 98–100, 191; keeper of premodern ethos, 205–6; life story as morality play, 96, 98–106, 108; "loud and colorful, but earthy," 30–32, 34–35; mythos placed in Catholic context, 106–8; Nicholas Sr. sidelined

in, 34, 100, 121; obituary, 121; OPA regulations, 60–61; partnership with Nicholas, 106; philanthropic leadership, 106–7; public face of grocers, 60, 61; shifts in Patsy's identity, 191; succession planning for business, 34–35, 81–82, 106; symbol of free enterprise, 61, 203; trinity of business, national pride, and family, 104–7; writer's choice of frame, 11–12, 103, 104–7; *Catholic Digest*, 75, 107; "The D'Agostino Brothers" (*Italamerican*), 104–7; *Food Marketing*, 120; "A Gospel for Independent Grocers" (*Business Week*), 97–98; "I Found $5,000,000 in a Pushcart" (*American Magazine*), 99–103, 203; "If Trouble Can Be Avoid" (*New Yorker*), 30–35, 60, 191–92, 205–6; "Independents on the Band Wagon" (*Food Marketing*), 79–82; *New York Times*, 121
media profiles, Stephen, 153–55
Metropolitan Life Insurance Company, 75, 83–86, 87, 262n43; 262n44, 262–63n51
Metropolitan Museum of Art, 135
Milken, Michael, 177
Minturno Aid Society, 114
Modern Bride, 158
Morton Williams, 214
Moses, Robert, 83–85, 261–62n42, 262–63n51, 268–69n146
Mrs. Gooch, 221
Murphy, Mark, 30–35, 60–61, 206
Mussolini, Benito, 59, 64, 99
mutual aid societies, 46, 113–14, 249n23.
  See also individual societies
MyWebGrocer.com, 199, 287n87

Nabisco, 229
National Association of Food Chains, 152, 277–78n84
National Association of Retail Grocers: Patsy's involvement in, 3, 60, 77, 106, 265n95; Stephen's involvement in, 151, 162
National Grocers Association, 284–85n12
Nevers, Ron, 181, 227, 233

New York City (NYC): American symbolism, 130–31; author's overview, 9; Bronx Terminal Market, 25–26, 31–32, 41–42, 89, 206; building campaign, 130; closure of small grocery stores, 238–39; corrosive social problems, 284n4; demographics, 108, 130–31, 162–63, 178, 201–2, 280nn118–19, 290–91n131; Department of Markets, 23; Elmhurst (Queens), 109-10, 147, 201; expansion of, 268–69n146; *Fortune* issue devoted to, 130–31; gentrification, 147, 165–67, 178, 216, 219, 224, 240–41, 281n131; "hippoisie," 166–67; "I Love New York" campaign, 165, 281n128; immigrant character, 2; immigrant labor, 15–16; infrastructure projects, 15–16, 110, 268–69n146; Italian immigration to, 9, 14–19, 26; localism of marketplace, 215, 217, 238; Long Island Expressway, 111–12; outward migration and upward mobility, 109–10, 268n144; Peter Cooper Village, 75, 84–86, 91, 114, 241, 262–63n51; racial tensions and segregation, 85, 163, 262–63n51, 282n141, 284n4, 289n112, 290–91n131; renaissance, 165–67, 177, 201–2, 284n6; retail superstores in, 215–17, 238, 241, 292n159; Roaring Twenties transforming, 23; Stuyvesant Town, 75, 84–86, 91, 114, 241, 262–63n51; urban decay, 131, 161, 162–65, 167, 280n117; 280–81n124; urban renewal, 75, 82–87, 91–92, 110–12, 261–62n42, 262n44, 268–69n146; vogue of Italian culture, 210–12, 213. *See also* D'Agostino Supermarkets; food retailers; immigrants and immigration

New Yorker, 31, 160

New York Food Group, 7, 242–43, 299n273

New York Public Library, 135

New York State Food Merchants Association: addressing chain store competition, 77; Nicholas Jr.'s involvement in, 180, 182–83, 284–85n12; Nicholas Sr.'s involvement in, 114; Patsy's involvement in, 3, 60, 106, 114; Stephen's involvement in, 151, 161–62; wholesale warehouses, 79

Nixon, Richard, 129, 135, 137, 258n89, 271n2

Office of Price Administration (OPA), 3, 60–64, 76, 257n85, 258n90

online shopping, 198–200, 239, 287n87, 288n89, 297n261

organic food movement, 220–21, 224

organized labor, 62, 258n89

Orsi, Robert, 109, 117

Packard, Vance, 111, 268n144

Parisi, Joe, 243

Patman, Wright, 61

Peale, Norman Vincent, 173

Peapod, 198

peddlers. *See* pushcart peddling

Pei, I. M., 241

philanthropy: demonstration of wealth and social power, 117; of immigrants, 114–15, 269–70n151; Mafia involvement, 116; means of communicating corporate culture, 181–83, 186; mutual aid societies, 113–14; of Nicholas Jr., 179, 181–83; of Nicholas Sr., 106–7, 114, 115–16, 117, 134–36; opportunities for ethnic fellowship, 115, 117; of Patsy, 106–7, 114, 115–16, 117

Philip Morris, 229

Piggly Wiggly, 24

Pillsbury, 143

Pipo, Zio, 49

Pius XII, 107, 118

Pope, Generoso, 59, 115–16

Powell, Adam Clayton, 258n89

Priceline.com, 199

Prodigy Services, 199

pushcart peddling, 68; advantages to, 251n51; ethnic entrepreneurship, 22–24, 26; Ignatius, 43, 49; Italian immigrant ascendancy, 20–21; new relevance of, 144; Nicholas Sr., 26, 49, 133, 267n122; Patsy, 22, 26, 33–34, 43, 65–66, 100, 253n7; pushcart markets,

95; reimagined as a frontier mentality, 100; social mobility, 22.
Puzo, Mario, 169

Reagan, Ronald, 173, 283n160
Red Apple (grocery chain), 242, 274n32
Red Apple Group conglomerate, 7, 242
Rite Aide, 298n265
R.J. Reynolds, 229
Roediger, David, 17
Rolling Stone, 157
Russell Sage Foundation, 268–69n146

Safeway, 25, 77, 79
Salemme, Irene. *See* D'Agostino, Irene (Patsy's wife)
Sam's Club, 218
Sayres, Paul, 79–80
Scorsese, Martin, 164
Servicemen's Readjustment Act (1944), 110, 268n140, 268n145
Shopwell, 145, 214
Silverzweig, Stanley, 295–96n233
Simon, Arthur, 262–63n51
Sinatra, Frank, 168
Singer, Caroline, 251n44
Sloan's, 154, 214, 218, 234, 242, 274n32
Smith, Patti, 241
Society for the Protection of Italian Immigrants, 114
Sons of Italy, 59
Spellman, Francis, 108, 134
Spiderman 2, 188
Standard Foods, 25
Staples, 215
Statue of Liberty, 160
St. Clare's Hospital and Health Center, 182
Sterling, Jack, 263n59
Sterling Investment Partners, 297n260
Stevenson, Adlai, 61, 64
St. Patrick's Cathedral, 125, 165
Super Market Institute, 152, 277–78n84
supermarkets: advertising, 156, 158, 226–27, 278–79nn95–96; anonymity and, 93–94; author's overview, 9–10; Big Three chains, 77, 79; chain supermarket model, 79, 146, 216; changing consumer behavior, 25–26; class distinctions, status, and, 90; in Cold War rhetoric, 129; compartmentalization, 26; competition from restaurants, 218; costs of move toward, 93–95; COVID-19 creating new opportunities for, 298n265; decline of, 141, 197, 218, 223–24; defined, 259n6; as department stores, 89–90; embodying mass market and progress, 129–30; employees, 276–77n68; gourmet food culture, 92, 142-43; great leveler for independents, 79; growing dominance, 74, 76–77, 138; imperiling niche retail institutions, 94; influence on store design, 89; innovations in, 24–25; prices, 89–90, 137; product selection, 217; sales figures, 136; specialty foods, 142; "story of America," 79; superette model, 78, 260n22; urban supermarkets, 78, 139; WWII influencing establishment of, 256n71. *See also* customers; D'Agostino Supermarkets; food retailers; *individual supermarkets*

Talese, Gay, 241
Tamm, Gus, 52
Target, 215
Tartt, Donna, 297–98n263
Taxi Driver (Scorsese), 164
Tedlow, Richard, 25, 259–60n10
Sopranos, 169
Thomas, David, 173
Tiro a Segno Rifle Club, 116, 270n156
Tishman Speyer, 241, 298n266
T.J. Maxx, 215
Tomasi, Lydio, 211
Tower Records, 215
Trader Joe's, 216, 237
Tricarico, Donald, 213
Trump, Donald, 177
Tucciarone, Adolpho "Adolph," 28, 43–44, 45, 53
Tucciarone, Frank, 28; debt issues, 55, 267n121; immigrant story, 43–45; limits of success, 57, 65, 103, 150; Nicholas

Tucciarone, Frank (*continued*)
    buying out, 34, 45, 55–56, 267n121;
    Patsy partner with, 34, 45, 102–3;
    relationship with Ignatius, 44
Tucciarone, John, 52
Tucciarone, Josephine. *See* D'Agostino,
    Josephine (Nicholas's wife)
Tucciarone, Marty (brother-in-law), 148
Tucciarone, Patsy, 253n7
Tucciarone Brothers store, 28, 44–45
Tyson, Jimmy, 101

Union League Club of New York, 151
unions, 15, 62, 163, 258n89
United Fruit, 275n40
United Hospital Fund, 182
United Way of New York, 181, 182, 186

Versace, 211, 212
Virgin Records, 215
Vogue, 158
Volper, Morris, 260–61n28

Wagner, Robert F., Jr., 95
Walgreen, 297n258
Walmart, 195, 198, 215, 218
Warhol, Andy, 191
Waters, Alice, 144–45
Waters, Mary, 213, 291n147

WebHouse Club, 199
Webvan, 198
Wegmans, 238, 298n265
Wells Rich Greene, 165
Western Growers Association, 264n69
whiteness, 17, 268n140
Whole Foods Market, 216, 218, 220–22,
    225, 237–39, 294n199, 298n265
Whyte, William Foote, 167
Whyte, William H., 266n119
Will and Grace, 188
women: American dream's disappointment,
    39, 45–46; changing consumer role,
    137, 142, 257n85; changing views of
    cooking, 143–44, 276n56; domestic
    cleanliness, 254n29; influencing Italian
    culture and identity, 37, 291n147;
    isolation of immigrant women, 39,
    112; wage labor, 16, 39, 142, 255n44,
    264n73, 275n37
Works Progress Administration (WPA), 19
World War II, 58–64, 76, 256n71

Yans-McLaughlin, Virginia, 248n13
Yorkville Food Shoppe. *See* D'Agostino
    Supermarkets
Yorkville Lions Club, 106

Zabar's, 145, 223, 278n92

Paul Schmitz is an Associate Teaching Professor in the History and Society Division at Babson College (MA) and has taught courses on the modern American city, the history and culture of American business, and immigration and race. His research focuses on issues of food, business, and identity within the Italian and immigrant communities of New York City.

EMPIRE STATE EDITIONS SELECT TITLES FROM EMPIRE STATE EDITIONS

Salvatore Basile, *Fifth Avenue Famous: The Extraordinary Story of Music at St. Patrick's Cathedral*. Foreword by Most Reverend Timothy M. Dolan, Archbishop of New York

Daniel Campo, *The Accidental Playground: Brooklyn Waterfront Narratives of the Undesigned and Unplanned*

Gerard R. Wolfe, *The Synagogues of New York's Lower East Side: A Retrospective and Contemporary View, Second Edition*. Photographs by Jo Renée Fine and Norman Borden, Foreword by Joseph Berger

Joseph B. Raskin, *The Routes Not Taken: A Trip Through New York City's Unbuilt Subway System*

Phillip Deery, *Red Apple: Communism and McCarthyism in Cold War New York*

North Brother Island: The Last Unknown Place in New York City. Photographs by Christopher Payne, A History by Randall Mason, Essay by Robert Sullivan

Robert Weldon Whalen, *Murder, Inc., and the Moral Life: Gangsters and Gangbusters in La Guardia's New York*

Joanne Witty and Henrik Krogius, *Brooklyn Bridge Park: A Dying Waterfront Transformed*

Sharon Egretta Sutton, *When Ivory Towers Were Black: A Story about Race in America's Cities and Universities*

Pamela Hanlon, *A Wordly Affair: New York, the United Nations, and the Story Behind Their Unlikely Bond*

Britt Haas, *Fighting Authoritarianism: American Youth Activism in the 1930s*

David J. Goodwin, *Left Bank of the Hudson: Jersey City and the Artists of 111 1st Street*. Foreword by DW Gibson

Nandini Bagchee, *Counter Institution: Activist Estates of the Lower East Side*

Susan Celia Greenfield (ed.), *Sacred Shelter: Thirteen Journeys of Homelessness and Healing*

Susan Opotow and Zachary Baron Shemtob (eds.), *New York after 9/11*

Andrew Feffer, *Bad Faith: Teachers, Liberalism, and the Origins of McCarthyism*

Colin Davey with Thomas A. Lesser, *The American Museum of Natural History and How It Got That Way*. Forewords by Neil deGrasse Tyson and Kermit Roosevelt III

Mike Jaccarino, *America's Last Great Newspaper War: The Death of Print in a Two-Tabloid Town*

Angel Garcia, *The Kingdom Began in Puerto Rico: Neil Connolly's Priesthood in the South Bronx*

Jim Mackin, *Notable New Yorkers of Manhattan's Upper West Side: Bloomingdale–Morningside Heights*

Matthew Spady, *The Neighborhood Manhattan Forgot: Audubon Park and the Families Who Shaped It*

Marilyn S. Greenwald and Yun Li, *Eunice Hunton Carter: A Lifelong Fight for Social Justice*

Jeffrey A. Kroessler, *Sunnyside Gardens: Planning and Preservation in a Historic Garden Suburb*

Ron Howell, *King Al: How Sharpton Took the Throne*

Jean Arrington with Cynthia S. LaValle, *From Factories to Palaces: Architect Charles B. J. Snyder and the New York City Public Schools*. Foreword by Peg Breen

Boukary Sawadogo, *Africans in Harlem: An Untold New York Story*

Alvin Eng, *Our Laundry, Our Town: My Chinese American Life from Flushing to the Downtown Stage and Beyond*

Stephanie Azzarone, *Heaven on the Hudson: Mansions, Monuments, and Marvels of Riverside Park*

Ron Goldberg, *Boy with the Bullhorn: A Memoir and History of ACT UP New York*. Foreword by Dan Barry

Peter Quinn, *Cross Bronx: A Writing Life*

Mark Bulik, *Ambush at Central Park: When the IRA Came to New York*

Matt Dallos, *In the Adirondacks: Dispatches from the Largest Park in the Lower 48*

Brandon Dean Lamson, *Caged: A Teacher's Journey Through Rikers, or How I Beheaded the Minotaur*

Raj Tawney, *Colorful Palate: Savored Stories from a Mixed Life*

Edward Cahill, *Disorderly Men*

Joseph Heathcott, *Global Queens: An Urban Mosaic*

Francis R. Kowsky with Lucille Gordon, *Hell on Color, Sweet on Song: Jacob Wrey Mould and the Artful Beauty of Central Park*

Jill Jonnes, *South Bronx Rising: The Rise, Fall, and Resurrection of an American City*, Third Edition

Barbara G. Mensch, *A Falling-Off Place: The Transformation of Lower Manhattan*

David J. Goodwin, *Midnight Rambles: H. P. Lovecraft in Gotham*

Felipe Luciano, *Flesh and Spirit: Confessions of a Young Lord*

Maximo G. Martinez, *Sojourners in the Capital of the World: Garifuna Immigrants*

Jennifer Baum, *Just City: Growing Up on the Upper West Side When Housing Was a Human Righ*

Davida Siwisa James, *Hamilton Heights and Sugar Hill: Alexander Hamilton's Old Harlem Neighborhood Through the Centuries*

Annik LaFarge, *On the High Line: The Definitive Guide*, Third Edition. Foreword by Rick Dark

Marie Carter, *Mortimer and the Witches: A History of Nineteenth-Century Fortune Tellers*

Alice Sparberg Alexiou, *Devil's Mile: The Rich, Gritty History of the Bowery*. Foreword by Peter Quinn

Carey Kasten and Brenna Moore, *Mutuality in El Barrio: Stories of the Little Sisters of the Assumption Family Health Service*. Foreword by Norma Benítez Sánchez

Kimberly A. Orcutt, *The American Art-Union: Utopia and Skepticism in the Antebellum Era*

Jonathan Butler, *Join the Conspiracy: How a Brooklyn Eccentric Got Lost on the Right, Infiltrated the Left, and Brought Down the Biggest Bombing Network in New York*

Nicole Gelinas, *Movement: New York's Long War to Take Back Its Streets from the Car*

Jack Hodgson, *Young Reds in the Big Apple: The New York Young Pioneers of America, 1923–1934*

Lynn Ellsworth, *Wonder City: How to Reclaim Human-Scale Urban Life*

Walter Zev Feldman, *From the Bronx to the Bosphorus: Klezmer and Other Displaced Musics of New York*

Larry Racioppo, *Here Down on Dark Earth: Loss and Remembrance in New York City*

Bonnie Yochelson, *Too Good to Get Married: The Life and Photographs of Miss Alice Austen*

David Brown Morris, *Ten Thousand Central Parks: A Climate-Change Parable*

Eve M. Kahn, *Queen of Bohemia Predicts Own Death: The Forgotten Journalist Zoe Anderson Norris, 1860–1914*

Miriam Chaiken, *Creative Ozone: The Artists of Westbeth*

Stefanie Mercado Altman, Claire Altman, and Stan Altman, *Twice Blessed: A Story of Unconditional Love*. Foreword by Stephen G. Post

Stephanie Azzarone, *Fabulous Fountains of New York*

Annik LaFarge, *Composing Olana: A Journey on Foot Through an American Landscape*

Larry Racioppo, *Memorial '76*. Foreword by Kevin Baker

Phyllis Ross, *Stories in Fabric: The Design Works of Bedford Stuyvesant*. Foreword by Judith Jones

For a complete list, visit www.fordhampress.com/empire-state-editions.